The Masonic Book Club

Vol. 11B

A Masonic Reader's Guide

Alphonse Cerza & Thomas Warden

Westphalia Press
An Imprint of the Policy Studies Organization
Washington, DC

THE MASONIC BOOK CLUB

The *Masonic Book Club* (MBC) was formed in 1970 by two Illinois Masons, Alphonse Cerza, 33°, and Louis L. Williams, 33°. The MBC primarily reprinted out-of-print Masonic books with scholarly introductions; occasionally they would print additional texts as "bonuses" (though none were marked specifically as such on the title pages); sometimes a reprint would be marked "Masonic Book Club Edition"; often an unnumbered bonus was published jointly with the Illinois Lodge of Research or the Supreme Council, 33°, NMJ, USA.

Most of the MBC volumes indicated on the title page, "Volume [*Number*] of the Publications of the Masonic Book Club," some were misnumbered, and some were unnumbered. Indeed, the numbering of the early volumes was inconsistent. For example, *A Serious and Impartial Enquiry* is "Volume Five" (1974) but *Masonic Membership of the Founding Fathers* is "The Masonic Book Club Edition" (1974). Then, *Masonry Dissected* is "Volume Eight" (1977), *The Trestleboard* is "Volume 8A" (1978), and *Anderson's Constitutions of 1738* is "Volume Nine" (1978). If nothing else, MBC books keep bibliophiles on their toes.

The first volumes had deckle-edged paper and pages of slightly different sizes, though eventually the MBC settled into a 6″×9″ trimmed-page format for their books. The books were bound in a dark blue fabric with gold lettering. Listed below are the fifty-nine MBC volumes published 1970–2010 with bonuses. N.B.: A number and letter, e.g. "Volume 8A," is a numbering for this reprint series.

The club originally was limited to 333 members, but the number grew to nearly 2,000, with 1,083 members when it dissolved in 2010. In 2017 MW Barry Weer, 33°, the last president of the MBC, transferred the MBC name and assets to the Supreme Council, 33°, SJ, USA. Under the editorship of Arturo de Hoyos, 33°, ɢ∴ᴄ∴, and S. Brent Morris, 33°, ɢ∴ᴄ∴, the revived Masonic Book Club has the goal of publishing classic Masonic books while supporting Scottish Rite, SJ, USA philanthropies.

Publications of the Masonic Book Club, 1970–2010

1	1970	*The Regius Poem*	Masonic Book Club
2	1971	*The Constitutions of the Free-Masons*	Benjamin Franklin
3	1972	*Ahiman Rezon*	Laurence Dermott
4	1973	*Illustrations of Masonry*	William Preston
5	1974	*A Serious and Impartial Enquiry into the Cause of the Present Decay of Free-Masonry in the Kingdom of Ireland*	Fifield D'Assigny
5A	1974*	*Masonic Membership of the Founding Fathers*	Ronald E. Heaton

6	1975	*The Signers of the Declaration of Independence*	David C. Whitney
7	1976	*The Signers of the Constitution of the United States*	David C. Whitney
7A	1976*	*Masonic Symbols in American Decorative Art*	Louis L. Williams & Alphonse Cerza
8	1977	*Samuel Prichard's Masonry Dissected, 1730*	Harry Carr
8A	1978*	*Trestle-Board (A facsimile of the original Trestle Board by the Baltimore Masonic Convention of 1843)*	Dwight L. Smith
9	1978	*Anderson's Constitutions of 1738*	Lewis Edward & W. J. Hughan
10	1979	*Sufferings of John Coustos*	Wallace McLeod
11	1980	*The Revelations of a Square*	George Oliver
11A	1980	*Biblical Characters in Freemasonry*	John H. Van Gorden
11B	1980*	*A Masonic Reader's Guide*	Alphonse Cerza & Thomas Warden
12	1981	*Three Distinct Knocks and Jachin and Boaz*	Harry Carr
13	1982	*Masonic Almanacs and Anti-Masonic Almanacs*	Plez A. Transou
13A	1982*	*Stephen A. Douglas: Freemason*	Wayne C. Temple
14	1983	*The Beginnings of Freemasonry in America*	Melvin M. Johnson
14A	1983*	*Bespangled, Painted & Embroidered: Decorated Masonic Aprons in America, 1790–1850*	Scottish Rite Masonic Museum & Library
14B	1983*	*Making a Mason at Sight*	Louis L. Williams
15	1984	*Masonic Concordance of the Holy Bible*	Charles Clyde Hunt
15A	1984*	*By Square and Compasses: The Building of Lincoln's Home and Its Saga*	Wayne C. Temple
16	1985	*The Old Gothic Constitutions*	Wallace McLeod

28	1997	*The Masonic Ladder or the Nine Steps to Ancient Freemasonry*	John Sherer
28A	1997*	*Freemasonry and Democracy: Its Evolution in North America*	Allen E. Roberts & Wallace McLeod
29	1998	*The Masonic Harp: Collection of Masonic Odes, Hymns, Songs*	George Wingate Chase
30	1999	*Symbolic Teachings of Masonry and Its Message*	Thomas Milton Stewart
31	2000	*Freemasonry Its Meaning and Significance, An Exposition of its Ethics, Religion and Philosophy*	Otto Caspari
32	2001	*K. R. Cama Masonic Jubilee Volume*	Jivanji Jamshedji Modi
33	2002	*Caementaria Hibernica*	W. J. Chetwode Crawley
34	2003	*A Daily Advancement in Masonic Knowledge*	Wallace McLeod & S. Brent Morris
35	2004	*The Craftsman, and Templar's Textbook and, also, Melodies for the Craft*	Cornelius Moore
36	2005	*The Text Book of Freemasonry*	Retired Member of the Craft
37	2006	*Orations of the Illustrious Brother Frederick Dalcho Esq., M.D.*	Frederick Dalcho
38	2007	*Antiquities of Freemasonry Comprising Illustrations of the Five Grand Periods of Masonry from the Creation of the World to the Dedication of King Solomon's Temple*	George Oliver
39	2008	*Diogenes' Lamp or an Examination of our Present-Day Morality and Enlightenment*	Adam Weishaupt
40	2009	*Proofs of Conspiracy Against All the Governments of Europe*	John Robison
41	2010	*The Evolution of Freemasonry*	Delmar Darrah

** indicates a bonus book*

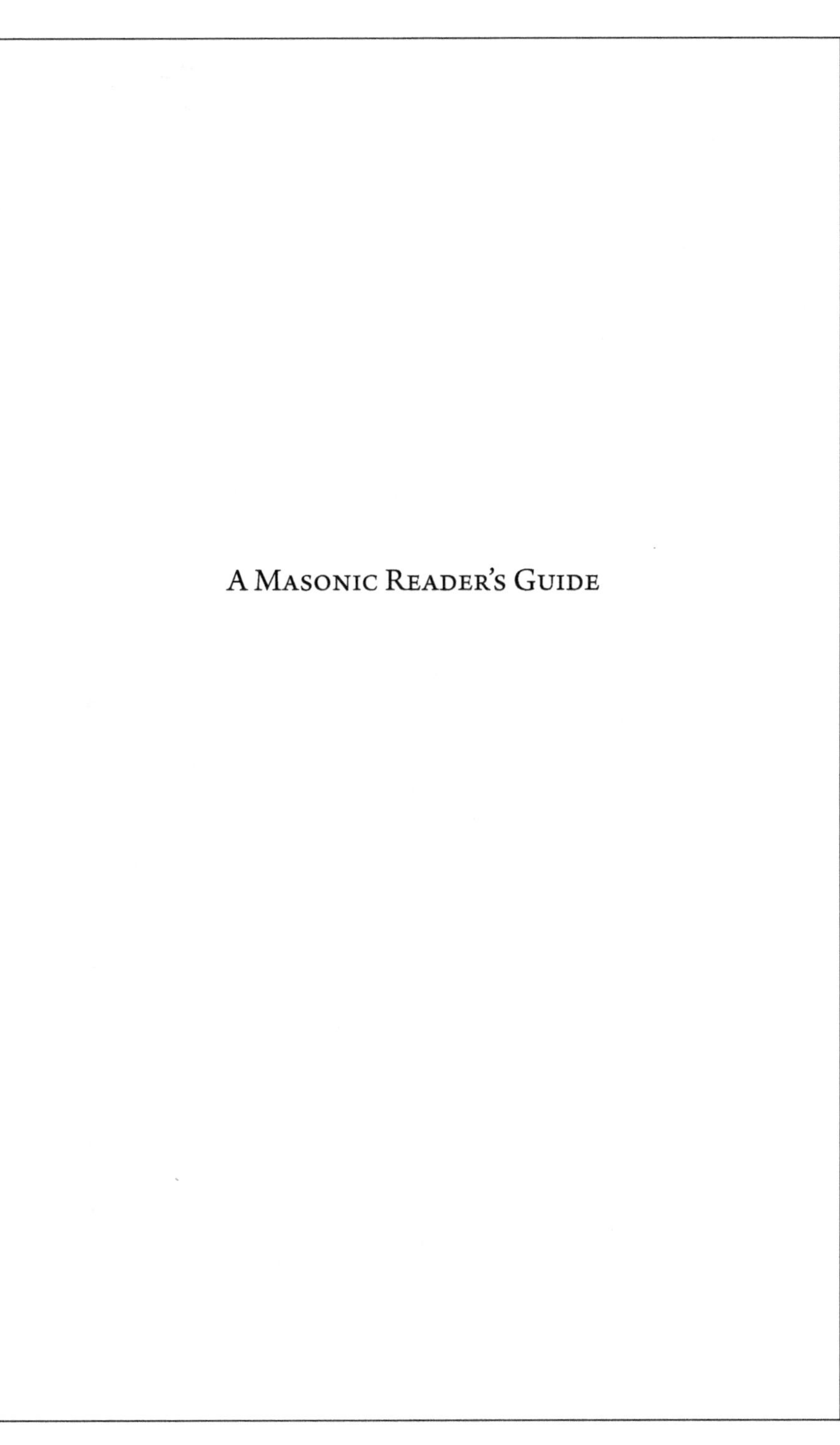

A Masonic Reader's Guide

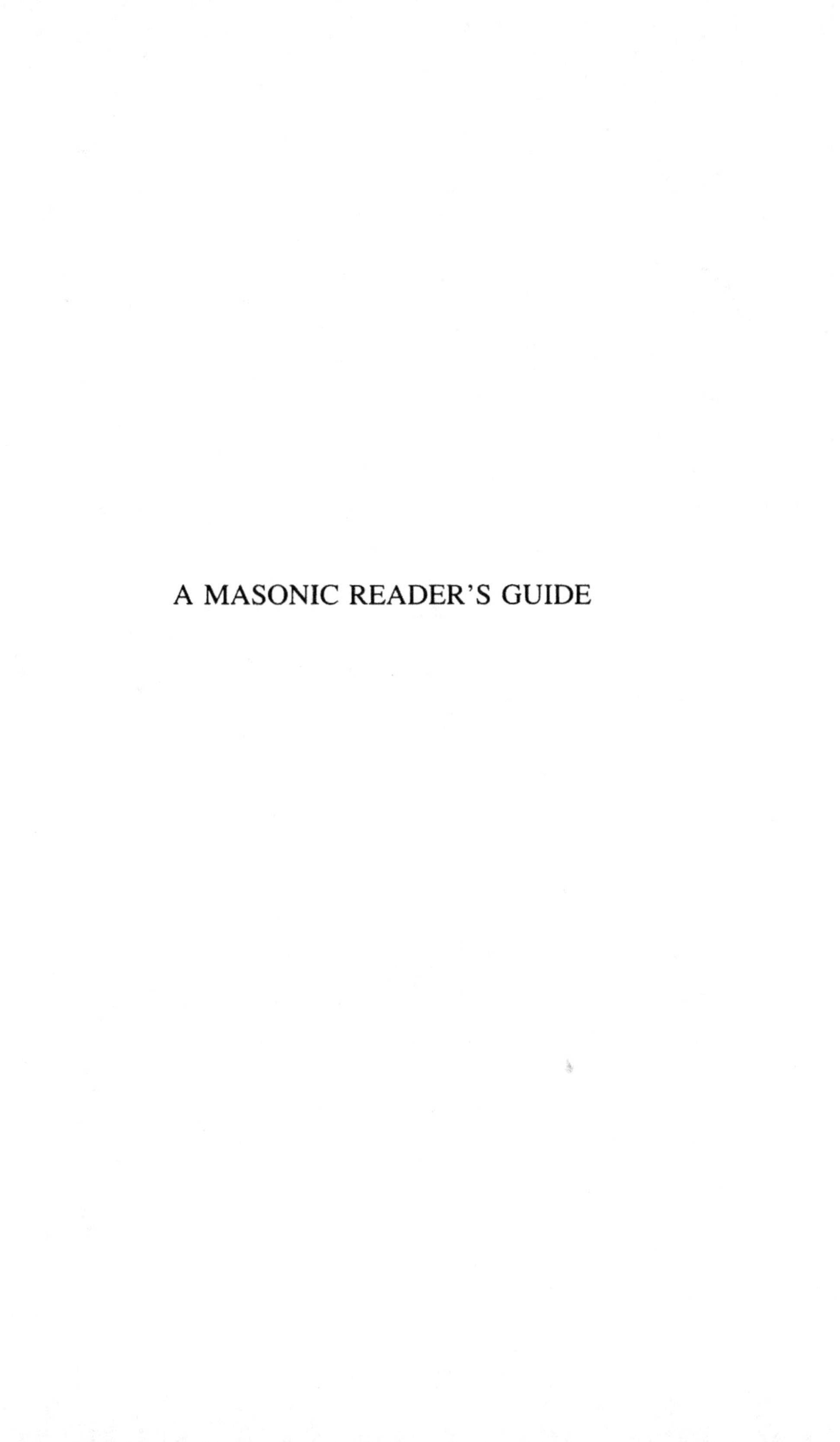

A MASONIC READER'S GUIDE

A MASONIC READER'S GUIDE

By
Alphonse Cerza

Thomas C. Warden, *Editor*

1978-1979

TRANSACTIONS OF THE MISSOURI LODGE OF RESEARCH
Volume No. 34

Printed in the United States of America

Foreword

The Missouri Lodge of Research is fortunate to present another volume by Alphonse Cerza. *A Masonic Reader's Guide* will become a useful reference for members of the fraternity in their search for Masonic knowledge.

Alphonse Cerza is a retired attorney and law professor, author of *Anti Masonry*, MLR-1962, and *A Masonic Thought for Each Day of the Year*, MLR-1971. He is also the author of numerous digests, booklets, and magazine articles, and is one of the founders of "The Masonic Book Club."

Brother Cerza is more than a student of Freemasonry. He is one of the fraternity's most outstanding scholars. *A Masonic Reader's Guide* will not only be a welcome addition to other Missouri Lodge of Research volumes, but will become a necessary reference in the continuing search for more light by many brothers of the Craft.

Bert W. Casselman, Master, 1978-79
Missouri Lodge of Research

Preface

An anonymous writer, referring to Alphonse Cerza the attorney and professor of law, once noted that he "is an exceedingly fine teacher . . . exemplifying those qualities of instruction and teaching methods which separate the merely competent from the exceedingly capable."

No better phraseology could more explicitly describe Alphonse Cerza the Freemason who, during some 30 years in the field of Masonic education and literature, has proven himself indeed to be a "fine teacher" as well as "exceedingly capable" in his endeavors.

A Masonic Reader's Guide is Mr. Cerza's third contribution to the Missouri Lodge of Research publications, and it well may be his most important.

This diligent effort by Mr. Cerza is precisely what the title suggests: A "guide," a literary index to the preponderance of Masonic literature in existence in the United States today. It is not just Cerza the author: It is Cerza the reader, Cerza the scholar, the interpreter, the book reviewer, the teacher, who presents the culmination of ten years' effort in a single volume of such immensity that it staggers the imagination to contemplate the scope of his perseverence.

While this competent itinerary of Masonic literature is as complete as ten years of labors will permit, the appendix of selected authors notably omits the credentials of one of Freemasonry's finest scholars — Alphonse Cerza himself.

His dedication to Freemasonry and its appendant bodies is too vast for recitation here. It must suffice to note that he is a recipient of the James Royal Case Medal of Excellence, and is one of four members of the Missouri Lodge of Research recognized as a "Fellow" of the Lodge.

Only a scholar of the stature of Alphonse Cerza, who has labored long in the literary quarries of Freemasonry, could deliver himself of a works of this magnitude. It will endure for decades to come as a guidepost that shines and beckons and illuminates the paths of those who seek the literary light that glows beyond the confines of our Masonic altars.

Thomas C. Warden, Editor

Introduction

Tʜɪs ʙᴏᴏᴋ is addressed to Masons with four types of literary interests: (1) The member who has learned for the first time about the world of Masonic books and wants to know what printed material has been published so he can start to do some reading and thus improve himself in Masonry; (2) The member who has discovered that he has time on his hands and wants to read Masonic material and thus become a better informed Mason; (3) The member who has become an officer and wishes to improve his skills and thus serve in a better way; and (4) The member who is interested in doing research in order to prepare a talk, an article for publication, or a book on a Masonic subject. In each instance this book is designed to be a starting point in one's quest for suitable printed material. Manifestly, a great many subjects are covered because of the many areas of Masonic interest, and no single area is covered extensively in order to keep this book within reasonable bounds. Those members who come within the third and fourth classification will get a good start but in most instances will be required to do additional exploring for material.

Receiving the degrees in the Craft makes one a member, but he does not become a Mason until he has learned the meaning of the degrees, the moral lessons taught in the degrees, and how to make them a part of his life. Engaging in the reading of Masonic books is designed to help make a member a Mason. It has been stated by a perceptive person that one who knows how to read and does not read is no better off than the person who does not know how to read. The Mason who does not engage in any Masonic reading is poor indeed, for he is depriving himself of the opportunity of becoming an informed person and thus a better Mason. Up to this time there has been no easily obtainable general tool to help the Masonic reader in making a start. It is hoped that this book will be helpful as a practical guide.

Most Masons are surprised when they learn for the first time that there are Masonic books. This is probably due to the wording of the Obligation which indicates there can be no Masonic books and also because rarely are new Masons told that there are good Masonic books available for them to read so they can learn more about Freemasonry. No one has ever taken the time to count the number of Masonic books. One person estimated years ago that about 800,000 such books had been published, but this was probably a typographical error because an 80,000 figure would have been closer to the correct number. In making such a count one would be presented with many problems because how would you define the term ''Masonic book''? In a strict sense, a book written by Masons for Masons would come under such a description. Should we consider books that have been written by non-Masons for the general reader which deal with subjects of interest to Masons? Under this category, for example, would be a book such as Chailley's *The Magic Flute*. At any rate, the number is not important, but it is worthy of note that there are many such books. A paradox exists in that there are so many Masonic books and so few Masons who read them. Can a book such as this bring a change?

One practical problem about Masonic books is finding the names of the books as well as the source to secure them. Many Masonic publications in recent years have been following the practice of publishing short reviews of Masonic books and this is a good way to learn about new Masonic books. There have been a number of bibliographies of Masonic books published over the years but these lists are not always readily available. With Masonic libraries being few and often located far from one's home, together with the fact that many books in Masonic libraries do not circulate, there is a serious problem for the Mason who wishes thus to improve himself in Masonry. It is suggested that this introduction be read carefully and completely so that you may be able to get the fullest benefit on how to use this book.

Inclusion of an item does not necessarily mean that such item is approved or recommended. This is especially true in some areas which are somewhat controversial, and books on both sides of the issue may be listed here. By the same token, the omission of certain material from this book does not mean that this material is not worthy of consideration. Everything of merit could not be included in the space available here. I have deliberately ignored certain areas which I felt were not worthy of our attention, such as the large amount of printed material dealing with occult, Rosicrucian, mystic, and related subjects that some of our enthusiastic and misguided members have sought to associate with the Craft.

On the surface, some topics are presented in greater number than others. This is partly due to the available material on the specific subject and also because of the perceived greater interest by our members about these subjects. I have been informed by Masonic librarians that requests for biographical information far outnumber all other inquiries combined. Consequently, the section dealing with individual biographies is a long one. No attempt has been made to cover the biographies of famous men who have been Masons as such material is available in most public libraries. The cut-off point for material included here was the end of the year 1979.

How to Use This Book

Frequently one will know in advance what subjects he is interested in and the main problem is ascertaining what printed material is available. But when one has no subject or subjects that stand out in one's mind for exploration, the following suggestions may be of help in making a choice.

One method is to study the Table of Contents at the beginning of this book. Start by reading the ten chapter headings and select the one that appears to be closest to your interest. Then read the sections under that chapter to find the specific area that describes your topic of interest. Then proceed to that part of the book to learn what is set forth there.

Another method is to secure a catalog from the Masonic Service Association, which is available free, and to study the various items that are published by the Association. This material has been published each month since the early 1920s and the subjects cover the entire field of Masonic interest. The cost of the materials is nominal and they can be secured as a first step in determining in an inexpensive way what subjects are of special interest to you. Not everyone will have the same interest and the printed material about the Craft is vast and covers so many facets that with a little effort one can find material that will satisfy his interest.

Another method is to consult a Masonic encyclopedia and briefly study the various topics. Make notes of the subjects that appear to be of interest to you and then go back and read the items carefully. By this time you can begin to focus your attention on the subjects of special interest to you.

There are some sources of material that are easily overlooked. The Grand Lodge Proceedings, the proceedings of appendant bodies, the transactions of research lodges, and the printed material of educational committees contain many golden nuggets of information. Among the formal reports of the official proceedings, for example, often are buried items of unusual interest. Some of these items have been noted in this book. Examples are the *Joseph Robbins Oration* considered by many Masons as the greatest exposition of the nature of the Craft, and the Opinion of Grand Master Grover C. Neimeyer regarding the supremacy of the Grand Lodge over appendant bodies.

DESCRIPTION OF ITEMS PRESENTED

When books are described certain features are covered. The name of the author is stated first, as most libraries have an author's index which is easy to use in locating the call number. The title of the book is then given as it will usually tell the reader the nature of the topic covered. The date of publication is given to indicate its age, and the number of pages is stated to describe the breadth of the coverage. Some books have been published in many editions; no attempt has been made to describe these editions. Whenever easily available, some biographical material or leads to material about the author is presented. Frequently this is valuable in weighing the qualifications of an author to deal with the subject contained in the book. In most instances it is stated where the book has been reviewed; this information may be desired by some readers to determine what others think about the book and whether it is worthy of their attention. In some instances brief comments by Masonic authors relating to the book are set forth as a guide. Then follows the selected libraries where the book was found. In order to save space the 15 selected libraries are identified by numbers only. The number and the name of the library is identified and listed later.

Many papers published in research lodge transactions and magazines are listed here. Where the item appears to cover the subject, the name of the author and the title of the item may not be given but only the place where it appears. No attempt has been made to list the libraries where these items can be found. This bit of exploration is left for the reader since I did not want to encumber this book with too many details.

Since the Table of Contents at the beginning of this book is detailed in relation

xi

to the subject matter, the index at the end of the book has been restricted to the names of authors of books covered and the pages where the items appear herein. This is designed to help you locate the place in this book where the specific volume is described, and to locate other books written by the same author that you may wish to read. This index can also be used to find additional books on the same subject by using the name of the author to locate quickly the part of the book where other material on the same subject can be found.

ABBREVIATIONS USED IN THIS BOOK

Throughout this book abbreviations are used to save space and also for ease in reading. Many of these abbreviations are easy to understand, but others may not be familiar to some of our readers.

By way of explanation, instead of stating Volume 10 of the Transactions of Quatuor Coronati Lodge, on page 100, the item will be described as follows: 10 AQC 100, followed by the date. Always when so stated the first number will indicate the volume number, and the ending number the page where the item appears. The year in parenthesis will refer to the year of publication. A list of abbreviations immediately precedes Chapter One.

MASONIC LIBRARIES

Libraries with Masonic books exist everywhere and it would be impossible to compile a complete list containing all of them which would be of any practical value. There are Masonic libraries maintained by some Grand Lodges, by appendant bodies, and lodges. A partial list of these libraries is published by the Masonic Service Association from time to time. There are also special collections of Masonic books in some public libraries. Here is an illustration: The Loewy collection at Cornell University; the Harry A. Williamson Collection of Prince Hall material at the New York Public Library Branch located at 103 W. 135th Street, New York City, as part of the Schomburg Collection. Individual Masons at times have maintained extensive collections of Masonic books; two illustrations are the former private collections of Dr. William J. Cummings and Dr. William G. Peacher, both of New York, which books are now located at the Scottish Rite Library at Lexington, Massachusetts. As a practical matter, the Masonic reader should make inquiry at the various libraries within a reasonable distance of his home to determine what books are located there, whether the books circulate, the rules of the library, the hours the library is open, etc. Do not overlook college and university libraries in your area, local historical societies, and appendant bodies.

Do not let state lines act as a deterrent. Persons living along the central boundary line of Illinois and Indiana might find it convenient to use the library of the Grand Lodge of Indiana located at Indianapolis; persons living in southern Illinois might find it convenient to use the Scottish Rite Library in St. Louis; and persons living in western Illinois might find it convenient to use the Iowa Masonic Library located at Cedar Rapids.

Here is a list of Masonic libraries that contain some of the books listed herein.

xii

Such a list is never current, as books are being added, lost, and misplaced with the passage of time:

1. California Grand Lodge Library.
2. Chicago Scottish Rite Library.
3. Iowa Grand Lodge Library.
4. King County Masonic Library, Seattle, Washington.
5. Massachusetts Grand Lodge Library.
6. Missouri Grand Lodge Library.
7. New York Grand Lodge Library.
8. Oregon Grand Lodge Library.
9. Pennsylvania Grand Lodge Library.
10. St. Louis Scottish Rite Library.
11. Scottish Rite Library, Lexington, Massachusetts.
12. Scottish Rite Library, Washington, D.C.
13. Southern California Masonic Library.
14. Texas Grand Lodge Library.
15. Utah Grand Lodge Library.

There are many other fine Masonic libraries throughout the United States as well as in various other parts of the world. Time and space did not permit covering these libraries. Some that quickly come to mind are those in Cleveland, South Dakota, the Scottish Rite in Milwaukee, the Scottish Rite in Oakland, the Scottish Rite in Dayton, Ohio, the Grand Lodge Library in Indiana, and the Masonic collection in Ann Arbor, Michigan.

Some Masonic libraries have lists of the most-circulated books. Others will mail books to readers. If it is not convenient to visit a Masonic library, consider making use of a modern device that can save time and money. In most Masonic libraries there is a co-operative librarian or worker who will be glad to arrange for a local photocopying firm to make copies of the item you need, upon payment of cost.

The Scottish Rite Library, located at 33 Marrett Street, Lexington, Massachusetts, is concentrating on acquiring books on Americana and aims to be the best library in the United States with material relating to American history. It has a considerable number of Masonic books and the number is growing each year as boxes are unpacked and books are placed on the shelves and indexed. In a few years this library will be one of the outstanding Masonic libraries in the United States. It has acquired the books of Dr. William J. Cummings, who spent a lifetime collecting Masonic rituals and material relating to the William Morgan and anti-Masonic period. The library also acquired the extensive library of Dr. William G. Peacher before he moved to California.

In Washington, D.C., the Library of Congress may be consulted for many Masonic books. The Folger Shakespeare Library, near the Capitol, has many books on the period when the Craft was evolving from an operative to a speculative organization. But the greatest storehouse of material is located in the House of the Temple, maintained by the Scottish Rite, Southern Jurisdiction, with its special collections of Robert Burns, Goethe, Grand Commanders Pike, Cowles, Luther A. Smith, and Henry C. Clausen. The contents of *The New Age Magazine* and the *Proceedings* of the Supreme Council have been indexed by Aemil Pouler. The library has many unpublished works of Albert Pike plus many original letters, certificates, etc.

It has taken ten years to gather the material contained in this book. I have learned that it is easy to overlook sources of Masonic material close at hand. For example, state historical societies often have Masonic material, and some municipalities maintain adequate libraries with local material. Most local public libraries will have some Masonic material. Do not overlook the private libraries in your area. For example, the Newberry Library, in Chicago, has a great collection of genealogical material, plus many Masonic books.

No attempt has been made to describe or include Masonic libraries outside the United States. Masonic libraries are maintained by the Grand Lodges of England, Scotland, and Ireland. There are Masonic libraries in Canada, New Zealand, Rome, and other places.

Publishers of Masonic Printed Material

Readers who are desirous of assembling a library of Masonic books will be interested in knowing that the sources are few at the present time. Here is a list:

Masonic Service Association,
8120 Fenton Street,
Silver Spring, Maryland 20910.

Macoy Masonic Publishing Co.,
3011 Dumbarton Road,
Richmond, Virginia 23228.

A. Lewis Ltd.,
Terminal House,
Shepperton, TW17 8AS,
London, England

Temple Publishing Co.
8120 Fenton Street,
Silver Spring, Maryland 20910.

Each of the above publishers periodically issues catalogs of the books sold by them.

There is no easy source for securing out-of-print Masonic books. In addition to having them photocopied, two suggestions are made in this connection. First, ascertain the names and addresses of several secondhand book stores in London and let them know what publications you seek. Second, find the name and address of a convenient ''book search'' person or firm and supply a list of books you want. These persons will then advertise and seek to locate the books; when they find one they will let you know the price and you can then decide whether or not you want to buy the book. There is no charge made for the service. The names of these firms can be located in the book review section of most newspapers and also in the *New York Times Book Review*.

At this time there is no national Masonic magazine being published such as *The Builder Magazine*, the official publication of the National Masonic Research Society, issued between 1915 and 1931. But there are many fine local Masonic magazines, including many Grand Lodge publications. In many states in recent years Grand Lodges have established Educational Committees that publish material of interest and can be of assistance in the literary querries. All these local sources should be explored. From time to time there is talk of establishing a national Masonic magazine and perhaps some day this will come to pass.

Acknowledged Help by Others

I gratefully acknowledge the help of many persons in the gathering of information contained in this book. In many instances because of distance I have had to rely on librarians and friends to check books in local libraries so the information could be recorded here. Eventually this phase of the work became a burden and had to be curtailed because it became a never-ending task that could never be completed or up-to-date as books were added or lost in each of the libraries.

I am especially indebted to the following persons for outstanding and devoted help in this phase of the work:

Chicago Scottish Rite Library: Samuel K. Zipp; Arthur J. Votava.

Iowa Masonic Library: Franklin J. Anderson; Keith Arrington; William Durow.

King County Masonic Library, Seattle, Washington: Albert L. Woody.

Massachusetts Grand Lodge Library: Abraham Feldman; John M. Sherman; Roberta Hankamer

Missouri Grand Lodge Library: John B. Vrooman; Doug Morin; Earl K. Dille.

New York Grand Lodge Library: Wendell K. Walker; Grace R. Curtis; Dr. Allan Boudreau.

Pennsylvania Grand Lodge Library: William A. Carpenter; Frank W. Bobb.

St. Louis Scottish Rite Library: John B. Vrooman; Earl K. Dille; Charles R. Coleman.

Scottish Rite Library, Lexington, Massachusetts: Dr. Clement Silvestro; Gloria Jackson.

Scottish Rite Library, Washington, D.C.: Aemil Pouler; Inge Baum.

Southern California Masonic Library: John R. Nocas.

Texas Grand Lodge Library: Dixie Milton.

Abbreviations

Here is a list of the more frequently used abbreviations:

ALR: Transactions of the American Lodge of Research.

Build. Mag.: *The Builder Magazine*, official magazine of the now defunct National Masonic Research Society.

Cal. Free: *The California Freemason*, official publication of the Grand Lodge of California.

Ind. Free.: *The Indiana Freemason*, official magazine of the Grand Lodge of Indiana.

Io. Res. L.: Research Lodge No. 2 of Iowa.

K. T. Mag.: *The Knight Templar Magazine*, official publication of the Grand Encampment of Knights Templar of the United States.

M. & P. M. L.: Masters and Past Masters Lodge No. 130, of New Zealand.

Mas. Mess. Ga.: *The Masonic Messenger*, official magazine of the Grand Lodge
of Georgia.
MLR: Missouri Lodge of Research.
MSA: Masonic Service Association of the United States.
New Age Mag.: *The New Age Magazine*, official publication of the Scottish
Rite, Southern Jurisdiction.
N.Y. Mas. Outl.: *New York Masonic Outlook*.
No. Light: *The Northern Light*, official publication of the Scottish Rite, North-
ern Masonic Jurisdiction.
Phil. Mag.: *The Philalethes Magazine*, official magazine of The Philalethes
Society.
RAM: *The Royal Arch Mason*.
TLR: Texas Lodge of Research.
Trans.: Transactions.

Contents

Chapter Nine. ORGANIZATIONS

Chapter Ten. ANTI-MASONRY

A MASONIC READER'S GUIDE

CHAPTER ONE

General Works

1.01 INTRODUCTION TO FREEMASONRY.

Carl H. Claudy, *Introduction to Freemasonry*. 1931; 182 pp. Temple Publishing Co., publishers. In one volume and in three volume editions.
Author: Appendix No. 6. Contents: Elementary material designed to be presented to the candidate after receiving each degree. Libraries: 1, 2, 3, 4, 5, 6, 7, 8, 9, 10, 11, 12, 13, 14.

H. L. Haywood, *Introduction to Freemasonry*. 1971. Reproduced by Iowa Research Lodge No. 2.
Author: Appendix No. 16. Libraries: 2, 3.

William E. Hammond, *What Masonry Means*. 1939; 170 pp. Macoy Publishing Co. With introduction by Joseph Fort Newton. Part of this book originally appeared in the Master Mason magazine.
Contents: Good description of what Freemasonry is and what it does to the individual member. Libraries: 1, 3, 4, 5, 6, 9, 10, 11, 13, 14.

A. Meeson, *An Introduction to Free Masonry*.
Contents: Presents the moral aspects of the Craft with the use of geometrical illustrations. Reviewed: Harry Carr, ed., Collected Prestonian Lectures, p. 87. Libraries: 3.

Knoop and Jones, *Introduction to Freemasonry*. 1937; 90 pp. Manchester University Press.
Authors: See Sec. 2.16 in this book.

Contents: Covers the origin of Freemasonry, the connection between the operative and the speculative masons and is a good introduction to the background of the Craft. Reviewed: New Age Mag., April, 1937, 352; Ill. Enlight., Sept., 1950, 2. Libraries: 1, 2, 3, 5, 7, 8, 9, 10, 11, 12, 14.

Henry W. Coil, Sr., *A Comprehensive View of Freemasonry*. 1954; 234 pp. Macoy Publishing Co.
Author: Appendix No. 8. Contents: Analysis of the Craft, its relationship with other groups, and a brief history. Reviewed: New Age Mag., Dec., 1954, 763; 67 AQC 141 (1954). Libraries: 1, 2, 3, 4, 5, 7, 8, 9, 10, 11, 12, 13, 14.

Robert J. Blackham, *Apron Men: The Romance of Freemasonry*. 1933; 275 pp. Rider & Co., London, publisher.
Contents: Presents a number of brief topics relating to the Craft in various parts of the world, covers some fables, and presents a number of topics of general interest such as the development of the degrees. Comment: L. B. Blakemore, "A loosely sketchy volume on a variety of topics, but valuable for its chapters on lodges in the British Empire." Libraries: 3, 5, 7, 8, 10, 11, 14.

Joseph Robbins, *What Freemasonry Is*. Oration delivered before the Grand Lodge of Illinois on October 6, 1869. Considered by many as the best exposition of what is Freemasonry. Reproduced in the Ill. Enlight., June 1952 to Feb. 1953 issues.

Dr. Robert J. Lewinski, *What Is Freemasonry?* 1961; revised and enlarged in 1973. MSA Digest.

M.A.R. Howard, *What Is Freemasonry?* 3 Walter F. Meier L. of Res. 71.

What Is Masonry? STB, Sept., 1924.

What Masonry Means. STB, Aug., 1928.

Fred J. W. Crowe, *Things a Free Mason Should Know.* 1909; 86 pp. G. Kenning & Son, London, publisher.

Author: See 22 AQC 198 (1909); 44 AQC 130 (1931). Contents: Collection of essays on basic Masonic information. A short history, the old charges, regalia, charities, literature, and other Grand Lodges. Comments: L. B. Blakemore, "A small book of excellent essays on such topics as the Apron by the revisor and editor of Gould's Concise History." Silas H. Shepherd, "One of the best elementary books." Reviewed: 3 Build. Mag. 285 (1917); 15 Build. Mag. 316 (1930); 23 AQC 196 (1910). Libraries: 1, 2, 3, 4, 5, 7, 8, 9, 10, 11, 12, 13, 14.

Alphonse Cerza, *What Can I Tell My Non-Masonic Friends.* New Age Mag., Aug., 1962, 30.

Marvin L. Isley, *What Can I Tell My Non-Masonic Friends,* Ind. Free., May, 1971, 6.

What To Tell Your Wife. STB, July, 1939.

What Is Masonry? Mas. J. of So. Africa, June, 1975, 3.

Stanley B. Crossland, *What Is Freemasonry?* Ind. Free., July, 1953, 6.

An Introduction to the Study of Freemasonry. Phil. Mag., March, 1952, 11.

How to Enjoy Masonry. New Age Mag., Feb., 1955, 109.

Gen. MacArthur, *Morality Is the Basis of Freemasonry.* 12 RAM 215 (1977).

Edwin Markham, N.Y. Mas. Outl., Dec., 1928, 100 (Has his picture).

Edgar A. Guest, *What Masonry Means to Me.* New Age Mag., 1931, 612.

Dr. Daniel A. Poling, *Journey Into Light.* Ind. Free., May, 1956, 9.

Walter J. Bunney, *Freemasonry and the Contemplative Art.* Reproduced in Harry Carr, ed., Collected Prestonian Lectures, 195.

K. G. S. Shepherd, *What Is Freemasonry?* Reproduced in Harry Carr, ed., Collected Prestonian Lectures, 377.

1.02 THE NATURE OF THE CRAFT

Joseph Fort Newton, *The Builders.* 1914. Originally published by the Grand Lodge of Iowa for presentation to each new Mason. Is probably the most widely read Masonic book of all times. Written in a fine style, it briefly covers the history, symbolism, and nature of the Craft.

Author: Appendix No. 26. Reviewed: The Master Mason, Feb., 1924; 76; 10 Build. Mag. 121 (1924); 30 AQC 215 (1917). Comments: Certain parts of this book should be read with reservations such as the mention of the Boston Tea Party and the cathedral builders. When an edition of this book was published in England certain changes were made in specific subjects to bring the material up-to-date. Soon after this book was published, the Cincinnati Masonic Study Club compiled a list of questions based on this book as an aid to studying Masonry; a list of these questions were printed in the first volume of the Build. Mag. (1915): 128-129; 166-168; 189-190; 227-228; 279-280; and in Vol. 2, 25-26. Comments by: L. B. Blakemore, "The Blue Lodge Classic. This is the most widely read Masonic book in modern times. Beautifully written. Covers the complete history of Freemasonry. In error as to the Comacine origin of Masonry." Carl H. Claudy, "This volume is in three sections devoted to Prophecy, History, and Interpretation, and, by the gentle genius of the author, whose wide reading, scholarship, and insight well equipped him for an almost impossible task, weaves Freemasonry into daily life and living, shows its place in history and in religion and puts into vivid English as much of the spirit of the Order as can be expressed in words." Norman B. Hickox, "The fundamentals of Freemasonry are presented in beautiful and expressive English. . . . Personally, if I had only one book to choose on Masonry it would be this classic. . . ."

Libraries: 1, 2, 3, 4, 5, 6, 7, 8, 9, 10, 11, 12, 13, 14, 15.

H. L. Haywood, *The Newly-Made Mason*. 1948; 220 pp. The Masonic History Co., Chicago, publisher.

Author: Appendix No. 16. Contents: An introduction to the Craft to the new Mason covering a variety of subjects. Comments: L. B. Blakemore, "What every Mason should know about Masonry. Excellent text for beginners." Libraries: 1, 2, 3, 4, 5, 6, 7, 8, 9, 10, 11, 12, 13, 14, 15.

H. L. Haywood, *More About Masonry*. 1948; 220 pp. The Masonic History Co., Chicago, publisher. The author told me that the material he wrote was intended to be one book but was too large for one volume so the company printed it in two volumes. This is a logical follow-up on the preceding book.

Libraries: 1, 2, 3, 4, 5, 7, 8, 9, 10, 11, 13, 14.

Rollin C. Blackmer, *The Lodge and the Craft*. 1923; 286 pp. Standard Masonic Publishing Co., St. Louis, Mo. Republished by Macoy Publishing.

Author: Was a physician. Brief sketch in 13 Build. Mag. 47 (1928). Contents: General description of Freemasonry: its laws, degrees, symbols, structure, and history. Reviewed: 9 Build. Mag. 349 (1923); New Age Mag., Feb., 1924, 124. Ind. Free., March, 1977, 17. Libraries: 3, 6, 8, 9, 10, 11, 15.

George Draffen, *The Making of a Mason*. 1978; 159 pp. A. Lewis Ltd., publisher.

Author: See Sec. 2.16 herein. Contents: Designed for use at each step as the candidate progresses from degree to degree. Reviewed: Mas. Sq., Sept., 1979, 125.

Ernest Beha, *A Comprehensive Dictionary of Freemasonry*. 1962; 207 pp. First American edition published in 1963 by Citadel Press.

Contents: Though written primarily for English Masons and slanted with British information, it has some items of general interest describing the Craft. The material is arranged in alphabetical order according to subjects. Reviewed: New Age Mag.,

March, 1964, 52. Libraries: 3, 5, 7, 9, 11, 12, 14.

William Preston Campbell-Everden. *Freemasonry and Its Etiquette*. 1919; 507 pp. A 1938 edition was published by A. Lewis Ltd., having 465 pp. It was reprinted in 1978 in the United States.

Contents: A general description of Freemasonry, how it is organized, qualifications for membership, duties of lodge officers, and related subjects. This book is apparently an expansion of a prior book issued on the same subject. Comment: Harry Carr, in his introduction to the 1973 ed. of Dr. E. H. Cartwright, *A Commentary on The Freemasonic Ritual*, on page 30 states: "It is got up in specious imitation of the Etiquette but the 'incorporation' consists of barely a quarter of the original matter and that merely such portions as were in general terms and had little or nothing to do with the actual ritual." Libraries: 1, 3, 4, 6, 7, 8, 9, 10, 11, 12, 13, 14.

Charles Gough, *The Etiquette of Freemasonry – Bro. Franklin Thomas*. 29 AQC 101 (1916).

George Draffen, *Masonic Etiquette and Scottish Usage*. 1966 Grd. L. of Scotl. Yrbk. 57.

H. L. Haywood, *Masonic Etiquette*, in Masonic Essays, 423.

Masonic Etiquette. Colo. leaflet reproduced in New Age Mag., June, 1947, 338.

Oswell G. Treadway, *The Nature of Freemasonry*. Ill. Enlight., Aug., 1956, 86.

George B. Clark, *Our Masonic Heritage*. 1936; 90 pp. Grand Lodge of Colo. publisher.

Contents: Presents early history of the Craft with many biographical sketches and leads into Colorado history. Has many pictures of persons and discussion of Masonic literature. Libraries: 2, 3, 5, 7, 8, 9, 12, 13.

Salem Town, *A System of Speculative Masonry*. 1818; 283 pp. Dodd and Stevenson, Salem, N.Y. publisher.

Author: Temple R. Hollcroft, Salem

Town; 5 ALR 240 (1944-1945). See The Civil War Letters of Salem Town. 8 ALR 180 (1961). Contents: A collection of lectures given at various times by the author in which the nature of the Craft is explained. Comment: Mackey's Ency., Vol. 2, 1045: "This work is of course tinged with all the legendary ideas of the origin of the Institution which prevailed at that period, and which would not now be accepted as authoritative; but it contains, outside of its historical errors, many valuable and suggestive thoughts." In 1828 there was published a book entitled *"Freemasonry,"* by A Master Mason (believed to have been Henry Dana Ward), consisting of 396 pages, in which the author reviews Salem Town's book critically and presents extracts from Barruel and Robison and quotes from many Masonic authors to prove his points against the Craft. Clearly an anti-Masonic book found in the following libraries: 3, 5, 7, 9, 12. Libraries with Town's book: 3, 7, 9, 11.

Alphonse Cerza, *Our Masonic Heritage.* Ill. Grd. L. Proc., 1969, 92.

Melvyn M. Johnson, *For All Men and All Times.* 1946; 50 pp. Supreme Council, NMJ, publisher. See MSA Digest, The Universality of Freemasonry.
Contents: Devoted to the theme that Freemasonry is universal. Libraries: 3, 5, 7, 10, 11, 12, 13.

J. A. Cockburn, *Freemasonry: What, Whence, Why, Whither.* n.d., 58 pp. The Masonic Record, Ltd., of London, publisher.
Contents: A short discussion of various aspects of Freemasonry with many personal opinions on debatable subjects. Reviewed: Mast. Mas., May, 1924, 335. Libraries: 3, 5, 7, 8, 9, 11, 12, 13, 14, 15.

What? When? Where? Why? Who? in Freemasonry. MSA Digest.

Alphonse Cerza, *The Attraction of Freemasonry.* No. Light, April, 1970, 7.

Why Do Men Join Lodges? New Age Mag., Feb., 1960, 31; 7 RAM 87 (1955).

Henry W. Coil, Sr., *Conversations On Masonry.* 1979; 282 pp. Edited by Wes Cook with a preface by W. R. Denslow. MLR publisher.
Author: Appendix No. 8. Contents: Contains ten chapters dealing with various aspects of the Craft with many perceptive observations.

Does Masonry Have Anything of Value to Offer? 1970 Grd. Mast. Conf. 52.

What Do Men Want and Expect From Masonry? 1969 Grd. Mast. Conf. 74.

How Does the Individual Mason Live Masonry Daily? 1969 Grd. Mast. Conf. 79.

What Is the Ultimate Purpose and End of Masonic Teaching? And Is It Being Achieved? 1970 Grd. Mast. Conf. 63.

What Are A Mason's Responsibilities to His Fraternity and to Mankind? 1968 Grd. Mast. Conf. 69.

What Is Involved In the Idea of the Brotherhood of Man? 1967 Grd. Mast. Conf. 97.

Is Freemasonry Really Making Good Men Better? 1967 Grd. Mast. Conf. 94.

What Are the Basic and Fundamental Ideals of Freemasonry? 1967 Grd. Mast. Conf. 93.

Charles G. Reigner, *The Meaning and Mission of Masonry.* (1966).

Andrew Caraker, *The Nature of Freemasonry.* 1956 Proc. Ill. Grd. L. 103.

What Can You Say? Ind. Free., Nov., 1976, 8.

What Should You Not Say? Ind. Free., Dec., 1976, 9.

F. W. Gregory, *An Interpretation of Masonry.* Trans. Leicester L. of Res., 1973-1974, p. 48.

Motivation. New Age Mag., April, 1962, p. 39.

Andrew Caraker, *Freemasonry In the Business of Character.* 1957 Proc. Ill. Grd. L. 99.

Statement made in 1938 by the Grand Lodges of England, Ireland, and Scotland. Reproduced in Ind. Free., Nov., 1976, p. 10.

The Tenets of Freemasonry. 1964 Yr. Bk. Grd. L. of Scot. Reproduced in Ind. Free., Feb., 1979, p. 12.

A Letter to the Petitioner. New Mexico Free., Nov., 1977, p. 5.

William Jacobson, *How Should Masons Act?* Ind. Free., May, 1974, 18.

Dr. Irving I. Lasky, *Masonry, Medicine and Dignity.* New Age Mag. March, 1979, p. 47.

A. Cerza, *The Benefits of Masonic Membership.* STB, Nov., 1978.

Norman C. Dutt, *What Do I Get Out of Freemasonry?* Phil. Mag., Feb., 1977, p. 20.

F. A. Kleinschmidt, *What A Privilege It Is to Be a Mason!* 3 Tex. L. of Res. 166 (1965-1968).

Richard W. Lottridge, *The Practical Application of the Principles of Masonry or the Hope of Mankind.* New Age Mag., Dec., 1978, p. 43.

Alex Horne, *English and American Freemasonry Compared.* Phil. Mag., April, 1977, p. 8.

H. L. Haywood, *This World of Masonry.* N.Y. Mas. Outl., Sept., 1929, p. 5.

H. L. Haywood, *Our Masonic Doctrine.* N.Y. Mas. Outl., July, 1929, 335.

A. A. Brill, *How Masonry Talks to Men.* N.Y. Mas. Outl., Feb., 1929, 164.

Frederick W. Kendall, *What the Mason of 1925 Can Learn From the Mason of 1390.* N.Y. Mas. Outl., Nov., 1925, p. 79.

H. L. Haywood, *Qualifications of A Master Mason.* N.Y. Mas. Outl., May, 1930, p. 263. Also in Phil. Mag., Feb., 1963, p. 14.

Albert A. Hughes, *Physical Disqualifications Arising Out of War Service,* 1944 Proc. Grd. Mas. Conf. 67.

John R. Hunter, *Physical Qualifications. Who Shall Be the Final Judge?* 1940 Proc. Grd. Mast. Conf. 45.

John A. Stormon and Harold R. Stephenson. *Should the War Change Our Viewpoint on Physical Qualifications?* 1947 Proc. Grd. Mast. Conf. 83, 92.

Dwight L. Smith, *Are the Physical Requirements Essential for Freemasonry?* Phil. Mag., April, 1971, p. 30.

George Rees, *The Physically Disabled and the Craft.* 11 ALR 371 (1971).

Ray E. Cummings, *Liquor Industry as a Bar to Membership.* 1950 Proc. Grd. Mast. Conf. 57.

William B. Ogden, *Persons Engaged in or Connected With the Sale or Manufacture of Intoxicating Liquor.* 1940 Proc. Grd. Mast. Conf. 86.

Carl W. Ellenwood and John H. Crooker, *Lodge Dues.* 1935 Proc. Grd. Mast. Conf. 34.

Harry A. Belt, *Dual and Plural Membership.* 1926 Proc. Grd. Mast. Conf. 11.

F. T. McFadden, *Dual Membership.* 1930 Grd. Mast. Conf. 43.

William O. Ware and Sanford M. Chilcote, *Should All Grand Lodges of This Conference Grant Their Members the Privilege of Dual, and Possibly Plural, Membership?* 1958 Proc. Grd. Mast. Conf. 86.

Life Membership and Automatic Granting of the Same. 1931 Proc. Grd. Mast. Conf. 38.

District Deputy Grand Master System; How Widespread and How Successful? 1931 Proc. Grd. Mast. Conf. 37.

Charity. 11 Build. Mag. 142 (1925).

Mystery. STB, Oct., 1942.

A. C. Parker, *Why All the Secrecy?* 9 Build. Mag. 362 (1923).

Freemasonry and the Computer. Mo. Free., Spring, 1972, p. 57.

"Busy Brotherly World of Freemasonry." Life Magazine, Oct., 1956, p. 104.

The Power of Freemasonry. Newsletter of the Grd. L. of India, Oct., 1970. Reproduced in The Freemasons' Chronicle, London. Also in the Ind. Free., April, 1971, p. 9.

Religion and Politics, Why Not Discussed in Lodge? New Age Mag., Dec., 1972, p. 3; United Masters Lodge No. 167, New Zealand, July, 1972, p. 207. 83 AQC 367 (1970).

Article in the Christian Science Monitor about Freemasonry, 1956. Reproduced in Ill. Enlight., May, 1956, p. 1.

Franklin J. Anderson, *The Soul of Masonry.* Phil. Mag., Feb., 1970, 10.

What A Fellow Craft Should Know. 10 Build. Mag. 35 (1924).

Occultism. 9 Build. Mag. 245 (1923).

Rev. W. W. Covey-Crump, *The Craft and the Kabalah.* 19 pp. in Vol. 3 Trans. Author's Lodge. Defines what is the Kabalah and relies on A. E. Waite. Discusses Gould's History, Vol. 2, p. 138. This material must be read with caution.

My Masonic Membership. 7 RAM 224 (1962).

"Once a Mason Always a Mason." 13 Build. Mag. 246 (1927).

"Naturalism" Defined. 7 Build. Mag., 270 (1921).

R. J. Meekren, *Mythology and Masonry.* 10 Build. Mag. 67 (1924).

Alchemy. 8 Build. Mag. 160 (1922).

1.03 MASONIC ENCYCLOPEDIAS

Albert G. Mackey, *Revised Encyclopedia of Freemasonry.* Two vols., 1929; 1217 pp.; Vol.3, by H. L. Haywood, 1946; 419 pp. Masonic History Co., Chicago, publisher. This work started out years ago as a Masonic Dictionary and was expanded as it was reprinted. It has been expanded and revised over the years by many distinguished Masons.
Author: Appendix No. 23. Comments: Silas H. Shepherd, "If a Mason would have one book on Masonry, this would be the most useful one to choose. If he has an extensive library, he needs this encyclopedia for constant reference. This is the best of the many encyclopedias that have been published." Norman B. Hickox, ". . . undoubtedly the best reference work in the 49 American Jurisdictions and,

although it has faults, is a most necessary basic item. Its few errors may be due to most of the work dating between 1845 and 1874, others to uncritical editing when it was revised for 1912 and 1929 printings. It furnishes a rich field of Masonic information within small compass and has no serious rival. . . . " Henry W. Coil, "Notwithstanding the scholarship and facile pen of Dr. Mackey, his encyclopedia could not avoid vast alterations after 1874. . . . The less said about Volume III by H. L. Haywood the better. . . . The result was some extreme partisan positions, and propositions and theories which were false or even absurd." Reviewed: 16 Build. Mag. 91 (1930); The Masonic Mirror, Vol. 1, page 11 (1874); Ill. Enlight., May, 1961, 235; New Age Mag., April, 1961, 56. Libraries: Most Masonic libraries have more than one edition of this work.

Henry W. Coil, Sr., *Masonic Encyclopedia.* 1961; 731 pp. Macoy Publishing Co. Edited by Dr. William L. Cummings, Dr. William Moseley Brown, and Harold V. B. Voorhis.
Author: Appendix No. 8. Comments: Louis L. Williams, "A fine work and the best presently available." Reviewed: New Age Mag., April, 1961, 56; Ill. Enlight., April, 1961, 56. Libraries: Will be found in most Masonic libraries.

E. L. Hawkins, *A Concise Cyclopedia of Freemasonry.* 1908; 251 pp. A. Lewis, London.
Author: 26 AQC 88 (1913). Comments: Silas H. Shepherd, "Accurate and instructive on the limited selection of subjects included." L. B. Blakemore, "Though it wants bringing up to date, this is perhaps the best dictionary of Masonry, and as a reference work ranks second after Mackey's Encyclopedia." Libraries: 1, 3, 4, 5, 7, 9, 10, 11, 12, 13.

Kenneth R. H. MacKenzie, *Royal Masonic Cyclopedia of History, Rites, Symbolism, and Biography.* 1877; 782 pp. John Hogg, London, publisher.
Author: 85 AQC 252 (1972). Comments: Silas H. Shepherd, "An excellent work, unfortunately out of print and scarce. Hughan says that the encyclopedias of Mackey, Kenning, and Mac-

Kenzie each possess special features not common to all." L. B. Blakemore, "A one-volume dictionary of brief paragraphs of information on thousands of Masonic subjects." A. E. Waite made some disparaging remarks about the author in his New Encyclopedia. Libraries: 1, 3, 5, 7, 9, 11.

Robert Macoy, *General History, Cyclopedia and Dictionary of Freemasonry*. 1970; 700 pp. Includes "A Dictionary of Symbolic Masonry" by George Oliver.
Libraries: 10.

Fred L. Pick and G. Norman Knight, *The Freemasons' Pocket Reference Book*. 1956; 283 pp. American ed. published by the Philosophical Library, New York.
Authors: 56 AQC 298 (1943); 79 AQC 93 (1966); Contents: A good short reference work arranged in alphabetical order. Libraries: 4.

Arthur Edward Waite, *New Encyclopedia of Freemasonry*. Two vols.; 458 pp. and 487 pp. Virtue & Co., London, publisher.
Author: The leading occultist of his day. Contents: Contains too many occult references and statements. Must be read with caution. Comments: Silas H. Shepherd, "Contains much material respecting the mystic and occult phases of Freemasonry, but has a tendency to be dogmatic." H. L. Haywood, " . . . is less about Masonry than about occultism." L. B. Blakemore, "This two-volume work is not so much an encyclopedia as a collection of essays on a variety of Masonic themes, most of them belonging to history and ritual." Libraries: 3, 4, 5, 6, 7, 9, 10, 11, 12, 15.

Alec Mellor, *Dictionaire de la Franc-Maconnerie et des Francs-Macons*. 1971; 321 pp. Editions Pierre Belfond, Paris, publisher.
Reviewed: 84 AQC 220 (1971); 91 AQC 111 (1979).

James Hastings, *Encyclopedia of Religion and Ethics*. 1917; 13 vols. Scribner Sons. publisher.
Comment: H. L. Haywood, " . . . such a work as Hasting's . . . contains nearly 150 subjects especially worth a Mason's study." Libraries: This work is found in most public libraries. Volume 8 of The Builder Magazine, page 218 (1922) contains a list of the topics in this work of interest to Masons. This set is in the following Masonic Libraries: 3, 5, 7, 14.

1.04 COLLECTED WORKS

Rob Morris, ed., *Universal Masonic Library*. Thirty large volumes which collected the standard works of the day. Published in various years around 1855.
Author: Appendix No. 25. Libraries: 2, 3, 4, 5, 7, 8, 11, 12, 13, 14.

British Masonic Miscellany. Compiled by George Martin of Dundee, Scotland.
Contents: Collection of many short items on a variety of Masonic subjects. Reviewed: New Age Mag., Dec., 1932, 761. Libraries: 3, 8, 11, 14.

Little Masonic Library. Originally published in 20 small volumes. 1924. The material was collected by Carl H. Claudy. Current edition issued by Macoy Publishing Co.
Author: Appendix No. 6. Comments: Carl H. Claudy, "The books are actually a reading course in Freemasonry, and their popularity . . . since their original publication has attested to their value. They are varied in content and in treatment and the brevity of the twenty treatments attracts and holds the readers who might otherwise be repelled by a too forbidding size." Reviewed: 11 Build. Mag. 92 (1925); Mast. Mas., Oct., 1924, 657. The Master Mason, Feb., 1925, 144, has a series of questions based on this set of books designed for use by Masonic study groups.

A revised edition of this work was published by Macoy Publishing Co., in 1978 with two major changes: The Samuel Goodwin article on Mormonism was substituted with one by Dr. Mervin B. Hogan and there was added an item by Harold V. B. Voorhis expressing a view on what happened to William Morgan. Libraries: 2, 3, 7, 8, 9, 10, 11, 12, 13, 14, 15.

George Oliver, *Golden Remains of Early Masonic Writers*. Six small volumes

containing a collection of old Masonic books and brochures.
Libraries: 4, 5, 7, 8, 9, 11, 12, 13, 14.

Harry Carr, ed., *The Collected Prestonian Lectures, 1925-1960.* 1965; 491 pp. Quatuor Coronati Lodge, publisher.
Author: Appendix No. 3. Contents: William Preston in his will left a sum of money to be devoted to paying for a lecture to be given each year. For some years this was not done and the fund grew. These lectures are now an annual event and the subjects and speakers have been selected with care. Comment: Louis L. Williams, ''A masterpiece for the advanced Masonic scholar.'' Reviewed: 8 RAM 283 (1966); 78 AQC 157 (1965). Libraries: 1, 2, 3, 4, 5, 6, 7, 8, 9, 10, 11, 13, 14, 15.

Dollar Masonic Library. Ten small soft-bound booklets containing a wealth of valuable material. This was a joint publishing project.
Reviewed: 13 Build. Mag. 347 (1927). Libraries: 3.

Henry Sadler, *Masonic Reprints and Revelations.* 1898; 91 pp. George Kenning, London, publisher.
Author: 23 AQC 328 (1910); 24 AQC 277 (1911). Contents: Explanatory notes and reproduction of some old important printed Masonic material: Letter from the Grand Mistress of the Female Free-Masons, A Defence of Free-Masonry, A Defence of Laurence Dermott and the Antients, and a discussion of Swift's connection with the Craft. Reviewed: 11 AQC 190 and 192 (1898). Libraries: 2, 3, 7, 9, 12, 15.

Roscoe Pound, *Masonic Addresses and Writings.* 1953; 384 pp. Macoy Publishing Co., publisher. With introduction by Melvin M. Johnson.
Contents: The main works of an outstanding student of the Craft. Has his picture. Author: Phil. Mag., Oct., 1964, 78; 8 RAM 92 (1964). Reviewed: New Age Mag., Oct., 1953, 636. Libraries: 1, 2, 3, 4, 5, 6, 7, 8, 9, 10, 11, 12, 13, 14.

Earl K. Dille, ed., *The Masonic Review of Bruce H. Hunt.* 1978; 220 pp. MLR, publisher.
Author, Bruce H. Hunt: Appendix 22.

Contents: Annually since 1962 Bruce H. Hunt has been making a summary of what has been taking place in various jurisdictions by reading the proceedings of these Grand Lodges. This volume contains the cream of the crop carefully and skillfully selected and combined by the editor.

Lewis C. Wes Cook, ed., *Masonic Portraits,* by Ray V. Denslow. 1972; 322 pp. MLR.
Contents: Twenty-one chapters collecting together a variety of items of perennial interest written over the years by Ray V. Denslow.

A Haywood Trio. 115 pp. Published by Iowa Res. Lodge No. 2. 115 pp.
Contents: Reproduces A Vest Pocket History of Freemasonry; Facts and Fables of the Craft; and The Walrus and the Carpenter.

Masonic Americana, 1975; 246 pp. Collection of patriotic Masonic articles which appeared originally in the Knight Templar Magazine.

Quatuor Coronatorium Antigrapha. Twelve volumes containing reproduction of original Masonic material of interest to researchers. Some of the items are reproduced in facsimile. Many of the ancient manuscripts are here, and most of the items have a commentary by a Masonic scholar.

1.05 QUIZZES

Harry Carr, *The Freemason at Work.* 1976; 425 pp. Two hundred questions and answers selected from the many sent to Quatuor Coronati Lodge over a period of years and answered.
Author: Appendix No. 3. Reviewed: 1977 Grd. L. of Scot. Yrbk. 111; Mas. Mess., Ga., Sept., 1977, 6; 12 RAM 278 (1978); 88 AQC 174 (1976); Ore. Free., Feb., 1977, 6; Tex. Free., March-April, 1977, 28.

Harold Van Buren Voorhis, *Facts for Freemasons.* 1951; revised ed. in 1979. Macoy Publishing Co., publisher.
Author: Appendix No. 33. Contents: Basic information about the Craft in question and answer form. Reviewed: New Age Mag., Aug., 1952, 501. Libraries: 1,

2, 3, 4, 5, 7, 8, 9, 10, 11, 12, 13, 14.

Herman A. Sarachan, *Dear Brother Herman*. 1979; 223 pp. Masonic Service Bureau, Rochester, N.Y., publisher.
Author: Biographical sketch appears in the book: pp. 216-218. Contents: Selection of questions and answers received by a Masonic publication with the answers given. Reviewed: No. Light, Nov., 1979, 15.

A. R. Chambers, ed., *Questions and Answers*. 1972; 369 pp. M. & P. M. L., publisher.
Contents: Collection of questions and answers, edited and re-arranged, which appeared over a long period of time in the Transactions of the Lodge.

Herbert F. Inman, compiler, *Masonic Problems and Queries*. 1933; 247 pp. A. Lewis, London, publisher.
Contents: Contains 1001 questions and answers on Masonic subjects. Libraries: 3, 4, 5, 7, 8, 9, 12, 13.

J. S. M. Ward, *Masonic Why and Wherefore*. 1929; 104 pp. Baskerville Press, publisher.
Contents: 101 questions and answers on Masonic subjects. Libraries: 3, 5, 7, 9, 11, 12, 13, 14.

Masonic Enquiry Within. 1925; 212 pp. The Masonic Record, publisher.
Libraries: 3.

E. R. Johnson, *Masonry Defined*. 1930; rev. ed. 1939; 911 pp. National Masonic Press, Shreveport, La., publisher.
Contents: The first 568 pages consists of 1025 questions and answers taken from the books of Albert G. Mackey; the balance of the book presents a summary of material in alphabetical order, followed by a pronouncing dictionary. Libraries: 1, 3, 5, 7, 8, 9, 11, 12, 14, 15.

101 Questions About Freemasonry. 1955; 66 pp. MSA.

160 Questions and Answers appear in the A. J. Holman edition of the Holy Bible.

Questions and Answers for Masonic Study Clubs. New Age Mag., July, 1951, 428; Aug., 1951, 481, Sept., 551; and Oct., 1951, 619.

Alphonse Cerza, *Use of Quiz or Audience Participation Programs in Lodge*. 1954 Proc. Midw. Conf. Mas. Ed. 46.

1.06 BIBLIOGRAPHY

August Wolfsteig, *Bibliographie der Freimaurerischen*. 1911-1913. Described in 24 AQC 294 (1911). Libraries: 3, 12.

Freemasons and Freemasonry. Reproduction of that part of Volume 184 of the National Union Catalog, pre 1956 Imprints entitled ''Freemasons and Freemasonry.'' Mansell Information/ Publishing Ltd., London, publisher. 1973; 194 large pages.
Reviewed: 86 AQC 300 (1973).

Edmund Hunt Dring, *English Masonic Literature Before 1751*. 1913. Quatuor Coronati Lodge, publisher.
Author: 25 AQC 384 (1912); 41 AQC 286 (1928). Libraries: 4.

Norman B. Hickox, *The Twelve Treasured Tomes of Freemasonry*. 1938; 43. Evanston Temple Topic, publisher.
Contents: Result of questionnaires sent by the author to a number of Masons. The 12 books receiving the largest number of commendations are reviewed here. Libraries: 2, 3, 4, 5, 7, 8, 9, 11, 12.

Lionel Vibert, *The Rare Books of Freemasonry*. 1923; 41 pp. The Bookman Journal, London, publisher.
Author: 34 AQC 217 (1921); 52 AQC 2 (1939). Contents: List of various items such as old constitutions, pocket companions, etc. with a short description of each. Libraries: 3, 5, 7, 8, 9, 12, 14, 15.

J. Hugo Tatsch, *A Reader's Guide to Masonic Literature*. 1930; 32 pp. Macoy Publishing Co., publisher.
Reviewed: 15 Build. Mag., 375 (1929). Libraries: 3, 5, 9, 10, 11.

Ray Baker Harris, *A Selection of the Rare Books of Freemasonry*. 1955; 29 pp. MSA Digest.
Contents: Facsimile of some pages of various old material. Libraries: 1, 3, 5, 6, 12.

List of Suggested Reading. Reproduced from the Masonic Record. of London.

N.Y. Mas. Outl., Dec., 1926, 123.

H. L. Haywood, *Annotated Reading List.* MSA Digest.

E. H. Dring, *Bibliography.* 25 AQC 345 (1912).

W. J. Hughan, *Bibliography of the Old Charges,* 9 AQC 85 (1890).

N. B. Spencer, *Some Rare Books of Freemasonry.* 78 AQC 210 (1965).

G. W. Speth, *A Masonic Curriculum.* 3 AQC 116 (1890).

Chronological Chart of Acquisitions of the Grand Lodge of England. 63 AQC 304 (1950).

Dr. William L. Cummings, *A Bibliography of Anti-Masonry.* 1963. Originally published in Volume 4 of Norcalore.

The Library of William L. Cummings. Phil. Mag., April, 1967, 38.

M. W. Hamilton, *Anti-Masonic Newspapers.* 1939; 97 pp. Bibliographical Society of Portland, Me., publisher. Vol. 32, pp. 78-97 of their Proceedings. Libraries: 3, 7, 9, 12.

Shadwell H. Clerke, *Catalogue of Books in the Library of Freemasons' Hall, London.* 1887; 49 pp. Supplement published in 1895.
Libraries: 3, 9, 12.

A Bibliography of Masonic Books. 6 Build. Mag. 52 (1920).

Paul Fesch, *Bibliography of Freemasonry and Secret Societies.* In French. 1976; 730 pp. Published in Belgium; not well organized.
Reviewed: 89 AQC 189 (1977); 91 AQC 108 (1979).

Alphonse Cerza, *A Survey of Masonic Literature,* 2 Mas. Papers of the Walter F. Meier Lodge of Research, Washington, 250 (1954); supplemented in Volume 5, June, 1976. List of Masonic books in chronological order.

1979 Proc. Mid. Conf., 123-159, list of contents of all proceedings to date.

Silas H. Shepherd, *Selected List of Masonic Literature.* 1923; 138 pp. Wis.

Grd. L. Comm. on Mas. Res., publisher.
Contents: Brief explanation of the Boyden book classification and then lists Masonic books with comments. A summary of this material appears in the Build. Mag., Vol. 2, pp. 7-10; 36-40 (1916).

Good Masonic Books. STB, Nov., 1945.

Alphonse Cerza, *Guide to Masonic Books.* Phil. Mag., Feb., 1972, 7.

H. H. Solf, *A Bibliographical Essay on Recent French Masonic Literature.* 91 AQC 101 (1979).

Your Personal Masonic Library. MSA Digest.

Alphonse Cerza, *American Masonic Literature.* 1952 Proc. Midw. Conf. Mas. Ed. 24; presented in chronological order.

Masonic Literature Before 1730. 25 AQC 345 (1912).

William L. Boyden, *Bibliography of the Writings of Albert Pike.* 1921 and 1957; 291 pp.

Enoch T. Carson, *Masonic Bibliography.* 1874.

Charles F. Gosnell, *Nine Rare Imprints in the New York State Library.* 7 ALR 171 (1958).

Old German Books of Interest. 5 ALR 47 (1947-1948).

Bibliography of Masonic Sermons. 3 ALR 227 (1939-1940); 4 ALR 343 (1941-1942).

List of Books by Knoop and Jones. Vol. 3, Mackey's Rev. Ency. of Free.

William J. Williams, *The Works of Robert F. Gould.* 44 AQC 246 (1934).

Bibliography of Histories of Grand Lodge of the U.S. MSA.

H. L. Haywood, *Beginnings of American Masonic Literature.* In his Masonic Essays, p. 302.

H. L. Haywood, *Oldest Book in Iowa Masonic Library.* In his Masonic Essays, p. 217.

Harold V. B. Voorhis, *Notes on Some Masonic Books.* 9 ALR 397 (1965).

What to Read in Masonry. 11 Build. Mag. 30, 62, 94, 126, 186, 220, 254, 284 (1924).

John T. Thorpe, *Bibliography of Masonic Catechisms and Exposures.* 1929 Trans. Leicester L. of Res.

Dr. William G. Peacher, *The Benno Loewy Masonic Library in Cornell University*, Ithaca, N.Y. 12 ALR 169 (1972).

E. Newton, *Masonic Writers and Their Influence.* 84 AQC 1 (1971).

Harold V. B. Voorhis, *Notes on Some Masonic Books.* Phil Mag., Aug., 1965, 63; Oct., 1965, 78; Dec., 1965, 96.

John B. Vrooman, *Our Proceedings as a Source of Masonic Information.* Phil. Mag., Aug., 1959, 52.

The Bibliography and Masonic Library of the Late Ward K. St. Clair. Phil. Mag, July-Aug., 1968, 72.

Bibliography and Masonic Library of Harold V. B. Voorhis. Phil. Mag., Dec., 1967, 102.

Books on Solomon's Temple. 8 Build. Mag. 386 (1922).

1.07 CLASSIFICATION OF MASONIC BOOKS

William J. Boyden, *Classification of the Literature of Freemasonry and Related Societies.* 1915; 23 pp.
Author: For many years he was the Librarian of the Scottish Rite Library, Southern Jurisdiction. Libraries: 1, 2, 3, 4, 5, 7, 9, 11, 12, 14.

Frank J. Thompson, *A System of Card Membership Records for Masonic Bodies and a Scheme of Classification for Masonic Books.* 31 pp. Uses the Dewey system as a base.

Alphonse Cerza, *The Classification of Masonic Literature.* Phil. Mag., Feb., 1951, p. 2.

Alphonse Cerza, *An Outline of Masonic Literature.* Phil. Mag., Aug., 1971, 74.

1.08 GUIDES FOR LODGE OFFICERS

H. L. Haywood, *Masonic Lodge Officers and How to Become One.* 1958; 224 pp. Masonic History Co., publisher.
Author: Appendix No. 16. Reviewed: New Age Mag., June, 1959, 374. Libraries: 2, 3, 4, 7, 10, 13, 14.

Louis B. Blakemore, *Masonic Lodge Methods.* 1953; 308 pp. Masonic History Co., publisher.
Author: He was a Past Grand Master of Ohio and for many years the president of the Masonic History Company. Reviewed: The Freemason (Canada), Dec., 1977, 7; New Age Mag., Sept., 1954, 572. Libraries: 1, 2, 3, 4, 5, 7, 8, 9, 10, 11, 12, 13, 14.

Carl H. Claudy, *The Master's Book.* 1935. 122 pp. Temple Publishers.
Author: Appendix No. 6. Reviewed: New Age Mag., Oct., 1935, 638. Libraries: 1, 2, 3, 4, 5, 7, 8, 9, 10, 11, 12, 13, 14.

Robert Macoy, *Worshipful Master's Assistant.* 1885; 1947; 302 pp.
Contents: Duties of officers, their public functions, parliamentary law, Masonic jurisprudence and forms. Reviewed: 11 Build. Mag. 92 (1925). Libraries: 1, 4, 5, 6, 7, 9, 11, 12, 13, 14.

Geoffrey S. Bakey, *The Worshipful Master.* 1975. A. Lewis Ltd., publisher.
Author: Sketch and picture in Mas. Sq., Sept., 1979, 128; he passed away on April 18, 1979. Reviewed: 88 AQC 106 (1975).

Henry G. Meachem, *Our Stations and Places.* 1938; 1949; 214 pp. Of special interest to New York officers.
Libraries: 2, 3, 4, 5, 7, 8, 9, 10, 11, 12, 13, 14, 15.

Fred J. W. Crowe, *The Master Mason's Handbook.* 1980; 83 pp. George Kenning & Co., London, publishers. Has an introduction by W. J. Hughan.
Author: 22 AQC 198 (1909); 44 AQC 130 (1931). Comment: L. B. Blakemore, "A concise reference work (83 pages) which, though it was prepared for use in England, has for years been much read in America. Its author was a Masonic scholar of high rank." Reviewed: 2 Build. Mag.

220 (1916). Libraries: 1, 3, 4, 5, 6, 8, 9, 10, 11, 12, 14.

Arthur R. Hermann, *Designs Upon the Trestleboard.* 1957; 147 pp. Press of Henry Emmerson, publisher.
Contents: Duties of Master and Wardens keyed to New York work. Reviewed: New Age Mag., June, 1959, 58. Libraries: 1, 4, 7, 9, 11, 12, 13, 14.

Art of Presiding. STB, Oct., 1939.

Lodge Courtesies. STB, Aug., 1924.

A. Cerza, *Securing a Speaker for That Special Occasion.* Phil. Mag., Oct., 1967, 92.

Carl H. Claudy, *Use and Abuse of Lodge Speakers.* 1951 Proc. Midw. Conf. Mas. Ed. 88.

Masonic Speakers and Speeches. STB, Dec., 1950.

Lodge Budget, N.Y. Mas. Outl., Jan., 1920, 135.

Lodge Secretary, STB, Sept., 1954.

Planning Lodge Rooms. N.Y. Mas. Outl., May, 1929, 269.

Modern Heating and Ventilating in Masonic Temples. N.Y. Mas. Outl., April, 1925, 174.

Safeguarding Against Fires. N.Y. Mas. Outl., Nov., 1928, 75.

Lodge Finances. STB, June, 1941.

The Learning and Delivery of the Ritual. STB, Oct., 1962.

Lodge Attendance. 1955 Proc. Midw. Conf. Mas. Ed. 21.

Increasing Lodge Attendance. STB, Oct., 1928.

Henry C. Kunz, *Incentives for Lodge Attendance and Participation.* 1963 Proc. Midw. Conf. Mas. Ed. 137.

Visitors and Visitor Committee. STB, Jan., 1947.

How to Use Short Talk Bulletins. STB, Sept., 1960.

Six Presentation Speeches. STB, Feb., 1950.

Jack F. Hewson, *The Use of Lodge Talent.* Ind. Free., Dec., 1956, 10.

Hugh A. Cole, *Making a Lodge Talent Survey.* 1977 Proc. Midw. Conf. 30.

Alphonse Cerza, *Utilizing Lodge Talent.* 13 RAM 52 (1979).

Rhetoric In the Realm of Freemasonry. Ill. Enlight., Aug., 1955, 51.

Financing the Temple. Mast. Mas., June, 1928, 389.

Think-Tank for Junior Wardens. 1978. 52 pp. MSA.

Arthur Markewich, *Duties, Powers, and Authority of A Grand Master.* 1975 Conf. of Grd. Mas. 129.

Duly and Truly Prepared. (To be a Worshipful Master). Ind. Free., Jan., 1976, 8.

David L. Griffiths, *A Successful Lodge Program.* 1975 Proc. Grd. Mast. Con. 59.

Dr. George H. T. French, *Hear Ye, Wardens!* Tex. Free., March-April, 1977, 18.

Dr. George E. Turner, *Hold High the Torch.* Discusses our troubles on the basis of having lowered our qualifications for membership. Ind. Free., April, 1977, 14.

Meeting the Challenge. The Lodge Officer at Work. 1977 publication of the Grand Lodge of Canada for the Province of Ontario. Has six chapters. Reviewed in 90 AQC 265 (1978).

Dwight L. Smith, *The All Important Question.* Ind. Free., Dec., 1978, 14.

Charles R. Brown, *Raising Our Sights.* Ind. Free., Sept., 1973, 6.

Blue Lodge Officers – Requirements as to Masonic Education. 1973 Proc. Grd. Mast. Conf. 121.

Ideas: A Part of the Program. STB, Oct., 1971.

Roger S. Brown, *Speak Now to Us of Masonry.* Phil. Mag., Dec., 1967, 112.

Advice in Forming a Research Lodge. Trans. M. & P. M. L., July, 1973, 60.

1.09 THE INTENDER PROGRAM

Albert L. Woody, *Our Present Need – The Scottish Intender System*. Phil. Mag., April, 1957, 19. Has picture of author.

Alphonse Cerza, *The Intender System*. 7 RAM 218 (1962).

Becker and Hiegel, *A Live Demonstration of the Wisconsin Counselor System*. 1964 Proc. Midw. Conf. Mas. Ed. 38.

Chester B. Steele, *A Discussion of the Intender System*. 1950 Proc. Midw. Conf. Mas. Ed. 55.

Laurence R. Taylor, *The Indiana Mentor Plan*. 1953 Proc. Midw. Conf. Mas. Ed. 41.

Albert L. Woody and R. W. Homann, *Live Demonstration*. 1963 Proc. Mid. Conf. Mas. Ed. 28.

Demonstration of Michigan Intender Program. 1967 Proc. Midw. Conf. Mas. Ed. 22.

Robert Hinshaw and R. C. Scofield, *Masonic Guidance – Ohio Technique*. 1965 Proc. Midw. Conf. Mas. Ed. 18.

1.10 LEADERSHIP

Allen E. Roberts, *Key to Freemasonry's Growth*. 1969; 170 pp. Macoy Publishing Co., publisher.
Author: Appendix No. 29. Contents: Presents business principles of leadership and administration as applicable to the Craft.

J. C. Morris, *Leadership Training and Development – A Masonic Purpose*. 1975 Proc. Grd. Mast. Conf. 74.

Edward G. Siems, *The Quest for Leadership*. Cal. Free., Autumn, 1974, 149.

Allen E. Roberts, *Masonic Leadership*. Phil. Mag., June, 1968, 54.

Allen E. Roberts, *How to Conduct a Leadership Seminar*.

Joseph A. Batchelor, *Masonic Leadership*. Phil. Mag., March, 1968, 34.

William S. Conaway, *The ABC of Masonic Leadership*. Phil. Mag., Feb., 1968, 15.

Carl H. Claudy, *Capable and Sensible*. Phil. Mag., Oct. 1955, 9.

Robert D. Caplinger, *Lodge Leadership*. STB, Jan., 1970.

Allen E. Roberts, *A Road to Success*. STB, June, 1972.

Planning for Progress. STB, Oct., 1972.

Dedication Through Education. STB, Dec., 1972.

The Individual. STB, Dec., 1972.

Allen E. Roberts, *More Light in Masonry: Who Needs It?* STB, Jan., 1972.

A Plan for Action. STB, Feb., 1972.

Working With Goals. STB, March, 1972.

Teamwork Makes a Difference. STB, May, 1972.

Growing the Leader. STB, June, 1972.

Why Communications Break Down. Cal. Free., Winter, 1975, 31.

Harris Bullock, *Creating New Interest Among the Men on the Sidelines*. 1975 Proc. Grd. Mast. Conf. 45.

W. LeRoy McKinley and Ira H. Coburn, *What Can We Do as Masons to Develop Leadership Within and Without Our Lodges?* 1963 Proc. Grd. Mast. Conf. 82.

Dr. S. Brent Morris, *Paying the Piper. The Use of Rewards to Secure Interested Workers*. 13 RAM 47 (1979).

1.11 MASONIC PUBLIC RELATIONS

Public Relations Activities of U.S. Grand Lodges in 1965. MDA Digest.

Dwight A. Dahmes and Daniel C. Jenkins, *What Can We Do as Masons to Give More Publicity to Our Craft and Its Activities?* 1962 Proc. Grd. Mast. Conf. 114, 119.

Clarence L. Batholic and William S. Christian, *What Public Relations Programs Should Be Adopted for Grand Lodges and Masonry in General?* 1963 Proc. Grd. Mast. Conf. 98.

William G. Neu, *How to Improve Public Image*. 1973 Proc. Grd. Mast. Conf. 41.

Public Relations. 1974 Proc. Grd. Mast. Conf. 103.

Arthur Gladstone, *The Case for Public Relations in Freemasonry*. Phil. Mag., April, 1966, 63.

Edwin P. Clark, *Public Image and Public Relations*. Phil. Mag., Feb., 1964, 18.

Albert L. Woody, *Publicity – Its Place in Masonry*. 1960 Proc. Midw. Conf. Mas. Ed. 85.

Myron K. Lingle, *How May We Influence Good Men to Petition for Degrees in Our Masonic Lodges?* No. Light, Jan., 1970, 16.

Alphonse Cerza, *Promoting the Craft*. Phil. Mag., Feb., 1976, 19.

Clyde E. Hegman, *Masonic Public Relations*. 1963 Proc. Midw. Conf. Mas. Ed. 67.

Thomas H. Davis, Jr., *The Image of Freemasonry – Public Relations Demonstrated*. 1972 Proc. Mid. Conf. Mas. Ed. 30.

What Are the Values of Grand Lodge Publications Among Masons and Non-Masons? 1968 Proc. Grd. Mast. Conf. 71.

Howard W. Moore, *Masonic Public Relations*. Phil. Mag., June, 1965, 45.

J. Fairbairn Smith, *Inviting A New Member to Join*. 1974 Masonic Review, supplement to Mo. Grd L. Proc. 5c-5d.

Prince Alexander of Yugoslavia, *What Can Freemasonry Bring to the Unsettled Youth of Today? 12 RAM 305 (1975)*.

William N. Love, The "Public Relations" Issue Directed Outward? No. Ind. Free., March, 1979, 4; April, 1979, 4. Expounds the view that public relations activities are wrong.

Allan D. Parsons, *Masonic Public Relations*. 1979 Proc. Midw. Conf. 27.

Dr. Larry Helms, *Wanted: A Masonic Apostolate*. 12 RAM 362 (1978).

Benjamin H. Priest, *Can the Image of Freemasonry Be Improved by Publicity?* No. Light, June, 1979, 6.

George L. Marshall, *A Question of Survival*. Phil. Mag., April, 1977, 12.

George W. Walker and Charles B. Folley, *Masonic Publicity*. 1937 Proc. Grd. Mast. Conf. 33.

1.12 MASONIC PROBLEMS DISCUSSED

What Are the Real Problems of Masonry? 1969 Prod. Grd. Mast. Conf. 75.

Dwight L. Smith, *Within Our Power*. Brief consideration of needed changes to bring the Craft up-to-date. The 1978 Anson Jones Lecture. 14 Trans. Tex. L. of Res. 17 (1978-1979).

What's the Matter With Freemasonry? 14 Build. Mag., 321, 353 (1928); 15 Build. Mag. 1, 34, 65, 97, 130 (1929).

What Is Right With Masonry? 1965 Trans. Grd. Mast. Conf. 47, 52.

Robert P. Joyce, *The Problems of Freemasonry and Their Solution*. Phil. Mag., Dec., 1973, 102. Also in 1973 Proc. Midw. Conf. Mas. Ed.

Dwight L. Smith, *Whither Are We Traveling?* Series of articles published in the Indiana Freemason in the year 1962. Later published in booklet form, and then reissued by the MSA.

Dwight L. Smith, *Why This Confusion in the Temple?* A follow-up on the preceding item, published in 1966.

Alphonse Cerza, *Is Ritualistic Work Enough?* Phil. Mag., June, 1964, 43.

An Introduction to the Problems of Declining Membership and Poor Attendance. MSA Digest.

What Price Life Membership? N.Y. Mas. Outl., March, 1927, 199.

Louis Block, *Shall a Mason Be Permitted to Belong to More than One Lodge?* N.Y. Mas. Outl., Jan., 1927, 160. His answer was "No."

Melvin M. Johnson, *A Plea for Plural Membership*. N.Y. Mas. Outl., Feb., 1927, 167.

H. L. Haywood, *Shall A Mason Be Permitted to Belong to More Than One*

Lodge? N.Y. Mas. Outl., Nov., 1926, 78.

Rubber Stamping Masons. (Attendance Problem). N.Y. Mas. Outl., July, 1925, 233.

K. O. Knudson and Herbert H. Eberle, *Should Constituent Lodges Be More Active in Non-Political and Non-Religious Affairs That Make for Community Betterment?* 1958 Proc. Midw. Conf. Mas. Ed. 32, 36.

Glenn B. Van Fleet and Floyd D. Richards, *Should There Be Uniform Qualifications for Masonic Membership?* 1958 Proc. Grd. Mast. Conf. 98, 102.

J. Carl Humphrey and Joseph Tye, *Should There Be Universal Instruction of Candidates After Being Elected, but Before Initiation?* 1960 Proc. Grd. Mast. Conf. 32, 36.

Doyn Inman, *The Economy and Freemasonry.* Ind. Free., June, 1977, 10.

Bliss Kelly, *More About Dropouts.* Phil. Mag., Feb., 1968, 6.

Henry J. Cooper and Ronald C. Nicolson, *Should Candidates Undergo Compulsory Instruction in Masonic Philosophy?* 1959 Proc. Grd. Mast. Conf. 106, 110.

August C. Ulrich and Robert L. Aronson, *Should Grand Lodges Exercise More Control Over Recognition and Activities of Organizations Requiring Masonic Affiliation for Membership?* 1959 Proc. Grd. Mast. Conf. 31, 40.

Rex P. Sackett and Leland D. Wilson, *Should There Be a Greater Co-operation Between Grand Lodges and Appendant Masonic Bodies?* 1960 Proc. Grd. Mast. Conf., 70, 74.

John H. Murphy and Herbert A. Ronin, *What Can We Do to Increase Lodge Attendance?* 1962 Proc. Grd. Mast. Conf. 64, 70.

William R. Weisinger, *Courtesy Work and the Problems Incident Thereto.* 1943 Proc. Grd. Mast. Conf. 155.

Ray Baker Harris and Harold M. Jayne, *Is Freemasonry Overextended, and Should Efforts Be Made to Discourage Formation of Organizations Dependent Upon Masonic Membership?* 1957 Proc. Grd. Mast. Conf. 110.

George T. Macklin, *Is Freemasonry Over-Extended?* 1938 Proc. Grd. Mast. Conf. 126.

John C. Hubbard, *Adaptation of Ancient Craft Masonry to Modern Requirements.* 1948 Proc. Grd. Mast. Conf. 45.

What Can We Do to Increase the Interest of Masons in Masonry? 1956 Proc. Grd. Mast. Conf. 45, 50.

What Policy Should Be Encouraged for Chartering New Lodges Geared to the Population Shift, in Order to Give More Members Convenience in Attending Lodge Meetings? 1966 Proc. Grd. Mast. Conf. 71, 75.

What, If Anything, Can Be Done About the Lack of Interest in Masonry by Non-Masons? 1966 Proc. Grd. Mast. Conf. 85, 89.

How Can We Improve Our Services to Our Youth Organizations? 1967 Proc. Grd, Mast. Conf. 64.

Is Masonic Relief a Principle of Individual Personal Action or Has It Been Embalmed in Institutions? 1967 Proc. Grd. Mast. Conf. 99.

How Well Is Freemasonry Propagating Its Ideals, Not Only With the Lodges But to the Larger World Outside? 1967 Proc. Grd. Mast. Conf. 102.

Problems of the Large City Lodges. 1968 Proc. Grd. Mast. Conf. 76.

What Are the Most Successful Programs Tried by Lodges and Grand Lodges Such as Scholarship Programs, etc.? 1969 Proc. Grd. Mast. Conf. 66.

Does Masonry Need to Consider the Challenge of Change in a Changing World? 1969 Proc. Grd. Mast. Conf. 71.

What Shall We Do to Revitalize Masonry; How to Stimulate Our Own Interest? 1969 Proc. Grd. Mast. Conf. 66.

How Can Masonry Best Deal With the Problem Created by the Social and

Moral Revolution Through Which We Are Living? 1969 Proc. Grd. Mast. Conf. 73.

What Is the Proper Role of Masonry in Relation to Modern Civil, Political, and Religious Problems? 1970 Proc. Grd. Mast. Conf. 47.

John W. Thornburgh and William J. Nash, Jr., *Should There Be A Waiting Period After Membership?* 1950 Proc. Grd. Mast. Conf. 89, 94.

Louis S. Thomas, Norman H. Smith, Hugh M. Craig, Henry O. Morgan, and Stuart Krebs, *Should There Be a Waiting Period Between Degrees?* 1949 Proc. Grd. Mast. Conf. 74, 78, 79, 81, 83.

Clarence D. Phillips, *Status of Territories.* 1943 Proc. Grd. Mast. Conf. 139.

Benjamin L. Hadley, *Discuss the Merits of Grand Lodge Regulations Which (1) Require Election of Candidates for Each Degree, or (2) Permit Election for All Three Degrees on One Ballot.* 1944 Proc. Grd. Mast. Conf. 40.

Gay H. Brown, *How Can We Promote Lodge Attendance?* 1947 Proc. Grd. Mast. Conf. 59.

Charles W. Littlefield and Lawson D. Willis, *Lodge Attendance.* 1935 Proc. Grd. Mas. Conf. 15.

Gurdon M. Butler, *Lodge Attendance.* 1940 Proc. Grd. Mast. Conf. 33.

Getting Masons on Sidelines Involved; Cooperation With Other Groups, Civic and Fraternal. 1972 Proc. Grd. Mast. Conf. 43.

Should There Be Easing of Requirements? 1973 Proc. Grd. Mast. Conf. 54.

How to Improve Blue Lodge Attendance. 1973 Proc. Grd. Mast. Conf. 76.

Howard J. Hunter, *Lowering the Age to Eighteen.* 1973 Proc. Grd. Mast. Conf. 85.

Grand Lodge-Blue Lodge Relationship. 1973 Proc. Grd. Mast. Conf. 111.

Flight to the Suburbs. 1973 Proc. Grd. Mast. Conf. 67.

Effect of Government Assistance on Masonry. 1973 Proc. Grd. Mast. Conf. 128.

Abolishment of Territorial Jurisdiction Within a Grand Jurisdiction. 1974 Proc. Grd. Mast. Conf. 48.

Grand Lodge Relationship to Subordinate or Appendant Bodies. 1974 Proc. Grd. Mast. Conf. 55.

Stewart W. Miner, *Various Forms of Masonic Charity.* 1974 Proc. Grd. Mast. Conf. 65.

Civil Rights Act of 1964 – Brought to Date. 1974 Proc. Grd. Mast. Conf. 89.

Should a Grand Lodge Regulate Advancement to the Higher Degrees? 11 Build. Mag. 161 (1925).

Edwin L. Holt, *Should Any Reduction Be Made in the Age Requirement of Candidates for Admission Into Freemasonry?* 1944 Proc. Grd. Mast. Conf. 101.

Lee Anon and Carey B. Wilson, *Should We Change Our Theory of Non-Solicitation for the Degrees?* 1956 Proc. Grd. Mast. Conf. 32, 37, 38.

What Is the Challenge Ahead for Masonry? 1964 Proc. Grd. Mast. Conf. 46, 52.

How May We Overcome the Passive and Complacent Attitude of So Many in the Craft? 1964 Proc. Grd. Mast. Conf. 70, 76.

Limited Membership in Masonic Lodges. 1964 Proc. Grd. Mast. Conf. 81, 86.

1.13 MASONIC STUDY CLUBS

Alphonse Cerza and Dr. William Moseley Brown, *Masonic Study Groups.* 1957. MSA Digest.

Dr. Russell C. Slater, *A Report on the Activities of an Active Study Club.* 1955 Proc. Midw. Conf. Mas. Ed. 83.

James R. Gale, *Indiana Lodge Sponsors Academy of Masonic Culture.* No. Light, Sept., 1972, 10. Also Phil. Mag., Dec. 1970, 116; Feb., 1971, 15; Feb., 1972, 22.

Louis A. Wiese, *Benefits of a Study Club.* N.Y. Mas. Outl., April, 1927, 256.

Research Lodge of New Zealand. New Age Mag., Dec., 1942, 729.

What Came We Here to Do? N.Y. Mas. Outl., Jan., 1920, 131.

Dr. George H. T. French, *Education in Freemasonry.* Ind. Free., Feb., 1979, 8.

R. H. Baxter, *Lodges and Associations for Masonic Education in England.* 13 Man. Assn. of Mas. Res. 81 (1922-1923).

John B. Vrooman, *Suggested Procedure for Masonic Study.* Phil. Mag., June, 1955, 15, and continuing in each issue for several years.

Donald G. Ingalls, *The Learning Center.* Cal. Free., Spring, 1978, 52.

List of Regional Conferences on Masonic Education. Ind. Free., Feb., 1972, 29.

How Can We Develop Masonic Educational Programs Which Will Really Reach the Membership of Our Constituent Lodges? 1965 Proc. Grd. Mast. Conf. 77.

Masonic Education. 1974 Proc. Grd. Mast. Conf. 114.

How to Develop a Masonic Educational Program That Will Really Work? 1965 Proc. Grd. Mast. Conf. 93.

How to Study Masonry; a Symposium. 1 Build. Mag. 75, 101, 127, 140, 152 (1915).

Ritualism and Masonic Information. Ill. Enlight., Feb., 1952, 4.

Thomas M. Stuart, *How to Study Masonry.* 1 Am. Free. 105, 155, 229, 368, 428, 518 (1910).

Alphonse Cerza, *What Constitutes Good Masonic Reading.* Phil. Mag., Dec., 1958, 95.

Burtis M. Little, *Between the Lines of the Masonic College Records.* 1943 Trans. MLR 151.

Some Aspects of Masonic Study. 53 AQC 316 (1942).

A Lodge of Instruction. 10 Build. Mag. 270 (1924).

Masonry and Education – The 14th to the 18th Century. 9 ALR 184 (1964).

A Study Club in Action. 15 Build. Mag., 182, 216, 376 (1929).

Study Club Constitution. 14 Build. Mag. 28 (1928).

Bruce W. Oliver, *The Freemason's Education.* In Harry Carr, ed., Collected Prestonian Lectures, 385.

Joseph A. Batchelor, *Let's Keep It Simple.* Ind. Free., Feb., 1955, 14.

Michigan's Unique Experiment in Masonic Education. 14 Build. Mag. 312 (1928).

A Study Lecture Course in Masonic Education. 14 Build. Mag. 337 (1938).

Guides to Masonic Study: Vol. 3 of Mackey's Rev. Ency. of Freemasonry, 1443-1454 (1946). For many years the Cleveland Masonic Library conducted forums at which Freemasonry was discussed as a "round table" program; mimeographed sheets with topics and references were mailed to the members in advance of each meeting. Also, the Builder Magazine in each issue had suitable material and suggestions for use by Masonic study groups.

1.14 MASONIC RESEARCH AND WRITING

Robert F. Gould, *Masonic Research.* New Age Mag., Dec., 1911, 585.

Joseph R. Gilbert and Ronald E. Heaton, *Masonic Research, How to Proceed.* Phil. Mag., Oct., 1972, 92.

Gilbert W. Daynes, *Untrodden Paths of Masonic Research.* 1924; 60 pp. Masonic Record, London, publisher.
Author: 43 AQC 253 (1930); 44 AQC 67 (1931). 11 Build. Mag. 43 (1925).
Comment: L. B. Blakemore, "An essay by an active and distinguished member of the Quatuor Coronati Lodge of Research." Review: Mast. Mas., June, 1924. 408. Libraries: 1, 2, 3, 4, 5, 7, 8, 9, 11, 12, 13, 14, 15.

Alphonse Cerza, *At Labor In the Quarries.* Phil. Mag., Feb., 1957, 9.

Charles S. Guthrie, *Some Research Techniques and Suggested Topics for Research.* Phil. Mag., Feb., 1971, 19.

Conrad Hahn, *Writing for Masonic Publications.* Phil. Mag., April, 1965, 30.

Alphonse Cerza, *On Becoming a Masonic Writer.* Phil. Mag., Feb., 1960, 9.

A. L. Vibert, *A Survey of Masonic Research.* 43 Trans. Leicester L. of Res. 62-82 (1933-1934).

H. L. Haywood, *Explanation of the Index Rarum in the Iowa Masonic Library;* in his Masonic Essays, 429.

R. I. Clegg, *Road to Masonic Research.* 1 Build. Mag. 65 (1915).

How to Study Freemasonry. 1 Build. Mag. 152 (1915).

John T. Thorp, *Masonic Research: What It Has Done and Can Still Do.* 2 Build. Mag. 73 (1916).

The Scope of Research. 14 Build. Mag. 212 (1928).

Lodges of Research. Phil. Mag., April, 1965, 37.

Ward K. St. Clair, *Masonic Research Groups.* 7 RAM 277, 305 (1963).

W. I. Grantham, *Masonic Research and Freemasonry in Sussex.* 55 AQC 326 (1942).

W. B. Hextall, *Masonic Research.* 27 AQC 224 (1914).

Boris Ivanoff, *Some Aspects of Masonic Study.* 53 AQC 316 (1940).

F. R. Radice, *Masonic Research,* 59 AQC 201 (1946).

J. R. Rylands, *Masonic Research.* 66 AQC 3 (1953).

J. E. S. Tuckett, *Masonic Research.* 32 AQC 164 (1919).

Masonic Research Societies in England. 8 Build. Mag., 353 (1922).

Albert C. Nilson, *Freemasonic Research.* Mas. J. of So. Africa, Sept., 1974, 20.

Keith Arrington, *Use of Masonic Reading Lists in Iowa.* 1978 Proc. Midw. Conf Mas Ed. 39.

H. L. Haywood, *Rare and Valuable Books in the Iowa Masonic Library;* in his Masonic Essays, 230.

Thomas C. Warden, *Whatever Happened to the Written Word?* 1978 Proc. Midw. Conf. Mas. Ed. 94.

Herbert A. Eggie, *Coordinate Masonic Education.* 1977 Proc. Midw. Conf. Mas. Ed., 59.

J. T. Thorp, *Masonic History, With Suggestions for Study and Research.* 5 March. Assn. for Mas. Res. 89 (1914-1915). Also in 3 Build. Mag. 206 (1917).

Outline for a Proposed Grand Lodge History. 1944 Trans. MLR 237.

Writing for Masonic Publications. 8 RAM 329 (1966).

What to Read in Masonry. 11 Build. Mag. 30, 62, 94, 126, 186, 220, 254, 284 (1924).

Wendell K. Walker, *The Grand Lodge Library as a Source of Masonic Research.* Phil. Mag., April, 1963, 28.

Wes Cook, *Masonic Research.* 1964 Trans. MLR 178.

Charles F. Gosnell, *Some Source Materials for Local, State, and National Masonic History.* Phil. Mag., June, 1959, 40.

Masonic Study. 4 ALR 424 (1946-1947).

Harold V. B. Voorhis, *Preliminary Efforts on Masonic Research.* 9 ALR 218 (1964).

Modern Historical Research and Its Application to Freemasonry. 1 ALR 56 (1930-1932).

Charles H. Jackson, *Masonic Education. What is the Best Way to Interest Members?* 1929 Proc. Grd. Mast. Conf. 39.

Herbert W. Dean, Charles H. Johnson, and Hiram F. Lively, *Masonic Educational Programs.* 1930 Proc. Grd. Mast. Conf. 11.

Dr. William G. Peacher, *Temple Hollcroft's Library and Aurora-on-Cayuga.* 12 ALR 153 (1972).

Walter E. Heller, *A Ritualistic Mind's Eye View of a Master Mason.* Draws a word picture of a Masonic library. Phil. Mag., Dec., 1978, 9.

Dwight L. Smith, *Researching and Writing the Masonic History of Indiana.* Phil. Mag., Dec. 1977, 6 Also see: 1977 Proc. Midw. Conf. Mas. Ed. 37.

Jack E. Kelly, *Writing a Lodge History.* With a detailed checklist or outline of matters to include. 1979 Proc. Mid. Conf. 45.

Paul E. Rudbeck, *Printing and Distribution of a Masonic Book.* 1979 Proc. Mid. Conf. 104.

David L. Laske, *Towards a Social History of Masonry – A Real Need.* Expresses the view that Masonic researchers should pay more attention to social events of interest to the Craft. Phil. Mag., April, 1978, 12.

Dr. George H. T. French, *Masonology – A Challenge,* Phil. Mag., Feb., 1971, 11; and June, 1979, 9.

Walter K. Belt, *How I Write Masonic Verse.* Phil. Mag., Dec., 1975, 118.

Jerry Marsengill, *Masonic Research – Iowa Style.* Phil. Mag., Oct., 1974, 83; and Dec., 1974, 104.

Arthur W. Barnett, *Research for a Purpose.* 30 Trans. Phoenix L. of Res. (Paris) 11.

Howard L. Knupp, *Putting Together a Film Catalogue.* 1975 Proc. Midw. Conf. Mas. Ed. 89.

Wes Cook, *The Art of Communication.* 1975 Proc. Midw. Conf. Mas. Ed. 84.

Jerry Marsengill, *Research Groups – Their Uses and Abuses.* 1975 Proc. Midw. Conf. Mas. Ed. 36.

Clyde E. Hegman, *Masonic Scholarships Essay Contests.* 1978 Proc. Midw. Conf. Mas. Ed. 104.

William B. Barnes, *Preparing and Presenting an Open House Program.* 1978 Proc. Midw. Conf. Mas. Ed. 80.

James R. Case, *Masonic Education Through Biography.* 1978 Proc. Midw. Conf. Mas. Ed. 73.

Silas H. Shepherd, *Masonic Study and Research.* 1920; Wisconsin Grand Lodge Com. on Masonic Research.

Alphonse Cerza, *Sources for Securing Masonic Printed Material.* 1977 Proc. Midw. Conf. Mas. Ed. 121.

Dr. Wayne C. Temple, *Historical Research for the George Rogers Clark Portrait.* 1977 Proc. Midw. Conf. Mas. Ed. 77.

Hugh A. Cole, *Masonic Audio Visuals.* 1978 Proc. Midw. Conf. Mas. Ed. 67.

Dr. Ross Hepburn, *Masonic Education in New Zealand.* Phil. Mag., June-July, 1950, 3. Also see: 86 AQC 267 (1973); 87 AQC 204 (1974).

James W. Welch, *The Foreign Correspondent and His Work.* 1 Res. L. of Ore. 301 (1933-1935).

J. Hugo Tatsch, *American Masonic Journalism, 1811-1840.* 3 ALR 48, 647 (1938-1939).

Richardson Wright, *American Masonic Journalism.* 4 ALR 202 (1944-1945).

Masonic Study and Research. 4 ALR 424 (1946-1947).

Harold V. B. Voorhis, *Preliminary Efforts on Masonic Research.* 9 ALR 218 (1964).

Richardson Wright, *Masonic Bypaths in American History.* 1 ALR 25 (1930-1932).

Modern Historical Research and Its Application to Freemasonry. 1 ALR 56 (1930-1932).

J. Heron Lepper, *A Suggestion for the Collection of Masonic Data.* 14 Build. Mag. 1 (1926).

Alphonse Cerza, *Techniques of Using Masonic Books.* Phil. Mag., Dec., 1971, 110.

R. H. Baxter, *A Course of Masonic Reading.* 2 Build. Mag. 298 (1916).

Alec Mellor, *What Is a Lodge of Re-*

search? Trans. Phoen. L. No. 30, Paris, 1 (1971-1972).

William R. Denslow, *Pitfalls and Pratfalls in Compiling Masonic Biographies*. Phil. Mag., April, 1960, 20.

Dr. Francis J. Scully, *Compiling Masonic Biographies*. Phil. Mag., April, 1960, 22.

William R. Denslow, *An Ideal Masonic Publication*. Phil. Mag., Dec., 1963, 92.

H. C. Arbuckle, *Advice on Writing a Lodge History*. 14 Trans. Tex. L. of Res. 232 (1978-1979).

L. L. Walker, Jr., *A Suggested Program of Oral History in the Grand Lodge of Texas*. 14 Trans. Tex. L. of Res. 29 (1978-1979).

1.15 MASONIC LIBRARIES

Five Great Masonic Libraries. STB, Nov., 1956.

Alphonse Cerza, *Masonic Libraries*. 1972 Proc. Midw. Conf. Mas. Ed. 44.

C. C. Adams, *Masonic Museums and Libraries*. 52 AQC 270 (1939).

Harry Carr, *Guide and Tour of the Grand Lodge Museum and Library*. 78 AQC 241 (1965).

Dr. William L. Cummings, *Masonic Libraries, Public and Private*. Phil. Mag., April, 1963, 31.

Texas Library and Museum. Tex. Free., March-April, 1977, 4.

Waco's Lee Lockwood Tribute. K. T. Mag., Dec., 1976, 19.

Ervin L. Hippe, *Masonic Library Story of Seattle*. Phil. Mag., Feb., 1976, 8.

Louis L. Williams, *So You Want to Start a Masonic Library?* No. Light, Jan., 1972, 10; No. Light, April, 1972, 10.

The William L. Cummings Library, New Age Mag., Oct., 1960, 53.

G. S. Draffen, *Library of the Grand Lodge of Scotland*, 71 AQC 3 (1958).

List of Masonic Libraries, 1973 Proc. Midw. Conf. Mas. Ed. 131.

Masonic Library of Research Lodge No. 104, Atlanta, Ga., Mas. Mess., March, 1972, 19.

Conference of Masonic Librarians at Cedar Rapids, Iowa, May, 1928. See: 14 Build. Mag., 279; has picture of group attending the Conference. Meeting in 1929. 15 Build. Mag. 119 (1929).

Charles T. Jackson, *Description of the Iowa Masonic Library*. Phil. Mag., April, 1972, 34.

H. L. Haywood, *The Library of the Grand Lodge of Iowa*. 1955 Proc. Midw. Conf. Mas. Ed. 36.

H. L. Haywood, on the *Library of Rob Morris*: "Morris accumulated a Masonic library of his own, an unusually rare and creditable collection for his time, of about 1200 titles. For years it vanished from view, and admirers of Morris, of whom he had many, searched everywhere for it. It transpired that he sent it, or had it sent, to the Grand Lodge Library, at Masonic Hall, New York City, which is in the custody of the Grand Lodge of New York."

Jerry Marsengill, *How Ted Parvin Lost a Girl and Gained a Library*. 10 RAM 327 (1972).

H. L. Haywood, *The Iowa Masonic Library*. In his Masonic Curiosa, 31; also in his Masonic Essays, 213.

Charles T. Jackson, *Grand Lodge Libraries, Their Uses and Benefits*. Phil. Mag., April, 1972, 34.

Masonic Library of Pennsylvania. Phil. Mag., March, 1950, 6; and April, 1963, 57.

Folger Shakespeare Library. Phil. Mag., June, 1966, 58.

Truman Library Dedicated. Phil. Mag., Oct., 1957, 75.

H. L. Haywood, *The Iowa Masonic Library*. Ill. Enlight., April, 1949, 2.

T. S. Southwick, *A Librarian on Libraries*. 12 Build. Mag. 149, 156 (1927).

Loral W. Pancake, *A Masonic Library*. Ind. Free., May, 1971, 8.

The Lee Lockwood Library and Museum. New Age Mag., July, 1978, 15.

Masonic Libraries. 52 AQC 270 (1941).

Ray Baker Harris, *The Iowa Masonic Library, 1845-1955.* New Age Mag., Sept. 1955, 531.

Los Angeles Library. 14 Build. Mag. 123 (1928).

Mildred Benton and Singe Otterson, *Roster of Federal Libraries.* (1970).

Anthony T. Kruzas, *Directory of Special Libraries and Information Centers.* 1968.

1.16 MASONIC MISINFORMATION

Alphonse Cerza, *Masonic Misinformation.* Phil. Mag., Aug.-Sept., 1951, 2.

Alphonse Cerza, *More Masonic Misinformation.* Phil. Mag., Oct., 1956, 73.

Jerry Marsengill, *Masonic Misinformation.* 10 RAM 145 (1971).

Alphonse Cerza, *Masonic Misinformation.* 1956 Proc. Midw. Conf. Mas. Ed. 67.

Alphonse Cerza, *Masonic Misinformation.* Ill. Enlight., August, 1952, 3.

Jerry Marsengill, *Kinnamon's Fraudulent Egyptian "Masonry."* Iowa Grand Lodge Bulletin, Nov., 1972, 655. Expanded with more details in 11 RAM 69 (1973).

Jerry Marsengill, *Truth Is a Divine Attribute.* Phil. Mag., Aug., 1973, 68.

Jerry Marsengill, *How to Kick a Sacred Cow.* 1973, Iowa Res. Lodge No. 2, publisher.

Harold V. B. Voorhis, *Two Historical "Myths" of Freemasonry.* 9 ALR 282 (1964).

For More Modern Records. N.Y. Mas. Outl., Feb., 1930, 170; March, 1930, 202.

James R. Case, *What's in a Name?* 1979 Proc. Conf. Grd. Mast. 44. Presents consideration of confusion of persons with similar names and claimed as Masons.

H. C. Arbuckle, III, *The Truth is Enough.* Cal. Free., Winter, 1976-77, 27. Also in K. T. Mag., April, 1976, 19.

Estel W. Brooks, *These Men Were Masons.* K. T. Mag., Sept., 1975, 7.

H. C. Arbuckle, III, *Tell It Like It Was.* Summary of STB of May, 1976; 12 RAM 247 (1977).

J. Fairbairn Smith, *It Just Ain't So.* Ind. Free., Sept., 1977, 14.

John A. Richardson, *The Great Message.* Touted for a time as the "greatest Masonic book of all times." Contains a great deal of pompous nonsense into which is woven mental telepathy and the existence of a "great school of the masters." Exposed in Dr. Sylvester A. West, *T-K and the Great Work in America.* Both these books are in at least the following libraries: Iowa Masonic Library, Chicago Scottish Rite Library, and Supreme Council Library, Washington, D.C. See: 1 Build. Mag. 113, 143, 181, 187, 203, 244, 248. Phil. Mag., 1955, 11.

1.17 NOVELTY

Alphonse Cerza, *The Truth is Stranger Than Fiction.* 1967. MSA Digest.

Alphonse Cerza, *Masonic Oddballs.* 12 RAM 330 (1978).

Wes Cook, ed., *Did You Know?* 1965; 269 pp. MLR Collection of Vignettes from the Royal Arch Mason, and many full page series of cartoon pictures with unusual Masonic items.

Edward A. Kotlar, *Norton, The First Emperor of the United States.* Cal. Free., Winter, 1979, 7.

Alphonse Cerza, *A Masonic Alphabet.* A Masonic poem modeled after the children's rime "A is for apple." With art work by L. Sherman Brooks. Phil. Mag., April, 1978, 8-9.

Stephen Knight, *Jack the Ripper: The Final Solution.* 1976; 284 pp. Harrap & Co., London. Advances the theory that the killing of five prostitutes was the result of a plan to silence them because they were blackmailing Queen Victoria by disclosing that her grandson had secretly married a shop girl and fathered her child. The Masons were blamed for the murders.

John Mauk Hilliard, *The "Ripper" and the Craft*. Discussion of the movie "Murder by Degree" and its Masonic connotations. 13 RAM 59 (1979).

Jack the Ripper a Freemason? 10 RAM 120 (1970).

Jerry Marsengill, *Union and Freemasonry*. Ore. Free., July, 1974, 25.

The Cup of Brotherly Love. K. T. Mag., June, 1976, 15. Also No. Light. Sept., 1972, 14. MSA Digest. Ill. Enlight., Sept., 1951, 1; May, 1958, 138; Aug., 1958, 147.

Alphonse Cerza, *A Lodge of Counterfeiters*. Phil. Mag., 1974, 44.

Masonic Clock. Mas. Mess., Ga., Aug., 1974, 13.

Travelling Bible. In the Walrus and the Carpenter, 110-111, edition published by Iowa Res. L. No. 2.

Jerry Marsengill, *Quackery and Masonic Ailments*. Ore. Free., April, 1975, 22.

Grand Lodge Convened on a Railroad Train. 1964-1965, Kansas Grd. L. Proc. 37.

J. Fairbairn Smith, *A Trolley Car to the Grave*. No. Light., Sept., 1973, 12.

Roy A. Wells, *The Interesting Name of Caducean*. 12 RAM 39 (1979).

Keith Arrington, *A Masonic Painting and Its Story*. Phil. Mag., Aug., 1978, 8.

Abraham Baum, *Symbols of Masonry: A Hobby That Has Won National Recognition*. Phil. Mag., Oct., 1978, 23.

Clowning. 9 RAM 142 (1968).

Burton Kessler, *Some Geographic Aspects of Freemasonry in Illinois*. 1970. 1975. In the following libraries: Iowa, Ill. Grd. L., Chicago Scott. Rite.

A Curious Peppercorn. Phil. Mag., Aug., 1976, 75.

The American Seal. K. T. Mag., June, 1975, 15.

Dr. Stephen R. Greenberg. *Masonic Pretensions*. Phil. Mag., Oct., 1970, 91.

Cross Word Puzzles and Cartoons, with solutions in N.Y. Mas. Outl., April, 1925, 182.

Masonic Calendars. New Age Mag., Sept., 1951, 536.

William L. Boyden, *The Goat in Freemasonry*. New Age Mag., April, 1925, 207.

Freemasonry in the Air. 5 RAM 295 (1957).

Jerry Marsengill, *The Strange End of Brother Soliman*. 10 RAM 202 (1971); 10 RAM 312 (1972). Also Sarastro Club Bulletin, May-June, 1963.

John G. Hanna, *The Mounties and Freemasonry*. Phil. Mag., Aug., 1949, 2.

Lawton E. Meyers, *The Hidden Meaning of "Nursery" Rhymes*. Phil. Mag., May, 1954, 3.

Those "Masonic" Chain Letters. 8 RAM 27 (1964); 13 RAM 10 (1979).

Robert Gollmar, *The Circus and Freemasonry*. 5 RAM 259 (1957); Phil. Mag., Feb., 1964, 12.

Jerry Marsengill, *Was the Conductor a Craftsman?* 10 RAM 26 (1970).

The Unknown Tattooed Mason. 3 RAM 170 (1938-1939).

Masonically Planted Tree. 3 RAM 146 (1950).

Suspended After Funeral. 5 RAM 349 (1957).

Masonic Slaves. 7 RAM 335 (1963).

Masonic Colors. Trans. No. Cal. Res. L., June, 1974, 12.

Lotteries. 13 RAM 31 (1979).

Harold V. B. Voorhis, *N.Y. Masonic Lotteries*. 12 ALR 100 (1972).

Masonic Forts. Phil. Mag., Feb., 1975, 10.

Alex Horne, *Curiosities of Masonic Literature*. No. Light, June, 1979, 20.

Roger F. Callejas, *A Masonic Session in Jail*. Phil. Mag., Dec., 1974, 110.

J. Fairbairn Smith, *Dream Lodges Add to Masonic Lore*. Mas. World, of Detroit, Sept., 1979, 5. Describes the imaginary lodges treated by Greenleaf, Claudy's Doric Lodge, and George's Friendship Lodge.

Bill Weisberger, *Mesmerism and Masonry*. 11 RAM 219 (1974).

Dr. L. C. Helms, *Mnemosyne*. New Age Mag., March, 1978, 40. Suggestions on how to improve memory.

Masonry Is . . . Art work by L. Sherman Brooks. Phil. Mag., Feb., 1976, 16.

Hugh A. Cole, *A Masonic Book a Month Club*. Phil. Mag., Oct., 1975, 97.

Masonic Bells. K. T. Mag., Dec., 1975, 12.

Knoop and Jones, *London Bridge and Its Builder*. 47 AQC 5 (1938).

Has the S.O.S. Call a Masonic Origin? 28 AQC 213 (1915).

G. W. Daynes, *A Masonic Foundation Stone at the Bank of England*. 41 AQC 160 (1928).

Dueling and Freemasonry. 6 Norcalore 9.

Jerry Marsengill, *The Mystic Art of Gold Making*. Ore. Free., Sept., 1973, 16.

Masonic Playing Cards. Mas. Sq., Dec., 1979, 168.

1.18 PLACES WITH MASONIC SIGNIFICANCE

Karl W. Kurts, *Sandusky, Ohio, Laid Out in the Form of Square and Compass by Founders*. Phil. Mag., Oct., 1968, 106.

The Statue of Liberty and Freemasonry. New Age Mag., June, 1956, 355. Also see 5 RAM 19 (1955); with picture of Bartholdi.

Fort Masonic. New Age Mag., Dec., 1964, 29.

Stonehenge. New Age Mag., Dec., 1958, 736. Also: William Simpson, The Threefold Division of Temples, 1 AQC 89, 166 (1886-1888); Henry Lovegrove, Notes on Stonehenge, 15 AQC 26 (1902).

Modern Vessels With Masonic Names. 6 ALR 413 (1956).

Sailing Vessels With Masonic Names. 9 ALR 381 (1965).

The Ship "Freemason." 4 ALR 130 (1942-1943).

Further Light on the Ship "Freemason." 7 ALR 241 (1908).

Street. 10 RAM 3, 90 (1970); 6 RAM 250 (1959).

William R. Denslow, *Masonic Place Names*. 5 RAM 104 (1955). Also: Ind. Free., Dec., 1956, 11.

Map With Places of Interest in Illinois. Ill. Enlight., Aug., 1964, 370.

CHAPTER TWO

Masonic History

2.01 GENERAL WORKS

Henry W. Coil, Sr., *Outlines of Freemasonry*. 1939; 256 pp. Walter P. Clark, Riverside, Cal., publisher.
Author: Appendix No. 8. Contents: Fourteen chapters covering the history of the Craft to 1730. Libraries: 1, 3, 5, 7, 8, 10, 11, 13, 14.

Henry W. Coil, Sr., *Freemasonry Through Six Centuries*. Two vols. 1968, 1969; MLR, publisher.
Author: Appendix No. 8. Contents: This book covers the history of the Craft in four periods: To 1717, 1717-1751, 1751-1813, 1813 to date. Comments: Louis L. Williams, "An excellent, up-to-date, modern history." Reviewed: New Age Mag., March, 1969, 55. Libraries: 1, 2, 3, 4, 5, 7, 9, 10, 11, 12, 13, 14.

Robert Freke Gould, *The History of Freemasonry*. Originally published in 1885 and reissued in many editions. The original edition had parts written by Josiah H. Drummond and T. S. Parvin, covering American history. In 1951 an edition edited by Herbert H. Poole was published in England. In 1936 a six-volume edition was published by Charles Scribner's Sons. This edition was sponsored by Melvin M. Johnson. It was supposed to have been a revision bringing the subject up-to-date but failed in this respect. Its greatest merit is the part covering the states of the United States written in each instance by a qualified person in the specific state.
Author: Appendix No. 12. Reviewed: 2 ALR 367 (1936); 62 AQC 327 (1951); 46 AQC 456 (1937). Comments: H. L. Haywood, "It was expected that when he came to revise Gould's History of Freemasonry . . . Bro. Dudley Wright would . . . make sure to revise completely Gould's Chapter on the Antients; for some reason which has not been explained he did not do so. . . . This failure in revision is regrettable to American readers because the Revised History elsewhere makes it clear that more than half of early American Masonry . . . was derived from Antient sources." Henry W. Coil, Sr., "The original and basic Masonic historical work on which all subsequent, realistic investigations have been based. Documented and exhaustive to use to the point of discouragement to all but scholars, and particularly lacking in an index." Regarding the 1936 ed., Henry W. Coil, Sr., "Some parts of the revised portions were distinctly antique and depreciated according to modern standards and should be avoided by the beginner." Libraries: 1, 3, 4, 5, 6, 7, 8, 9, 10, 11, 12, 13, 14.

Robert Freke Gould, *Concise History of Freemasonry*. 1902; 430 pp. Gale & Polden, Ltd., London, publisher. Summary of his larger work.
Author: Appendix No. 12. Comments: Silas H. Shepherd, "This work is one of the best ever written. It omits some of the details to be found in his larger history, but appearing many years later was revised in many respects. A recent review has been issued by W. J. Crowe." H. L. Haywood, "In the 1920s Fred J. M. Crowe issued a new revised edition of the Concise History, and in it he deleted Gould's chapter on the Antients and replaced it by one written by himself."

L. B. Blakemore, "Contains in condensed form and in one volume materials in the same author's large work on the subject. One of the standard works of modern Masonic scholarship." Reviewed: 7 Build. Mag. 23 (1921); 8 Build. Mag. 183 (1922); 18 AQC 230 (1905); 20 AQC 88 (1907); New Age Mag., July, 1904, 208. Libraries: 1, 2, 3, 4, 5, 7, 9, 10, 11, 12, 13, 14, 15.

A. R. Hewitt, *R. F. Gould's "History of Freemasonry," a Bibliographical Puzzle*. Considers the early printed editions of the book. 85 AQC 61 (1972).

Albert G. Mackey, *The History of Freemasonry*. 1898; seven vols. Printed in several editions.
Author: Appendix No. 23. Comments: Silas H. Shepherd, "Many histories of Freemasonry have been written but few writers have had the faculty of elucidation of Mackey. Although this history was written before the scholarly school of which Hughan, Gould, Speth, Lane, and Sadler are examples, began to develop, it was a useful work." Henry W. Coil, Sr., " . . . began his labors some years before the effects of the realistic investigators in Britian appeared in America and caught his history about midway of his career. His History was practically contemporaneous with Gould's, but he was distinctly at a disadvantage as to the information possessed by Gould, Hughan, Sadler, Speth, and other British writers, though he was in a superior position as to conditions in the United States. Libraries: 2, 3, 5, 7, 8, 9, 10, 11, 12, 14.

Alexander Lawrie, *The History of Freemasonry*. 1804; 340 pp. Reproduced in Vol. 8 of the Universal Masonic Library.
Contents: This book aims at being a sober and realistic appraisal of Masonic history but turns out to be the opposite. After describing the details of the Mysteries of Greece and Egypt and the Dionysians, as a prelude, he then states that the Craft existed at the time of King Solomon and, as stated by Alex Horne, "is by no means so pregnant with absurdity, as some men would wish it to believe." Comments: Henry W. Coil, Sr., "Alexander

Lawrie, who was a bookseller and who, it is agreed, employed David Brewer to write the book, Edinburgh, Scotland, 1804. Rich with Scots' history and legend." L. B. Blakemore, "A history in the old style now of special interest only; chiefly valuable for details not found in many other books." Libraries: 1, 2, 3, 4, 5, 7, 9, 10, 15.

Capt. George Smith, *The Use and Abuse of Freemasonry*. 1914; 191 pp. This edition published by Macoy Publishing Co. Reproduced in Vol. 23 Universal Masonic Library.
Contents: The title of this book is misleading. It covers the antiquities of the Craft, its ceremonies, and the early history in a number of European countries. Of interest is that the author requested permission of the Grand Lodge to publish the book (as was the rule at that time, i.e., when originally published in 1783) but it was refused; he published the book anyway and established the custom of not seeking Grand Lodge permission from that time on. Comments: See Essays of H. L. Haywood, 401; Harry Carr, ed., Collected Prestonian Lectures, 78. Libraries: 3, 4, 7, 8, 9, 11, 12, 13, 14.

Bernard E. Jones, *Freemasons' Guide and Compendium*. 1950; 552 pp. American ed. published by Macoy Publishing Co.
Contents: An excellent book with a good history of the Craft, its medieval background, the years of transition, the origin of certain words, the formation and development of Grand Lodge, the ritual, and related subjects. Author: 74 AQC 9 (1961); 78 AQC 146 (1965). Reviewed: New Age Mag., Jan., 1951, 63. Comments: Louis L. Williams, "Positively the finest one-volume study of Masonry ever written." Libraries: 1, 2, 3, 4, 5, 6, 7, 8, 9, 10, 11, 12, 13, 14.

Eugen Lennhoff, *The Freemasons. 1934;* 357 pp. Methuen & Co., London, publisher. Originally written in German but translated into English by Einar Frame. Reprinted by A. Lewis Ltd. in 1979.
Contents: A good general one-volume history with fine coverage of European countries. Comment: L. B. Blakemore, "A concise account of Freemasonry in

Europe, with special reference to the period between the two World Wars.'' Reviewed: 16 Build. Mag. 94 (1930); N.Y. Mas. Outl., May, 1929, 287; 91 AQC 213 (1979); New Age Mag., Nov., 1934, 699. Libraries: 1, 4, 5, 6, 7, 8, 9, 10, 11, 14, 15.

Jacob Katz, *Jews and Freemasons in Europe*, 1723-1939; 1970; Harvard University Press. Reviewed: William Weisberger, in the Duquesne Review, Fall, 1973, pp. 62-64. 83 AQC 322 (1970).

Pick, Knight and Smyth, *Pocket History of Freemasonry*. The sixth edition of this book was published in 1977, by Frederick Muller, Ltd., London, England.
Authors: F. L. Pick: 56 AQC 298 (1943); 79 AQC 93 (1966). Smyth, Appendix No. 32. G. Norman Knight: Mas. Sq., Dec., 1978, 180. Contents: Excellent one-volume history but too brief on material relating to the United States. Reviewed: New Age Mag, Jan., 1970, 58; also Feb., 1954, 118; Ind. Free., Jan., 1956, 23; 66 AQC 66 (1953); 76 AQC 73 (1960); 81 AQC 250 (1965). Libraries: 2, 3, 4, 6, 10, 11, 12.

H. L. Haywood and James E. Craig, *A History of Freemasonry*. 1927; 326 pp. Much of the material in this book originally appeared in The Builder Magazine; see Vols. 7, 8, 9, 10.
Authors: Haywood: Appendix No. 16. Craig: 9 ALR 182 (1964); 11 ALR 188 (1971). Comments: L. B. Blakemore, ''One of the most solid and modern one-volume general histories of Freemasonry. Written by Americans and from the American point of view. Scholarly and authentic but written for the average reader.'' Reviewed: 13 Build. Mag. 285 (1927). Mast. Mas., July, 1927, 571. Libraries: 1, 3, 4, 5, 6, 7, 8, 9, 11.

Delmar D. Darrah, *The Evolution of Freemasonry*. 1920; 409 pp. The Masonic Publishing Co., Bloomington, Ill., publisher.
Author: A Past Grand Master of Illinois; the best book with biographical material is Louis L. Williams, The American Passion Play. Comment: Silas H. Shepherd, ''As a history of the present institution, this work is a worthy production, but the good features are somewhat offset by the materialistic views of the author. The 'Old Charges' are very lightly handled although their importance is fully recognized by the school Darrah claims to follow.'' Reviewed: 7 Build. Mag. 360 (1921). Libraries: 1, 2, 3, 4, 5, 6, 7, 8, 9, 10, 11, 12, 14.

Sir Alfred Robbins, *English Speaking Freemasonry*. 1930; 367.
Author: 86 AQC 100 (1973). Contents: History of the Craft in various parts of the world. Reviewed: 15 Build. Mag. 135 (1930), and has picture of the author. New Age Mag., Nov., 1930, 689. Libraries: 2, 3, 4, 5, 6, 7, 8, 9, 10, 12, 13, 14.

J. Hugo Tatsch, *Short Readings in Masonic History*. 1926; 55 pp. The Torch Press, Cedar Rapids, Iowa, publisher.
Author: See Sec. 2.16 herein. Comment: L. B. Blakemore, ''A collection of brief chapters on salient events in history of Masonry by an American Masonic bibliographer.'' Reviewed: 12 The Build. Mag. 349 (1926). Libraries: 1, 2, 3, 4, 5, 7, 8, 9, 11, 12, 13, 14.

Ray V. Denslow, *Freemasonry in the Eastern Hemisphere*. 1954; 375 pp. MLR Trans.
Author: Appendix No. 10. Contents: Brief history in the countries of Europe, Asia, Australia, and surrounding areas.

Ray V. Denslow, *Freemasonry in the Western Hemisphere*. 1952-1953; 402 pp. MLR Trans.
Author: Appendix No. 10. Contents: Brief history of the Craft in Canada, states of the United States, Hawaii, Mexico, Central and South America.

Frederick Armitage, *A Short Masonic History*. 1911. H. Weare & Co., London. Two vols. 338 pp.
Author: 71 AQC 124 (1961). Comments: Silas H. Shepherd, ''One of the best short histories.'' L. B. Blakemore, ''A work in two short volumes which gives a simple and rapid outline of the more important events of Masonic history.'' Reviewed: 25 AQC 132 (1912). 2

Am. Free. 384 (1910). Libraries: 3, 9, 12, 13, 14, 15.

J. G. Findel, *History of Freemasonry.* 1871; 700. Asher & Co., London. Originally published in German.
Author: 19 AQC 72 (1906); 2 Build. Mag., 221 (1916). Contents: The book is divided into three periods. In the first period various theories are set forth. Comments: Silas H. Shepherd, ''The best history at the time of its publication. Much of the historical matter has been rendered obsolete by subsequent research and critical analysis, but there is left a wealth of good material for study. L. B. Blakemore, ''A once popular work, now out of date, but required reading for students of Masonic history. . . . one of the best mid-nineteenth century writers.'' Libraries: 1, 2, 3, 4, 5, 7, 9, 10, 11, 12, 14, 15.

Emmanuel Rebold, *A General History of Freemasonry.* 1883; 464 pp. J. F. Brennan, Toledo, Ohio, publisher.
Comments: Silas H. Shepherd, ''Contains much useful information concerning rites not treated in English and American works.'' Henry W. Coil, Sr., ''It is indeed general and lacking in detail but a work of longstanding.'' L. B. Blakemore, ''An old-fashioned history, now somewhat out of date, but very interesting and still useful for reference purposes.'' Libraries: 2, 3, 4, 5, 6, 7, 8, 10, 11, 12, 14, 15.

J. W. S. Mitchell, *History of Freemasonry and Masonic Digest.* 1869; privately published.
Author: 8 MLR Trans. 121 (1950). Comments: Silas H. Shepherd, ''This work was written before the era of critical scholarship in Masonic historical writing. It follows that the old idea of giving credence to transcendental and allegorical matter.'' L. B. Blakemore, ''A book of reference. Not much weight.'' H. L. Haywood, ''Has been unjustly criticized for setting forth a number of impossible theories of the origin of the Craft, but these criticisms overlooked the fact that during the years in which he worked on his book he had use of almost no Masonic literature.'' Libraries: 1, 2, 3, 4, 5, 7, 8, 9, 10, 11, 12, 13, 14.

Henry Leonard Stillson and William James Hughan, *History of the Ancient and Honorable Fraternity of Free and Accepted Masons, and Concordant Orders.* 1906; 986 pp. Originally published in 1890; revised in 1898; this was a reprint of the 1898 ed. It is a collection of many fine articles by many authors.
Comments: Silas H. Shepherd, ''This is the work of a number of eminent American brethren assisted by Hughan. The chapters dealing with the history of Freemasonry in general are concise and reasonably authentic and the chapters about the concordant orders are valuable.'' Libraries: 2, 3, 4, 5, 6, 7, 8, 9, 10, 11, 12, 13, 14, 15.

Alphonse Cerza, *Historical Parallels.* 1955. MSA Digest. General historical events and Masonic events presented in adjoining columns.

Knoop and Jones, *Masonic History Old and New.* 55 AQC 285 (1942).

Knoop and Jones, *Begemann's History of Freemasonry.* 54 AQC 86 (1943).

Alphonse Cerza, *Our Masonic Heritage.* Series of articles in the 1967 issues of the Phil. Mag.: Feb., Our Ancestors; April, The Transition from the Operative to the Symbolic Craft; June, The Formation of the First Grand Lodge; Aug., Colonial Freemasonry; Oct., Anti-Masonry and the Revival; Dec., Freemasonry in the Modern World.

J. Fairbairn Smith, *Michigan Masonic Trestleboard;* 1976; 84 pp. Grand Lodge of Michigan, publisher. Collection of articles and pictures originally published in the Masonic World, of Detroit, and arranged in chronological order resulting in a good short history with emphasis on Michigan items.

Ross Hepburn, *The Value of Masonic History.* Trans. M. & P. M. L. March, 1973, 28.

John Yarker, *Masonic History – Let Us Seek the Truth.* 20 AQC 15 (1907).

J. R. Clarke, *External Influence on the Evolution of English Masonry.* 82 AQC 263 (1969).

Norman Rogers, *The Years of Develop-*

ment. In Harry Carr, ed., The Collected Prestonian Lectures, 439.

Louis L. Williams, *The History (When and How?) and Philosophy (Why?) of Masonry.* No. Light, June, 1971, 10.

H. L. Haywood, *A Bird's-Eye View of Masonic History.* 6 Build. Mag. 236 (1920).

Robert J. Meekren, *Evolution of the Lodge.* 11 Build. Mag. 273 (1925).

Alex Horne, *Some of the Influences Behind the Rise of Modern Masonry.* New Age Mag., Nov. 1964, 14.

2.02 THEORIES OF THE ORIGIN OF FREEMASONRY

In reading books on this subject one must be careful in what he accepts as being correct. About 24 theories have been advanced on this subject with various degrees of imagination. (See H. W. Coil, Freemasonry Through Six Centuries, Vol. 1, pp. 5-10, for a classification and discussion of these theories; also see Pick, Knight, and Smyth, Pocket History of Freemasonry, 6th ed., 13-18).

Alec Mellor, *Methods and Scope of Masonic History.* 5 Trans. Phoenix L. (Paris) 29.

Robert H. Lowe, *Primitive Societies.* 1920; 462 pp. Boni & Liveright, N.Y., publisher.
Contents: Presents description of ritual and ceremonies of early societies. Comments: L. B. Blakemore, "A masterpiece in anthropology, with many pages on primitive societies. A companion to Hutton Webster's Primitive Secret Societies."

Simon Greenleaf, *A Brief Inquiry Into the Origin and Principles of Freemasonry.* 1820; 117. Arthur Shirley, Portland, Me., publisher.
Contents: Collection of talks given by the author in 1817-1818 to the lodges of the ninth Masonic District of Massachusetts, over which he presided as District Deputy Grand Master. Comment: Silas H. Shepherd, "One of the best short histories of the times." H. L. Haywood, Masonic Curiosa, 168. H. L. Haywood,

"Our British Brothers in the Craft have used, revered, honored, and countlessly quoted Calcott's Disquisition, Hutchinson's Spirit of Freemasonry, Preson's Illustrations, and Laurence Dermott's Ahiman Rezon . . . but not one of these books is on a level with A Brief Inquiry; nor was one of those writers possessed of Greenleaf's massive scholarship, power and greatness of mind, or literary ability." Libraries: 3, 9, 12, 14.

John Fellows, *The Mysteries of Freemasonry.* 1866; 366 pp. Reeves and Turner, London, publisher. Originally published in 1835.
Contents: Expounds the theory that Freemasonry is a descendant of the Ancient Mysteries of Egypt. Comments: Silas H. Shepherd, "One of the best books rendered obsolete by subsequent research and critical analysis, but there is left a wealth of good material for study." H. W. Coil, Sr., "Thoroughly mystical and conforms to most other books of this kind. Libraries: 4, 7, 11, 13.

J. N. Casavis, *The Greek Origin of Freemasonry.* 1955; 208 pp.
Contents: Presents the theory that the Craft evolved from the Ancient Mysteries of Greece. He quotes from a large number of published works and took pictures of statues in Greece to support his theory. The Mysteries are described briefly. Libraries: 1, 2, 3, 4, 5, 7, 8, 9, 10, 11, 12, 13, 14.

A. Le Plongeon, *Sacred Mysteries Among the Mayas and the Quiches.* 1909; 153 pp. Macoy Publishing Co.
The theory advanced in this book is examined in 10 Build. Mag. 7 (1924). Contains picture of Le Plongeon. Comments: Silas H. Shepherd, "Contains results of researches in Yucatan." L. B. Blakemore, "At the time of its publication this strange book made a small sensation. Unsound about the Mayas, still more unsound about Freemasonry, but very interesting to read." Reviewed: Am. Free., Vol. 1, Sept., 1910, 533. See: Carl H. Claudy, Some American Masonic Myths, Ind. Free., Dec., 1958, 12. Libraries: 1, 2, 3, 5, 6, 7, 8, 9, 12, 13.

Morton Deutsch, *From Whence Came You.* 1958; 231 pp. Philosophical Library, N.Y., publisher.

Contents: Presents the theory that Freemasonry was organized after many of the Masons went to the Holy Land with the Crusades. He got the idea while on a trip to one of the Mediterranean islands and weaves it into the words of the ritual "from a Lodge of the Holy Sts. John of Jerusalem." See New Age article Jan., 1954. Reviewed: 71 AQC 123 (1961). Libraries: 2, 3, 5, 7, 9, 11, 12, 14, 15.

Charles H. Vail, *Ancient Mysteries and Modern Masonry.* 1909; 214 pp. Macoy Publishing Co., publisher.

Contents: A series of lectures delivered before a church in Albion, N.Y. Comments: Silas H. Shepherd, "One of the best works treating of the connection between the mysteries of antiquity and the modern symbolic teaching of which Freemasonry is the custodian." Libraries: 8, 9, 15.

J. S. M. Ward, *Freemasonry and the Ancient Gods.* 1926; 577 pp. Simpkin, Marshall, Hamilton, Kent & Co.

Contents: Examines many aspects of ancient history, symbols, practices, and religions seeking to find traces of Masonic origin. Presents the theory that Freemasonry originated before the operative masons of the middle ages. Must be read with caution. Comments: L. B. Blakemore, "A large book in one volume which develops the theory that the origins of Freemasonry are to be found among the cults and rites of primitive people." Silas H. Shepherd, "One of the most interesting and thought compelling works of recent years on the use of signs and symbols throughout the world." Reviewed: 8 Build. Mag. 151 (1922). Libraries: 2, 3, 4, 5, 7, 9, 10, 11, 12, 14, 15.

Mrs. C. M. Pott, *Bacon and His Secret Society.* 1891; 421 pp. Francis J. Schulte & Co., Chicago, Ill., publisher.

Contents: Presents the theory that Francis Bacon was the founder of the Craft. Must be read with caution. Comment: L. B. Blakemore, "An attempt to prove that Freemasonry originated in a secret society founded by Francis Bacon. Unreli-

able, but brilliant in spots, and full of out of the way information." Reviewed: 10 Build. Mag. 380 (1924). Libraries: 3, 7, 9, 10, 11, 12, 14.

George V. Tudhope, *Bacon Masonry.* 1954; 121 pp.

Comments: The book states "Much cumulative evidence discloses that Francis Bacon . . . is the original designer of Freemasonry and that he discovered the meaning of the Mystic Word and introduced it into the Order of Freemasonry as the Lost Word." Must be read with caution. Reviewed: 5 RAM 106 (1955). Libraries: 1, 3, 5, 7, 8, 9, 12.

Alfred Dodd, *Shakespeare, Creator of Freemasonry.* 1936; 276; Rider & Co., London, publisher.

Contents: The author made a detailed study of the works of Shakespeare and quotes all parts that sound like Masonic thoughts. He advanced the interesting theory that the Craft was started by Shakespeare on the basis of these quotations. Libraries: 1, 2, 3, 5, 9, 12, 14. See: Clegg, *Was William Shakespeare a Freemason?* 2 Build. Mag. 125 (1916); 5 Build. Mag. 32 (1919); A. Cerza, *Freemasonry and Shakespeare,* Phil. Mag., Aug., 1964, 60; Raymond B. Pease, *Masonic Parallels in Shakespeare,* 1952, MSA Digest; A. Cerza, *William Shakespeare and Freemasonry,* an imaginary interview with Shakespeare in which pertinent questions are asked and he answers in his own words, New Age Mag., Nov., 1973, 8.

Augustus C. L. Arnold, *Philosophical History of Freemasonry and Other Secret Societies.* 1854; 283 pp. Clark, Austin & Smith, New York, publisher.

Contents: Discussion of the Ancient Mysteries, the Carbonari, and other groups. Comments: Silas H. Shepherd, "This is a work of considerable merit. The author has enriched it with a large fund of historical matter bearing on the probable derivation of our teaching from the ancient mysteries. The work includes a reproduction of the essay by Thomas Paine on Freemasonry." L. B. Blakemore, "Published in 1854. Valueless as history, but filled with interesting material on the ancient mysteries.'' Libraries: 2, 3, 5, 7, 9, 11, 13, 14.

Albert Churchward, *The Arcana of Freemasonry*. 1915; 326 pp. George Allen & Unwin, London, publisher.
Contents: Expounds the theory that the Craft originated with the ancient mysteries; uses charts, pictures, figures to support his view. Must be read with caution. Libraries: 1, 2, 3, 4, 5, 7, 8, 9, 10, 11, 12, 13, 14.

Albert Churchward, *The Origin and Evolution of Freemasonry*. 1898; 75 pp.; a 1920 edition was expanded to 231 pp.
Contents: Offers theory that the Craft originated in the lost continent of Atlantis. Comment: Silas H. Shepherd, ''Although Brother Churchward's theories appear extravagant to many, he has gathered much important data on the signs and symbols of antiquity.'' L. B. Blakemore, ''An attempt in a large book, to show that Freemasonry began thousands of years ago among the Mayas, on the lost continent of Atlantis. . . . '' Reviewed: 12 AQC 40 (1899). Libraries: 2, 3, 5, 7, 12, 14, 15.

Albert Churchward, *Signs and Symbols of Primordial Man*. 1913; 491 pp.
Comment: Silas H. Shepherd, ''This is Dr. Churchward's most pretentious work. The many illustrations are of importance in learning about symbolic teaching in general. Although most readers probably will not concede the antiquity of the signs and ceremonies described by Dr. Churchward, all will be enlightened by this book.'' Mas. Sq., Dec., 1976, 150, '' . . . the writings of Dr. Albert Churchward should be treated with caution.'' Reviewed: 6 Build. Mag. 267 (1920); Am. Free., Aug., 1910, 485. Libraries: 2, 3, 4, 5, 7, 11, 12, 13, 14.

The Missing Link. Best physical description of the Obelisk in Central Park, New York City, but creating the unfounded inference that Egypt is the source of the Craft. 1977; published by the Springfield Temple Association, Spring, Va. Reviewed: New Age Mag., July, 1977, 53

New York's Silent Sentinel, K. T. Mag., July, 1978, 13.

Alphonse Cerza, *The Origin of Freemasonry*. 1 Trans. Ill. L. of Res. 181 (1978).

Whence Came Freemasonry? 7 Build. Mag. 90 (1921).

William E. Parker, *The Antiquity of Freemasonry*. Phil. Mag., April, 1975, 43.

The Origin of Freemasonry, New Age Mag., Aug., 1958, 461.

Dr. Sidney Vatcher, *The Origin of Speculative Freemasonry*. 3 Trans. Phoe. L., Paris, 85 (1971-1972).

H. P. Marriott, *The Secret Tribal Societies of West Africa*. 12 AQC 66 (1899).

Gerald Fitzgibbon, *The Classic Writers on the Mysteries*. 8 AQC 190 (1895).

Masonry and the Mysteries. Mas. J. of So. Africa, 683 (1927).

The Mystery Degrees. New Age Mag., Aug., 1946, 471; April, 1961, 51.

The Dionysiac Artificers; A Masonic Myth. 14 Build. Mag. 75 (1928).

Henry R. Evans, *The Mysteries of Isis and Osiris and Modern Masonry*. Mast. Mas., Jan., 1928, 21.

W. Graham Brown, *Freemasonry and the Ancient Mysteries*. 1974 Grd. L. Scot. Yrbk. 57.

George F. Greene, *Masonry and the Mysteries*. 2 Build. Mag. 19 (1916).

Alex Horne, *The Ancient Mysteries*. New Age Mag., Oct., 1964, 21.

Ross Hepburn, *Freemasonry and the Ancient Mysteries*. Trans. M. & P. M. L., Sept., 1970, 159.

W. W. Covey-Crump, *Egyptian Mysteries and English Masonry*. 26 Leic. L. of Res. 86 (1917-1918).

Goblet D'Alviella, *Mithraic Rites*. 13 AQC 90 (1900).

W. W. Westcott, *The Resemblance of Freemasonry to the Cult of Mithra*. 29 AQC 336 (1916).

The Mysteries of Mithra, New Age Mag., Oct., 1928, 609.

H. G. Burows, *Some Links Between Mithraism and Freemasonry*. 4 Author's L. 322 (1928).

Harold V. B. Voorhis, *A Third Theory About Freemasonry*. Phil. Mag., April, 1976, 58.

The Culdees. 57 AQC 23 (1944).

Oliver D. Street, *The Charles Martel Legend and Freemasonry*. 1 Build. Mag. 250 (1915).

C. Bud White, *The Druses*. Quart. J. of No. Car. L. of Res., March, 1974.

Atlantis. 13 Build. Mag. 65 (1927).

Haskett Smith, *The Druses of Syria and Their Relation to Freemasonry*. 4 AQC 7, 63, 175 (1891).

Henry Lovegrove, *Notes on Stonehenge*. 15 AQC 26 (1902).

William Simpson, *The Threefold Division of the Temples*. 1 AQC 89, 166 (1886-1888).

Russell A. Herner, *Stonehenge; an Ancient Masonic Temple*. Annual Proc. Ohio L. of R., 1979, 5.

Robert J. Meekren, *The Essenes in Masonic Literature*. 13 Build. Mag. 361 (1927).

The Essenes and Freemasonry. New Age Mag., Dec., 1972, 24.

The Essenes and Freemasonry. Phil. Mag., Aug., 1958, 56.

William C. Blaine, *The Essenes and Freemasonry*. New Age Mag., Dec., 1928, 195.

Freemasonry and the Aborigines, N.Y. Mas. Outl., March, 1925, 140.

Masonry Among Primitive People. 3 Build. Mag. 38 (1917).

Alphonse Cerza, *From Whence Came Freemasonry*. 2 Mas. Papers of Walter F. Meier L. of Res., Wash., 223 (1954).

W. E. Heaton, *Masonic Antiquities*. 59 AQC 23 (1946).

J. W. Hobbs, *Antiquity of Masonic Symbolism*. 3 AQC 7 (1890).

Herbert Poole, *Antiquity of the Craft*. 51 AQC 6, 126 (1938).

J. Austin Evans, *Official Origin of Speculative Craft*. 2 RAM 6 (1946).

F. F. Schnitzer, *Evidence of Steinmetzen Esoterica*. 3 AQC 33 (1890).

G. W. Speth, *The Steinmetzen Theory Critically Examined*. 1 AQC 17 (1886-1888).

P. Fischel, *Le Compagnonnage and Its Survival in France Today*. 79 AQC 203 (1966).

W. H. Rylands, *A Word on the Legends of the Compagnonnage*. 1 AQC 116 (1886-1888); 2 AQC 52 (1889).

A. L. Vibert, *The Compagnonnage – A Tentative Enquery*. 33 AQC 191 (1920).

A. F. A. Woodford, *Freemasonry and Hermeticism*. 1 AQC 28 (1886-1888).

Kress and Meekren, *Gilds, Collegia, and Comacines*. 12 Build. Mag. 14 (1926).

George Atkinson, *De Quincey and the Origin of Freemasonry*. 3 Mas. Assn. for Mas. Res., 71; Also in 10 Mas. Miscellany 109.

Douglas Knoop, *The Genesis of Speculative Masonry*. 55 AQC 4 (1942).

Eric Ward, *The Birth of Free-Masonry*. 91 AQC 77 (1979).

2.03 THE CATHEDRAL BUILDERS

Leader Scott, *The Cathedral Builders*. 1899; 2nd ed; 426 pp. Sampson Low, Marston & Co., London, publisher.
Contents: Presents the theory that with the fall of Rome certain skilled workers went to the Isle of Como and preserved the skills of the stonemasons. Comments: L. B. Blakemore, "In this widely-read book an Englishwoman tried to prove that Freemasonry originated in the school of builders established near Lake Como. Required reading by the students of 'the Comacine theory.' " H. L. Haywood, "Lucy Baxter married an archeologist . . .

and with her husband lived some years in Italy. While there she became fascinated by the history of Italian architecture, and in 1899, she published . . . a large, sumptuous, and richly illustrated book entitled The Cathedral Builders. She signed the book with her pen name 'Leader Scott.' "
Note: The full name of the author was Lucy E. Baxter; in Haywood's vol. 3 of Mackey's Encyclopedia, he states her name as "Mrs. Webster"; this is in error. Reviewed: 12 AQC 124 (1899); 3 Build. Mag. 380 (1918). Libraries: 1, 2, 3, 4, 7, 8, 9, 10, 11, 12, 13, 14.

W. Ravenscroft, *The Comacines: Their Predecessors and Successors*. 1910; 80. Elliott Stock, London, publisher. Reproduced in the Little Masonic Library, vol. 2, p. 3.
Reviewed: 23 AQC 194 (1910); Am. Free., Aug., 1910, 484; The subject of this book was debated in a series of articles in the Builder Magazine: Vol. 4, p. 195; vol. 7, p. 247; vol. 10, p. 14; vol. 12, p. 14, 112, 145, and p. 363; vol. 9, p. 304; Libraries: 2, 3, 7, 8, 9, 15.

Ossian Lang, *The Comacine Masters*. 1925; 24 pp.
Libraries: 2, 3, 7, 11, 12, 13, 14.

J. Walter Hobbs, *The Travelling Masons and Cathedral Builders*. 40 AQC 140 (1927).

Jean Gimpel, *The Cathedral Builders*. 1961; 184 pp.
Reviewed: 74 AQC 104 (1961). Libraries: 7, 11, 14.

2.04 TRANSITION FROM THE OPERATIVE TO THE SYMBOLIC CRAFT

Alex Horne, *The York Legend in the Old Charges*. 1978; 152 pp. A. Lewis Ltd., publisher.
Author: Appendix No. 20. Reviewed: Cal. Free., Autumn, 1979, 170; 90 AQC 325 (1978).

Ray Baker Harris, *The York Problem*. MSA Digest.

Alex Horne, *Prince Edwin, 926 A.D. – Our First Speculative Freemason*. Phil. Mag., Oct., 1975, 100.

The Regius Poem. Facsimile published by the Masonic Book Club. 1970.
Reviewed in 83 AQC 331 (1970).

Frederick Hunter, *The Regius Manuscript*. 1952; 96 pp. Facsimile and commentary; published by the Research Lodge of Oregon.

Alphonse Cerza, *The Discoverer of the Regius Poem*. Phil. Mag., Feb., 1976, 23.

Harry Carr, *Transition from Operative to Speculative*. 69 AQC 161 (1956), also in Collected Prestonian Lectures, 421.

A. L. Miller, *Notes on the Early History and Records of the Lodge, Aberdeen*. 1919; 74 pp. University press, Aberdeen, publisher.
Contents: Description of the minute book and other records of the lodge with some pages reproduced. Comments: Silas H. Shepherd, "Besides many interesting notes . . . this work contains valuable photographic reproduction of old minutes and other documents of one of the oldest Scotch lodges. Only three lodges have precedence over it." L. B. Blakemore, "A beautifully-written, illustrated history of one of Scotland's oldest lodges; a graphic picture of Masonic practices about the years 1650-1700." H. L. Haywood, "It is written modestly, with a fine spirit, and with a just sense of proportion; it is a model for a lodge historian everywhere to pattern on; moreover it contains the clearest picture of a lodge of the Transition Period, as it was and it worked, a century before the first Grand Lodge of 1717." This lodge is of special interest since James Anderson was a member of it; and because John Skene, first Mason to come to the United States, was enrolled as a member. Reviewed: 9 Build. Mag. 347 (1923). Libraries: 2, 3, 4, 7, 9, 11, 12, 14.

Harry Carr, *Lodge Mother Kilwinning*. 1961; 324 pp. Quatuor Coronati Lodge, publisher.
Author: Appendix No. 3. Contents: A study of the minutes of this lodge from 1642 to 1842; some minutes are reproduced, others are summarized. Reviewed: 73 AQC 127 (1962). Libraries: 1, 2, 3, 4, 5, 7, 8, 9, 10, 11, 13, 14, 15.

Kilwinning, *The Lodge Without a Charter*. 5 RAM 17, 84 (1955).

W. J. Ashley, *English Economic History*. Good background on guilds.
Library: 5.

William J. Hughan, *Origin of the English Rite*. 1909; 198 pp.
Comments: Silas H. Shepherd, "This is one of the best works on Freemasonry. The second edition is corrected and reviewed in accord with the later studies of the author. The history of the rise of the degrees is so obsure that most careful study must be made to enable one to reach any satisfactory conclusion. Hughan's works are all Masonic classics. This one is particularly valuable." L. B. Blakemore, "The documents and records of the early period of Speculative Freemasonry in England by a Masonic scholar of great eminence." Reviewed: 22 AQC 205 (1909). Libraries: 3, 4, 5, 7, 9, 10, 11, 14.

Toulmin Smith, *English Guilds*, 1870; 462 pp.
Libraries: 3, 7, 9, 10, 12, 14.

Frederick Armitage, *Old Guilds of England*. 1918; 219 pp. Weare & Co., publishers.
Comment: Silas H. Shepherd, "One of the best works obtainable containing a concise account of the connection between the guilds and Masonry." L. B. Blakemore, "A pleasant, easy to read account of the old guilds with special reference to Masonic guilds by a distinguished English Masonic writer." Libraries: 3, 5, 9, 10, 12, 14, 15.

Norman Rogers, *The Lodge of Elias Ashmole*. 66 AQC 35 (1952).

Louis L. Williams, *Elias Ashmole, The First Recorded Initiate*. No. Light, Jan., 1979, 13.

Plot's Book, *Extracts*. New Age Mag., March, 1908, 272.

J. H. Tatsch, *Plot's Natural History of Staffordshire*. Mast. Mas., July, 1924, 487.

Thomas H. S. Escott, *Club Makers and Club Members*. 1914; 352 pp. Sturgis & Walton, New York, publisher.
Comments: L. B. Blakemore, "Club life in 17th and 18th century England, helped to shape the system of Speculative Lodges in 1717 and after. The author is an authority." Libraries: 3, 5, 7, 9, 14.

Knoop, Jones and Hamer, *Early Masonic Pamphlets*. 1945; 335 pp. Manchester University Press.
Comments: Henry W. Coil, "This . . . our principal sources of information about the internal workings of Masonry in the early Grand Lodge era. . . . " Libraries: 3, 4, 11.

Knoop and Jones, *The Medieval Mason*. 1949; 278 pp. Manchester University Press.
Contents: Economic consideration of the operative masons and their building projects. Reviewed: 44 AQC 191 (1934); 80 AQC 293 (1977). Libraries: 1, 2, 3, 4, 5, 6, 7, 8, 9, 10, 11, 12, 14.

Knoop and Jones, *The Scottish Mason and the Mason Word*. 1939; 109 pp. Manchester University Press. Reproduced in Collected Prestonian Lectures, 243.
Comments: L. B. Blakemore, "A brochure on an obscure subject which throws much light on the beginning of Speculative Masonry." Libraries: 1, 2, 3, 4, 5, 7, 8, 9, 11, 12, 14.

Knoop and Jones, *The Genesis of Freemasonry*. 1947; 323 pp. Manchester University Press, publisher.
Reviewed: 59 AQC 197 (1948). Libraries: 1, 2, 3, 4, 5, 7, 9, 10, 11, 12, 14.

Knoop, Jones and Hamer. *The Two Earliest Masonic Manuscripts*. 1938; 204 pp. Manchester University Press, publisher.
Contents: Detailed analysis of the Regius and Cooke Manuscripts. Reviewed: 47 AQC 115 (1938). Libraries: 1, 2, 3, 4, 5, 7, 8, 9, 10, 11, 12, 13, 14.

Elias Ashmole, His Autobiography & Historical Notes, His Correspondence, and Other Contemporary Sources Relating to His Life and Works. 1968; 5 vols. Oxford University Press, publisher.
Contents: Of special interest in places because he was an early member of the Craft and was a famous antiquarian of his day. Reviewed: A prior book on the sub-

ject was reviewed in 11 Build. Mag. 322; see also Elias Ashmole and the Craft, 7 Build. Mag. 158. J. H. Tatsch, The Diary of Elias Ashmole, Mast. Mas., June, 1924, 416. Louis L. Williams, Elias Ashmole, The First Recorded Initiate. No. Light, Jan., 1970, 13.

W. R. Lethaby, *Westminster Abbey and the King's Craftsmen.* 1906; 383 pp. Duckworth & Co., London, publisher. Comment: L. B. Blakemore, "A vivid and authentic picture of Operative Masons as they were actually at work by a master of the history of architecture." Libraries: 3, 5, 14.

The Minutes of the Lodge of Edinburgh, Mary's Chapel No. 1. 1962; 354 pp. Quatuor Coronati Lodge, publisher. Contents: Edited minutes of the lodge, with a note and introduction by Harry Carr; covering the years 1598 to 1738. Libraries: 2, 3, 7, 11.

Knoop and Jones, *The London Mason of the Seventeenth Century.* 43 AQC 5, 305 (1935).

George W. Speth, *Builders Rites and Ceremonies.* 1894; 52 pp. Contents: Two lectures on the folklore of Masonry delivered on October 30 and November 13, 1893 to the members of the Church Institute, Margate. Comments: Silas H. Shepherd, "Everything of Brother Speth is well done. This work is for the deeper reader." Libraries: 3, 4, 9.

Edward Conder, Jr., *Records of the Hole Crafte and Fellowship of Masons.* 1894; 312 pp. Author: 13 AQC 184 (1900); 47 AQC 172 (1934); 3 Build. Mag. 251 (1918). Contents: Covers the history of the Worshipful Company of Masons of London. Comments: L. B. Blakemore, "A large and learned book about a London lodge with Speculative members prior to the first Grand Lodge of 1717." Silas H. Shepherd, "One of the most important of the works giving the connection between the 'operative' and 'speculative' Masons. In this work we find evidence of an inner circle in the Mason company which is of vital importance." Reviewed: 3 Build. Mag. 251 (1918); 7 AQC 178 (1894). Li-

braries: 2, 3, 5, 6, 7, 8, 9, 11, 12, 14.

A. C. F. Jackson, *Our Predecessors; Scottish Masons of About 1660.* 91 AQC 10 (1979).

A. C. F. Jackson, *Our Predecessors – The English Non-Operative Masons of the Mid-17th Century.* 89 AQC 23 (1976).

A. C. F. Jackson, *Our Predecessors; The Medieval Masons of the Regius Manuscript.* 88 AQC 1 (1975).

Dr. William Moseley Brown, *Lodge of Antiquity No. 2.* MSA Digest.

Dr. William Moseley Brown, *From Operative to Speculative.* MSA Digest.

W. F. Kuhn, *Evolution of the Operative Into the Speculative.* 3 Build. Mag., 337 (1917).

J. A. Ness, *Kilwinning Abbey.* Mas. Sq., Dec., 1978, 174.

Eric Ward, *Dassigny, Younghal and All That.* 88 AQC 20 (1975).

Alex Horne, *The Medieval Guilds and Freemasonry.* Phil. Mag., Dec., 1971, 100.

B. E. Jones, *Freemasonry's Debt to the Guilds.* 74 AQC 1 (1961).

W. J. Hughan, *The York Grand Lodge.* 13 AQC 4 (1900).

T. H. Wytehead, *The Grand Lodge at York.* 2 AQC 110 (1889).

Alex Horne, *The Saga of York.* Phil. Mag., Feb., 1975, 8.

Alfred E. Robbins, *The Earliest Years of English Organized Freemasonry.* 22 AQC 67 (1909).

Herbert Poole, *The Medieval Mason and the Parish Churches of England.* 44 AQC 236 (1931).

W. J. Williams, *The King's Master Mason.* 43 AQC 75 (1930); 44 AQC 123 (1931).

Wylie B. Wendt, *The City of York and Freemasonry.* K. T. Mag., July, 1976, 19.

Cyril N. Batham, *The London Company of Masons.* 7 Trans. Phoe. L. (Paris) 44.

G. H. Robertson, *The Making of a Cathedral*. 88 AQC 195 (1975).

Lionel Vibert, *Freemasonry in the Two Kingdoms*. (Scotland and England). 85 AQC 11 (1972).

J. Fairbairn Smith, *Transition of Freemasonry*. Masonic World, Detroit, July-Aug., 1978, 10.

Charles S. Guthrie, *The Medieval Guilds and Freemasonry*. Phil. Mag., Dec., 1971, 100.

John R. Nocas, *Musical Society Confers Third Degree*. Phil. Mag., Dec., 1973, 111; and Cal. Free., Summer, 1975, 132.

Lionel Vibert, *A Lodge in the 14th Century*. 89 AQC 253 (1976).

W. E. McLeod, *St. Alban and St. Amphibal in the Medieval Masonic Tradition;* a review article. 89 AQC 113 (1976).

Arthur Barnet, *A Social Background of the Transition to Speculative Freemasonry.* 6 Trans. Phoe. L. (Paris) 12 (1974-1975).

Alex Horne, *The Medieval Guilds*. Mas. Sq., Dec., 1977, 156.

James B. Gale, *A Master Mason Builds a Great Medieval Abbey*. 1972 Proc. Midw. Conf. Mas. Ed. 12. Also in Phil. Mag., Aug., 1972, and Oct, 1972.

Harry Carr, *The Mason and the Burgh*, 67 AQC 30 (1954).

Robert J. Meekren, *The Aitchison Haven Minutes and Early Scottish Freemasonry*. 53 AQC 147 (1940).

Kenneth F. Curtis, *Active Transition From Operative to Speculative Freemasonry*. Phil. Mag., Dec., 1972, 100.

William J. Hughan, *Freemasonry Before 1723*. New Age Mag., Oct., 1908, 352.

E. E. Thiemyer, *The Transition: Some Reflections on Early Grand Lodge History*. 42 AQC 188 (1929).

A. J. Arkell, *The Genesis of Operative Masonry*. 77 AQC 169 (1964).

Harry Carr, *Apprenticeship in England and Scotland in 1700*. 69 AQC 46 (1956).

H. G. Clarke, *Folklore Into Masonry*. 76 AQC 147 (1963).

Edward Conder, *Benedict Biscop and the Introduction of Freemasonry Into England*. 9 AQC 109 (1896).

G. W. Daynes, *A Masonic Contract of A.D. 1432*. 35 AQC 34 (1922).

J. W. Hobbs, *The Travelling Masons and Cathedral Builders*. 40 AQC 140 (1927).

William J. Hughan, *A Masonic Contract of A.D. 1378*. 10 AQC 70 (1897).

Douglas Knoop, *The Connection Between Operative and Speculative Masonry*. 48 AQC 292 (1935).

T. H. Lewis, *Operative Masonry*. 5 AQC 195 (1892).

Herbert Poole, *The Trail of the Operative*. 41 AQC 289 (1928).

Knoop and Jones, *The Bolsover Castle Building Account*. 49 AQC 24 (1936).

J. H. Lepper, *Records of Operative Masons, Trinity College, Dublin*. 33 AQC 242 (1920).

Douglas Knoop, *London Bridge and Its Builders*. 47 AQC 5 (1934).

W. J. Williams, *Masons and the City of London*. 45 AQC 117 (1932).

J. W. Horseley, *An Account of Rebuilding the Cathedral Church of St. Paul's, London*. 17 AQC 102 (1904).

William Schaw, *Master of the Works of King James VI*. 50 AQC 220 (1937).

William Schaw, *Master of the Works*. New Age Mag., Dec., 1909, 551.

R. H. Holme, *Masons' Marks at Wetheral*. 12 AQC 33 (1899).

The Secret of the Old Operative Mason. 10 Build. Mag. 42 (1924).

The Mystery of the Unidentified Entered Apprentice. 6 ALR 312 (1956).

R. E. Wallace-James, *The Minute Book of Aitchison's Haven Lodge*. 24 AQC 30 (1911)

A Note on Medieval Masonry in York, England, and the Early Organization of the Lodge. 8 ALR 444 (1962).

O. Lang, *Speculative Masonry in the 17th Century*. 4 Build. Mag. 229, 286 (1918).

Operative vs. Speculative. 15 Build. Mag. 272 (1929).

The Lodge of Edinburgh-Mary's Chapel. 2 RAM 358 (1948).

J. P. Simpson, *Old City Taverns and Masonry*. 19 AQC 28 (1907).

Some Old Suburban Taverns and Masonry. 21 AQC 38 (1908).

S. L. Coulhurst and P. H. Lawson, *The Lodge of Randle Holme at Chester*. 45 AQC 68 (1932).

The Operatives Mason and His Work. 9 ALR 233 (1964).

Alex Horne, *Architectural Symbolism in the Middle Ages*. New Age Mag., Aug., 1970, 44.

Dudley Wright, *The First Recorded Initiation in England*. 7 Build. Mag. 185 (1921).

Background of Masonic History in the 18th Century. 12 Build. Mag. 102, 366 (1926).

William L. Boyden, *Ancient Taverns and Lodge Names*. New Age Mag., Aug., 1924, 463.

2.05 START OF THE GRAND LODGE SYSTEM

Albert F. Calvert, *The Grand Lodge of England*. 1917. 300 pp. Herbert Jenkins, London, publisher.
Comments: Silas H. Shepherd, "A useful book giving the essential features of the history of the Grand Lodge era." Libraries: 2, 3, 5, 7, 8, 9, 11, 12, 14.

Grand Lodge 1717-1967. 1967; 295 pp. United Grand Lodge of England, publisher.
Contents: Has five chapters, Freemasonry Before Grand Lodge, by Harry Carr; The Formation, by T. O. Haunch (1717-1751); 1751 to 1813, by J. R. Clarke; The Union and After, by P. R. James; The Last Fifty Years, by J. W. Stubbs; plus much more in the appendix. Reviewed: 79 AQC 234 (1968). Libraries: 1, 2, 3, 4, 7, 8, 10, 11.

Frederick Smyth, *Report on the 250th Anniversary Celebration of the United Grand Lodge of England*. 10 ALR 372 (1968).

The 250th Anniversary Celebration. 80 AQC 169 (1967).

England, The Mother of Modern Freemasonry. 5 RAM 142 (1956).

The Four Original Lodges. 5 RAM 99 (1955).

Alphonse Cerza, *The World of 1717*. Phil. Mag., May, 1954, 7.

William Weisberger, *Speculative Freemasonry and the Culture of Hanoverian England*. Phil. Mag., June, 1970, 64.

The Four Old Lodges. 6 Build. Mag. 53 (1920).

J. R. Clarke, *The Establishment of the Premier Grand Lodge: Why in London and Why in 1717?* 81 AQC 1 (1968).

Harry Carr, *Grand Lodge and the Significance of 1717*. 79 AQC 289 (1966).

William J. Songhurst, *Minutes of the Grand Lodge of England*. 1913; 360 pp. Quatuor Coronati Lodge, publisher.
Contents: Summary of the minutes of the early years of the 1717 Grand Lodge. Libraries: 3, 6, 9,

George Draffen, *A Register of Grand Lodges Active and Extinct*. 1972. Reviewed: 84 AQC 230 (1972).

Early Grand Lodges of England. Phil. Mag., Feb., 1970, 18.

J. H. Lepper, *Relations Between the Grand Lodges of England and Ireland*. 37 AQC 297 (1924).

W. I. Grantham, *The Title of the United Grand Lodge of England and the "Antients" and "Moderns."* 64 AQC 76 (1951).

Henry Sadler, *An Unrecorded Grand Lodge*. 18 AQC 69 (1905); 22 AQC 133 (1909).

Gilbert Y. Johnson, *The Grand Lodge*

South of the River Trent. Reproduced in The Collected Prestonian Lectures, 283.

Gilbert W. Daynes, *The Birth and Growth of the Grand Lodge of England*. 1926; 187 pp. The Masonic Record, London, publisher.
Comment: L. B. Blakemore, "A brief but carefully prepared account of the more important events in the history of the Grand Lodge in which the system of Speculative Freemasonry began." Reviewed: 12 Build. Mag 315 (1926); and 13 Build. Mag. 59 (1927). Summarized in N.Y. Mas. Outl., March, 1927, 205.

A. R. Hewitt, *A Relic of the York Grand Lodge*. 75 AQC 66 (1962).

W. J. Hughan, *The York Grand Lodge – a Brief Sketch*. 13 AQC 4 (1900).

G. Y. Johnson, *The Subordinate Lodges Constituted by the York Grand Lodge*. 52 AQC 195 (1940).

2.06 THE ANCIENT GRAND LODGE

Henry Sadler, *Masonic Facts and Fictions*. 1887; 210 pp. Dipose & Bateman, London, publisher.
Contents: This is an important book because the author explored the existing records and discovered that the Ancient Grand Lodge was not a "schism" as contended up to that time. Comment: Silas H. Shepherd, "When Brother Sadler made known the facts he discovered in regard to the origin of the 'Ancient' Grand Lodge, it revolutionized the opinion generally held at that time." L. B. Blakemore, "An epoch-making book. Consists largely of documents which show the origin of the Ancient Grand Lodge." Libraries: 1, 2, 3, 4, 5, 7, 8, 9, 11, 12, 14.

Robert Freke Gould, *Atholl Lodges*. 1879; 102.
Contents: Contains a list of the lodges formed by the Ancient Grand Lodge. Comments: L. B. Blakemore, "Lists and discussions of lodges which worked under charters of the Ancient Grand Lodge; a reference work for the professional historian." Silas H. Shepherd, "Hughan says that there is nothing better of the junior rival Grand Lodge of A.D. 1751 to 1813." Libraries: 1, 3, 4, 5, 7, 8, 9, 10, 11, 12, 14, 15.

The Ancients and Moderns, Ind. Free., Nov., 1958, 14.

J. R. Clarke, *The Formation of the Grand Lodge of the Antients*. 79 AQC 270 (1966).

Sixty-Two Years of Masonic Dissent (1751-1813). 8 Trans. Phoe. L. (Paris) 5 (1977).

Henry Sadler, *The "Irish Question" Settled*. Reproduction of Chapter 5 of Masonic Facts and Fictions. 85 AQC 184 (1972).

Lionel A. Seemungal, *The Fictitious "Great Schism."* Phil. Mag., Feb., 1974, 5.

The Union of 1792. Mas. Sq., March, 1976, 11.

Arthur Heiron, *The Craft in the 18th Century With Specific Relation to Dermott's Criticism*. 14 Man. Assn. for Mas. Res. 69 (1923-1924).

J. R. Dashwood, *Notes on the Early Records of the Grand Lodge of the Ancients*. 70 AQC 63 (1957).

John Lane, *Date of the Origin of the Grand Lodge of Antients, 1751*. 5 AQC 166 (1892).

2.07 THE UNION OF 1813

William James Hughan, *Memorial of the Masonic Union of 1813*. 1874; 119 pp. Second ed. in 1913.
Comments: L. B. Blakemore, "Documents covering the Union of the Modern and Antient Grand Lodges of England." Silas H. Shepherd, "Brother Hughan had a rare gift of discrimination and was able to place the important facts relating to Freemasonry before the Craft in a clear and forceful manner. The introduction is an historical essay of great value for reference." Libraries: 3, 5, 6, 7, 8, 9, 10, 11, 14.

J. H. Lepper, *The Union of the Grand*

Lodges of England in 1813. 56 AQC 128, 308 (1943).

W. B. Hextall, *The Special Lodge of Promulgation, 1809-1911.* 23 AQC 37 (1910).

J. M. Hammill, *Consolidation and Change – The Union of 1813.* 1977 Trans. Leic. L. of Res. 49. Discusses the necessity for the Union, the changes it brought about, and its effect on the Craft in England and elsewhere.

William Wonnacott, *The Lodge of Reconciliation.* 23 AQC 215 (1910).

E. H. Cartwright, *The Lodge of Reconciliation and the Ritual.* 54 AQC 115 (1941).

Royal Freemasons at Kew. Mas. Sq., Dec., 1976, 139.

C. N. Batham, *Unusual Masonic Ceremonies.* 1977 Trans. Leic. L. of Res. 40. Explains changes in the ritual brought about by the Union.

J. M. Hammill, *The Duke of Sussex and the Union.* 86 AQC 286 (1073) Text of a newly discovered document.

2.08 FREEMASONRY IN COUNTRIES OUTSIDE THE UNITED STATES.

Afghanistan: 15 Build. Mag., 115 (1929).

Africa: *On the African Gold Coast;* 2 RAM 23 (1946).

Antarctica: New Age Mag., Jan., 1964, 40.

Arabia: John Yarker, *Arab Masonry.* 19 AQC 243 (1906). J. A. Haywood, Freemasonry in the Arab World. Mas. Sq., March, 1976, 20.

Argentina: A. S. Hall-Johnson, *A Century of English Freemasonry in Argentina,* 65 AQC 98 (1952). Miranda, *San Martin and Freemasonry in Argentina,* 3 RAM 296 (1951). 5 RAM 145 (1956). 4 RAM 137, 172 (1953). 4 ALR 415 (1946-1947). Arthur W. Warren, *Freemasonry in Argentina,* 1954 Proc. Grd. Mast. Conf. 129. 1953 Proc. Grd. Mast. Conf. 30.

A. J. Goode, *Freemasonry in Argentina,* 14 Leic. L. of Res. 134 (1905-1906).

Australasia: 2 RAM 19 (1945).

Australia: 4 RAM 195 (1953). Charles R.S. Craig, *History of the Craft in South Australia,* 1977, 357 pp. Published by the Grd. L. of Australia. Norman C. Dutt, *The First Masonic Certificate in Australia,* Phil. Mag., Dec., 1974, 108. Robert S. Barnett, *Masonry in Australia,* New Age Mag., Oct., 1930, 607. E. H. Burne, *Freemasonry-Australia, 1820-1840.* Lodge of Res., Dublin, 84 (1922).

Austria: Frank Bernhart, *Freemasonry in Austria,* 76 AQC 1 (1963). *Austria's Masonic Museum,* 12 RAM 154 (1977). New Age Mag., Feb., 1926, 103. 10 Build. Mag. 376 (1924). Ladislas de Malczvich, *A Sketch of the Earlier History of Masonry in Austria and Hungary,* 4 AQC 20, 181 (1891). 5 AQC 15, 68, 187 (1892), 6 AQC 85 (1893), 7 AQC 18, 77, 184 (1894), 9 AQC 129 (1896). 2 RAM 28 (1946). *Persecution of Freemasons in Austria and Czechoslovakia,* 3 RAM 5 (1949). *The Last Days of the Grand Lodge of Austria,* 15 (1949). *Attacks on Freemasonry in Austria,* 11 Build. Mag. 307 (1925). *Thoughts on Reading 18th Century Viennese Masonic Trans.* 4 ALR 595 (1946-1947). William Weisberger, *Joseph von Sonnenfels: A Symbol of Austrian Freemasonry and the Enlightenment:* Phil. Mag., Aug., 1972, 78.

Belgium: Maurice F. Verbist, *The Development of Craft Masonry in Belgium: 1830-1960,* New Age Mag., 1975, 17; Charles F. Adams, *Freemasonry in Belgium,* 1957 Proc. Grd. Mast. Conf. 78.

Bengal: W. K. Firminger, *Some Fresh Light on the Old Bengal Lodges,* 18 AQC 157 (1905).

Bermuda: A. J. B. Milborne, *Freemasonry in Bermuda,* 74 AQC 11 (1961). 4 RAM 163 (1953). 7 ALR 279 (1959). Stanley Q. Wentz, *Bermuda, Alias Somers Island,* Ore. Free., Nov., 1973, 19, April, 1974, 4, May, 1974, 26 and subsequent issues to Oct. 1974. *Brothers in Bermuda,* N.Y. Mas. Outl., March, 1930, 205.

Bolivia: 5 RAM 302 (1957). Aubrey L.

Burbank, *Freemasonry in Bolivia*, 1957 Proc. Grd. Mas. Conf. 71.

Brazil: E. E. Cromack, *English Freemasonry in Brazil — A Short History*, *80 AQC 224 (1967). Connecticut Mason Introduced Scottish Rite in Brazil, No. Light, June, 1973, 16.* Denis I. Duveen, *English Freemasonry in Brazil*, Mas. Sq., Sept., 1975, 80, 95. Alfred C. Knight, *Freemasonry in Brazil*, Empire St. Mas., Feb., 1978, 8. Thomas S. Roy, *Freemasonry in Brazil*, 1957 Proc. Grd. Mast. Conf., 82.

Canada: J. Ross Robertson, *The History of Freemasonry in Canada.* 1900; 2 vols. Author: The Free. (Canada) Jan. 1974, 40; 31 AQC 178 (1918). John M. Cunningham, *Canadian Freemasons Who Served as Prime Minister*, 11 RAM 264 (1975). Gordon Morrison, *Canadian Freemasonry Today*, 1975 Proc. Grd. Mast. Conf. 38. John H. Graham, *Outline of the History of Freemasonry in Quebec;* 1892. *Early Years of Freemasonry in Canada*, No. Light, June, 1973, 10. Osborn Sheppard, *Freemasonry in Canada*, 1924. J. G. Hanna, *The Mounties and Freemasonry*, Phil. Mag., Aug.-Sept., 1949, 2. William Douglas, *Freemasonry in Manitoba*, 1925. William Kirk Bailey, *Beyond the Pillars* (History of the Craft in Ontario); 1972. *Review of the History of the Grand Lodge of British Columbia, 1871-1970*, 84 AQC 217 (1971). A. J. B. Milborne, *The Provincial Grand Lodge of Quebec*, 68 AQC 15 (1955), 71 AQC 104 (1958). *Oldest Masons' Mark Believed Discovered in Manitoba*, 5 RAM 146 (1956). J. E. Taylor, *Freemasonry in Upper Canada and the 1812 War.* 73 AQC 99 (1960), 74 AQC 105 (1961). James Vroom, *Ancient York Masons in British America*, 24 AQC 268 (1911). *Freemasonry in Ontario*, 9 Build. Mag. 267, 301, 332 (1923). *The Grand Lodge of Alberta*, 9 Build. Mag. 237 (1923). *Freemasonry in Prince Edward Island*, 9 Build. Mag. 238 (1923). *Freemasonry in the Province of Quebec*, 9 Build. Mag. 243 (1923). *Freemasonry in British Columbia*, 9 Build. Mag. 246 (1923). *The Early History of Freemasonry in Eastern Canada*, 10 Build. Mag. 227 (1924). *Freemasonry in Alberta*, 1 RAM 356 (1945). *Freemasonry in Saskatchewan*, 1 RAM 325 (1945). 10 Build. Mag. 273 (1924). *The Grand Lodge of New Brunswick*, 10 Build. Mag. 272 (1924).

Canal Zone: *Masonry in the Canal Zone.* 14 Tex. L. of Res. 128 (1978-1979).

Caribbean: *The Craft Covers the Caribbean Islands.* 5 ALR 330 (1947-1948).

Central America: 2 RAM 102, 153, 172, 208, 234, 264 (1948).

Ceylon: J. R. Dashwood, *Notes on Freemasonry in Ceylon.* 59 AQC 129 (1946); 60 AQC 99 (1947).

Chile: George Lanzarotti, *Freemasonry in Chile*, 9 Build. Mag. 8 (1923). Oreste Froden, *Freemasonry in Chile*, 1950 Proc. Grd. Mast. Conf. 26.

China: Chaloner Alabaster, *Freemasonry in China*, 2 AQC 119 (1889). J. M. Campbell, *Chinese Secret Societies*, 6 AQC 193 (1893). *Revival of a Dormant Lodge in China*, 5 Build. Mag. 259 (1919). *History of Masonry in China*, 11 Build. Mag. 12 (1925). *Massachusetts Freemasonry in China*, 11 Build. Mag. 3 (1925). Herbert Allen Giles, *Freemasonry in China* — reviewed in 9 Build. Mag 60 (1923). Phil. Mag., Dec., 1956, 91; Feb., 1970, 4. 3 RAM 260 (1951). 4 RAM 218 (1953). *Freemasonry in Shanghai*, 7 Norcalore 25. George W. Chen, *Freemasonry in China*, Mas. Sq., June, 1976, 48. 5 RAM 140 (1956). *Massachusetts Masonry in China*, Master Mason, Nov., 1924, 74. *Series of Persecution of Freemasons in China by the Japanese*, 2 RAM 332 (1948). H. A. Mets, *Chinese Secret Societies*, New Age Mag., Jan., 1909, 50; Sept., 1926, 540; Oct., 1926, 601; May, 1956, 278; Feb., 1928, 105, April, 1926, 215. *Masonic Clubs in China*, New Age Mag., Dec., 1945, 494. Arthur W. Warren, *Freemasonry in China*, 1956 Proc. Grd. Mast. Conf. 93.

Colombia: Robert H. Gollmar, 1956 Proc. Grd. Mast. Conf. 88. J. R. Dashwood, *Union Lodge of Colombia*, 60 AQC 78 (1947). Americo Carnicelli, *Historia* *de la Masoneria Colombiana,* 1833-1940; 2 vols., 1975, 1000 pp. with many pictures.

Costa Rica: Jaimes Granados, *Freemasonry in Costa Rica,* 1953 Proc. Grd. Mast. Conf. 76. 8 RAM 201 (1965). 8 Norcalore 30.

Cuba: *The Beginnings of Freemasonry in Cuba,* 12 Build. Mag. 115 (1923). Charles A. Brockway, 1 ALR 202 (1933). Dr. Carlos Manuel Pineiro, *Freemasonry in Cuba,* 1950 Proc. Grd. Mast. Conf. 67. *Military Lodges in Cuba,* 4 Build. Mag. 54 (1918). *A Cuban Viewpoint of World Freemasonry,* 6 Build. Mag. 217 (1920). 1 ALR 202 (1930-1932). *History of Freemasonry in Cuba,* 8 ALR 449 (1962). *Royal Arch Masonry in Cuba,* 5 RAM 82 (1955). *Cubans Dedicate Temple,* 5 RAM 36 (1955). 7 RAM 184, 241 (1962). 8 RAM 304 (1966).

Cyprus: Phil. Mag., Feb., 1969, 9. 15 Build. Mag. 193 (1929).

Czechoslavakia: *Masonry in Czechoslavakia,* N.Y. Mas. Outl., April, 1929, 233. E. Winterburgh, *Prague, A Centre of Freemasonry,* 77 AQC 65 (1964), 15 Build. Mag. 45, 79, 257, 289 (1929). *Freemasons in Austria and Czechoslavakia,* 3 RAM 5 (1949). New Age Mag., July, 1924, 401; Aug., 1924, 472. Felix A. Lenhart, *Freemasonry in Czechoslavakia,* 1 RAM 84 (1943).

Denmark: T. M. Jaeger, *Rasmus Rask: A Famous Danish Mason,* 59 AQC 188 (1946). A. J. Lange, *A Danish Freemasons' Lodge Unknown in Denmark,* 12 AQC 166 (1899). 9 ALR 119 (1963). Phil. Mag., Oct., 1945, 7. Ray V. Denslow, *Freemasonry in Denmark,* 1 RAM 111 (1943). W. P. Tange, *Freemasonry in Denmark,* New Age Mag., Dec., 1960, 24. Danish Bicentennial Visited by English Masons, 2 RAM 187, 366 (1947). Revival of Danish Freemasonry, 2 RAM 3 (1946).

Dominican Republic: Thomas S. Roy, *Freemasonry in the Dominican Republic,* 1956 Proc. Grd. Mast. Conf. 86.

East: Christopher Haffner, *The Craft in the East,* 1977; 419 pp. District Grd. L. of Hong Kong and the Far East. Reviewed: 90 AQC 259 (1978).

Ecuador: Arthur N. Warren, *Freemasonry in Ecuador,* 1957 Proc. Grd. Mast. Conf. 81, J. E. Levi-Castillo, *Ecuador Freedom and Masonry,* Mas. Sq., Dec., 1979, 160.

Egypt: Stevenson-Drane, *Freemasonry in Egypt,* 81 AQC 209 (1968) 82 AQC 51 (1969). R. C. Wright, 16 Build. Mag., 65 (1930). New Age Mag., 1926, 489. Albert Kudsi-Zadeh, *Afghani and Freemasonry in Egypt,* Journal of the American Oriental Society, Jan.-March, 1972, 25.

El Salvador: Einar W. Johnson, *Masonic Situation in El Salvador.* 1956 Proc. Grd. Mast. Conf. 81.

England: A. C. F. Jackson, *Freemasonry in Jersey,* 86 AQC 177 (1973). *Freemasonry in Warwickshire,* 1978, 319 pp. with pictures and charts; many interesting facts. *Hampton Court Palace,* Mas. Sq., June, 1977. J. W. Stubbs, *Building a Temple, 1927-1933,* the story of the construction of the Grand Lodge Building in London, 89 AQC 123 (1976). *The Dedication of Freemasons' Hall,* on May 23, 1776, 88 AQC 179 (1975).

Europe: P. A. Tunbridge, *The Climate of European Freemasonry, 1730-1750,* 81 AQC 88 (1968); *1750-1810,* 83 AQC 248 (1968). 14 Build. Mag. 302 (1928). *The Freemason in Northern Europe,* 13 Build. Mag. 231 (1927). *Freemasonry in Europe,* 2 RAM 3 (1946). Bill Weisberger, *Studies in Central European Freemasonry,* Iowa Res. L. No. 2; reviewed in 87 AQC 217 (1974).

Far East: Melvin M. Johnson, *Freemasonry in the Far East,* 3 Build. Mag. 305 (1917). See above under East.

Fiji: Freemasonry in Fiji, 1963 Grd. L. of Scot. Yrbk. 61. J. Wright, *Anecdotes of the Fiji Islands,* 1976 Trans. Leic. Lodge of Res. 23.

Finland: *The Grand Lodge of Finland,* N.Y. Mas. Outl., March, 1925, 138. Dudley Wright, *Freemasonry in Finland,* Master Mason, Sept., 1927, 730. Jaako Vory, *Freemasonry in Finland,* 1974 Gr. L. of Scot. Yrbk, 119. *Freemasonry in*

Finland, Mas. Sq., March, 1978, 23. George Draffen, *New Supreme Council for Finland*, No. Light, Nov., 1973, 18. Frederick Smyth, *Freemasonry in Finland*, 78 AQC 87 (1965); 7 RAM 207 (1962). *Highlights in the History of American Freemasonry in Finland, 1922-1949*, 6 ALR 22 (1952-1953). 9 ALR 415 (1965). 2 RAM 309 (1948). 6 RAM 49 (1948).

France: George W. Baird, *Freemasonry in France*, 4 Build. Mag. 106 (1918). W. E. Moss, *Freemasonry in France, 1725-1735*, 47 AQC 84, 87 (1934). William Bruce Warne, *Regular Freemasonry in France*, Mas. Sq., March, 1978, 26. C. N. Batham, *A Famous French Lodge* (6 sisters), 86 AQC 312 (1973). William E. Parker, *Lodge of the Nine Muses* (a summary of the Batham article) Phil. Mag., Feb., 1975, 21. G. W. Speth, *The English Lodge at Bordeaux*, 12 AQC 6, 105 (1899). Alex Parker, *Two Epochs in the French National Grand Lodge*, Trans. Phoe. Lodge (Paris) 7 (1974-1975). Alec Mellor, *Freemasonry and the French Compagnonnage*, 7 Trans. Phoe. (Paris) 25 (1974-1975). C. N. Batham, *The Compagnonnage and the Craft*, 86 AQC 1 (1973); 87 AQC 242 (1974). Ossian Lang, *The National Grand Lodge of France*, N.Y. Mas. Outl., Aug., 1928, 360. Alec Mellor, *Emulation Working in French Regular Masonry*, 7 Trans. Phoe. L. (Paris) 2 (1974-1975). Cyril N. Batham, *The Nine Muses*, New Age Mag., Aug., 1974, 50. Mildred J. Headings, *French Freemasonry Under the Third Republic;* 1949. William E. Parker, *The Compagnonnage of France*, 12 RAM 17 (1979). William Weisberger, *Littre and Borgeois, Masons Who Defended the Third Republic of France*, Phil. Mag., June, 1973, 60. Albert Pike, *Materials for the History of Freemasonry in France:* Series of articles in the New Age Mag. starting with Dec., 1904 issue, p. 577, and continuing until Oct., 1909, p. 337. J. E. S. Tuckett, *The Early History of Freemasonry in France*, 31 AQC 7 (1918).

Germany: Carl Wiebe, *Notes on German Freemasonry*, 9 AQC 146 (1896). G. W. Speth, *Freemasonry in Prussia*, 4 AQC 192 (1892). *Freemasonry in Germany*, 1946-1947, New Age Mag., Oct., 1947, 591, Nov., 1947, 677. Frederick P. Stevenson, *The Dark Ages of German Masonic History*, 10 Trans. Tex. L. of Res. 188. Ellic Howe and Helmut Moller, *Theodor Reuss, Irregular Freemasonry in Germany*, 91 AQC 28 (1979). *Freemasonry in the City of Berlin*, 3 RAM 130 (1950). *Revival of Freemasonry in Germany*, 3 RAM 135 (1949). *German Grand Lodges Unite to Form a National Grand Lodge*, 3 RAM 107 (1949). Robert W. Orr, *Masonry and the Third Reich*, Phil. Mag., Dec., 1978, 4.

Ghana: *Mark Lodges Formed in Ghana.* 6 RAM 55 (1958).

Gibraltar: Herbert Poole, *A Sketch of Freemasonry in Gibraltar Before the Union.* 64 AQC 116 (1951).

Greece: John J. Lampos, *Freemasonry in Greece*, Phil. Mag., April, 1973, 45. New Age Mag., June, 1964, 15. 7 Build. Mag. 188 (1921). J. W. Burness, *Freemasonry's Influence on Greek Independence, 1821-1829*, Phil Mag., Oct., 1956, 72.

Guam: *Royal Arch Chapter Established in Guam*, 4 RAM 149 (1953). *Templary Established in Guam*, 5 RAM 149 (1956).

Guatemala: Phil. Mag., Aug., 1972, 77.

Hawaii: *A Century of Masonry in the Hawaiian Islands*, New Age Mag., Dec., 1940, 719. John R. Nocas, *Grand Chapter of Hawaii Constituted*, 11 RAM 133 (1977).

Holland: J. P. Vaillant, *Freemasonry in Holland*, 4 AQC 157 (1891). H. W. Dierpernink, *Freemasonry in Holland*, 4 AQC 23 (1891); 5 AQC 23 (1892). J. P. Vaillant, *A Last Word on Freemasonry in Holland*, 5 AQC 114 (1892). *Freemasonry in Holland*, 5 AQC 114 (1892). 11 New Age Mag., Jan, 1924, 11. E. A. Boerenbeker, *The Relations Between Dutch and English Freemasonry From 1734 to 1771*, 83 AQC 149 (1970). 2 RAM 366 (1948). 4 RAM 99 (1952). 7 RAM 9 (1961).

Hungary: Arthur W. Keil, *Hungarian*

Masonry, New Age Mag., March, 1963, 41. 10 ALR 327 (1968). 11 ALR 245 (1969). William Weisberger, *Hungary in the Late 18th Century*, Phil. Mag., Oct., 1972, 95. Ossian Lang, *The Craft Under Fire in Hungary*, N.Y. Mas. Outl., March. 1928, 203. Ladislas de Malxzovich, *A Sketch of the Earlier History of Masonry in Austria and Hungary*, 4 AQC 20 (1891), 5 AQC 15, 68, 187 (1892), 7 AQC 184 (1894), 8 AQC 180 (1895), 9 AQC 129 (1896). D. Wright, *The Hungarian Persecutions*, 6 Build. Mag. 274 (1920).

Iceland: Einar Loftson and Sidney Pope, *Freemasonry in Iceland*, 60 AQC 206 (1947). *Masonic Experience in Iceland*, 1 RAM 330 (1945). New Age Mag., Sept., 1952, 529.

India: *Freemasonry in India*, New Age Mag., Jan., 1935, 35. G. E. Walker, *Who Must Have Otherwise Remained at a Perpetual Distance*, 1979 Prestonian Lecture, a brief history of the Craft in India; reviewed in New Age Mag., Dec., 1979, 53. Frasee B. Musa, *The First Indian Freemason: R. W. Bro. Manockjee Cursetjee*, 81 AQC 317 (1968). *Grand Lodge of India Established*, 7 RAM 246 (1962). Ward K. St. Clair, *Some Masonic Experiences in India*, 1 RAM 258 (1945). *Lodge Proves Universality of Freemasonry*, 6 RAM 167 (1959).

Indonesia: Paul W. Van der Veur, *Freemasonry in Indonesia*, 1762-1961; 1976; 37 pp. Ohio University Center for International Studies, South East Asia Program.

Iran: Harry Carr, *The Foundation of the Grand Lodge of Iran*, 81 AQC 226 (1968). J. D. Payne, *Freemasonry in Iran*, 1 RAM 289 (1945).

Ireland: J. H. Lepper and P. Crossle, *History of the Grand Lodge of Ireland;* 1925; 2 vols. P. Crossle, *Irish Masonic Records, Grand Lodge of Ireland*, 1973. *Illustrious Masons of Ireland*, 10 Build. Mag. 144 (1924). 6 RAM 272 (1960). J. H. Lepper, *Freemasonry in Ulster*, 12 Build. Mag. 272 (1926). J. L. Carson, *Irish Freemasonry*, 1 Build. 6 (1915). J. H. Edge, *A Short Sketch of the Rise and Progress of Irish Freemasonry*, 28 AQC 131 (1913). *The Effects of "Home Rule" on Freemasonry in Ireland*, 6 Build. Mag. 31 (1920). W. Begemann, *A Few Remarks on the Establishment of the Grand Lodge of Ireland*, 12 AQC 164 (1899). J. H. Lepper, *Relations Between the Grand Lodges of England and Ireland*, 37 AQC 297 (1924). H. F. Berry, *Some Historical Episodes in Irish Freemasonry*, 1790-1830, 26 AQC 196 (1913). J. W. Hobbs, *Irish Lodge Minute Book*, 34 AQC 74 (1921). W. J. Chetwode Crawley, *Notes on Irish Freemasonry*, 8 AQC 53, 56, 79, 110 (1895); 9 AQC 4 (1896), 13 AQC 142 (1900), 15 AQC 100 (1902), 16 AQC 69 (1903), 17 AQC 137, 230 (1904). J. H. Edge, *Short Sketch of the Rise and Progress of Irish Freemasonry*, 26 AQC 131 (1913).

Israel: Rob Morris, *Freemasonry in the Holy Land;* 1879. Lawrence Meyer, *The Grand Lodge of the State of Israel*, 13 ALR 135 (1975). *Foundation of the Grand Lodge of Israel*, 1954 Gr. L. of Scot. Yrbk. 78. Thomas Dryer, *The Grand Lodge of Masons of the State of Israel*, 12 ALR 457 (1974). Max Silverstone, *The Centenary of Freemasonry in the Holy Land*, 89 AQC 211 (1977). Dr. Stephen R. Greenberg, *The History of the Grand Lodge of Israel*, Phil. Mag., June, 1970. J. Bar-Ner, *The Order of Freemasons in Israel*, 80 AQC 275 (1967). *Royal Solomon Moyher Lodge No. 293, Jerusalem*, 10 ALR 414 (1968). *New Grand Lodge of Israel Formed*, 4 RAM 323 (1954). *Grand Chapter RAM of Israel Is Established*, 9 RAM 337 (1969).

Italy: Bruno S. Guglielmo, *The History of Freemasonry in Italy*, Phil. Mag., March-April, 1968, 40. 1973 Grd. L. of Scot. Yrbk, 57. *The Carbonari, An Offshoot of Freemasonry*, Mast. Mas., Aug., 1926, 719. F. J. W. Crowe, *Curious Carbonari Certificate*, 16 AQC 163 (1903). R. R. Radice, *An Introduction to the History of the Carbonari*, 51 AQC 37 (1938), 52 AQC 63 (1939), 53 AQC 48 (1940), 54 AQC 35, 122 (1941), 60 AQC 106 (1947). *Freemasonry and Fascism in Italy*, 11 Build. Mag. 196 (1925). 12 Build. Mag. 97 (1926). 13 Build. Mag.

244, 256 (1927). *Signor Mussolini Receives Masons,* 10 Build. Mag. 17 (1924). *Mussolini and Freemasonry,* Mast. Mas., Sept., 1925, 586. *Mussolini and Italian Freemasonry,* New Age Mag., Sept., 1924, 544. May, 1925, 281. Alfred Robbins, *Mussolini and English Freemasonry,* Mast. Mas., April, 1928, 247. *Persecutions in Italy,* 13 Build. Mag., 278 (1927). New Age Mag., Dec., 1924, 747; Nov., 1925, 669; Dec., 1925, 716; Jan., 1926, 15, Feb., 1926, 85, July, 1927, 461, Sept., 1927, 539. *Italian Government Decree Restores Masonic Property,* 6 RAM 9 (1952). *What Happened to Italy?* 2 RAM 213 (1947). *Grand Chapter of Italy Organized,* 8 RAM 67 (1964). William J. Hughan, *The Jacobite Lodge at Rome, 1735-1737,* 1910; reviewed in 23 AQC 198 (1910).

Jamaica: F. W. Seal-Coon, *An Historical Account of Jamaican Freemasonry;* 1976; reviewed in 89 AQC 185 (1977). 3 ALR 126 (1938-1939). Phil. Mag., Feb., 1970, 8. Mast. Mas., July, 1926, 653. F. W. Seal-Coon, *Island in the Sun,* Mas. Sq., Sept., 1977, 116. Royal Lodge Jamaica, Mas. Sq., Sept., 1979, 105.

Japan: Nohea O. A. Peck, *Masonry in Japan; the First Hundred Years: 1866-1966.* Author: New Age Mag., July, 1979, 33. Reviewed: New Age Mag., Feb., 1967, 54. Nohea A. Peck, *Masonry in Japan,* New Age Mag., March, 1972, has picture of author. Shigeru Nishiyama, *Freemasonry in Japan,* Mas. Sq., Dec., 1976, 124. *Japanese Reaction Towards Freemasonry,* 2 RAM 24 (1946). *The First Masonic Lodge in Japan Since World War II,* 2 RAM 366 (1951), 198 (1950), 4 RAM 45, 182, 210 (1953), 279 (1954). *Freemasonry in Japan in 1870,* 6 RAM 133 (1959). *Japan's About Face,* 7 RAM 38 (1961). *Premier Hatoyama of Japan Made a Mason,* 5 RAM 38 (1955). *Count Hayashi, Japan's Great Mason,* 6 RAM 99 (1958).

Korea: New Age Mag., Oct., 1953, 595, Nov., 1953, 687. Theodore R. Gerdner, *Reminiscences From Korea,* New Age Mag., April, 1977, 51.

Malta: 4 RAM 292 (1954). A. M.

Broadley, *History of Freemasonry in Malta,* mentioned in remarks of the subject in 85 AQC 173 (1972).

Mecca: 4 RAM 269 (1954).

Mediterranean: *Freemasonry in the Eastern Mediterranean.* 5 RAM 183 (1956).

Mexico: Thomas B. Davis, *Aspects of Freemasonry in Modern Mexico, 1976;* 421 pp. Reviewed in 89 AQC 191 (1976); Mas. Sq., Sept., 1979, 126. *A Sketch of Mexican Masonic History,* 8 RAM 107 (1964). Phil. Mag., June, 1970, issue devoted entirely to Mexico. O. D. Street, *Masonry in Mexico,* 6 Build. Mag. 264 (1920). Charles Albert Adams, *Report on Masonry in Mexico,* 1921 Proc. Grd. L. of Cal. Alford Ross, *Masonry in Mexico,* New Age Mag., June, 1963, 51. *Freemasonry and the Mexican War,* Trans. MLR, 1948, 5. *A Forgotten Episode,* 5 RAM 369 (1957). New Age Mag., Jan., 1957, 43, Feb., 1927, 81, June, 1928, 351, 359, July, 1928, 416, Aug., 1928, 469. W. J. Allen, *Masonry in Mexico,* 21 Leic. L. of Res. 109 (1912-1913). *A Sketch of Masonic History,* 8 RAM 107 (1964). *Freemasonry's Influence on Mexican History,* 6 RAM 343 (1960). *Early Freemasonry in Mexico,* 10 Build. Mag. 205 (1924). *Masonry and Religious Persecution in Mexico,* 13 Build. Mag. 129 (1928). R. F. Gould, *Freemasonry in Mexico,* 6 AQC 113 (1893), 7 AQC 72 (1895), 10 AQC 46 (1897). F. E. Young, *Mexican Masonry in 1909,* 22 AQC 214 (1909).

Monterrey: W. S. Turnpaugh, *The Masonry of Monterrey,* 1 RAM 96 (1943).

Netherlands: Edward Armitage, *Early Netherland Lodges,* 10 AQC 61 (1897). *Netherlands Freemasonry in Court,* 5 AQC 163 (1892). F. J. W. Crowe, *Masonic Certificates of the Netherlands,* 16 AQC 17 (1903). Andrew Oliver, *Masonic Certificates of the Netherlands,* 17 AQC 20 (1904). *Royal Arch in the Netherlands,* 5 RAM 301 (1957). J. D. Oortman-Gerlings, *Early History of the High Degrees of the Netherlands,* 5 AQC 158 (1892). Van Der Laan, *Freemasonry in the Netherlands East Indies,* 1 RAM 40

(1943). W. Van Emden, *Freemasonry in the Netherlands*, Mas. Sq., March, 1977, 30. Sept., 1977, 105.

New South Wales: H. L. Thomas, *The Old Grand Lodge of New South Wales*, 84 AQC 7 (1971).

New Zealand: F. W. Northern, *History of Grand Lodge, 1890-1970;* 1973; 173 pp. Grand Lodge of New Zealand, publisher; copy in Iowa Masonic Library; reviewed: Trans. United Masters Lodge, Sept., 1972, 248 and Trans. M. & P. M. L., March, 1973, 25. A. B. Croker, *History of the Grand Lodge of New Zealand*, 1940. *Freemasonry in New Zealand*, New Age Mag., April, 1969, 18. Ross Hepburn, *Masonic Education in New Zealand*, Phil. Mag., June, 1950, 3. Col. N. G. Barclay, *The Extinct Lodges of New Zealand*, 1935; 197 pp. A. E. Rogers, *A Brief History of Masonic Education in New Zealand*, Trans., United Masters Lodge, March, 1973, 5. Ross Hepburn, *Freemasonry in New Zealand*, Phil. Mag., April, 1956, 18 and subsequent issues. 6 RAM 83 (1958).

Nicaragua: W. Ralph Howard, *Grand Lodge of Nicaragua*, 1956 Proc. Grd. Mast. Conf., 85.

Nigeria: *Freemasonry Marches On*, 1979; 31 pp.; copy in the Iowa Masonic Library.

Norway: A. J. Lange, *A Sketch of Norway Masonic History*, 13 AQC 35 (1900). *Freemasonry in Norway During World War II*, Phil. Mag., April, 1972, 40. 10 RAM 172 (1971). *Freemasonry in Norway Emerges From German Occupation*, 2 RAM 131, 366 (1947-1948). New Age Mag., June, 1957, 359, Feb., 1960, 43.

Okinawa: *Now Has All York Bodies*, 5 RAM 211 (1956). *Knights Templar Organize in Okinawa*, 5 RAM 135 (1956). 6 RAM 263 (1960).

Panama: Jose Oller, *Freemasonry in Panama*, 9 Build. Mag. 301 (1923). Melvin M. Johnson, 3 Build. Mag. 327 (1917). *Masons Prominent in Government*, New Age Mag., Nov., 1924, 679. *Rioters Damage Cristobal Masonic Temple*, 8 RAM 8 (1964).

Paraguay: Robert H. Gollmar, *Freemasonry in Paraguay*, 1957 Proc. Grd. Mast. Conf. 76.

Persia: *Freemasonry in Persia*, New Age Mag., Oct., 1964, 17.

Peru: 7 RAM 202 (1962). Dr. Gilberto Morey Sotomayor, *Freemasonry in Peru*, 1954 Proc. Grd. Mast. Conf., 39.

Philippines: Teodoro Kalaw, *Philippine Masonry*, 1955. *The Beginnings of Freemasonry in the Philippines*, 5 RAM 25 (1955). *The Story of Philippine Masonry*, 9 Build. Mag. 239 (1923). New Age Mag., Aug., 1923, 461, Sept., 1927, 543. Juan Causing, *Freemasonry in the Philippines*, 1969, 308 pp.; copy in Iowa Masonic Library. Edward A. Dolph, *Tragedies of the Early Filipino Masons*, N.Y. Mas. Outl., March, 1927, 208, April, 1927, 237. *American Masonry in the Philippines*, New Age Mag., Dec., 1938, 723, Jan., 1939, 35. Dr. Frederick H. Stevens, *Philippine Freemasonry*, New Age Mag., Aug., 1976, 10. Ray V. Denslow, *Through Fire and Sword, The Story of Freemasonry in the Philippines*, 1941. Leo Fischer, *Masonry in the Philippines*, New Age Mag., Sept., 1927. William C. Councell, *The 75th Anniversary of Manila Lodge No. 1*, 1901-1976; has brief history of the Craft in that country; 1976; 195 pp. Reviewed in New Age Mag., July, 1977, 52 and in 90 AQC 267 (1977). William C. Councell, *The Establishment and Growth of Masonry in The Philippines and the Contribution of Sojourning Freemasons*, New Age Mag., Feb., 1978, 8. Lobingier and Rodriquez, *Early Philippine Masonry*, 20 AQC 82 (1907). *The Story of Philippine Masonry*, 9 Build. Mag. 239 (1923). Mauro Baradi, *Freemasonry and the Filipinos*, New Age Mag., Aug., 1954, 456. Alvin J. Lee, *Freemasonry Alive in the Philippines*, 2 RAM 9 (1946). Antonio Gonzales, *As I Look Back*, Phil. Mag., Sept., 1946, 6. *Japanese Persecution of Freemasons in the Philippines*, 2 RAM 292 (1948). *Masonic Activities During the Japanese Occupation of the Philippines*, 9 ALR 66 (1963). Frederick H. Stevens, *San Tomas, the Story of Survival During the Japanese*

Occupation. Mauro Baradi, *Freemasons and Freemasonry.*

Poland: Zygmunt Frenkiel, *Freemasonry in Poland,* Mas. Sq., March, 1977, 12. Boris Telepneff, *A Few Leaves From the History of Polish Freemasonry,* 44 AQC 179 (1931); 59 AQC 192 (1946). *Brief History of Freemasonry in Poland,* New Age Mag., April, 1923, 209, Sept., 1906, 246.

Portugal: H. T. C. De Lafontaine, *Freemasonry in Portugal,* 42 AQC 293 (1929). G. W. Speth, *Freemasonry in Portugal,* 8 AQC 24 (1895). G. W. Baird, *Freemasonry in Portugal,* New Age Mag., Feb., 1917, 61; 3 Am. Free., 154 (1912). W. I. Grantham, *A Portuguese Lodge in England,* 66 AQC 24 (1953). *The Modern Persecution of Freemasonry in Portugal,* New Age Mag., Nov., 1919, 519. Dr. S. Vatcher, *A Lodge of Irishmen at Lisbon,* 1738, 84 AQC 75 (1971). A. R. Hewitt, *Tribulations of an English Lodge at Lisbon,* 1799, 84 AQC 110 (1971).

Puerto Rico: New Age Mag., May, 1925, 287; Jan., 1964, 287. Phil. Mag., Dec., 1966, 104.

Rhodesia: Phil. Mag., Feb., 1948, 3.

Rumania: New Age Mag., June, 1924, 337. Ossian Lang, *Story of the Founding of the Grand Orient of Rumania;* has picture of author; N.Y. Mas. Outl., Aug., 1926, 358.

Russia: Dr. Ernest Friedrichs, *Freemasonry in Russia and Poland,* 1908. Boris Telepneff, *Freemasonry in Russia,* 35 AQC 261 (1922). Boris Telepneff, *Some Aspects of Russian Freemasonry During the Reign of the Emperor Alexander I,* 38 AQC 6 (1925). John Yarker, *Patent of a Russian Grand Lodge,* 16 AQC 160 (1903). Boris Ivanoff, *Cagliostro in Eastern Europe,* 40 AQC 45 (1927). G. W. Speth, *A Relic of Russian Freemasonry,* 8 AQC 231 (1895). G. W. Speth, *A Russian Anecdote,* 10 AQC 72 (1897). 2 Build. Mag. 254 (1916). 8 Build Mag. 290. 13 Build. Mag. 187, 251 (1927). *Freemasons in Russia,* New Age Mag., Feb.-March, 1945, 79. A. G. Gross, *British Freema-sons in Russia During the Reign of Catherine the Great,* 84 AQC 239 (1971). Dr. Stephen R. Greenberg, *Ivan Yelaguin and the Masonic Bear,* Phil. Mag., Oct., 1972, 94. Henry L. Zelchenko, *Freemasonry in Russia,* New Age Mag., Feb., 1973, 49. Albert Van Damm, *The Masonic Movement in Russia in Brief,* Phil. Mag., Feb., 1976, 20. William Weisberger, *Comments and Thoughts on Russian Freemasonry During the Reigns of Catherine II and Alexander I,* Phil. Mag., April, 1975, 47. G. S. Blakey, *A Russian Ceremony,* Mas. Sq., Dec., 1978, 172. Aemil Pouler, *Grand Lodge of Astrea,* New Age Mag., Oct., 1973, 52. Lauren G. Leighton, *The Grand Lodge of Astrea,* New Age Mag., May, 1979, 44. *Catherine II and Freemasonry,* New Age Mag., Dec. 1939, 733. D. K. Chamberlain, *A Russian Initiation,* 87 AQC 229 (1974). Constantin de Grunwald, *Russian Freemasonry – Its Death and Resurrection,* 5 Trans. Phoe. Lodge, Paris, 18. John S. Chesebro, New Age Mag., Dec., 1978, 15.

Scotland: George S. Draffen, *Scottish Masonic Records 1736-1950;* 1950. Fred J. W. Crowe, *The Grand Lodge of Scotland and Its History in 1813,* 11 Build. Mag., 149 (1925). George S. Draffen, *Freemasonry in Scotland in 1717,* 83 AQC 367 (1970). *Early Scotch Masonry,* N.Y. Mas. Outl., Sept., 1929, 12. L. A. Seemungal, *The Edinburgh Rebellion, 1808-1813,* 86 AQC 322 (1973). Edward MacBean, *Formation of the Grand Lodge of Scotland,* 3 AQC 172 (1890). George S. Draffen, *Scottish Masonic Records,* 64 AQC 63 (1951). G. W. Speth, *Scottish Freemasonry Before the Era of Grand Lodge,* 1 AQC 139 (1886-1888). L. Vibert, *The Early Freemasons of England and Scotland,* 43 AQC 195 (1930).

South Africa: *Masonry in South Africa,* Mas. J. of So. Africa, May, 1972, 17. Ivor F. Sander, *Masonry in the Transvaal,* Mas. J. of So. Africa, Jan., 1975, 15. *Travelling Among the South Africa Lodges,* N.Y. Mas. Outl., Sept., 1925, 12. *Three German Lodges in South West Africa,* 1977 Grd. L. Scot. Yrbk, 62. Paul H. Butterfield, *The First Hundred Years of English Freemasonry in the Transvaal,*

1878-1978; 1978; 296 pp. Reviewed in 91 AQC 212 (1979). Stephen Underwood, *Capetown Revival,* Mas. Sq., June, 1977, 68. A. T. Penman, *Freemasonry in So. Africa,* 80 AQC 280 (1967). D. H. Botha, *South Africa Commission of Enquery into Secret Organizations,* 78 AQC 74 (1965).

South America: Americo Carnicelli, *La Masoneria En La Independecia de America;* 1970; in Spanish; a comprehensive work. J. H. Lepper, *The First Masonic Procession in South America,* 57 AQC 280 (1944). H. B. Hemenway, *The Relationship of Masonry to the Liberation of Spanish America,* 1 Build. Mag. 259 (1915), *The Political Pseudo Masonry of South America,* 2 Build. Mag. 147, 233 (1916). Dr. Richard A. Kern, *Freemasonry in South America,* Pa. Grd. L. Proc., 1970; 1974 Proc. Sup. Counc., NMJ, 253. Dr. J. R. Levi-Castillo, *Masonry in South America,* Mas. Sq., Dec., 1978, 152.

Spain: J. H. Lepper, *Freemasonry in Spain Under Fernando VII,* 61, AQC 212 (1948), 62 AQC 292 (1949). S. T. Klein, *Vestiges of the Craft in Spain,* 32 AQC 57 (1919). *Spain, Franco, and Freemasonry,* 1 RAM 325 (1945). *The Inquisition in Spain; Persecution in Recent Years,* 6 RAM 108 (1958). Pierre Lutrec, *Spanish Freemasonry in the 18th Century,* Trans. Phoen. L. (Paris), 40 (1974-1975).

St. Helena: R. F. Gould, *Freemasonry in St. Helena,* 3 AQC 187 (1890).

Sweden: *Freemasonry in Sweden and Its Dependency, Finland,* New Age Mag., Dec., 1906, 544. *Sweden's First Grand Master,* New Age Mag., Jan., 1965, 16. 4 Build. Mag. 126 (1918). *Swedish Freemasonry,* New Age Mag., March, 1953, 1 2.

Switzerland: John W. Barkley, *1957 Proc. Grd. M. Conf.* 72. F. Chancellor, *Swiss Freemasonry's Fight for Life,* 1933-1937, 60 AQC 211 (1947). H. O. Mauerhofer, *150 Years of Lodge "Zur Goffnung" in Berne, Switzerland,* 67 AQC 60 (1954). H. R. Hilfiker, *Historical Sketch and the Origin and Development of the Scottish Rectified Rite in Switzerland,* 68 AQC 85 (1955). *Swiss Freemasonry in the Years 1937-1947,* Phil. Mag., Feb., 1949, 3. Edward Quar-tier-la-Tente, *Freemasonry in Switzerland,* 2 Am. Free., 120, 157, 244, 288 (1911).

Tasmania: G. Widdowson, *The Rise of Freemasonry in Tasmania,* 76 AQC 28 (1963).

Thailand: Charles R. Kramer, *Freemasonry in Thailand,* New Age Mag., May, 1974, 53.

Transvaal: See above under South Africa.

Trinidad: *The Beginnings of Freemasonry in Trinidad,* 88 AQC 199 (1975).

Turkey: Albert E. Carasso, *Freemasonry in Turkey,* 4 Am. Freemason 404 (1913). *Freemasonry in Turkey,* New Age Mag., April, 1965, 23, March, 1966, 44. Roger E. Hopkins, *Freemasonry in Turkey,* 3 Trans. Ann. L. No. 175 (N.H.) 56.

Venezuela: *Masonic Conditions in Venezuela,* 5 RAM 73 (1975). *Masonic Temple,* 5 RAM 209 (1956). Edward M. Selby, *Capitular Masonry Arrives in Venezuela,* 11 RAM 195 (1974). Charles F. Adams, *Freemasonry in Venezuela,* 1956 Proc. Grd. Mast. Conf. 90.

Virgin Islands: New Age Mag., Jan., 1949, 13, Feb., 1949, 95.

West Indies: Johs. Rasmussen, *A Contribution to the History of Freemasonry in the Former Danish West Indies Islands,* 37 AQC 144 (1924). N. S. H. Sitwell, *Some Mid-Eighteen Century French Manuscripts,* 40 AQC 91 (1927). T. G. G. Valette, *The Island of St. Eustatius and Its Lodges,* 44 AQC 57 (1931).

Yugoslavia: New Age Mag., March, 1956, 158.

2.09 FREEMASONRY DURING THE COLONIAL PERIOD IN THE UNITED STATES

William R. Denslow, *Freemasonry and the American Indian;* 1956; 248 pp. Foreword by Carl H. Claudy.

Author: Appendix No. 11. Comments: Henry W. Coil, Sr., "Facts instead of fancies about the Red men." Reviewed: 6 RAM 20 (1958). Libraries: 1, 2, 3, 5, 6, 10, 11, 12, 14.

William R. Denslow, *Secret Societies of the American Indian*, 4 RAM 199 (1953); 5 RAM 49 (1955).

John A. Mirt, *Freemasonry and the American Indian*, Ind. Free., July, 1955, 9; has picture of author.

An Oft-Told Tale, Ind. Free., Nov., 1958, 12. (About Joseph Brant).

A. C. Parker, Ill. Enlight., June, 1953, 2.

Joseph Brant, Ill. Enlight., April, 1951, 2.

Ely S. Parker, Ill. Enlight., Feb., 1951, 4.

Red Jacket, Ill. Enlight., Dec., 1952, 6.

Chief John Ross, New Age Mag., Aug., 1963, 15.

Masonic Incident in Unadilla, 9 ALR 203 (1964).

William L. Boyden, *Freemasonry Among the American Indians; 1931;* 12 pp. Libraries: 7, 9, 12, 14.

Lewis Annance, *Indian Chief of Maine Tribe*, No. Light, April, 1973, 9

Robert C. Wright, *Indian Masonry*, 1907; 123 pp. Libraries: 3, 4, 7, 8, 9, 10, 11, 12, 14.

Silas H. Shepherd, *Notes on Indian Masonry;* Phil. Mag., March, 1946, 3; has picture of author.

Dr. Oscar A. Kinchen, *Indian Secret Societies*, 3 Trans. Tex. L. of Res. 135 (1965-1968).

Tecumseh, The Indian Chief and Mason, New Age Mag., April, 1949, 225.

Arthur C. Parker, *New York Indians and the Craft*, N.Y. Mas. Outl., Oct., 1928, 40.

J. M. Spainhour, *Excavation of An Indian Mound*, 1 AQC 106 (1886-1888).

A. C. Parker, *Freemasonry Among the American Indians*, 6 Build. Mag. 295 (1920). 8 Build. Mag. 71 (1922). 10 Build. Mag. 137, 169 (1924).

Indian Freemasonry, 2 Build. Mag. 371 (1916).

C. F. Willard, *Indian Freemasonry*, Phil. Mag., March, 1947, 8.

Leo Fisher, *An Indian Chief as Provincial Grand Master*, Phil. Mag., May, 1947, 6.

The Masonic Stone of 1606, 10 Build. Mag. 295 (1924).

Melvin M. Johnson, *The Beginnings of Freemasonry in America*. 1924; 410 pp. Masonic Service Association, publisher.
Author: See Gould, *History of Freemasonry Throughout the World* (1936), 472. Some of the material in this book relating to the United States appeared originally in the Build. Mag., Vols. 4 and 5, with his picture in Vol. 9, 196. Comments: L. B. Blakemore, "Based on every known published item about Freemasonry in America prior to 1750. A standard work on American Masonic history by the Sovereign Grand Commander, Northern Jurisdiction, Scottish Rite." Silas H. Shepherd, "The talented author has searched the records very carefully and has accumulated a vast amount of information. The conclusions he arrives at, however, are to be accepted only after comparison with the views of others. The established jurisprudence of the Twentieth Century is hardly the correct basis on which to judge regularity in the Eighteenth." Carl H. Claudy, ". . . a monumental volume in a class by itself in American Masonic literature . . . The book is fully documented. Unlike many contemporaneous volumes of history of Masonry, it indulges in no speculations, guesses, hopes, beliefs. It is essentially a book of facts, so well attested that they might easily be evidence in a law court. No Masonic student interested in the arcana of the Craft and none who wish a sound background against which to evaluate the speculations, theories, beliefs of Masonic writers on historical matters can do work without this work." Reviewed: 10 Build. Mag. 315 (1924). Mast. Mas., Aug.-1924, 505. Libraries: 1, 2, 3, 4, 5, 6, 7, 8, 9, 10, 11, 12, 13, 14, 15.

J. Hugo Tatsch, *Freemasonry in the Thirteen Colonies;* 1929; 225 pp. Macoy Publishing Co., publisher.
Author: See Sec. 2.16 herein. Comments: Norman B. Hickox, " . . . has been prepared with the thought of giving the average American Mason a graphic

picture of our Fraternity as a whole, and its introduction into the United States from the earliest days to the formation of independent Grand Lodges after the Revolution.'' Carl H. Claudy, '' . . . a delightful book of early Masonic history in what was to become the United States.'' Reviewed: 16 Build. Mag. 27 (1930). 42 AQC 121 (1932). Libraries: 1, 2, 3, 4, 5, 7, 8, 9, 10, 11, 12, 13, 14, 15.

Colonial Freemasonry, 1977; 241 pp. MLR, publisher.
Contents: With several preliminary paragraphs for background, there follows thirteen chapters covering each of the original thirteen colonies with basic facts about Freemasonry in each of them, then followed by several chapters or related subjects such as the Boston Tea Party, military lodges, etc. Reviewed: 90 AQC 262 (1977).

C. Dawson, *The Making of the Earl of Moura,* 1976 Trans. Leic. L. of Res. 56. Presents biographical sketch with details of his service in the American War of Independence on the British side.

Conrad Hahn, *American Literature During the Revolution,* Ind. Free., Nov., 1976, 6.

Robert L. Lowell, *Bicentennial Reflections on the U.S. Navy,* Ind. Free., June, 1976, 6.

John R. Nocas, *Brother John Glover and His Marblehead Fishermen,* New Age Mag., Aug., 1975, 17.

Alphonse Cerza, *The Moral Dilemma of Freemasonry 200 Years Ago.* No. Light, June, 1977, 10.

Ronald E. Heaton and James R. Case, *The Lodge at Fredericksburgh.* 1975; 95 pp. Digest of the early records of this lodge which conferred the Masonic degrees on George Washington. Reviewed in 89 AQC 184 (1976).

James R. Case, *Colonial Governors of the Thirteen Original Colonies,* 7 ALR 192 (1958). Phil. Mag., Dec., 1960, 84.

Ralph J. Pollard, *Freemasons in American History.* MSA Digest.

Ronald E. Heaton, *Masonic Membership of the Founding Fathers.* 1965; 164 pp. Masonic Service Association, publisher.
Author: Appendix No. 17. Libraries: 1, 2, 3, 4, 5, 7, 8, 9, 10, 11, 12, 14, 15.

Sidney Morse, *Freemasonry in the American Revolution;* 1924; 134 pp. Masonic Service Association, publisher. Reproduced in the Little Masonic Library. Libraries: 1, 3, 5, 7, 8, 12, 14.

Samuel Oppenheim, *The Jews and Masonry in the United States Before 1810;* 1910; 100 pp. American Jewish Historical Society, publisher.
Contents: The author, a non-Mason, presents many brief sketches of the part played by Jewish Masons in colonial times. Reviewed: 1 Build. Mag. 277 (1915). Libraries: 3, 5, 7, 11, 12

Ralph J. Pollard, *One Nation Under God.* Biographical sketches of Masonic leaders of the period.

Alphonse Cerza, *Freemasonry in the American Revolution,* New Age Mag., July, 1973, 20.

Case and Milborne, *Loyalist Masons,* 3 ALR 208 (1939).

Gayle S. Eads, *Lodges and Colonial Taverns.* Ind. Free., April, 1979, 6.

James R. Case, *Loyalists and Freemasonry.* Three installments starting with June, 1978 issue of Ind. Free.

John R. Nocas, *Brother Henry Knox and His Big Guns.* New Age Mag., Sept., 1974, 12.

Alphonse Cerza, *Effects of the War of Independence on American Freemasonry.* 13 Trans Tex. L. of Res. 23 (1978).

Members of St. John's Lodge Heroes of the Revolution. New Age Mag., May, 1946, 289.

Wilmer E. Bresee, *Col. Cary Goes to Lodge.* New Age Mag., Dec., 1950, 737.

Wilmer E. Bresee, *A Masonic Tale of Washington's Time.* New Age Mag., May, 1950, 287.

Masons Who Fought for the United States.
New Age Mag., May, 1942, 275.

*Gen. Lafayette's Visit to Fredericksburg,
Va. in 1824,* N.Y. Mas. Outl. Jan.
1925, 92.

William L. Boyden, *Masonry of the Revolutionary Period.* New Age Mag.,
Oct., 1936, 607.

Sidney Morse, *The Drums of '75.* Reprinted by Iowa Res. L. No. 2. Reprinted in installments with annotations
by Jerry Marsengill in the Oregon
Freemason, March, 1973, and four
issues thereafter.

James R. Case, *American Union Lodge,*
11 ALR 333 (1971).

H. L. Haywood, *Masonry and the Bunker
Hill Monument.* In his Masonic
Curiosa, 78.

H. L. Haywood, *Masonic Books Published During the Revolutionary
Period;* in his Masonic Essay, 307.

Robert P. Southerland, *The Valley of Freedom.* The battle of 1777 for the Mohawk
Valley. N.Y. Mas. Outl., Aug., 1927,
340.

William L. Lyons, *The Covered Wagons
of Freemasonry.* The westward movement. N.Y. Mas. Outl., Sept, 1927, 15.

R. J. Meekren, *Masonry and the Revolution.* N.Y. Mas. Outl., April, 1925,
166.

Mansfield Hobbs, *The Constitution of
Freemasonry and Freemasons in the
American Revolution.* N.Y. Mas. Outl.,
Sept., 1925, 3, 44.

Norris G. Abbott, Jr., *The Adventures of
Silas Talbot During the War of Independence,* No. Light. Nov., 1973, 4.

C. L. Rothwell, *St. Andrew's Lodge,
Headquarters of the Revolution,* K. T.
Mag., May, 1975, 13.

Benjamin Woods Labaree, *The Boston
Tea Party.* 1964; Oxford University
Press.

John C. Vyn, *St. Andrew's Lodge and the
Boston Tea Party.* Ill. Enlight. May,
1957, 106.

J. Hugo Tatsch, *About That Tea Party,*
No. Light, Jan., 1974, 10. Sets out copy
of minutes.

Alphonse Cerza, *The American War of
Independence and Freemasonry,* 89
AQC 169 (1976).

Frederick G. Spiedel, North Carolina
Masons in the American Revolution;
1975; 77 pp.

Loral W. Pancake, *The Masonic Convention at Morristown.* Ind. Free., Dec.,
1979, 10.

Henry W. Coil, Sr., *Provincial Grand
Masters and Provincial Grand Lodges.*
Phil. Mag., Aug., 1972, 72.

K. Edwin Applegate, *Start of the Beginning.* Ind. Free., Sept., 1974, 10.

Richard Tutt, Jr., *Paul Revere's Most Important Ride.* 12 ALR 145 (1972).

Harold V. B. Voorhis, *Those Husbands of
Betsy Ross.* 12 ALR 97 (1972).

Harold V. B. Voorhis, *The First Wife of
William Franklin, the Last Provincial
Governor of New Jersey.* 12 ALR 131
(1972).

Jack Budett, *The Shot Heard Round the
World.* K. T. Mag., Aug., 1974, 25.

Dwight L. Smith, *Philadelphia in Colonial Days.* Ind. Free., June, 1974, 8.

William E. Parker, *Lafayette – Man of
Two Nations.* Mas. Mess., Ga., July,
1974, 11.

Benedict Arnold, Traitor-Freemason.
Mas. Mess., Ga., July, 1974, 10.

Roger Lacy, *Provincial Grand Master of
Georgia?* Trans. Mas. Res. L. No. 4,
Atlanta, Ga., Nov., 30, 1973.

Dwight L. Smith, *Boston Two Centuries
Ago.,* Ind. Free., May, 1974, 10.

Ralph J. Pollard, *Foreign Officers in the
Continental Army.* Phil. Mag., Feb.,
1978, 14.

Jerry Marsengill, *Freemasonry and the
Founding Fathers.* Phil. Mag., Oct.,
1976, 90.

Alex Horne, *Financing a Revolution, The
Epic of Haym Salomon.* Phil. Mag.,

June, 1977, 8. Has picture of monument in Chicago.

Harry Barnard, *This Great Triumvirate of Patriots*. 1971; 105 pp. Story of the Washington-Robert Morris-Haym Salomon monument in Chicago.

Conrad Hahn, *The Beginnings of Freemasonry in the American Colonies*. Phil. Mag., June, 1975.

Alphonse Cerza, *Bicentennial Chronology*. Phil. Mag., Feb., 1975, 16.

Masons at War, 1775-1781. Mas. Sq., March, 1976, 12.

The Daylight Ride of Paul Revere. New Age Mag., Oct., 1974, 10.

George E. Burow, *Illinois Mason Proud of Apron Made by Martha Washington*. No. Light, Jan., 1976, 16.

Ralph W. Lichty, *Masons and the Surrender at Yorktown*. K. T. Mag., Oct., 1975, 25.

Laurence Scott, *There Is a Turbulence in Boston*. New Age Mag., March, 1976, 16.

Alphonse Cerza, *The American War of Independence and Freemasonry*, 89 AQC 169 (1976).

What Is a Provincial Grand Lodge? 3 RAM 279 (1951).

Scottish Lodges in the American Colonies. 16 RAM 181 (1959).

Freemasonry in Early America. 9 RAM 35, 67, 99, 133 (1967).

James R. Case, *Freemasonry at Yorktown*. 8 RAM 153 (1965).

William H. Knutz, *Colonial Freemasonry*. Phil. Mag., Oct.-Nov., 1949, 5.

Henry W. Coil, Sr., *Early Freemasonry in North America*. Phil. Mag., Feb., 1971, 18. Comment on this article is in Phil. Mag., June, 1971, 56.

Ronald E. Heaton, *Freemasonry and Freemasons at Valley Forge*. Ind. Free., Feb., 1972, 6.

C. S. Lobingier, *Freemasons in the American Revolution*. 4 Build. Mag. 67 (1918). *Bunker Hill Monument*, 7 Build. Mag. 269 (1921).

C. A. Brockway, *American Union Lodge and Its Meeting Places*. New Age Mag., Sept., 1908, 274.

William Peartree Smith, *First Provincial Grand Master of New York*. 3 ALR 269 (1939-1940).

George Harison, *Fourth Provincial Grand Master of New York*. 8 ALR 285 (1961).

Ronald E. Heaton, *Masonic Membership of the General Officers of the Continental Army*. MSA Digest.

A Tentative Roster of Revolutionary Soldier-Masons. 5 ALR 125 (1947-1948).

James R. Case, *Roll of American Union Lodge*. 6 ALR 356 (1956).

A. J. B. Milborne, *"Hessian" Regiments and Freemasons in America; 1776-1783*. 10 ALR 177 (1967).

Richardson Wright, *Refugee Lodges*. 3 ALR 81 (1938-1939).

Three Soldiers of the Revolution Who Later Became Generals. 8 ALR 401 (1962).

Concord Masons and the Revolution. 2 ALR 547 (1936-1938).

Richardson Wright, *Masonic Contacts With the Early American Theatre*. 2 ALR 161 (1936).

James R. Case, *Freemasons at the First Inauguration of George Washington*. MSA Digest.

Benedict Arnold's Marble Boot. No. Light. Nov., 1970, 17.

During the Bicentennial period the Philalethes Magazine has in each issue at least one article relating to this period of American history.

2.10 MASONIC SIGNERS OF FAMOUS DOCUMENTS

Ronald E. Heaton, *Masonic Membership of the Signers of the Articles of Confederation*. MSA Digest.

Ronald E. Heaton, *Masonic Signers of the Declaration of Independence*. MSA Digest.

The Declaration of Independence, STB, July, 1943.

Ronald E. Heaton, *Masonic Membership of the Signers of the Articles of Association.* MSA Digest.

William L. Boyden, *Signers of the Articles of Confederation.* New Age Mag., Dec., 1936, 733.

Masons Signing the Declaration of Independence. STB, Jan., 1957.

Dr. George H. T. French, *Masonic Signers of the Declaration of Independence.* 12 Trans. Tex. L. of Res. 34 (1976-1977).

William L. Boyden, *Signers of the Declaration of Independence,* New Age Mag., Nov., 1936, 657.

E. Van Krugel, *Masonic Signers of the Declaration of Independence.* Presents a chart showing how eight authors have classified the signers. New Age Mag., Dec., 1974, 44. In later issues of the New Age Magazine Brother Krugel has biographical sketches of each of the Masonic signers.

2.11 THE WAR OF 1812.

William M. Stuart, *Freemasonry in the War of 1812.* 1 ALR 213 (1930-1932); 2 ALR 107 (1933-1937). N.Y. Mas. Outl., July, 1926, 330.

Masonic Forts in the War of 1812. 3 ALR 25 (1938-1939).

2.12 MASONIC HISTORY IN THE STATES OF THE UNITED STATES OF AMERICA

GENERAL

H. L. Haywood, *Well-Springs of American Freemasonry;* 1953; 156 pp. Masonic Service Association, publisher. Presents a brief statement on the early days of the Craft in each state. Libraries: 1, 2, 3, 4, 5, 7, 8, 9, 10, 11, 12, 14, 15.

H. L. Haywood, *A Study of American Masonry.* N.Y. Mas. Outl., April, 1925, 163.

Ray V. Denslow, *Freemasonry in the Western Hemisphere;* 1925; MLR. Has short chapter on each state.

Freemasonry and the Santa Fe Trail; 1948; MLR.

Ray V. Denslow, *Territorial Freemasonry.* Story of the Louisiana Purchase. 1925; 267 pp. Masonic Service Association, publisher.
Reviewed: 11 Build. Mag. 380 (1925).

J. Fairbairn Smith, *America's First Railroad.* Ind. Free., July, 1978, 8.

H. L. Haywood, *The Vigilante;* in his Masonic Essays, 208.

American Railroads and Freemasonry. Ind. Free., Aug., 1959, 4; and Sept., 1959, 10.

Erwin L. Hippe, *Masons Who Helped Develop the Pacific Northwest.* Ore. Free., Sept., 1977, 25, Oct., 1977, 21.

Short state histories prepared by an author in each state appear in the six-volume edition of Gould's History published by Scribner's in 1936.

STATE HISTORIES

Alabama: Joseph A. Jackson, *Masonry in Alabama.* 1970; 238 pp. Grand Lodge of Alabama, publisher. Oliver Day Street, *Historical Sketch of Freemasonry in Alabama.* In, The Masonic Manual of Alabama, 1956; pp. 387-433. David L. Conley, *The Formation of the Alabama Grand Lodge.* The Masonic Monthly Mag., May, 1978, 11. Don Lavender, *John Ross, Cherokee Leader and Mason.* 13 RAM 110 (1979).

Alaska: Paul W. Harvey, *Not Made With Hands;* 1958. This book is a history of the Craft in the State of Washington; the lodges in Alaska are chartered by this Grand Lodge. *Alaska and Hawaii.* STB, May, 1959. Ill. Enlight., Aug., 1960, 211. 3 RAM 105 (1949). 4 RAM 147 (1953). 9 RAM 242 (1968). *The Fellowship of Masonry in Alaska.* 11 Build. Mag. 11 (1925).

Arizona: Mervin B. Hogan, *Freemasonry Comes to Arizona;* New Age Mag., June, 1971, 18. *When Hostile Indians Upset Arizona Freemasonry.* 6 RAM 294

(1960). Mervin B. Hogan, *Mormons and the Founding of the Grand Lodge of Arizona.* 11 ALR 287 (1970).

Arkansas: Fay Hempstead, *History of Arkansas.* 1890. Clarence E. Ross, *The Grand Lodge of Arkansas.* Phil. Mag., April, 1979, 4. Dr. Francis J. Scully, *History of the Cryptic Rite in Arkansas;* 1948. F. W. Kidd, *Arkansas Freemasonry;* 1908. William M. Shepherd, *The Seven Honor Men;* 1979. Biographical sketches of the Scottish Rite leaders of the state.

California: Edwin A. Sherman, *Fifty Years of Masonry in California.* 2 large volumes; 1898. *One Hundred Years of Masonry in California;* 4 vols.; 1950. Edward Stansel, *History of the Grand Lodge of California,* 1850-1975; 227 pp. A one-volume summary of the four-volume history. Arthur R. Anderson and Leon O. Whitsell, *California's First Century of Scottish Rite Masonry;* 1962. Reviewed in H. L. Haywood's Masonic Curiosa, 270. *A Perfect Ashlar in the Making;* 1971. Dr. Eugene S. Hopp, *How Freemasonry Came to California and Hawaii.* Phil. Mag., April, 1975, 32. Ellsworth Meyer, *A Century of Masonry in California.* Cal. Free., Summer, 1975, 103. *California and Hawaii in Masonic Partnership.* Cal. Free., Spring, 1977, 59. J. E. Behrens, *The San Francisco Earthquake and Fire.* K. T. Mag., April, 1979, 9. J. R. Wilson, *Unique Carving Tops California Masonic Temple,* 2 RAM 229 (1947). *California Modernistic Masonic Temple.* 6 RAM 67 (1958). John R. Nocas, *San Francisco Earthquake Closed Grand Chapter in "Short Form."* 9 RAM 244, 282 (1968). Dr. Granville K. Frisbie, *Gold Dust and Trowels;* 1978; story of the first six years of the Craft during the gold rush days. *Who Really Discovered Gold in California?* Cal. Free., Autumn, 1978, 157.

Colorado: George B. Clark, *The Story of Freemasonry in Colorado.* 11 Build. Mag. 260, 302 (1925). *Centennial Celebration,* 1861-1961. Published by the Grand Lodge of Colorado. *Chapter of Western Frontier Observes Centennial.* 10 RAM 231 (1971-1972).

Connecticut: Arthur F. Lewis, *Histor-ical Address.* 1940 Proc. of the Grd. L. of Conn., pp. 99-115. James R. Case, *A Historical Sketch of the Grand Lodge of Connecticut,* 1963. James R. Case, *Freemasonry in Connecticut: Connecticut Masons in the American Revolution;* 1975. Joseph K. Wheeler, *One Hundredth Anniversary of the Grand Lodge of Connecticut:* 1890; 310 pp. Dorothy A. Lipson, *Freemasonry in Federalist Connecticut,* 1789-1935. 1977; 380 pp. Princeton University Press, publisher. James R. Case, *Connecticut Masons in Eastern New York.* 9 ALR 212 (1964). James R. Case, *New York Roots of Fairfield County Masonry.* 9 ALR 227 (1964). *Early New York Documents Relating to Connecticut.* 9 ALR 71 (1963). *New York Part of the Formation of the Grand Lodge of Connecticut.* 2 ALR 352 (1936). *Connecticut Chapter Observes 175th Birthday.* 6 ALR 131 (1959). Dr. William G. Peacher, *New York, the Mother of Grand Lodges,* 11 ALR 205 (1969). *Connecticut Masons Convene in 18th Century Lodge Room.* No. Light, April, 1975, 18. *Connecticut Has Lodge in Germany.* 3 RAM 303 (1951). James R. Case, *A "Barney Medal" Comes Home.* 11 RAM 248 (1974-1975). The Proceedings of the Grand Lodge of Connecticut from 1954 to date contain papers written by James R. Case, Grand Historian.

Delaware: Charles E. Green, *History of the Grand Lodge of Delaware;* 1956; 300 pp. *The First State — Delaware.* K. T. Mag., Jan., 1978, 28. *Delaware Masons Acclaim One of Revolutionary Heroes.* No. Light, June, 1970, 4.

District of Columbia: Kenton N. Harper, *History of the Grand Lodge of the District of Columbia;* 1911; 458 pp. Reviewed in 25 AQC 124 (1912). Ray Baker Harris, *Sesqui-Centennial History of the Grand Lodge of the District of Columbia;* 1962; 197 pp. Reviewed in the New Age Mag., Nov., 1962, 57. Ralph H. G. Auker, *History of the Scottish Rite Bodies of the District of Columbia;* 1970. Reviewed in the New Age Mag., April, 1971, 58. Renah Camalier, *Masonic Stones From Renovation of the White House.* 1953 Proc. Grd. Mast. Conf. 73. *Stones From the White House.* Phil. Mag., Dec., 1973, 112.

Florida: *History of Freemasonry in Florida,* 1830-1852; 1962; 56 pp. *Masonry, Territorial and State, in Florida.* 13 Build. Mag., 108 (1927). Philip C. Tucker, *Freemasonry in Florida.* Master Mason., Nov., 1926, 738. *Early Masonry in the Provinces of East and West Florida.* 13 Build. Mag. 48 (1927). R. F. Gould, *The 31st Foot and Masonry in West Florida.* 13 AQC 69 (1900).

Georgia: William B. Clarke, *Freemasonry in Georgia;* 1933. Reviewed in the New Age Mag., June, 1950, 381. *Birth of Grand Lodge,* Mas. Mess., Ga., Oct., 1974, 6. T. C. McDonald, *Freemasonry and Its Progress in Atlanta and Fulton Counties, Georgia, 1786-1925. Georgia;* Trans. Res. Lodge No. 104, Atlanta; July, 1971. *An Old Georgia Charter,* 2 Build. Mag. 193 (1926). Roger Lacy, *Provincial Grand Master of Georgia?* Trans. Mas. L. of Res. No. 104, Nov., 30, 1973. J. H. Williamson, *Masonic Home of Georgia, a History.* Mas. Mess., Ga., May, 1974, 6, 19. John W. Zuber, *The Atlanta Scottish Rite Hospital for Crippled Children.* New Age Mag., June, 1977, 17.

Hawaii: See under California above; lodges in Hawaii are chartered by the Grand Lodge of California. Edward Towse, *Le Tellier's Lodge in Hawaii;* 1930. Comment by H. L. Haywood, "It is one of the most interesting books in the Iowa Masonic Library." Reviewed in 10 Build. Mag. 340 (1924); has a picture of the author. Aemil Pouler, *Freemasonry in Hawaii.* New Age Mag., Jan., 1961, 26. Harold W. Kent, *Masonry in Hawaii, 1900-1975.* K. T. Mag., April, 1975, 13. *Masonry and Royalty in Hawaii.* New Age Mag., July, 1968, 26; Aug. 1968, 23. *A Masonic Event to Remember,* New Age Mag., Oct., 1964, 19. 3 RAM 248 (1950) 6 RAM 259 (1960).

Idaho: Frank J. Kester, *Beginnings of Masonry in Idaho;* 1953. Will H. Gibson, *How Masonry Came to Idaho.* Mast. Mason, Sept., 1926, 788. *Chinese Masons in Idaho.* 1971 Proc. Grd. L. Idaho.

Illinois: John C. Reynolds, *History of Masonry in Illinois;* 1869. John C. Smith, *History of Freemasonry in Illinois;* 1903. E. R. Turnbull, *The Rise and Progress of Freemasonry in Illinois;* 1952. Alphonse Cerza, *A Concise History of Freemasonry in Illinois;* 1968 Grd. L. Proc. 85. Alphonse Cerza, *Freemasonry Comes to Illinois.* Journal of the Ill. State Hist. Soc., Summer, 1968, 182. George W. Warvelle, *Compendium of Freemasonry in Illinois;* 1897. Alphonse Cerza, *A History of the Ancient Accepted Scottish Rite in Illinois;* 1966. George W. Warvelle, *History of Scottish Rite Masonry in Chicago;* 1907. Louis L. Williams, *The American Passion Play;* the story of the play presented by the Scottish Rite Bodies of Bloomington. Robert Bruce Flanders, *Nauvoo, Kingdom on the Mississippi;* 1965; presents the Mormon experience in Illinois. E. R. Turnbull, *The First Masonic Cornerstone Laid in Illinois;* 4 Norcalore 219 (1934). Burton Kessler, *Some Geographic Aspects of Freemasonry in Illinois.* 1970. A detailed study of geographic aspects of Masons in Illinois. Summary presented in Phil. Mag., Dec., 1976, 108. *Valley of Southern Illinois Dedicates New Scottish Rite Cathedral;* No. Light, Nov., 1972, 18. E. R. Turnbull, *Western Star Lodge No. 107, Kaskaskia, Illinois;* 2 Norcalore 193. *Illinois Lodge Displays Civil War Masonic Jewels.* No. Light, April, 1973, 14. In preparation is, George E. Burow, *The Scottish Rite Deputies in Illinois.*

Indiana: Daniel McDonald, *History of Freemasonry in Indiana;* 1898; 473 pp. Dwight L. Smith, *Goodly Heritage;* 1968; 525 pp. Gayle S. Eads, *Masonic Jewels Survive Civil War Raid.* No. Light, Jan., 1975, 16. George A. Seipp, *When a Confederate General Saved Jewels of a Masonic Lodge.* 11 RAM 238 (1974-1975). Dwight L. Smith, *Grand Lodge of Indiana Dedicates Its Restored Birthplace.* No. Light, June, 1975, 12. Alphonse Cerza, *Indiana Law and Freemasonry.* Ind. Free., Feb., 1951, 16.

Iowa: Joseph E. Morcombe, *History of the Grand Lodge of Iowa,* 1910; 310 pp. William F. Cleveland, *History of the Grand Lodge of Iowa;* 1913; 375 pp. William F. Cleveland, *History of the Grand Lodge of Iowa;* 1915; 424 pp. Ernest R. Moore, *History of the Grand Lodge of Iowa;* 1939; 310 pp. Ralph E. Whipple,

History of the Grand Lodge of Iowa; 1969; 371 pp. New Age Mag., May, 1928, 287. Jerry Marsengill, *The Iowa Mormon Lodges.* Gr. L. Bull. of Iowa, March, 1975, 67.

Kansas: Charles S. McGinness, *Once in a Hundred Years;* 1964. Ben W. Graybill, *History of Kansas Masonry;* 1975; 133 pp. *The Founding of Kansas Masonry.* 10 Norcalore 21.

Kentucky: H. B. Grant, *Doings of the Grand Lodge of Kentucky,* 1800-1900; 427 pp. *History of Freemasonry in Kentucky,* 1900-1935. A compilation of articles from the Masonic Home Journal. A. E. Orton and Dr. Charles A. Keith, *History of the Old Masons' Home of Kentucky;* 1960; 211 pp. Rob Morris, *History of Freemasonry in Kentucky;* 1859. *The Birth of Kentucky Grand Lodge.* Phil. Mag., Feb., 1950, 10. J. Winston Coleman, *Masonry in the Blue Grass;* 1933; 264. Charles S. Guthrie, *Lafayette's Visit to Kentucky Masonic Lodges in 1825.* Phil. Mag., Feb., 1973, 18. Charles S. Guthrie, *Rob Morris and the Early Years of the Grand Lodge of Kentucky.* Phil. Mag., Feb., 1975, 18. *Lexington Lodge No. 1 Celebrates Its 175th Anniversary.* 7 RAM 363 (1963). 8 RAM 333 (1966). Morrison L. Cooke, *A Brief History of the Masonic Home Journal.* Phil. Mag., April, 1976, 45.

Louisiana: Ray V. Denslow, *Territorial Masonry;* 1925. Story of the Louisiana purchase. Glen Lee Greene, *Masonry in Louisiana; 1962;* 310 pp. Thomas Ewing Dabney, *Marching Through the Years;* 1963. Peter D. Laguens, Jr., *Latin American Freemasonry and Its Influence Upon the State of Louisiana.* Phil. Mag., Jan., 1970, 58. Martin E. Krantz, *Masonry in New Orleans.* Phil. Mag., Feb., 1969, 22. Articles by Lee A. Strickland: New Age Mag.: June, 1928, 357; Dec., 1958, 715; Aug., 1962, 19. William R. Denslow, *Famous Lodges – Louisiana No. 109,* 5 RAM 150 (1956). 9 RAM 152 (1968). Dr. William G. Peacher, *New York, The Mother Grand Lodge.* 11 RAM 215 (1969). *New Orleans Receives Washington Statue From Louisiana Freemasons.* 6 RAM 291 (1960).

Maine: Ralph J. Pollard, *Freemasonry in Maine, 1762-1945;* 170; 310 pp. Charles B. Davis, *Proceedings of the Centennial Celebration of the Grand Lodge of Maine,* May 5, 1920. 10 RAM 43 (1970).

Maryland: Edward T. Schultz, *History of Freemasonry in Maryland,* 4 vols.; 1888. Carl N. Everstine, *History of Grand Lodge of Maryland,* 2 vols.; 1950; Charles Francis Stein, Jr., *History of the Grand Lodge of Maryland, 1951-1975;* 1979; 640 pp. Henry R. Evans, *The Grand Lodge of Maryland and Jacobism.* Mast. Mas., May, 1924, 281. May 10, 1887, Proc of Grd. L. of Md. has an Oration by John M. Carter, which is a history of the Craft in the state. Aemil Pouler, *DeMolay in Maryland,* 1921-1968; 1969; 124 pp.

Massachusetts: Dr. Thomas S. Roy, *Stalwart Builders.* A summary of the Grand Lodge Proceedings, 1733-1970; 1971; 411 pp. Biographical sketch of author p. 411; reviewed in 84 AQC 221 (1971). John M. Sherman, *John Coleman and the Revival Movement in "Ancient" Freemasonry in Boston,* 1769-1770. 10 ALR 423 (1968). Muriel Taylor, *The Beteilhe Manuscript.* 7 ALR 143 (1958). *Forefathers Monument at Plymouth, Massachusetts, Dedicated by Freemasons.* 5 RAM 303 (1957). *Freemason Lost in Storm Erects Road Marker.* 4 RAM 153 (1953). *Early Royal Arch in Boston.* 9 RAM 299 (1969). *The 200th Anniversary of the Grand Lodge of Massachusetts;* 1933. Laurence A. Scott, *There Is a Turbulence in Boston.* New Age Mag., March, 1976, 16. *Lodge of St. Andrew,* Bicentennial Memorial Volume; 1958. *Honor in an Urn.* No. Light, Jan., 1975, 18. John B. Vrooman, *St. John's Day Festival in December, A Splendid Massachusetts Celebration.* Phil. Mag., Dec., 1973, 100.

Michigan: Jefferson Conover, *Freemasonry in Michigan;* 1897. Author's picture and his biographical sketch appear in 1903 Proc. of Sup. C., NMJ, 289, 294. J. Fairbain Smith and Charles Fey, *History of Freemasonry in Michigan;* 1963. 1972 Proc. of Sup. C., NMJ, 415 has biographical sketch of Fey. F. Fairbairn

Smith, *Dateline 1764;* 1979; 280 pp. Continues story presented in preceding volume. J. Fairbairn Smith, *Stoney Creed Lodge.* No. Light, Jan., 1975, 8. L. B. Winsor, *Masonry in Michigan;* Mich. History Mag., Oct., 1936, 227. J. Fairbain Smith, *150 Epic Years;* history of Detroit Lodge No. 2, 1821-1971; 1972. J. Fairbairn Smith, *Chapter Builds First Detroit Masonic Temple.* 1 RAM 305 (1945). J. Fairbairn Smith, *Michigan Grand Lodge Dedicates New University Building.* No. Light, Sept., 1974, 12. J. Fairbairn Smith, *Michigan Masonic Trestleboard. A Bicentennial Tribute.*

Minnesota: *Masonry Comes to Minnesota,* New Age Mag., Dec., 1972, 15. Edward Johnstone, *Centennium: 1853-1953;* 1953; 114 pp. Larry Offenbecker, *Out of the Wilderness — Minnesota Freemasonry Is 125 Years old.* 11 RAM 170 (1974). Dr. Raymond W. Miller, *Brought to Light.* New Age Mag., April, 1975, 7. Ralph Turtinen, *More Than Bricks and Mortar;* 1975. Larry Offenbecker, *Development of the Capitular Rite in Minnesota.* 11 RAM 205 (1974).

Mississippi: Dr. Allen Cabaniss, *The Beginnings of Masonry in Mississippi;* in the 1943 Grd. L. Proc., 46; also in 4 ALR 250 (1944-1945). William R. Denslow, *"Monmouth," Home of the Father of Mississippi Freemasonry.* 4 RAM 266 (1954). *Historic Connelly Tavern.* 4 RAM 243 (1953).

Missouri: *Beginnings of Freemasonry in Missouri;* 1944 Trans. MLR. *Birth of Freemasonry in Missouri;* 12 RAM 67 (1976). Ray V. Denslow, *A Missouri Frontier Lodge* (Franklin Union Lodge No. 7). 1929; 92 pp. *Centennial History of the Grand Lodge of Missouri;* 1921; 367 pp. Ray V. Denslow, *Civil War and Masonry in Missouri;* 1930. *Biographies and Engravings of Grand Masters, Grand Treasurers, and Grand Secretaries of the Grand Lodge of Missouri, 1821-1920;* 185 pp. *Freemasonry in Kansas City;* 1945 Trans. MLR. Henry C. Chiles, *The Masonic College of Missouri;* 1935. *Beginnings of Templary in Missouri.* 1946 Trans. MLR. A. Lloyd Collins, *Anti-Masonry in Missouri;* 1950 Trans. MLR.

Chronology of Missouri Masonic History Before 1835. 1943 Trans. MLR. *Early Masonic History in Missouri.* 1944 Trans. MLR. *Missouri Masons Who Have Been Governors.* 1943 Trans. MLR. *The Story of Golden Square Lodge.* 1945 Trans. MLR. *Davenport Frontier Chapter.* 1945 Trans. MLR. *A History of St. Louis Commandery No. 1, K.T., 1847-1947.* 1947 Trans. MLR. *Missouri Military Lodges.* 1948 Trans. MLR. *Freemasonry in Grundy County.* 1949 Trans. MLR. *Western Star Lodge – A Far West Lodge.* 5 RAM 364 (1957).

Montana: Walter Ray Kohls, *Attempts to Start Masonic Lodges in Montana;* 1964. Nathaniel P. Langford, *Vigilante Days and Ways;* 1957. Robert S. Miller, *The Hands of the Workmen;* 1966. Harold Axford, *Four Firsts for a Modest Hero.* The autobiography of Paris Swazy Pfouts; 1970. Robert E. Miller, *Ninety Years of the Scottish Rite in Montana;* 1972; 174 pp. Reviewed in New Age Mag., Feb. 1973. *Rugged Men Forged Early History of Freemasonry in Montana,* 10 RAM 355 (1972-1973); 11 RAM 39 (1973). J. E. Norecombe, *Planting Masonry in Montana;* 5 Am. Free. 62, 143, 190, 238, 351 (1913-1914). *Army Lodge.* 14 Build. Mag. 228 (1928). *Masonry Survives Montana Ghost Town.* No. Light., June, 1974, 6. *Montana Because of Masonry.* New Age Mag., March, 1977, 24. *A Landmark Story (Pompey's Pillar).* New Age Mag., Dec., 1975, 38.

Nebraska: Dr. George W. Rosenlof, *Masonry in Nebraska;* 1962; 179 pp. *A Mason Escapes Nebraska Lynching.* 12 RAM 201 (1977). Walter Miller, *De-Molay in Nebraska.* K. T. Mag., March, 1976, 25.

Nevada: Clarence W. Torrence, *History of Freemasonry in Nevada;* 1944; reprinted in 1975; 365 pp. Silas E. Ross, *Biographical Sketches of Nevada Grand Masters;* 1970. Silas E. Ross, *The Pathway Through an Era,* New Age Mag., July, 1970, 41. Marvin Scher and R. Raymond Lowe, *William Morris Stewart, Legal Colossus.* Cal. Free., Spring, 1977, 76.

New Hampshire: Harry W. Cheney, *Symbolic Freemasonry in New Hampshire;* 1934; 289 pp. Gerald D. Foss, *Three Centuries of Freemasonry in New Hampshire;* 1972. *Capture of Fort William and Mary.* No. Light, Jan., 1975, 4. Gerald D. Foss, *History of Columbia Lodge No. 2.* 3 Trans. of Ann. L. No. 175, 1 (1978). Stanley A. Johnson, *Rising Sun Lodge of Keene, N.H.* 3 Trans. Ann. L. No. 175, N.H. 14 (1978). Gerald D. Foss, *Three St. Johns – The Lodge, The Church, and The Feast.* 12 RAM 113 (1976-1977).

New Jersey: David MacGregor, *History of Freemasonry in New Jersey, 1787-1937.* William Davis and Lewis M. Parker, *A History of the Grand Lodge of New Jersey;* 1961; 167 pp. *The Story of Freemasonry in New Jersey.* 9 Build. Mag. 329 (1928). Melvin M. Johnson, *Concerning ''The Story of Freemasonry in New Jersey.''* 10 Build. Mag, 109 (1924); 11 Build Mag., 166 (1925). Harold V. B. Voorhis, *A New Jersey ''Tea Party'' in 1774.* 10 ALR 260 (1967). *The Will of William Franklin.* 11 ALR 77 (1969). Harold V. B. Voorhis, *New Jersey Masonic Governors.* 11 ALR 259 (1969). Harold V. B. Voorhis, *History of Scottish Rite in New Jersey.* Harold V. B. Voorhis, *History of Washington Lodge 8.* 11 ALR 233 (1969).

New Mexico: La Moine ''Red'' Langston, *A History of Masonry in New Mexico;* 1977; 289. *Some Early Freemasons in New Mexico.* 1948 Trans. MLR. *Formation of the Grand Lodge of New Mexico.* 1948 Trans. MLR. *Col. Ceran St. Vrain.* 11 Build. Mag. 324, 353 (1925). Paul A. F. Walter, *Masonic History of New Mexico.* 8 Build. Mag. 211 (193). W. Peter McAtee, *Masonry in New Mexico,* K. T. Mag., Aug., 1975, 19. *Gov. Bent, A Masonic Martyr of New Mexico,* 9 Build. Mag. 358, (1923) *A Century of Freemasonry in New Mexico.* Published in 1950 by Montezuma Lodge No. 1. See New Age Mag., Sept. 1951, 535.

New York: Charles T. McClenachan, *History of the Most Ancient and Honorable Fraternity of New York;* 1888. Ossian Lang, *History of Freemasonry in the State of New York;* 1922. See biographical sketch of author in 3 Build. Mag. 361 (1917). Peter Ross, *Standard History of Freemasonry in New York;* 2 vols.; 1899, 1901. Howard P. Nash, *Origins of the Grand Lodge of New York;* many installments in 3-6 ALR. James E. Craig, *An Outline of the History of the Grand Lodge of New York;* 175th Anniversary issue of the Empire State Mason; 1956; 9. Wilmer E. Bresee and Wendell K. Walker, *The Livingston Years;* Empire State Mason, Dec., 1978, 2. *A Study of Masonry in New York State.* Mas. Out., July, 1925, 236; August, 1925, 262; Sept., 1925, 18; Nov., 1925, 77; Aug., 1926, 365. Daniel de Noyelles, *Early History of Rockland County and the Annals of Freemasonry;* 1974; 36 pp. Richard H. Brown, *Freemasonry on Staten Island.* 12 ALR 131 (1972). John H. Stelter, *The Erie Canal and Freemasonry.* 12 ALR 477 (1972). Herman A. Sarachan, *History of Masonry in Monroe County;* 1971; 282 pp. Joe C. Hays, Jr., *Schisms in the Grand Lodge of New York.* 3 Trans. Tex. L. of Res. 302 (1965-1968).

North Carolina: Marsall De Lancey Haywood, *The Beginnings of Freemasonry in North Carolina and Tennessee;* 1906. Thomas C. Parramore, *Launching the Craft; The First 50 Years of North Carolina History of Freemasonry;* 1975; 238 pp. E. Timber Lake, *The Rise of Freemasonry in North Carolina.* 3 Norcalore 13. Frederis G. Spiedel, *North Carolina Masons in the American Revolution;* 1975; 77 pp. *North Carolina Masonic Governors.* 7 Norcalore 14. *Masonic Marker in Waynesville.* 4 RAM 277 (1954).

North Dakota: Harold S. Pond, *Masonry in North Dakota, 1804-1864;* 1964. Edward J. Franta, *Secrets and Mysteries.* Phil. Mag., Oct., 1972, 88. *When North Dakota Established a Military Lodge in the Philippines.* 4 RAM 206 (1953).

Ohio: W. M. Cunningham, *A History of Freemasonry in Ohio;* Vols. 2 and 3, by John G. Reeves; 1914. *In Preparation:* one-volume history by Allen E. Roberts. Selby & Walker, *History of Royal Arch*

Freemasonry in Ohio. 2 vols. 1965. William R. Pringle, *A History of Ancient and Accepted Scottish Rite in Ohio;* 1972. *Historical Notes on the Grand Lodge of Ohio.* 13 Build. Mag. 1; 1927. *The Snow House, where the York Rite started in Ohio.* 9 RAM 91 (1967). William R. Pringle, *Ohio Military Lodges in the Civil War.* 11 ALR 91 (1969). *Grand Lodge Building of Ohio Has Interesting History.* Phil. Mag., June, 1973, 57. *An Early Ohio Masonic Record.* 10 Build. Mag., 357 (1924). *Mark Lodges Authorized in Ohio.* 10 RAM 102 (1970-1971). *Clandestine Masonry in Ohio.* New Age Mag., Mov., 1912, 521.

Oklahoma: C. A. Sturgeon, *Beginnings of Freemasonry in Oklahoma.* 3 ALR 477 (1941-1942). Clarence Brain, *Indian Territory.* 2 RAM 18 (1946). *Royal Arch Masonry at Work in Oklahoma.* 1 RAM 16 (1943). *History of Freemasonry in Oklahoma;* 1935; reviewed in New Age Mag., September 1937, 575. J. Fred Latham, *The Story of Oklahoma Masonry,* 1874-1949; 1978; 547 pp.

Oregon: John C. Wilkinson, *History of the Grand Lodge of Oregon,* 1846-1967; 2 vols. Elmer G. Wendling, *Beginning of Masonry in Oregon.* 1 Res. L. of Ore. 379. William R. Kennell, *Oregon's Masonic Genealogy.* Ore. Free., March, 1979, 6. Stanley O. Wentz, *Oregon Military Lodge,* Ore. Free., Dec., 1975, 7. *Early History of Portland Lodge No. 55,* Ore. Free., Oct., 1974, 16. Aemil Pouler, *John C. Ainsworth,* New Age Mag., Aug., 1961, 50.

Pennsylvania: Julius F. Sachse, and N. S. Barratt, *Freemasonry in Pennsylvania, 1727-1907;* 3 vols. 1908. Henry S. Borneman, *Early Freemasonry in Pennsylvania;* 1931; 102 pp. *125th Memorial Volume, 1786-1911;* 1912; 252 pp. *Washington Sesqui-Centennial Celebration.* Nov. 5, 1902; 382 pp. *Franklin Bi-Centennial Celebration;* 1906; 323 pp. *Bi-Centennial Celebration, 1731-1831;* 226 pp. *Dedication Memorial Book of Masonic Temple;* 1875; 236 pp. *Minutes of Grand Lodge of Pennsylvania, 1779-1962. The Philadelphia Masonic Temple,* No. Light, Sept., 1971, 4. *Penn's Woodland.* K. T. Mag., Feb., 1978, 28. William E. Mont-

gomery, *150 Years of Freemasonry in Chambersburg, Pa.,* No. Light, April, 1971, 14. Walter H. Jenkins, *The Grand Master's Jewel and John Pine, the Engraver,* 13 RAM 123 (1979).

Rhode Island: Henry W. Rugg, *Freemasonry in Rhode Island,* 1895; 869 pp. *Reprint of the Early Proceedings;* 3 vols.; 1909. Winfield S. Solomon, *History and Roster of Rhode Island Masonry in World War II;* 166 pp. Harold R. Curis, *Rhode Island Freemasonry in the Revolution;* Master Mason, Oct., 1928, 647; Nov., 1928, 744, Dec., 1928, 829. Aemil Pouler, *Fort Hiram,* New Age Mag., Oct., 1968, 44. No. Light, June 1970, 7. *Did Rhode Island Have a Masonic Lodge in 1658?* 9 RAM 207 (1968). Gerald D. Foss and Royal R. Case, *George Richards, Masonic Missionary and Thomas Thompson, His Sponsor.* 11 ALR 34 (1969). *The Lodge Newport.* 7 RAM 86 (1957). Henry G. Jackson, *The Story of an Ancient Lodge.* 6 RAM 11 (1958). C. C. Hunt, *Prehistoric Freemasonry in Rhode Island.* 5 Norcalore 112. Norris G. Abbot, *La Fayette and Rhode Island.* No. Light, April, 1975, 16.

South Carolina: Albert G. Mackey, *History of Freemasonry in South Carolina;* 1861; reprinted in 1936; 584 pp. *An Early Masonic Document of South Carolina.* 9 Build. Mag. 204 (1923). *Early History of Walhalla Lodge No. 66.* 8 ALR 97 (1960). *John Drayton, Governor and Botanist.* 4 ALR 604 (1946-1947).

South Dakota: Harold L. Tisher, *100 Years of Masonry in South Dakota;* 1974; 236 pp. Reviewed in New Age Mag., Jan., 1975, 55. E. R. McDowell, *The Beginnings of Masonry in the Dakotas.* New Age Mag., Feb., 1906, 175. David Graham, *Some Footnotes to the History of the Grand Lodge of South Dakota.* 1961 Trans. So. Dakota L. of Res. *Scottish Rite Masonry in So. Dakota and the New Temple at Yankton.* New Age Mag., March, 1906, 263.

Tennessee: Charles A. Snodgrass, *History of Freemasonry in Tennessee,* 1799-1943. 1944; 542 pp. Reviewed in New Age Mag., Feb.-March, 1945, 118. Marshall De Lancey Haywood, *The Beginnings of Freemasonry in North Carolina and Tennessee;* 1906. Charles Comstock, *Tennessee's Earliest Pioneer Lodge.* 2 Norcalore 31.

Texas: James D. Carter, *Education and Masonry in Texas to 1846;* 1963; 249 pp. James D. Carter, *The First Century of Scottish Rite Masonry in Texas, 1867-1967;* 1967; 508 pp. Reviewed: New Age Mag., Jan., 1967, 53. 79 AQC 253 (1968). Edwin S. Malo, III, *The First Masonic Monument in Texas.* 14 Trans. Tex. L. of Res. 195 (1978-1979). *Early Texas Masons,* Master Mason Mag., July, 1928, 475. J. C. Kidd, *History of the Grand Commandery of Knights Templar of Texas;* 1899. *Grand Lodge Temple.* 5 RAM 355 (1957). Dr. George H. T. French, *The Formation of the Texas Lodge of Research.* 14 Trans. Tex. L. of Res. 227 (1978-1979). John W. Denny, *A Century of Freemasonry in El Paso;* 1956. James M. Day, *Masonry and the Texas Rangers.* 13 Trans. Tex. L. of Res. 51 (1978). John E. Kelly, *Behold, How Good;* a history of Blue Bonnet Lodge No. 1219; 1976; 346 pp. Howard R. Stewart, *The Scottish Rite Learning Center of West Texas.* New Age Mag., Aug., 1978, 39. William T. Parmer, *The Influence of Freemasonry Upon the Institution of Protestantism in Texas.* Tex. Free., Nov., 1972, 8. *Presidents of Texas Who Were Masons.* 7 Build. Mag. 207 (1921). *The Story and Achievement of Freemasonry in Texas.* 9 Build. Mag. 133 (1923).

Utah: Mervin B. Hogan, *The Grass Roots of Utah Masonry.* New Age Mag., April, 1955, 239. Also in Rocky Mountain Mason, Aug.-Sept., 1954, 5. *Utah Dedicates Monument at Early Masonic Site.* 6 RAM 75; 338 (1960). S. H. Goodwin, *Freemasonry in Utah.* Various booklets published 1924-1933. *A Short History of Freemasonry in Utah;* 100th Anniversary; 1972; 2 pp. *Outline History of Freemasonry in Utah.* Phil. Mag., 1973; 15.

Vermont: Lee B. Tillotson, *Ancient Craft Masonry in Vermont;* 1920; 139 pp. H. L. Haywood, *Masonic Curiosa,* 162. *Three Dates in Vermont History.* 11 Build. Mag. 336 (1925). *Confederates Raid Town of St. Albans, Vt.,* 2 RAM 369 (1948). The No. Light, Nov., 1970, 10. John Spargo, *The Rise and Progress of Freemasonry in Vermont, 1765-1944;* 1944. Welland S. Horn, *Masonic Monument Once Stood on Vermont's Bird Monument.* No. Light, Sept., 1974, 6. Glen Buzzell, *Masonry in Vermont During and After the Morgan Affair and You Are There.* Unpublished skit on file in the Grand Lodge Library, at Burlington, Vermont; 1974.

Virginia: Dr. William Moseley Brown, *Freemasonry in Virginia;* 1936; 327 pp. Reviewed in New Age Mag., April, 1936, 249. George E. Kidd, *Freemasonry in Williamsburg, Va.;* 1957; 251 pp. John Dove, *Reprint of Minutes of Grand Lodge of Virginia, 1778-1823.* Dr. John B. Sperry, *The Grand Lodge of Virginia.* New Age Mag., June, 1977, 45. *How Cascade Lodge Was Closed; an Improbable Tale;* Phil. Mag., Feb., 1972, 20. *Richmond-Randolph Lodge No. 19;* 14 Build. Mag., 206 (1928). Franklin L. Brockett, *The Lodge of Washington;* 1876. Allen E. Roberts, *A Chronicle of Virginia Research Lodge No. 1777;* 1978; 81 pp. Allen E. Roberts, *Brotherhood in Action;* the story of the Virginia Craftsmen; 1977; 77 pp.

Washington: Paul W. Harvey, *Not Made With Hands;* 1958.

West Virginia: *A Century of Freemasonry;* 1956; 111 pp. Allen E. Roberts, *A Daughter of the Grand Lodge of Virginia.* Trans. Va. L. of Res., Dec. 28, 1957.

Wisconsin: Robert O. Jasperson, *Centennial of the Grand Lodge of Wisconsin;* 1944; 110 pp.

Wyoming: A. J. Mokler, *History of Freemasonry in Wyoming, 1874-1924;* 1924; 280pp. Walter C. Reusser, *Grand Lodge of A.F. & A.M. of Wyoming, 1925-1956;* 1959; 292 pp. *History of Wyoming.* 11 Build. Mag. 252 (1925). *Historic Independence Rock.* 4 RAM 227.

2.13 THE WAR OF 1860

Allen E. Roberts, *House Undivided;* 1961; 356 pp. MLR, publisher.

Author: Appendix No. 29. Comments: Henry W. Coil, Sr., ''A painstaking and abundant reproduction of Masonic action and policy during the American Civil War, a long neglected subject. Reviewed: 74 AQC 101 (1962). Libraries: 1, 2, 3, 4, 5, 6, 7, 9, 10, 11, 12, 14.

Allen E. Roberts, *Masonry Under Two Flags;* series of articles published between June 1961 and Dec. 1962 in the Philalethes Magazine.

Allen E. Roberts, *Freemasonry Aids Reconstruction;* series of articles published in the Philalethes Mag. between Feb. 1964 and Feb. 1965.

War Did Not Break Masonic Tie. 5 RAM 370, 373 (1957).

How the Yankee Colonel Saved the General's Library. Phil. Mag., Feb., 1972, 11.

Wilmer E. Bresee, *Masonry and the Civil War.* 7 RAM 355 (1959).

Albert G. Mackey, *Freemasonry in the Civil War.* 8 Build. Mag. 370 (1922).

Allen E. Roberts, *Freemasonry Attempts to Prevent the Civil War.* 7 RAM 35 (1961).

Federal Officers Confer Masonic Degrees on Confederate Officers. 4 RAM 103 (1952).

Confederates Raid Town of St. Albans, While Chapter Meets. 2 RAM 369 (1948).

Robert H. Gollmar, *Civil War Riots Charged to Masons.* Phil. Mag., June, 1955, 6.

Fraternal Courtesies in War Time. Phil. Mag., Feb., 1971, 22.

Robert J. Clegg, *How Masons Attempted to Stop Civil War in Paris.* N.Y. Mas. Outl., Aug., 1925, 266.

Frank Strickland, *Historical Notes on Masonry in the Civil War.* 16 Build. Mag. 8, 38 (1930).

A Masonic Incident. K. T. Mag., March, 1975, 24.

Albert Pike, *Freemasonry in the Civil War.* 16 Build. Mag. 8, 130 (1930).

Jacob Jewell, *Heroic Deeds of Noble Master Masons During the Civil War;* 1916.

Deed L. Vest, *One Texan's View of Masonry in the Civil War.* 14 Trans. Tex. L. of Res. 110 (1978-1979).

Deed L. Vest, *Texas Military Lodges in the Confederate Army.* 13 Trans. Tex. L. of Res. 129 (1977-1978).

Dr. Stephen R. Greenberg, *The War Between the States.* Phil. Mag., July-Aug., 1968, 70; has picture of author.

2.14 GENERAL MASONIC BIOGRAPHIES

William R. Denslow, *10,000 Famous Freemasons;* 4 vols.; 1957-1960; MLR, publisher.
Author: Appendix No. 11. Reviewed: New Age Mag., May, 1958, 297; May, 1960, 53; 6 RAM 4 (1958). Libraries: 1, 2, 3, 5, 8, 9, 10, 11, 12, 14.

George W. Baird, *Great American Masons;* 1924; 109 pp. Reproduced in the Little Masonic Library.
Author: Sketch and picture, 8 Build. Mag. 263 (1922).

Alphonse Cerza, *Masonic Biographical Sketches.* MSA Digest.

Dudley Wright, *Masonic Who's Who;* 1926; 512 pp. A. Lewis, London, publisher. Copy in Iowa Masonic Library.

Henry C. Clausen, *Messages for a Mission;* 1977; 227 pp. Supreme Council, 33°, S.J., publisher.
Author: Appendix 7. Reviewed: 90 AQC 264 (1977). Libraries: 2, 3, 5, 7, 8, 9, 10, 11, 12, 14.

Hubert S. Banner, *These Men Were Masons;* 1934; 258 pp. Chapman & Hall, London, publisher.
Contents: Sketches of famous men who have been Masons. Libraries: 3, 4, 5, 7, 9, 10, 11, 12, 14.

James Alexander Bell, *Famous Masons;* 1928; 273 pp. Judd & Detweiler, London, publisher.
Contents: Biographical sketches of 20 famous Masons. Libraries: 3, 7, 9, 10, 12, 14, 15.

Dudley Wright, *England's Masonic Pioneers;* 1925; 138 pp. George Kenning & Son, London, publisher.

Contents: Sketches of the early leaders of the Craft. Comments: L. B. Blakemore, "Biographical sketches of founders and leaders of early speculative Masonry." Reviewed: Master Mason, March, 1925, 258. Libraries: 3, 5, 7, 9, 10, 11, 12, 14.

Sydney Hayden, *Washington and His Masonic Compeers.* 1905; 395 pp. Macoy Publishing Co. Many editions have been published. Some editions have copy of Anderson's Constitutions of 1723.
Comments: Henry W. Coil, Sr., "Contains interesting facts." Silas H. Shepherd, "Many interesting facts connected with the Masonic career of Washington and other prominent Masons of the Revolutionary period." Libraries: 1, 2, 3, 4, 5, 6, 7, 8, 11, 12, 13, 14.

William M. Stuart, *Masonic Soldiers of Fortune;* 1928; 276 pp. Macoy Publishing Co., publishers.
Contents: Twenty-one biographical sketches of famous Masons. Reviewed: 15 Build. Mag. 121 (1929). Libraries: 2, 3, 4, 5, 7, 8, 9, 11, 12, 13, 14.

Are These the Greatest Masons? MSA Digest.

G. P. G. Hills, *Notes on Some Masonic Personalities at the End of the 18th Century.* 25 AQC 141 (1912).

W. G. Fisher, *A Cavalcade of Freemasons in 1731.* 74 AQC 32 (1961); 76 AQC 44 (1963).

Edward Newton, *Brethren Who Have Made Masonic History.* 78 AQC 130 (1965).

W. J. Williams, *Masonic Personalities, 1723-1739.* 40 AQC 30, 126, 138, 230 (1927); 44 AQC 198 (1931).

C. L. Rothwell, *Masonry and English Rulers.* K. T. Mag., Oct., 1972, 7.

List of Famous Persons Who Were Masons. 8 RAM 210 (1965).

2.15 PRESIDENTS AND VICE PRESIDENTS OF THE UNITED STATES WHO HAVE BEEN MASONS

William L. Boyden, *Masonic Presidents, Vice Presidents and Signers;* 1927; 68 pp.
Reviewed in 13 Build. Mag. 124 (1927). Libraries: 2, 3, 5, 7, 8, 9, 10, 12, 13, 14.

J. Fairbairn Smith, *Masonic Presidents of the United States;* 1945; 33 pp.
Author: Appendix No. 31. Contents: Has etching of each person covered. He includes Jefferson and Madison in the list; this is highly debatable. Libraries: 7, 9, 10, 11, 12, 14.

Ray V. Denslow, *Freemasonry and the Presidency;* 1951; 306 pp. MLR, publisher.
Author: Appendix No. 10. Contents: Seventeen chapters devoted to each of the known Presidents who have been Masons up to that time. There is coverage of some anti-Masons also. Many pictures relating to the subject. Libraries: 1, 2, 3, 4, 5, 7, 9, 10, 11, 12, 13, 14.

H. L. Haywood, *Famous Masons and Masonic Presidents;* 1944; 310 pp., The Masonic History Co., Chicago, publisher.
Author: Appendix No. 16. Reviewed: New Age Mag., Dec., 1944. Libraries 2, 3, 4, 5, 7, 8, 9, 10, 11, 13, 14.

Our Masonic Presidents. STB, July, 1933.

Composite picture of *Masons Who Have Been Presidents of the United States;* suitable for framing. MSA.

Ward K. St. Clair, *Masons Who Were Presidents.* Phil. Mag., Aug., 1959, 60.

J. Hugo Tatsch, *How Many Presidents Have Been Masons?* N.Y. Mas. Outl., Jan., 1926, 144.

Al Dapsauski, *The Presidential Trestleboard.* Phil. Mag., June, 1973, 53; statistics and map with burial places indicated.

Jerry R. Erikson, *Masonic Facets of the Presidential and Vice Presidential Elections.* 1788-1960. 6 RAM 323, 369 (1960); 7 RAM 14, 51 (1961).

United States Presidents and Master Masons; Cal. Free., Autumn, 1976, 179.

1. GEORGE WASHINGTON

Dr. William Moseley Brown, *George Washington: Freemason;* 1952; 542 pp. Grand Lodge of Virginia, publisher.
Author: Appendix No. 2. Reviewed: Ind. Free., April, 1953, 19; New Age Mag., June, 1953, 378. Libraries: 1, 2, 3, 4, 5, 8, 9, 10, 11, 12, 13, 14, 15.

Charles H. Callahan, *Washington, the Man and the Mason;* 1913; 366 pp. Memorial Temple Committee of the George Washington Masonic Memorial Association, publisher.
Comments: Henry W. Coil, Sr., ''The author was a Past Master of Washington-Alexandria Lodge No. 22 at Alexandria, Virginia, and sponsored by the Washington National Monument Association.'' Reviewed: 2 Build. Mag. 60 (1916). Libraries: 1, 2, 3, 4, 5, 6, 7, 8, 9, 10, 11, 12, 13, 14.

J. Hugo Tatsch, *The Facts About George Washington as a Freemason;* 1932; 98 pp. Macoy Publishing Co., publisher.
Author: See Sec. 2.16 herein. Reviewed: 43 AQC 187 (1933). Libraries: 2, 3, 4, 5, 7, 8, 9, 10, 11, 12, 13, 14.

Allen E. Roberts, *George Washington: Master Mason;* 1976; 207 pp. Macoy Publishing Co., publisher.
Author: Appendix No. 29. Libraries: 2, 3, 10, 11, 12.

Julius F. Sachse, *Masonic Correspondence of Washington;* 1915; 139 pp. Grand Lodge of Pennsylvania, publisher.
Contents: Reproduction of the letters found by the compiler in the Library of Congress which relate to the Craft. Reviewed: 28 AQC 211 (1915). Libraries: 2, 3, 5, 7, 9, 12, 14, 15.

Facts for Speakers About Washington. STB, Feb., 1932.

George Washington, Master Mason. MSA Packet of material.

H. L. Haywood, *The Changes in the Calendar and George Washington;* in his Masonic Curiosa, 74.

Henry C. Clausen, *Washington Chronology of Masonic Events.* New Age Mag., Feb., 1973, 2.

J. Hugo Tatsch, *Facts About Washington.* 2 Norcalore 66.

A. V. Swartz, *The Masonic Activities of George Washington.* New Age Mag., Feb., 1953, 77; March, 1953, 169.

When Washington Became President. N.Y. Mas. Outl., Feb., 1925, 117.

George Washington, Surveyor. New Age Mag., Feb., 1978, 28.

Masonry's Finest Hour. The Story of the Washington at Prayer Monument at Valley Forge. 12 RAM 280 (1978).

Dr. Stephen R. Greenberg, *The Human George Washington.* Phil. Mag., Feb., 1976, 18.

R. Baker Harris, *Chronological Facts Concerning the George Washington Gavel.* 5 ALR 315 (1951-1952).

Harold V. B. Voorhis, *Amusement in Masonic Research.* Discussion of Washington's Aprons. Phil. Mag., Aug., 1977, 13.

H. C. Arbuckle, *A George Washington Book Review.* K. T. Mag., Feb., 1977, 13.

Dr. Irving I. Lasky, *Washington's Physician, Dr. Samuel Bard.* K. T. Mag., April, 1979, 28.

James R. Case, *James Craik, 1730-1814, Friend and Physician of Washington.* New Age Mag., Oct., 1976, 22.

Harry S. Truman, *George Washington the Mason.* 11 RAM 131 (1974).

Frederick Smyth, *Worshipful Brother George Washington of Virginia.* 88 AQC 181 (1975).

George Washington, Altar Light, Sept.-Oct., 1977.

R. T. S. Kitwood, *Washington's Masonic Bible.* Mas. Sq., March, 1977, 18.

Frank W. Bobb, *The Lafayette-Washington Apron.* Pa. Free., Aug., 1977, 10; with color reproduction of the apron.

Portraits and Painters of Washington. Mast. Mas., Nov., 1927, 823.

James R. Case, *Washington's Doc-*

umented *Lodge Visits.* 10 ALR 440 (1968).

Harold V. B. Voorhis, *Washington Miscellanea.* 6 ALR 407 (1956).

Washington for Grand Master. 4 ALR 126 (1942-1944).

Washington Masonic Lodges. 9 ALR 105 (1963).

Gerald D. Foss, *Masonic Sidelights on Washington's Visit to New Hampshire in 1789.* 9 ALR 131 (1931).

Laying the Cornerstone of the U.S. Capitol. 4 RAM 84 (1952).

Pennsylvania Masons to Erect Statue of Washington. 8 RAM 344 (1966).

Freemasons Assisted in Dedication of Washington Monument. 4 RAM 259 (1954).

The Paul Revere Urn. 5 RAM 374 (1957); has picture of the urn which is in the possession of the Grand Lodge of Massachusetts and has a lock of Washington's hair.

How George Washington Died. 4 RAM 261 (1953).

Questions and Answers About George Washington. Phil. Mag., Feb., 1959, 8.

Washington Grand Master Pro Tem? Phil. Mag., April, 1972, 46.

Washington a Mason at Twenty? Phil. Mag., April, 1972, 47.

The George Washington Masonic National Memorial at Alexandria, Virginia. MSA Digest.

George Washington's Official Masonic Portrait. No. Light, Nov., 1971, 12.

Ronald E. Heaton, *Masonic Membership of Washington's Military Aides and Secretaries.* MSA Digest.

Washington, the Man. STB, Oct., 1952.

2. JAMES MONROE

New Age Mag., April, 1969, 47. Has his picture

Ind. Free., Oct., 1954, 4; reproduces article by G. W. Baird.

Master Mason, Aug., 1926, 671.

James R. Case, *The Mystery of Monroe the Mason.* No. Light, Sept., 1977, 6. Presents the view that he was not a Mason on the basis of presently available evidence. Reproduced in Ind. Free., Dec., 1978, 6.

3. ANDREW JACKSON

New Age Mag. articles: May, 1925, 291; Aug., 1946, 465; Sept., 1946, 547; March, 1979, 23; Jan., 1919, 3; June, 1904, 71 (has his picture in Masonic regalia); Dec., 1923, 717.

11 Build. Mag. 164, 206 (1925).

William M. Stuart, *Andrew Jackson and Freemasonry.* 1 ALR 110 (1930-1931).

Baynard Baker, *The Romance of Andy and Rachel.* Ind. Free., Nov., 1958, 4.

Cal. Free., Autumn, 1972, 155.

4. JAMES K. POLK

New Age Mag., Aug., 1969, 17; April, 1928, 234.

C. L. Rothwell, *Harding and Polk.* K. T. Mag., Nov., 1974, 11.

5. JAMES BUCHANAN

New Age Mag., Dec., 1969, 47.

K. T. Mag., June, 1974, 7.

6. ANDREW JOHNSON

Carl Swanson, *Early Days of Andrew Johnson: The Bound Boy of Raleigh.* No. Light, June, 1979, 4.

New Age Mag., Sept., 1953, 523; Oct., 1953, 609.

James R. Case, *Andrew Johnson (1808-1875),* K. T. Mag., June, 1978, 7.

Who Saved Andrew Johnson From Vote of Impeachment? New Age Mag., Sept., 1950, 543.

Mystery Surrounds President Andrew Johnson's Masonic Membership. 2 RAM 329 (1948). Has his picture in Masonic regalia.

New Age Mag., Jan., 1963, 46; April, 1970, 14.

William Stuart, *The Anti Masonic Phase of Johnson's Impeachment.* 2 ALR 146 (1936).

Ind. Free., April, 1959, 12.

K. T. Mag., Dec., 1972, 7.

7. JAMES A. GARFIELD

New Age Mag., Sept., 1970, 20; May, 1958, 291.

Ind. Free., June, 1959, 4.

The Garfield Memorial. 5 RAM 292 (1957). 7 RAM 142 (1962). K. T. Mag., July, 1972, 7.

Philalethes Mag., Aug., 1959, 56.

K. T. Mag., Sept., 1975, 29.

John M. Sherman, *A Relic of President James Abram Garfield Preserved in the Archives of the Grand Lodge of Massachusetts.* Phil. Mag., Oct., 1973, 90.

Dr. Irving I. Lasky, *The Baleful Aspects of the Assassination.* K. T. Mag., Nov., 1973, 21.

Proc. of Grd. L. of Mass., Dec., 13, 1882; report of lock of his hair and an urn presented to Grand Lodge.

8. WILLIAM MCKINLEY

K. T. Mag., Jan., 1976, 22.

New Age Mag., Dec., 1970, 47.

4 Build. Mag., 81 (1918).

How He Became a Mason. 8 Build. Mag., 186 (1922).

3 RAM 35 (1949); has his picture in Masonic regalia.

Proc. Ohio L. of Res., Vol. 2, 8.

9. THEODORE ROOSEVELT

New Age Mag. Articles: March, 1961, 41; July, 1958, 416; March, 1971, 44.

6 Build. Mag. 11 (1920).

Wendell K. Walker, *Theodore Roosevelt's Masonic Influence.* 7 RAM 238 (1958).

Personal Memories of Brother Theodore Roosevelt. 7 ALR 230 (1958).

Corinne Roosevelt Robinson, *Recollections of My Brother as a Mason.* N.Y. Mas. Outl., Sept., 1926, 41.

10. WILLIAM HOWARD TAFT

New Age Mag., Sept., 1911, 288; May, 1971, 42.

How William Howard Taft Became a Mason. 5 RAM 131 (1956); has his picture in Masonic regalia.

C. L. Rothwell, *Bro. William Howard Taft.* K. T. Mag., Sept., 1974, 7.

11. WARREN G. HARDING

STB, Sept., 1923.

C. L. Rothwell, *Harding and Polk.* K. T. Mag., Nov., 1974, 11.

John R. Nocas, *President Harding's Last Address.* Cal. Free., Winter, 1977, 12.

12. FRANKLIN D. ROOSEVELT

George Rees, *F. D. R. – The Mason.* 12 ALR 280 (1973).

C. L. Rothwell, *Bro. Franklin Delano Roosevelt.* K. T. Mag., Jan., 1975, 7.

13. HARRY S. TRUMAN

The RAM, Spring, 1973, is devoted completely to his life and work.

The Freemason of Mo., Spring, 1973.

Phil. Mag., Feb., 1973, 17.

Truman Memorial Service, House of Representative, 1974.

George W. Burch, Jr., *Plain Speaking Harry S. Truman,* Cal. Free., Summer, 1975, 118.

Truman Performs Masonic Ritual. K. T. Mag., June, 1975, 15.

Harry Truman, The Mas. J. of So. Africa, Sept., 1973, 11.

Walter S. Turnpaugh, *Truman and the Mexican Masons.* K. T. Mag., Aug., 1972, 28.

1 RAM 287 (1945).

MSA Digest plus a colored picture with Masonic regalia.

14. LYNDON B. JOHNSON

K. T. Mag., Oct., 1974, 14.

Why He Never Advanced Beyond the First Degree? Letter from a White House Associate answering this question. Phil. Mag., June, 1964, 49.

8 RAM 91 (1964).

15. GERALD R. FORD

K. T. Mag., Sept., 1974, 12.

Mas. World, Detroit, Dec., 1973, 12.

Phil. Mag., June, 1975, 59.

11 RAM 104 (1973-1974).

VICE PRESIDENTS

J. Robert Watt, *Vice Presidents Who Have Been Masons.* Phil. Mag., April-May, 1970.

Adlai Ewing Stevenson. 10 Build. Mag. 18 (1924). Also see 1 Trans Ill. Lodge of Res. 70.

Vice President Gerald R. Ford, K. T. Mag., Jan., 1974, 12.

MISCELLANEOUS

C. F. Willard, *Was Jefferson a Mason?* New Age Mag., June, 1928, 341.

Jefferson and Madison Masons? K. T. Mag., 1975, 6.

Jefferson and Hamilton – Were They Freemasons? Ind. Free., Oct., 1953, 11.

Zachary Taylor a Mason? 6 RAM 153 (1959).

Dwight D. Eisenhower Signs Petition for Degrees. 10 RAM 291 (1972).

2.16 INDIVIDUAL BIOGRAPHIES

Aasen, John: Mast. Mas., July-Aug., 1934, 431; has his picture.

Adams, C. C.: 52 AQC 283 (1939); 76 AQC 158 (1963).

Adams, John: *Not a Mason.* 9 Build. Mag., 29 (1923). 4 RAM 373 (1954).

Adams, John Quincy: *He Was an Anti-Mason.* Jerry R. Erikson has compiled a list of Masons with this name; 8 ALR 455 (1962).

Aguinaldo, Emilio: 5 RAM 11 (1955), 237 (1956), with his picture. 6 RAM 3 (1958), 8 RAM 35 (1964). New Age Mag., April, 1955, 232.

Ainsworth, John C.: New Age Mag., Aug., 1961, 50.

Aldrin, Jr., Edwin E.: New Age Mag., Nov., 1969, 18. See Sec. 2.17 herein.

Aleman, Miguel: 2 RAM 182 (1947); has his picture with Harry S. Truman.

Allen, Chester E.: Phil. Mag., April, 1976, 38.

Allen, J. Edward: *Gould's History of Freemasonry Throughout the World,* Vol. 6, p. 455 (1936).

Allende, Salvador: 10 RAM 361 (1972-1973).

Anderson, Franklin J.: 8 RAM 123 (1964); has his picture. 12 RAM 87 (1976). Phil. Mag., April, 1970, 33; June, 1970, 60.

Anderson, James: Altar Light, Dec.-Feb., 1978-1979. 36 AQC 86 (1923). 23 AQC 6 (1910). 18 AQC 28 (1905). 20 AQC 84 (1907). 78 AQC 130 (1965). 23 AQC 6 (1910). 18 AQC 9 (1905). 80 AQC 36, 271 (1967). 9 Build. Mag. 227 (1923).

Armitage, Edward: 26 AQC 294 (1913); 42 AQC 137 (1929).

Armstrong, Neil: New Age Mag., Nov., 1969, 32. See Sec. 2.17 herein.

Arne, Dr. Thomas (Composer of "Rule Britannica"): Mas. Sq., Dec., 1978, 166.

Arnold, Benedict: 80 AQC 120 (1967). 3 ALR 179, 390 (1938-1939). No. Cal. Res. L. Quart. J., Dec., 1976.

Arnold, Remmie Le Roy: Book by Dr. William Moseley Brown, *From These Beginnings;* 1953; 634 pp. McClure Printing Co., Staunton, Va.

Arrington, Keith: Phil. Mag., Oct., 1979, 3; 12 RAM 68 (1979).

Ashmole, Elias: 1 Author's Lodge Trans. 239 (1915). 78 AQC 83 (1965). 11 AQC 3 (1898). 65 AQC 35 (1952). 25 AQC 237 (1912). 7 Build. Mag. 158 (1921). STB, Oct., 1921.

Astor, Jacob: Mast. Mas., July, 1927, 545. 12 Build. Mag. 80 (1926). K. T. Mag., Aug., 11 (1975).

Atholl, Dukes of: 80 AQC 58 (1967).

Atwood, Henry Clinton: 8 ALR 89 (1960).

Austin, Stephen Fuller: New Age Mag., Dec., 1955, 747.

Bache II, Richard: Tex. Free., March-April, 1977, 7.

Bacheller, Irving: N.Y. Mas. Outl., May, 1930, 271.

Baird, George W.: 15 Build. Mag., Jan., 1930, 7.

Ballou, Hosea: No. Light, April, 1977, 6.

Barney, John: K. T. Mag., Feb., 1974, 11. 13 RAM 273 (1979). Masonic Americana, 81 (1974). 9 Proc. Chap. of Res of Ohio.

Bartlett, Robert E.: New Age Mag., Nov., 1976, 35.

Bartholdi, August: Mast. Mas., March, 1928, 192; Reader's Digest, April, 1977, 27.

Barthelmess, Dr. Richard: 11 ALR 281 (1970)

Baxter, R. H.: 35 AQC 301 (1922); 59 AQC 127 (1946).

Baylies, Hodijah: Ind. Free., Sept., 1977, 10.

Bedford, Jr., Gunning: No. Light, April, 1976, 14.

Beaumont, William: 11 ALR 262; has his picture. New Age Mag., July, 1972, 41. Phil. Mag., April, 1969, 42. 5 RAM 337 (1957).

Bede, Elbert: See Appendix No. 1.

Beethoven: 80 AQC 144 (1967).

Belcher, Jonathan: 10 RAM 165 (1971).

Bell, Andrew: 24 AQC 248 (1911).

Bell, G. Wilbur: 10 RAM 74 (1970).

Bell, Ovid: 4 ALR 590 (1946-1947).

Bellamy, Francis: Book by Margarette S. Miller *Twenty-Three Words;* 1976; 422 pp. *I Pledge Allegiance,* 11 RAM 81 (1973); has picture of both contenders, both Masons). K. T. Mag., June, 1977, 5. Cal. Free., Winter, 1974, 32. New Age Mag., June, 1972, 9.

Berlin, Irving: No. Light, April, 1971, 10. 6 RAM 5 (1958).

Besant, Walter: 14 AQC 105 (1901).

Birkhead, Mathew: 42 AQC 130 (1929).

Blair, Jr., John: 4 RAM 267 (1954).

Blanchard, Jonathan (Anti-Mason): Book by Clyde S. Kilby, *Minority of One,* 1959.

Boaz, Hiram Abiff: Cal. Free., Autumn, 1972, 165. 7 RAM 254 (1962).

Bolivar, Simon: 6 RAM 118 (1958). Ind. Free., Sept., 1959, 4. New Age Mag., Nov., 1966, 13; July, 1960, 45; Feb., 1952, 97.

Boone, Daniel: 11 Build. Mag. 31 (1925).

Booth, Edwin: 1 Build. Mag. 99 (1915). Phil. Mag, Oct. 1964, 75. Mast. Mas. Mag., April, 1925, 309. New Age Mag., June, 1959, 389.

Booth, H. C.: 64 AQC 2 (1953); 75 AQC 75 (1962).

Borglum, Gutzon: Mast. Mas. Mag., Feb., 1925, 103; has his picture.

Borgnine, Ernest: New Age Mag., July, 1956, 422.

Boswell, James: 79 AQC 90 (1966). New Age Mag., Feb., 1975, 32.

Bradley, Herbert: 34 AQC 10 (1921); 36 AQC 148 (1923).

Bradley, Preston: K. T. Mag., Jan., 1972, 22. *Along the Way,* by Harry Barnard; 1962; 280 pp.

Brant, Joseph: New Age Mag., Sept., 1959, 487. K. T. Mag., Nov., 1977, 5.

Breckinridge, John Cabell: K. T. Mag., May, 1976, 9; Feb., 1978, 19.

Bristowe, H. C.: 58 AQC 126 (1945).

Broek, Renier Jan Vanden: 3 ALR 649 (1941-1942).

Brown, Buster: K. T. Mag., March, 1973, 19.

Brown, Jacob: 11 ALR 222 (1933).

Brown, Moses: 5 ALR 62 (1947-1948).

Brown, Dr. William Moseley: See Appendix No. 2.

Browne, John Mills: Cal. Free., Summer, 1976, 117.

Brownson, Nathan: New Age Mag., May, 1978, 29.

Bruce, Eli: Book by Rob Morris, *The Biography of Eli Bruce;* 1861; 312 pp.

Brucker, Wilbur M.: K. T. Mag., 13; Sept., 1974, 28. 8 RAM 99 (1964); has his picture. 9 RAM 241 (1968). 11 RAM 260 (1970).

Bryan, William Jennings: K. T. Mag., April, 1976, 13.

Buck, J. D.: 3 Build. Mag. 46 (1917).

Bulkeley, Eliphalet: K. T. Mag., Feb., 1979, 25.

Burbank, Luther: 9 Build. Mag. 350 (1923). Phil. Mag., Dec., 1947, 6. New Age Mag., March, 1975, 18.

Burns, Robert: New Age Mag., Jan., 1975, 38. New Age Mag., Jan., 1977, 20. Altar Light, July-Aug., 1977. STB, June, 1923. 14 Build. Mag. 9 (1928). 5 AQC 46 (1892). 2 Build. Mag. 3 (1916). 6 Build. Mag. 190 (1920). Ind. Free., Jan., 1954, 6. 1 RAM 102 (1943); 3 RAM 3 (1949). William Harvey, *Robert Burns as a Freemason;* 1921; 92 pp. T. M. Sparks, London & Glasgow, publisher.

Burr, Aaron: 5 ALR 365 (1947-1948).

Burton, Sir Richard: Mas. Sq., Dec., 1977, 164.

Bushnell, George E.: 8 RAM 233 (1965).

Butterfield, Gen. Daniel Adams: 6 ALR 424 (1962).

Bywater, W. M.: 3 AQC 182 (1890); 23 AQC 66 (1911).

Byrd, Richard E.: K. T. Mag., Aug., 1974, 7.

Cagliostro: 16 Build. Mag., 71, 109, 130 (1930). 40 AQC 45 (1927). New Age Mag. articles: May, 1919, 215; June, 1919, 265; July, 1919, 314; Aug. 1919, 368. Francois R. Dumas, *Cagliostro;* 1967; 308 pp. Orion Press, N.Y.; reviewed in: 79 AQC 255; 80 AQC 289; New Age Mag., June, 1971, 58. Phil. Mag., Aug., 1965. W. R. H. Trowbridge, *Cagliostro,* 307 pp. Libraries: 3, 5, 7, 9, 11, 12, 14.

Calvert, Albert Frederick: Phil. Mag., Nov., 1946, 9.

Cameron, Simon: K. T. Mag., March, 1978, 19.

Carles, Abbee Antoine: Cal. Free., Summer, 1972, 132.

Carr, Harry: See Appendix No. 3.

Carson, Kit: K. T. Mag., Nov., 1976, 9. 8 Build. Mag. 366 (1922). Mast. Mas., Dec., 1926, 1056. New Age Mag., April, 1967, 47; Sept., 1971, 29.

Carter, Dr. James D.: See Appendix No. 4.

Carter, T. M.: 43 AQC 49 (1930).

Cartwright, Alexander Joy: 7 RAM 210 (1962).

Cartwright, E. H.: 66 AQC 40 (1953).

Case, James R.: See Appendix No. 5.

Cass, Lewis: Phil. Mag., Aug.-Sept., 1950, 5. New Age Mag., Feb., 1972, 25. The Masonic World, Detroit, Nov., 1972, 5.

Cerneau, Joseph: 8 Build. Mag., 60 (1920).

Cerza, Alphonse: Altar Light, Jan.-Feb., 1979. Phil. Mag., Oct., 1964, 6 ALR 276 (1952-1953).

Chakrabongse, Prince Chula: 8 RAM 375 (1966); has his picture.

Chang: 12 AQC 106 (1899).

Cherubini, Luigi: K. T. Mag., Sept., 1974, 19.

Chesterfield, Lord: Phil. Mag., April, 1971, 38. 4 Trans. Phoe. L. (Paris), 29.

Chivington, John Milton: Phil. Mag., Dec., 1948, 8. Reginald S. Craig, *The Fighting Parson:* 1959; 278 pp. Copy in Iowa Masonic Library.

Chu, Shi-Ming: 8 RAM 280 (1936).

Churchill, Winston: Phil. Mag., Feb., 1971, 5. K. T. Mag., 1974, 29. Harry Carr, *The Freemason at Work,* p. 151.

Clark, George Rogers: Ind. Free., Dec., 1977, 8. New Age Mag., 1979, 20.

Clark, Gen. Mark W.: 9 RAM 282 (1969).

Clark, Gen. William: 1942 Trans. MLR 40.

Clarke, Bascombe: 15 Build. Mag. 118 (1929).

Clarke, Casper: 11 AQC 215 (1898); 24 AQC 118 (1911).

Claret, George: 87 AQC 1 (1974).

Clay, Henry: Phil. Mag., Dec., 1973, 108. 13 Build. Mag. 223 (1926).

Claudy, Carl H.: See Appendix No. 6.

Clegg, Robert Ingham: Ia. Grd. L. Bulletin, Feb., 1926, 56; has his picture. 14 Build. Mag. 40 (1929). Ill. Enlight., May, 1955, 47.

Clinton, De Witt: 1 ALR 87 (1930-1932). 2 ALR 551 (1936-1938). 14 Build. Mag., 261 (1928); has his picture. 2 RAM 335 (1948), has his picture. K. T. Mag., July, 1973, 25. New Age Mag., March, 1953, 153.

Clinton, Henry: Ind. Free., May, 1977, 13.

Clinton, James: Ind. Free., Sept., 1974, 16.

Coburn, Charles: 5 RAM 341 (1957).

Cody, William (Buffalo Bill): 7 RAM 154 (1962). Trans. MLR, 1945, 8. Phil. Mag., July-Aug., 1968, 67. 6 Build. Mag., 198 (1920).

Coffey, Rich: Tex. Free., Nov., 1971, 13; Jan., 1972, 27.

Cole, Thomas: K. T. Mag., Feb., 1978, 21.

Coil, Sr., Henry W.: See Appendix No. 8.

Collins, Ray Bidwell: 8 RAM 220 (1965).

Colt, Samuel: K. T. Mag., Oct., 1973, 25.

Conder, Edward: 13 AQC 184 (1900). 48 AQC 172 (1934).

Cook, Wes: See Appendix No. 9.

Coontz, Robert Edward: New Age Mag., Dec., 1977, 42.

Cooper, James Fenimore: 7 RAM 221 (1962); not a Mason.

Corcoran, William Wilson: 5 ALR 170 (1947-1948).

Corwin, Thomas: K. T. Mag., Dec., 1977, 21; has his picture.

Cowles, John H.: New Age Mag., Jan., 1976, 12. 40th Ann. Celebration; 1948; 92 pp., published by the Supreme Council, S.J.

Cox, Allyn: 5 RAM 68 (1955).

Coxe, Daniel: 10 Build. Mag. 328, 368 (1924). 11 Build. Mag. 200 (1925). No. Light, Jan., 1972, 4; has his picture.

Craig, James Edward: 9 ALR 182 (1964); has his picture. 11 ALR 188 (1974).

Crawley, F. J. W. Chetwode: 2 Build. Mag. 217, 281 (1916). 11 Build. Mag. 140 (1925); has his picture. 22 AQC 198 (1909); 44 AQC 130 (1931).

Crockett, David: Ind. Free., May, 1955, 8.

Cromwell, Oliver: 21 AQC 181 (1908).

Cross, Jeremy Cross: K. T. Mag., Aug., 1976, 19. No. Light, June, 1974, 14.

Crossle, Philip: Phil. Mag., Oct., 1954, 10.

Crothers, George E.: New Age Mag., March, 1977, 16.

Crudeli, Tommaso: 58 AQC 4 (1945).

Cummings, Dr. William J.: Phil. Mag., Aug., 1966, 69.

Cunningham, John D.: Phil. Mag., Oct., 1977, 3.

Dallas, George Mifflin: New Age Mag., Jan., 1977, 48.

Dana, James Freeman: K. T. Mag., Oct., 1978, 9.

Dante: *Rivista Massonica*, in Italian, June, 1972, 357.

Darwin, Erasmus: Master Mason, grandfather of Charles; Cal. Free. Summer, 1976, 106.

Davies, Joseph Hamilton: New Age, May, 1956, 283. Phil. Mag., June, 1975, 69.

D'Alviela, Goblet: 38 AQC 223 (1925).

Dashwood, J. R.: 69 AQC 9 (1956); 74 AQC 87 (1961).

Davis, Jefferson: 11 Build. Mag. 174 (1925). 3 RAM 251 (1950).

Day, David Fisher: 10 ALR 97 (1966).

Dayton, Elias: Ind. Free., Oct., 1974, 12.

Daynes, Gilbert Williams: 43 AQC 253 (1930); 44 AQC 67 (1931). 11 Build. Mag. 47 (1921); 14 Build. Mag. 47 (1925); both have his picture.

Dean, Paul: 2 RAM 184 (1947).

Decatur, Stephen: K. T. Mag., Jan., 1975, 6. 5 RAM 305 (1957). Ind. Free., March, 1955, 12.

De Grasse, Auguste: New Age Mag., May, 1970, 19, 40.

Dearborn, Henry: No. Light, Sept., 1973, 4.

De Kalb, Major General: New Age Mag., Jan., 1933, 34. N.Y. Mas. Outl., March, 1926, 204.

Del Ruth, Roy: Cal. Free., Winter, 1974, 40.

De Lafontaine, H. T. C.: 42 AQC 308 (1929); 51 AQC 2 (1938).

DeMolay: H. L. Haywood, *Life and Times of Jacques DeMolay;* 1925; 54 pp. National Masonic Research Society, publisher. Libraries: 1, 3, 4, 5, 7, 8, 9, 12, 13, 14. 8 RAM 339 (1966). 2 Build. Mag. 163, 329, 355 (1916). 91 AQC 56 (1979).

Denslow, Ray V.: See Appendix No. 10.

Denslow, William R.: See Appendix No. 11.

D'Eon, Chevalier: Mast. Mas., Aug., 1928, 503. New Age. Mag., Jan., 1919, 7. 17 AQC 63 (1904); 16 AQC 231 (1903). Mas. Sq., June, 1976, 50.

Depew, Chauncey: N.Y. Mas. Outl., April, 1927, 240.

Derby, George Horatio: Cal. Free., Autumn, 1977, 179; Winter, 1977, 34.

Desaguliers, John Theophilus: 25 AQC 278 (1912). 38 AQC 285 (1925). 40 AQC 170 (1927). 78 AQC 130 (1965). STB, May, 1936. Ill. Enlight., June, 1953, 6. 9 Build. Mag. 86 (1923).

Dick, Elisha Cullen: 4 ALR 132 (1942-1944).

Dickinson, John: New Age Mag., Dec., 1979, 22.

Dickson, Joseph: Phil. Mag., April, 1961, 23.

Dirksen, Everett M.: New Age Mag., Feb., 1970, 47.

Dixon, John: 5 ALR 83 (1957).

Dodd, William: 19 AQC 181 (1906). 20 AQC 352 (1907). No. Cal. Res. L. Quarterly J., March, 1975, 1.

Do-Ne-Ho-Ga-Wa: 12 RAM 235 (1978-1979), has his picture. See Ely S. Parker, below.

Doolittle, Amos: STB, Sept., 1936. Ind. Free., Dec., 1958, 10; has his picture. Ill. Enlight., March, 1951, 2. New Age Mag., April, 1960, 54. K. T. Mag., May, 1979, 13.

Doolittle, Jimmy: New Age Mag., Dec., 1976, 44.

Douglas, Stephen A.: Phil. Mag., Feb., 1958, 8. Ind. Free., March, 1960, 12. 3 Norcalore 135 (1933).

Doyle, Arthur Conan: 15 AQC 27 (1902).

Dow, Lorenzo: New Age Mag., May, 1955, 297.

Draffen, George S.: 71 AQC 8 (1958). 79 AQC 12 (1966).

Drayton, John: 4 ALR 604 (1946-1947).

Dring, E. H.: 25 AQC 384 (1912); 41 AQC 286 (1928).

Drummond, George: 1968 Grd. L. Scot Yrbk. 93.

Drummond, Josiah Hayden: 9 Build. Mag. 137 (1923). STB, Oct., 1964. 1 RAM 360 (1945), has his picture. 10 AQC 165 (1897). 16 AQC 105 (1903).

Drummond, Malanzo J.: 10 ALR 90 (1966).

Duke of Lorraine: 37 AQC 107 (1924). 76 AQC 44 (1963).

Duke of Sussex: Mas. Sq., June, 1977, 66.

Duke of Wharton: 89 AQC 273 (1977).

Dunckerley, Thomas: Henry Sadler, *Thomas Dunckerley, His Life, Labours, and Letters;* 1891; 310 pp. H. L. Haywood, Masonic Essays, 83. 30 AQC 125 (1917). 18 AQC 43 (1905). 56 AQC 138 (1943). 57 AQC 264 (1944). 78 AQC 130 (1956). 7 AQC 52 (1894). 56 AQC 59 (1943). 45 AQC 104 (1932). 5 ALR 370 (1947-1948). 4 RAM 109 (1952).

Dunlap, John: No. Light, Sept., 1975, 4.

Dyas, Joseph E.: 2 RAM 269 (1948).

Eaton, Gen. William: N.Y. Mas. Outl., Aug., 1925, 270. 10 ALR 20 (1966).

Edward VII: 91 AQC 225 (1979).

Edwards, Lewis: 54 AQC 226 (1941).

Elbert, Samuel: Mas. Mess., Ga., Sept., 1977, 15. New Age Mag., Aug., 1978, 46.

Ellery, William: New Age, May, 1975, 49. Ind. Free., Dec., 1973, 24.

Ellis, Tom Q.: 10 RAM 201 (1971), has his picture.

Emmerson, Henry: 9 ALR 15 (1963).

Engle, Willis Darwin: H. V. B. Voorhis, The Eastern Star, 92-94, 127-128 (1976 ed.)

Erikson, Jerry R.: Phil. Mag., June, 1963, 45.

Farragut, David Glasgow: K. T. Mag., July, 1976, 5. New Age Mag., Dec., 1954, 735. Ind. Free., Feb., 1955, 7. 2 ALR 543 (1936-1937).

Fenton, S. J.: 51 AQC 221 (1938). 65 AQC 96 (1952).

Fey, Charles: Phil. Mag., Aug.-Sept., 1950, 5; Dec., 1950, 1, 10, has his picture.

Field, Robert: 5 ALR 172 (1947-1948).

Field, Stephen J.: K. T. Mag., Aug., 1975, 23.

Fierer, Charles Frederick: 4 ALR 601 (1946-1947).

Firminger, W. K.: 46 AQC 448 (1933). 53 AQC 45 (1940).

Fisher, W. G.: 80 AQC 240 (1967).

Fitzgerald, John: Ind. Free., Oct., 1977, 17.

Flather, David: 45 AQC 309 (1932). 61 AQC 115 (1948).

Fleming, Sir Alexander: New Age Mag., March, 1972, 10. Ind. Free., May, 1958, 8.

Florence, William Jermyn: Alexander Ureland, *Shriner and Humanitarian,* 1958; 86 pp. Christopher Publishing Co., Boston, publisher. 2 Build. Mag. 242, 286, 350 (1916).

Folkes, Martin: 8 Build. Mag. 108 (1922). Mast. Mas., Dec., 1924, 850.

Ford, Henry: Ind. Free., April, 1958, 4.

Fort, George Franklin: 11 ALR 259 (1970).

Foster, Stephen: 2 RAM 29 (1946).

Franchot, Paschal: 5 ALR 173 (1947-1948).

Francken, Henry Andrew: 3 ALR 159 (1938-1939).

Franklin, Benjamin: Julius F. Sachse, *Benjamin Franklin as a Freemason;* 1906; 15 pp. STB, Oct., 1933. STB, Jan., 1974. K. T. Mag., Jan., 1974, 13. Ind. Free., Jan., 1974. No. Light, April, 1975, 20. New Age Mag., Feb., 1923, 106; Jan., 1963, 15. 41 AQC 3 (1928). 11 ALR 77 (1969). 9 ALR 431 (1965). 10 ALR 89 (1966). 5 RAM 296 (1957). 9 RAM 296 (1957). 10 RAM 205 (1971).

Frederick the Great: New Age Mag., Oct., 1930, 589; Dec., 1912, 568; Jan., 1912, 25, Feb., 1913, 137. 10 AQC 188 (1897). 11 AQC 168, 199 (1898). 7 Build. Mag. 211 (1920). 13 Build. Mag. 41 (1927). 13 Build. Mag. 7, 225 (1927). 12 Build. Mag. 294, 333 (1926). 3 RAM 69 (1949).

French, Benjamin Brown: New Age Mag., Sept., 1953, 549.

French, Dr. George H. T.: 11 Trans. Tex. L. Res. 184 (1975-1976).

Frizzell, John: 2 RAM 25 (1946).

Frye, Joseph: Ind. Free., Nov., 1974, 20.

Gaine, H.: 3 ALR 11 (1938-1939).

Gamble, Hamilton R.: 1945 MLR Trans. 135, 945.

Garibaldi, Giuseppe: Detailed biography by Carol W. Masterman; appeared in instalments in the New Age Magazine, starting in May 1908 and continuing for several years. New Age Mag., Feb., 1933, 89; March, 1960, 40; March, 1970, 43. 11 ALR 241 (1974). Ind. Free., April, 1959, 8. 2 RAM 248 (1947).

Ghirardelli, Domenico: Cal. Free., Summer, 1978, 107.

Gibbon, Edward: 10 Build. Mag. 287 (1924). 17 AQC 22 (1904).

Gilbert, William Schwenck: 66 AQC 104 (1953).

Gilkes, Peter: 84 AQC 260 (1916). Albert F. Calvert, *Peter Gilkes, 1765-1833*, 1916; 35 pp.

Gilman, Charles: 2 RAM 242 (1947).

Girard, Stephen: 9 Build. Mag. 54, 61 (1923). New Age Mag., Nov., 1959, 621. N.Y. Mas. Out., March, 1928, 199. 1 Trans. Res. L. of Ore., 313, K. T. Mag., May, 1977, 11.

Gist, Mordecai: Ind. Free, Dec., 1974, 11.

Givan, Noah M.: Ind. Free., Sept., 1972, 31.

Glass, William: New Age Mag., Dec., 1975, 14.

Glover, John: Ind. Free., Jan., 1975, 15.

Godfrey, Arthur: 7 RAM 156 (1962).

Goethe: N.Y. Mas. Outl. March, 1930, 199. 9 Build. Mag. 259 (1923). STB, Sept., 1932. Mast. Mas., Sept., 1928, 597. Phil. Mag., Jan., 1951, 6. New Age Mag., June, 1908, 548. Cal. Free., Summer, 1972, 129.

Golby, F. W.: 50 AQC 218 (1937); 56 AQC 205 (1943).

Goldwater, Barry: New Age Mag., Oct., 1964, 10.

Gompers, Samuel: K. T. Mag., Jan., 1979, 23.

Gosnell, Charles F.: 10 ALR 176 (1967); has his picture.

Gourgas, John James Joseph: J. Hugo Tatsch, *John James Joseph Gourgas, 1777-1865;* 1938; 68 pp. Originally published in Sup. C. Proc., NMJ. Reviewed in 48 AQC 200 (1939). No. Light, Sept., 1970, 4.

Gould, Robert Freke: See Appendix No. 12.

Gowan, Robert: 7 RAM 332 (1963).

Grantham, W. T.: 55 AQC 338 (1942).

Grant, Melville R.: New Age Mag., Jan., 1933, 9.

Gray, Harold Lincoln: 6 RAM 74 (1958). 9 RAM 181 (1968).

Greaton, John: Ind. Free., Feb., 1975, 16.

Greenberg, Dr. Stephen R.: See Appendix No. 13.

Greene, Nathaniel: 12 Build. Mag. 139 (1926).

Gregg, Gen. John: K. T. Mag., Oct., 1978, 11.

Gridley, Col. Richard: No. Light, Nov., 1977, 14.

Grofe, Ferde: New Age Mag., July, 1977, 26.

Guest, Edgar A.: K. T. Mag., Aug., 1977, 5. Ind. Free., Sept., 1959; has his picture.

Guion, Isaac: New Age Mag., June, 1953, 353.

Hahn, Conrad: See Appendix No. 15.

Hale, Nathan: Not a Mason; No. Light, Sept., 1972, 9. Ind. Free., Nov., 1972, 6.

Hallett, E. H.: 62 AQC 30 (1949); 66 AQC 67 (1953).

Halliwell-Phillips: Phil. Mag., Feb., 1976, 23.

Hamilton, Alexander: Not a Mason; 12 RAM 371 (1978).

Hamilton, James R.: 6 ALR 52 (1952-1953). Ind. Free., April, 1972, 6.

Hamtramck, Col. John Francis: 12 ALR 101 (1972).

Hancock, John: Ind. Free., Feb., 1974, 12; April, 1955, 10. New Age Mag., June, 1975, 48, Feb., 1960, 19, Sept., 1954, 553. No. Light, June, 1975, 10. K. T. Mag., Aug., 1976, 7. 12 RAM 105 (1976-1977).

Hancock, Winfield Scott: K. T. Mag., Feb., 1977, 19.

Haggard, Rev. Forrest: See Appendix No. 14.

Hand, Dr. Edward: Ind. Free., March, 1975, 30.

Harned, Harold H.: Phil. Mag., April, 1978, 23.

Harison, George: 8 ALR 285 (1961).

Harper, Thomas: 18 AQC 147 (1905). 84 AQC 177 (1971).

Harris, Ray Baker: Phil. Mag., June, 1964, 50. New Age Mag., June, 1963, 21.

Harris, Reginald V.: Phil. Mag., Oct., 1968, 89. 14 Build. Mag. 47 (1929); has his picture.

Hatfield, Mark O.: 9 RAM 227 (1968); has his picture. 10 RAM 10 (1970).

Haunch, T. O.: Mas. Mess., Ga., Aug., 1974, 16; has his picture.

Haupt, Henry L.: Cal. Free., Autumn, 1972, 166.

Hawkins, E. L.: 26 AQC 88 (1912).

Haydon, N. W. J.: 14 Build. Mag. 40; has his picture.

Hays, Moses Michael: No. Light, Sept., 1977, 76.

Haywood, Harry Leroy: See Appendix No. 16.

Heaton, Ronald E.: See Appendix No. 17.

Heaton, W. E.: 60 AQC 204 (1947); 70 AQC 32 (1952).

Hedblom, Edward E.: Phil. Mag., June, 1964, 52.

Heiron, Arthur: 44 AQC 130 (1931).

Hemming, Rev. Samuel: 86 AQC 147, 152, 168, 258, 266, 320 (1973).

Hextall, W. B.: 27 AQC 228 (1914); 36 AQC 146 (1923).

Hepburn, Ross: See Appendix No. 18.

Hogan, Dr. Mervin B.: See Appendix No. 19.

Hoban, James: K. T. Mag., April, 1978, 5.

Hobart, Garrett Augustus: 3 ALR 243 (1939-1940).

Hobbs, J. W.: 42 AQC 69 (1929).

Hoe, Sang Mun: 5 RAM 140 (1956).

Hogarth, William: 77 AQC 1 (1964). 21 AQC 230 (1908). 23 AQC 334 (1910). 2 AQC 146. MSA Digest. 9 Build. Mag. 67 (1923).

Hogun, James: Ind. Free., April, 1975, 21.

Holbrook, Dr. Moses: New Age Mag., Feb., 1960, 15. K. T. Mag., Dec., 1979. (Note: picture shown is that of Gourgas, not of Holbrook).

Holme, Randle: 42 AQC 312 (1929).

Holland, Floyd: New Age Mag., Feb., 1977, 26.

Holland, John Henry: Phil. Mag., Oct., 1977, 8.

Holmes, William: 4 ALR 606 (1946-1947).

Hooper, William: Ind. Free., April, 1974, 14.

Hoover, J. Edgar: Phil. Mag., Aug., 1972, 68. No. Light., Sept., 1971, 8, has his picture.

Hornby, John: 39 AQC 107 (1926).

Horne, Alex: See Appendix No. 20.

Horsley, J. W.: 17 AQC 227 (1904); 35 AQC 2 (1922).

Houdini, Harry: Ind. Free., June, 1977, 6. Mast. Mas., April, 1926, 293, has his picture. K. T. Mag. April, 1978, 9. N.Y. Mas. Outl., March 1927, 206. New Age Mag., March, 1976, 41.

Sam Houston: Ind. Free., June, 1955. New Age Mag., Feb., 1905, 213; has his picture. 3 Trans. Tex. L. of Res. 317 (1965-1968). K. T. Mag, March, 1975, 7.

Howe, Robert: New Age Mag., March, 1978, 24.

Howland, Humphrey: 5 ALR 367 (1947-1948).

Hughan, William J.: See Appendix No. 21.

Humphrey, Hubert: K. T. Mag., Feb., 1978, 27.

Humphreys, David: K. T. Mag., Feb., 1978, 27.

Hunt, Bruce: See Appendix No. 22.

Hunt, Charles Clyde: 14 Build. Mag. 41 (1928); has his picture. Phil. Mag., Nov., 1946, 1, has his picture; Oct., 1948, 5.

Hunter, Andrew: 13 RAM 119 (1979).

Hutchinson, William: New Age Mag., Oct., 1904, 381.

Hyslop, Wellwood: 89 AQC 92 (1977).

Irving Brothers: 7 ALR 130 (1958).

Irvin, Capt. Francis George: 6 AQC 167 (1893); 85 AQC 251 (1972).

Ivanoff, Boris: 53 AQC 327 (1940); 71 AQC 27 (1958).

Jackling, Daniel C.: 5 RAM 46 (1955).

James, Percival Rowland: 80 AQC 6 (1907).

Jefferson, Thomas: Ind. Free., May, 1976, 10.

Jenner, Edward: New Age Mag., March, 1978, 46.

Jesus Christ: 9 RAM 49 (1967).

Joffre, General: 7 Build Mag. 229 (1921).

Johnson, C. Y.: 58 AQC 288 (1945); 79 AQC 11 (1966); 80 AQC 239 (1967).

Johnson, Melvin M.: Phil. Mag., April, 1958, 18, 21.

Johnson, Sir William: New Age Mag., Jan., 1955, 41.

Johnson, Samuel: 9 Build. Mag. 10, 46, 71, 109 (1923); 10 Build. Mag. 207 (1924).

Jones, Dr. Anson: 3 Trans. Tex. L. of Res. 501 (1965-1968); 14 Trans. Tex. L. of Res. 179 (1978-1979). Herbert Gambrell, *Anson Jones, The Last President of Texas*, 1947, 1964; 440 pp. University of Texas, publisher.

Jones, Bernard E.: 74 AQC 9 (1961); 78 AQC 146 (1965).

Jones, John Paul: K. T. Mag., July, 1975, 7. No. Light, Sept., 1975, 8. *The Final Voyage of Admiral John Paul Jones*, Proc. of Dist. of Col.; reproduced in 1974 by the Iowa L. of Res. 5 RAM 366 (1957).

Juarez, Benito: 5 RAM 75 (1955).

Kahanamoku: 9 RAM 150 (1968), has his picture.

Kalakaua, King: 3 RAM 345 (1951). Phil. Mag., April, 1962, 26.

Kamatoy, Dr. Roman: Cal. Free., Summer, 1976, 127.

Kane, Elisha Kent: Cal. Free., Autumn, 1978, 173. New Age Mag., Feb., 1978, 44. Ind. Free., Feb., 1959. 3 Build. Mag. 83 (1917).

Keith, Marshall James: New Age Mag., Dec., 1966, 47.

Kendall, Dr. Albert A.: No. Light, Sept., 1979, 8.

Kennedy, Charles Rann: N.Y. Mas. Outl., Dec., 1927, 108; has his picture.

Kent, Harold W.: K. T. Mag., March, 1975, 13.

Kern, Dr. Richard A.: 1966 Proc. Sup. C., NMJ, 241.

Kerr, William T.: K. T. Mag., June, 1978, 5.

Key, William Scott: 8 Build. Mag. 355 (1922).

King, Karl L.: 7 RAM 275 (1963); has his picture.

King, William Rufus: New Age Mag., Dec., 1925, 739.

Kipling, Rudyard: K. T. Mag., Dec., 1976, 7. New Age Mag., May, 1953, 285, 1954. Proc. Midw. Conf. 81. Phil. Mag., Aug., 1975, 78. STB, Oct., 1964. 8 RAM 310 (1966). 77 AQC 213 (1964); 78 AQC 207 (1965).

Kirby, Ephraim: K.T. Mag., Aug., 1973, 19. 3 RAM 17 (1949). Brochure published in 1972 by the Grand Chapter of Conn.

Kirkland, Samuel: N.Y. Mas. Out., May, 1928, 268. 4 ALR 615 (1946-1947).

Kirtland, Turnhan: 12 Build. Mag. 9 (1926).

Klein, S. T.: 10 AQC 207 (1890); 47 AQC 249 (1934).

Kleinknecht, C. F. Sr.: New Age Mag., March, 1969, 16.

Knocker, G. S.: 65 AQC 82 (1952).

Knoop, Douglas: 48 AQC 300 (1935); 62 AQC 2 (1949).

Knox, Henry: Ind. Free., May, 1975, 20. 12 ALR 88 (1972). No. Light, June, 1976, 8. K. T. Mag., Nov., 1976, 21. Phil. Mag., June, 1974, 60.

Kossuth, Louis: 8 Build. Mag. 78 (1922). 4 RAM 57 (1952).

Kresge, Floyd L.: Ind. Free., Feb., 1973, 10.

Kress, A. L.: 14 Build. Mag. 46 (1929); has his picture.

Kuck, Johnny: N.Y. Mas. Out., Oct., 1928, 47.

Lafayette: No. Light, June, 1977, 4, 6, 8. Ind. Free., June, 1975, 21. Phil. Mag., Feb., 1973, 18. STB, July, 1928. STB, April, 1934. 3 RAM 71 (1949). 2 ALR 25, 309 (1934-1935).

Land, Frank S.: Herbert Ewing Duncan, *Hi . . . Dad!*, 1970; 168 pp. MLR, publisher. Reviewed in New Age Mag., Aug., 1971, 56. Ind. Free., Feb., 1976, 18.

Lane, John: 13 AQC 41 (1900).

Lassen, "Uncle Pete": New Age Mag., April, 1977, 10; and Jan., 1957, 49.

Lauck, Chester: 10 RAM 213 (1971).

Laurens, Henry: New Age Mag., Oct., 1927, 64.

Lavender, Don: New Age Mag., Feb., 1977, 48.

Lawrie, Wilfred Theodore: 5 RAM 72 (1955).

Le Jeune, John A.: K. T. Mag., Feb., 1977, 9.

Lemert, R. J.: 15 Build. Mag. 142, 149 (1929).

Le Page, Marius: Phil. Mag., Aug., 1972, 71.

Lepper, J. H.: 37 AQC 303 (1924); 66 AQC 9 (1933).

Lessing, Gotthold: 88 AQC 98 (1975).

Le Strange, Hannon: 19 AQC 236 (1906); 31 AQC 66 (1918).

Levander, F. W.: 29 AQC 382 (1916); 30 AQC 2 (1917).

Lewis, John L.: 2 RAM 24 (1946). 7 RAM 331 (1962). 9 RAM 329 (1969).

Lewis, Meriwether: 5 RAM 19 (1955).

Lewis, T. N.: 5 AQC 222 (1892); 12 AQC 4 (1899).

Lewis, Morgan: 1 Trans. MLR 131 (1930-1931). 1 ALR 243 (1930-1931). 7 ALR 163 (1958).

Lichliter, M. M.: Phil. Mag., April, 1961, 21, 27; has his picture.

Light, Elias: 8 ALR 280 (1961).

Lincoln, Abraham: 3 Build. Mag. 93 (1917). 10 Build. Mag. 361 (1924). Ill. Enlight., Feb., 1952, 3. No. Light, Jan., 1971, 14. Ind. Free., Feb., 1952, 14. 6 RAM 345 (1960). 1 Trans. Ill. L. of Res. 79. Phil. Mag., Feb., 1978, 8.

Lincoln, Benjamin: Ind. Free., July, 1975, 20.

Lindbergh, Charles A.: New Age Mag., May, 1976, 50; Feb., 1975, 48. K. T. Mag., May, 1974, 7. Altar Light, May-June, 1977.

Little, R. W.: 85 AQC 250 (1972).

Livingston, Edward: 2 RAM 149 (1947); has his picture. Mast. Mas., Nov., 1924, 711. 11 ALR 217 (1970).

Lloyd, Harold C.: 10 RAM 212 (1971).

Lobingier, Charles S.: New Age Mag.,

May, 1978, 37, has his picture. Phil. Mag., Aug., 1972, 73.

Locke, John: 78 AQC 168 (1965).

Logan, John A.: K. T. Mag., June, 1974, 11; Phil. Mag., Oct., 1978, 10.

Luckner, Count Felix Von: 8 RAM 308 (1966); has his picture.

Luther, Martin: 7 Build. Mag. 238 (1921).

MacArthur, Gen. Douglas: K. T. Mag., Jan., 1976, 9. K. T. Mag., Feb., 1976, 14. New Age Mag., Nov. 1976, 9. No. Light, Nov., 1977, 4. 8 RAM 35 (1964).

Mac Bean, Edward: 8 AQC 250 (1895); 32 AQC 145 (1919).

MacDonald, Sir Alexander: 12 RAM 173 (1977).

Macfadden, Bernar: 9 RAM 269 (1969).

Mackey, Albert G.: See Appendix No. 23.

Major, John: Ind. Free., April, 1972, 10; has his picture.

Malczovich, Ladislas: 44 AQC 130 (1931).

Malotte, Albert Hay: New Age Mag., Sept., 1976, 42. 8 RAM 126 (1964).

Markham, Edwin: Phil. Mag., Aug., 1957, 58. New Age Mag., April, 1971, 11.2 Build. Mag. 118 (1916).

Marsengill, Jerry: See Appendix No. 24.

Marshall, John: K. T. Mag., July, 1975, 21. STB, July, 1955.

Marshall, Thomas R.: K. T. Mag., July, 1976, 11. 11 Build. Mag. 246, 320 (1925). Ind. Free., Feb., 1959, 9.

Marshall, William: K. T. Mag., Dec., 1979, 25.

Mavrick, Samuel: 10 ALR 380 (1968).

Maughan, Col. Russell L.: New Age Mag., May, 1977, 20.

Maxwell, William: Ind. Free., Aug., 1975, 19.
Mazzini, Giuseppe: 10 RAM 155 (1971).

McBride, Priestly: Trans. MLR, 1943, 141.

McClurg, Dr. James: New Age. Mag., Aug., 1961, 17.

McHenry, James: Ind. Free., June, 1977, 15.

McKane, Allen: Cal. Free., Summer, 1974, 121.

McClellan, Gen. Geo.: K. T. Mag., Oct., 1978, 11.

McLoughlin, Emmett J.: 7 RAM 317 (1960). 10 RAM 186 (1971).

Meekren Robert J.: Ind. Free., April, 1953, 12. 11 Build. Mag. 256 (1925). 14 Build. Mag. 45; has his picture. Phil. Mag., June, 1964, 51. 76 AQC 160 (1963).

Meigs, Jonathan: K. T. Mag., Feb., 1976, 19. New Age Mag., March, 1977, 53.

Mellon, Andrew W.: N.Y. Mas. Outl., March, 1929, 202.

Mellor, Alec: Phil. Mag., Oct., 1972, 96.

Mercer, Hugh: New Age Mag., Dec., 1976, 17. Va. Mas. Herald, June, 1978, 4, has his picture. N.Y. Mas. Outl., Feb., 1925, 122.

Milborne, Alfred John Bidder: 10 ALR 232 (1968); has his picture. 88 AQC 222 (1976).

Miles, Nelson A.: Cal. Free., March, 1979, 63; has his picture.

Mitchell, J. W. S.: Trans. MLR, 1950, 121. New Age Mag., Oct., 1973, 12.

Mix, Tom: 4 RAM 263 (1954). Ind. Free., May, 1957, 14. Mast. Mas., April, 1926, 360; has his picture. New Age Mag., Nov., 1972, 48.

Montesquieu: 5 ALR 176 (1947-1948). 11 RAM 270 (1975).

Montfort, Joseph: 4 RAM 14 (1952).

Moody, James: 2 ALR 338 (1936).

Moore, Charles Whitmore: *A Printer From Boston;* published by the Mass. Chapter of Research.

Montgomery, Richard: Ind. Free., Oct., 1975, 23.

Morcombe, Joseph Edgerton: 14 Build. Mag. 41 (1929); has his picture.

Morgan, John Hunt: 2 RAM 261 (1948).

Morin, Stephen: 11 Build. Mag. 257 (1925). 14 Build. Mag. 293 (1928). New Age Mag., Sept., 1926, 536; Oct., 1926, 605.

Morris, Rob: See Appendix No. 25.

Morse, John: 5 ALR 288 (1947-1948). 6 ALR 54 (1952-1953).

Morton, Jacob: K. T. Mag., Oct., 1974, 23. Empire St. Mas., Feb., 1979, 2, has his picture.

Muhlenberg, John P. G.: No. Light, Nov., 1975, 8. Ind. Free., Nov., 1975, 14. New Age Mag, July, 1979, 41.

Murphy, Audie: Harold B. Simpson, *American Soldier;* 466 pp. published by Hill Junior College Press, Hillsboro, Texas, in 1975. Phil. Mag., 1971, 80; Dec., 1971, 112.

Naismith, Dr. James: New Age Mag., June, 1972, 28. Ind. Free., Feb., 1973, 12.

Napoleon: 8 AQC 188 (1895); 27 AQC 96 (1914). 10 Build. Mag., 76 (1926). New Age Mag., Nov., 1955, 664.

Nash, Howard P.: 4 ALR 375 (1946-1947).

Nelson, Horatio: 12 AQC 109 (1899). 11 Build. Mag. 155 (1925).

Newbury, George A.: 1966 Proc. Sup. C., NMJ, 255.

Newton, Joseph Fort: See Appendix No. 26.

Ney, Marshall: 3 Trans. Ann. L. of Res., N.H. 10 1978.

Nye, Jonathan: Phil. Mag., Oct., 1956, 79.

Nicholas, Samuel: New Age Mag., Aug., 1952, 464.

Nickerson, Jr., Herman: K. T. Mag., June, 1976, 7.

Norcombe, J. E.: 14 Build. Mag. 41 (1928).

Norman, George: 70 AQC 7 (1957).

O'Brien, Jeremiah: No. Light, Jan., 1976, 4. New Age Mag., Sept., 1917, 408. 10 ALR 361 (1968).

Oglethorpe, James: 14 Build. Mag. 165 (1928). New Age Mag., Aug., 1912, 475.

Oliver, B. W.: 70 AQC 7 (1957).

Oliver, Rev. George: See Introduction to the 1980 book of the Masonic Book Club, being a reproduction of his *Revelations of a Square*.

Os-ke-Non-Ton: N.Y. Mas. Out., Feb., 1928, 173.

Oswald, Eleazer: 9 ALR 285 (1964).

Paine, Robert Treat: Ind. Free., May, 1974, 20. New Age Mag., May, 1976, 42.

Palfrey, William: Ind. Free., Oct., 1977, 17.

Palmer, Henry L.: No. Light, April, 1972, 4; has his picture.

Parker, Arthur C.: 10 Build. Mag. 137 (1924). 14 Build. Mag. 44; has his picture. Phil. Mag., April, 1955, 3; has his picture.

Parker, Ely S.: K. T. Mag., May, 1977, 7. 8 ALR 229 (1961); has his picture. 1 Trans. Ill. Lodge of Res. 172 (1978).

Parker, Fess: 8 RAM 347 (1966).

Parsons, Samuel Holden: K. T. Mag., June, 1976, 19.

Parvin, Newton Ray: 11 Build. Mag. 81 (1925).

Parvin, Theodore S.: New Age Mag., June, 1878, 30. (Erroneously states his first name to be Thomas). Joseph E. Morcombe, *The Life and Labors of T. S. Parvin;* 1906; 349. Published by the Grand Lodge of Iowa. 15 AQC 20 (1902). 1 Build. Mag. 38 (1915); has his picture.

Paterson, John: Ind. Free., Feb., 1976, 26. Phil. Mag., Oct., 1979, 6.

Patterson, William A.: 10 RAM 10 (1970); has his picture.

Paulding, Major John: Cal. Free., Summer, 1976, 110.

Ralls, John: Trans. MLR, 1948, 10.

Ramsey, Chevalier: 91 AQC 53 (1979). 81 AQC 280 (1968). 26 AQC 45, 146, 221 (1913). 35 AQC 76 (1922). 4 Norcalore 178 (1934). Ind. Free., July, 1977, 9. No. Light, Sept., 1974, 4.

Red Jacket: Ind. Free., Feb., 1959, 10.

Reigner, Charles G.: *Who's Who in America.* Phil. Mag., Aug.-Sept., 1950; has his picture.

Revere, Paul: STB, Jan., 1923. 5 ALR 13 (1947-1949), has his picture. Phil. Mag., Feb., 1972, 18. 1 RAM 3 (1943). Ill. Enlight., Feb., 1965, 390. Cal. Free., Summer, 1973, 108. No. Light, April, 1975, 6. Review of Esther Forbes book, *Paul Revere and the World He Lived In,* New Age. Mag., July, 1943, 373.

Rhodes, Cecil John: New Age Mag., Sept., 1972, 26. H. L. Haywood, *Masonic Curiosa,* 150.

Richard, F. M.: 57 AQC 262 (1944); 70 AQC 31 (1957).

Richards, George: 11 ALR 34 (1969).

Richardson, B. W.: 10 AQC 4 (1897).

Rickenbacker, Eddie: New Age Mag., Jan., 1969, 55. K. T. Mag., July, 1977, 5; has his picture. New Age Mag., Jan., 1969, 55 (Review of his biography).

Rizal, Jose: Austin Coates, *Philippine Nationalist and Martyr;* 1968; 378 pp. Published by Oxford University Press. 2 Build. Mag. 230 (1916). New Age Mag., July, 1955, 407; July, 1910, 159.

Roberts, Allen E.: See Appendix No. 29.

Robertson, John Ross: 2 AQC 137 (1890); 31 AQC 178 (1918).

Robbins, Sir Alfred: 36 AQC 274 (1923); 44 AQC 131 (1931). 86 AQC 100 (1973).

Robinson, Yankee: 5 RAM 323 (1957).

Rodgers, Jimmie: New Age Mag., Sept., 1978, 21. Tex. Free., Sept., 1973, 9.

Rogers, Norman: 68 AQC 9 (1955); 85 AQC 314 (1972).

Rogers, Will: K. T. Mag., Nov., 1975, 11. Altar Light, June-Aug., 1979. New Age Mag., May, 1962, 29; Feb., 1959, 114. Ind. Free., Oct., 1958, 4; has his picture.

Romberg, Sigmund: 4 RAM 49 (1952).

Rosetti, Gabriel: 1 ALR 232 (1930-1932).

Ross, Edmund G.: Cal. Free., Summer, 1975.

Rotch, C. D.: 65 AQC 15 (1952); 74 AQC 106 (1961).

Royall, Anne: 1 ALR 175 (1930-1932).

Rumford, Count: 10 RAM 79 (1970).

Rush, Benjamin: Cal. Free., Spring, 1975, 85.

Ruspini, The Chevalier Bathomew: 86 AQC 87 (1973).

Russell, William Hepburn: Trans. MLR, 1945, 4. K. T. Mag., Sept., 1977, 5.

Rylands, J. P.: 26 AQC 117 (1923).

Rylands, J. R.: 66 AQC 7 (1953).

Rylands, W. H.: 4 AQC 236 (1891); 35 AQC 258 (1922).

Sadler, Henry: 23 AQC 328 (1910); 24 AQC 277 (1911).

Salomon, Haym: Vick Knight, Jr., *Send for Haym Salomon;* 1976; 96 pp. Ill. Enlight., Nov., 1950, 3. No. Light, Jan., 1976, 12. New Age Mag., April, 1951, 229; Dec. 1953, 745. Harry Barnard, *This Great Triumvirate of Patriots,* 1972; story of the monument in Chicago. 11 RAM 296 (1975); the Haym Salomon stamp.

Sanders, Harlan: K. T. Mag., Jan., 1972, 13.

San Martin: New Age Mag., Jan., 1954, 19.

Sartain, John: 3 ALR 645 (1941-1942).

Saunders, George M.: New Age Mag., June, 1969, 31.

Sayre, Anthony: 14 AQC 181 (1901). 37 AQC 134 (1956). 41 AQC 158 (1928) 42 AQC 132 (1929). 89 AQC 264 (1977). 88 AQC 65 (1975). STB, April, 1941.

Sawyer, Judge Lorenzo: New Age Mag., Dec., 1978, 52.

Scammel, Alexander: New Age Mag., Aug., 1956, 475.

Schaw, William: 50 AQC 220 (1937).

Schiller: 13 Build. Mag. 342 (1927). 14 Build. Mag. 190 (1928).

Schirra, Jr., Walter M.: New Age Mag., Nov., 1969, 26. See Sec. 2.17 herein.

Schilt, Gen C. Frank: 12 RAM 207 (1977).

Scott, Sir Walter: 20 AQC 209 (1907). 21 AQC 69 (1908). 26 AQC 217 (1913). New Age Mag., Feb., 1023, 78. 3 RAM 3 (1949), has his picture.

Scott, Winfield: K. T. Mag., March, 1976, 7. 4 ALR 135 (1942-44).

Scully, Dr. Francis: Phil. Mag., Aug., 1975, 86.

Selby, Edward Martin: 12 RAM 111 (1976-1977). Proc. Sup. C., NMJ, 1976, p. 492; has his picture.

Sexson, W. Mark: New Age Mag., April, 1976, 27. 12 RAM 14 (1976).

Seymour, Thomas Henry: K. T. Mag., July, 1977, 13.

Sgabolt, William: 87 AQC 136 (1974).

Shackles, G. L.: 18 AQC 225 (1905); 39 AQC 61 (1926).

Sharp, Arthur: 75 AQC 8 (1962); 78 AQC 147 (1965).

Shays, Daniel: 3 ALR 185 (1938-1939).

Sherburne, Samuel: 3 Trans. Ann. Lodge, N. H., 49 (1978).

Shepherd, Silas H.: Phil. Mag., May, 1956, 12; Sept., 1946, 12.

Shetgar, Capt. John: 8 ALR 198 (1961).

Shyrock, Thomas Jack: New Age Mag., Oct., 1953, 581. 4 Build. Mag. 99 (1918).

Sibelius: No. Light, Jan., 1974, 4; has his picture. Phil. Mag., March, 1948, 1; April, 1956, 25.

Simpson, J. P.: 24 AQC 284 (1911); 52 AQC 35 (1938).

Skene, John: New Age Mag., Aug., 1951, 483; Aug., 1974, 23. N.Y. Mas. Outl., Sept., 1926, 13.

Sketchley, James: 50 AQC 94 (1937).

Skelton, Richard "Red": Altar Light, March-April, 1978. 9 RAM 266 (1969).

Smart, Christopher: 7 Trans. Phoe. L., Paris, 23.

Smith, Caleb B.: Ind. Free., Feb., 1955, 10. Phil. Mag., March-April, 1968, 38.

Smith, Dwight L.: See Appendix No. 30.

Smith, J. Fairbairn: See Appendix No. 31.

Smith, John Corson: New Age Mag., March, 1911, 302; has his picture.

Smith, John Stafford: Mas. Mess., Ga., July, 1974, 19.

Smith, Luther A.: New Age Mag., Jan., 1976, 5.

Smyth, Frederick H.: See Appendix No. 32.

Soliman: Sarastro Club Bulletin, Austria, May-June, 1963. 10 RAM 202 (1971).

Songhurst, W. J.: 47 AQC 257 (1934); 52 AQC 59 (1939).

Sousa, John P.: New Age Mag., March, 1962, 42. N.Y. Mas. Outl., Aug., 1927, 366. Mas. J. of So. Africa, Sept., 1973, 9.

Spalding, Dr. Lyman: 12 ALR 79 (1972). 12 ALR 164, 188 (1976). 13 ALR 188 (1976). No. Light, June, 1974, 8.

Spalding, Rufus Paine: 4 ALR 132 (1942-1943).

Spencer, Norman B.: 73 AQC 8 (1960); 80 AQC 109 (1967).

Speth, G. W.: 14 AQC 97 (1901).

St. Clair, Gen Arthur: New Age Mag., Feb., 1979, 46. Ind. Free., May, 1976, 17. Phil. Mag., Oct., 1966, 94. 8 Build. Mag. 201, 387 (1922).

St. Clair, Ward K.: 2 ALR 128 (1934-1935). 7 ALR 277 (1959). Phil. Mag., Dec., 1966, 103.

Schweitzer, Dr. Albert: Not a Mason. 7 RAM 26 (1961). Received a Masonic medal.

Stark, John: Ind. Free., June, 1976, 17.

Starr, Floyd: No. Light, Jan., 1973, 14.

Steele, Richard: New Age Mag., Sept., 1949, 551. Rae Blanchard, *Sir Richard Steele a Mason?* In Publications of Modern Language Association of America, 1948, pp. 903-917.

Stephens, James: 5 ALR 291 (1947-1948).

Stephens, William: Mas. Mess., Ga., Oct., 1977, 12.

Steuben, Baron: Ind. Free., Dec., 1977, 6; July, 1976, 10. Cal. Free., Autumn, 1976, 150. No. Light, June, 1974, 4.

Stevens, Frederick H.: New Age Mag., May, 1978, 14.

Stevens, Thaddeus: (Anti Mason) New Age Mag., Feb. 1955, 105. Ralph Korngold, *Thaddeus Stevens*, 1955; Chapter 5, "Anti-Mason."

Stewart, William Morris: New Age Mag., June, 1978, 43.

Stockton, Richard: New Age Mag., July, 1976, 49. No. Light, Sept., 1974, 16.

Stokes, John: 38 AQC 307 (1925); 48 AQC 210 (1935).

Stone, John: 26 AQC 301 (1913).

Stone, W. Clement: 11 RAM 67 (1973).

Storey, Edward Farris: Cal. Free., Summer, 1976, 123.

Story, Joseph: New Age Mag., Feb., 1942, 76; Sept., 1974, 4.

Stratton, Charles Sherwood (Tom Thumb): 10 ALR 245 (1967). K. T. Mag., Jan., 1972, 11. 3 RAM 22, 276 (1950); has his picture. New Age Mag., Feb., 1964, 19.

Stribling, William Laurence "Young": Mas. Mess., Ga., Aug., 1972, 13.

Stukeley, William: 8 Build. Mag. 40 (1922). H. L. Haywood, *Masonic Curiosa*, 177. Phil. Mag., Oct., 1971, 87.

Stuart Piggott, *William Stukeley – 18th Century Antiquarian;* 1950; 228 pp. Clarendon press, Oxford, publisher.

Sullivan, Arthur: Cal. Free., Autumn, 1972, 169.

Sullivan, Gen. John: 9 ALR 411 (1965). Ind. Free., Aug., 1976, 12. N.Y. Mas. Outl., Aug., 1929, 363.

Sumner, Jethro: Ind. Free., Sept., 1976, 16.

Talmadge, Capt. Samuel: 3 ALR 644 (1941-1942).

Tatsch, Jacob Hugo: 14 Build. Mag. 45 (1928); has his picture. Phil. Mag., Dec., 1963, 98.

Taxil, Leo: *Palladism and the Papacy,* in Journal of Church and State, Autumn, 1970, 453. Phil. Mag., Aug., 1958, 57; June, 1970, 61.

Taylor, Laurence R.: Phil. Mag., June, 1961, 43; has his picture. Dec., 1961, 103.

Telford, Thomas: New Age Mag., Sept., 1979, 42.

Thatcher, Maurice H.: New Age Mag., Oct., 1972, 5.

Thomas, David: 7 ALR 343 (1959).

Thomas, Lowell: Cal. Free., Autumn, 1972, 177. Empire St. Mas., June, 1976, 7; has his picture.

Thompson, Laurence: 84 AQC 116 (1971).

Thompson, Thomas: 11 ALR 34 (1969). K. T. Mag., April, 1975, 11.

Thompson, William: Ind. Free., Oct., 1976, 15.

Thoreau: Phil. Mag., April, 1972, 41. Not a Mason, 7 Build. Mag. 205 (1921).

Thorp, J. T.: 21 AQC 261 (1908); 45 AQC 114 (1932). 14 Build. Mag. 205 (1928).

Thory, Claude-Antoine: 4 ALR 140 (1942-1944).

Thumb, Tom: See Charles Sherwood Stratton, above.

Thurston, Howard: Mast. Mason, Jan., 1927, 13. New Age Mag., Sept., 1907, 274. 5 RAM 32 (155). N.Y. Mas. Outl., Aug., 1929, 377.

Tice, Harry E.: Phil. Mag., Oct., 1967, 90; Dec., 1967, 89. Mas. Mess., Ga., June, 1972, 7.

Tolstoy: Master Mas., Sept., 1927, 675. 10 RAM 241 (1971-1972).

Tompkins, Daniel D.: New Age Mag., Jan., 1906, 65. K. T. Mag., Sept., 1975, 29.

Toombs, Robert: Mas. Mess., Ga., April, 1976, 18.

Torrigiani, Domizio: Mas. Sq., June, 1976, 49.

Town, Salem: 1 RAM 370 (1945). 5 ALR 240 (1947-1948). Phil. Mag., Aug., 1965, 66.

Trotsky: *Was Trotsky a Mason?* 7 ALR 78 (1957).

Trumbull, Henry Clay: K. T. Mag., Oct., 1975, 13.

Tucker, William: 83 AQC 124 (1970).

Tuckett, J. E. S.: 32 AQC 167 (1919); 47 AQC 172 (1934).

Turnbull, Everette R.: Phil. Mag., Dec., 1962, 7; Ill. Grd. L. Proc., 1962, p. 57.

Tupper, Benjamin: Phil. Mag., Oct., 1979, 7.

Twain, Mark: New Age Mag., Nov., 1952, 663. K. T. Mag., Oct., 1974, 7. 1 RAM 352 (1945). 2 RAM 146 (1947). 10 RAM 172, 273 (1971). Ind. Free., Sept., 1954.

Vance, Arthur "Dazzy": N.Y. Mas. Outl., July, 1927, 336.

Vance, Gov. Zebulon: Phil. Mag., Feb., 1976, 15.

Van Dervanter, Willis: New Age Mag., Jan., 1943, 21.

Van Rensselaer, Killian Henry: 7 ALR 55 (1957). 8 ALR 459 (1962).

Varum, James: Ind. Free., Nov., 1976, 15.

Vibert, A. L.: 34 AQC 217 (1921); 52 AQC 2 (1939).

Voltaire: Phil. Mag., April, 1967, 34. New Age Mag., May, 1954, 283. 6 RAM 37 (1958). 7 Trans. Phoen. L., Paris, 52.

Voorhis, Harold Van Buren: See Appendix No. 33.

Vrooman, John B.: Phil. Mag., Aug.-Sept., 1948, 4; has his picture. June, 1967, 58; April, 1972, 44.

Waddell, William B.: Trans. MLR, 1945, 4.

Waite, A. E.: *Shadows of Life and Thought* (1918); autobiography mentioned in 85 AQC 242 (1972).

Walker, Dr. Thomas, Phil. Mag., Dec., 1971, 102.

Walker, Wendell K.: See Appendix No. 34.

Wallace, Lew: Ind. Free., Sept., 1959, 8. New Age Mag., March, 1960, 38. 6 RAM 237 (1959).

Walton, George: New Age Mag., March, 1976, 48.

Wannamker, John: Mast. Mason, March, 1928, 163. N.Y. Mas. Outl., Sept., 1927, 12.

Warburton, Frederick R.: Autobiography, *The Masonic Home Boy,* 1971; 287 pp. Vantage Press, N.Y.

Ward, Bilious: 3 ALR 187, 632 (1938-1939).

Ward, Eric: 77 AQC 18 (1964).

Warren, Joseph: J. H. Cary, *Physician, Politician, Patriot:* 1961. Thomas J. Fleming, *Now We Are Enemies* (1960), the story of the Battle of Bunker Hill. No. Light, June, 1975, 20. MSA Digest. 21 AQC 182 (1908). Phil. Mag., June, 1974, 58. Ind. Free., June, 1975, 6. New Age Mag., Dec., 1973, 48. K. T. Mag., June, 1973, 25.

Watson, Elkanah: 12 ALR 250 (1976).

Wayne, Anthony: New Age Mag., Sept., 1976, 52. N.Y. Mas. Outl., March 1925, 151; April, 1925, 172.

Wayne, John: 13 RAM 70 (1979).

Reader's Digest, Oct., 1979, 114.

Webb, Thomas Smith: Herbert T. Leyland, *Freemason – Musician – Entrepreneur*; 1965; 465 pp. H. L. Haywood, *Masonic Curiosa*, 108, 115, 161. H. L. Haywood, *Masonic Essays*, 113.

Weedon, George: Ind. Free., Dec., 1976, 18.

Weems, Mason: 16 Build. Mag. 76 (1930). New Age Mag., Feb., 1955, 81.

Wellington, Arthur: 15 AQC 108 (1902). Ind. Free., July, 1954, 4.

Wendt, Wylie B.: Phil. Mag., Aug., 1966, 80; Oct., 1968, 105; Oct., 1979, 7.

Wesley, John: Not a Mason. 15 AQC 102 (1902). 2 Build. Mag. 317 (1916).

Westcott, W. W.: 6 AQC 205 (1893); 38 AQC 224 (1925).

Whipple, William: New Age Mag., April, 1976, 46; July, 1973, 32.

White, Dr. Joseph: 5 ALR 292 (1947-1948).

Whittlesey, Elisha: 1 RAM 123 (1943).

Whytehead, T. B.: 12 AQC 213 (1899); 20 AQC 204 (1907).

Wilkes, John: Mas. Sq., March, 1977, 22. Phil. Mag., April, 1972, 30.

Wilkie, Wendell: Ind. Free., March, 1958, 6.

Willard, Archibald: Cal. Free., Autumn, 1976, 166.

Williams, David: 6 ALR 57 (1952-1953).

Williams, Louis L.: See chapter in Illinois Scottish Rite Deputies; now being prepared for publication.

Williams, W. J.: 44 AQC 250 (1931); 62 AQC 77 (1949).

Williams, Walter: 6 RAM 116 (1958).

Williams, William: 86 AQC 221 (1973).

Wilson, Charles: 7 RAM 126 (1961). Ind. Free., April, 1972, 26.

Wilson, Gavin: 25 AQC 258, 277 (1912).

Wilson, H. C. B.: 62 AQC 13 (1950); 76 AQC 159 (1963).

Withers, Robert Enoch: Phil. Mag., June, 1969, 63.

Witherspoon, Dr. John: Mast. Mas., March, 1928, 181.

Wonnacott, E. W. P.: 28 AQC 208 (1915); 39 AQC 206 (1926).

Wood, Leonard: Phil. Mag., April, 1970, 36. K. T. Mag., April, 1975, 7.

Wood, Walter: 9 ALR 222 (1964).

Woodford, A. F. A.: 1 AQC 85, 133 (1886-1888).

Woody, Albert L.: 1980 volume of the Masonic Book Club; introduction has his biographical sketch.

Wollstein, Dewey: See Appendix No. 35.

Wooster, David: Ind. Free., March, 1977, 16. 7 ALR 81 (1957). Phil. Mag., April, 1977, 23.

Worts, F. N.: 78 AQC 15 (1965).

Wren, Christopher: Phil. Mag., Feb., 1964, 8. 78 AQC 201 (1965). Ill. Enlight., Oct., 1950, 8. 10 Build. Mag. 336 (1924). 16 Build. Mag. 3 (1930). Mas. Sq., March, 1976, 18.

Wright, Waller Rodwell: 85 AQC 145 (1972).

Wynn, Ed: Mast. Mas., Sept., 1924, 537; has his picture.

Yates, Giles Fonda: 8 Build. Mag. 387 (1922).

Yeager, William E.: Phil. Mag., Aug., 1974, 77.

Yeaton, Capt. Hopley: 12 RAM 163 (1977). No. Light, June, 1973, 12.

You, Dominique: 4 RAM 3 (1952). New Age Mag., 1941, 470.

Young, Brigham: 9 ALR 123 (1963).

Young, Robert H.: Mast. Mas., Oct., 1925, 833.

2.17 MISCELLANEOUS

The Adams Family and Freemasonry. Ind. Free., March, 1952, 16.

Freemasons, Aviators, and the Air. Trans. M. & P. M. L. No. 130, Jan., 1973, 3.

Masons Who Have Been Astronauts. 13 RAM 12 (1979). 6 RAM 241; 7 RAM 367, 368, 380, 188, 47, 273, 323, 124; 8 RAM 245, 346; 9 RAM 14, 123.

Freemasonry in the Space Age. New Age Mag., 1969, 14.

Brethren Who Made Masonic History. 78 AQC 130 (1965).

Magicians and Freemasonry. Mast. Mas., April, 1925, 277.

Three Masonic Charlatans: D'Eon, Cagliostro, and Thomson. Ind. Free., June, 1959, 10.

Dukes of Atholl and Freemasonry. 1969 Yrbk. Grd. Lo. of Scot., 68.

Three Early Grand Masters. 58 AQC 226 (1945).

National Commanders of the American Legion Who Were Masons. 2 Norcalore 244.

Delegates to the Constitutional Convention, 1787. New Age Mag., Jan., 1937, 21 and May, 1938, 280.

Ray V. Denslow and William R. Denslow, Altar Light, Nov.-Dec., 1977.

Masonic Elephant Trainers. 11 RAM 227 (1974-1975).

Governors Who Are Masons. N.Y. Mas. Outl., Dec., 1926, 106.

Three Senatorial Grand Masters. K. T. Mag., Oct., 1975, 24.

Grand Masters of Missouri. 1947 Trans. MLR.

The Hall of Fame. K. T. Mag., April, 1975, 30.

Hall of Fame Players. Phil. Mag., Feb., 1973, 21.

Founders of Professional Dentistry, Harris Hayden. New Age Mag., Feb., 1977, 41.

Jewish Grand Masters in the United States. STB, March, 1967.

Justices of the Supreme Court Identified as Masons. MSA Digest.

Masonic Membership of Supreme Court Justices. New Age Mag., Dec., 1934, and many issues that follow; Also: April, 1940, 250.

Chief Justices Who Were Masons, by Carl H. Claudy. Ind. Free., Oct., 1955, 6.

Masonic Magicians. 7 RAM 318 (1963).

Masons in the Movies. N.Y. Mas. Outl., Aug., 1928, 368.

The Medical Profession in Freemasonry. 7 AQC 145 (1894).

The Discovery of Penicillin and Sir Alexander Fleming. New Age Mag., March, 1972, 10.

Four Doctors Mayo in Masonry. Paper No. 100, Ed. L. No. 1002, Minn. Oct., 1979.

Four Stars of the Diamond and of the Square. N.Y. Mas. Outl., Sept., 1926, 16.

Two Magician Masons. (Houdini and Hermann). New Age Mag., Aug., 1933, 481.

Monks and Masons. 15 Build. Mag. 8 (1929).

Masons Who Helped Shape Our Nation, by Henry C. Clausen; 1976; 113 pp. Reviewed in Journal of Church and State, Autumn, 1978, 598.

The Medical Profession and Early Freemasonry. 85 AQC 298 (1972).

Masonic Musicians. 4 AQC 90 (1891).

Masonic Dramas and Playwrights. Mast. Mas., Feb., 1926, 135.

Famous Men – Nobel Prize Recipients – Masons. New Age Mag., Feb., 1969, 25.

Craftsmen on Radio. N.Y. Mas. Outl., April, 1930, 234.

English Royal Freemasons. 81 AQC 348 (1968).

Royalty and Their Part in the Craft. 11 Build. Mag. 133 (1925).

Hollywood's "233 Club." N.Y. Mas. Outl., Nov., 1927, 76.

Shrine Potentates Who Have Served in the U.S. Congress as Senators or Representatives. 12 RAM 24 (1976).

Speakers of the House. 7 RAM 145, 177 (1962). New Age Mag., July, 1964, 23.

Statues of Great Men in our Nation's Capital. Phil. Mag., April, 1973, 32.

The Unknown Tattoed Mason. 2 ALR 170 (1938-1939).

Birthdays of Famous Masons. New Age Mag., each month during 1958.

Fifty Early American Freemasons. Reviewed in the New Age Mag., Sept., 1956, 567.

Long and Short of It. 5 RAM 93 (1955).

Long and Short Freemasons. 9 RAM 425 (1965).

A Tentative Roster of Revolutionary Soldier-Masons. 5 ALR 125, 267, 351 (1947-1948); 6 ALR 61, 233 (1952-1953).

Rollins "Walk of Fame." 7 ALR 65 (1957).

Merchants as Masons. 4 ALR 243 (1944-1945).

Masonic Teachers of the 18th Century. 1928 Prestonian Lecture.

Concord Masons and the Revolution. 2 ALR 547 (1936-1938).

Early Masonic Engravers in America. 2 ALR 97 (1938-1939).

Notes on Masonic Silversmiths. 5 ALR 21 (1947-1949).

Many Freemasons in Our Statuary Hall. 6 RAM 101 (1958).

Last of Peary Expedition Dies. 5 RAM 173 (1956).

Masonic Musicians. 4 AQC 90 (1891).

Daniel Vinton, Author of Solemn Strikes, etc. 2 Build. Mag. 31 (1916).

Continental Navy Masons. Phil. Mag.; April, 1969, 38; June, 1969, 54; Aug., 1969, 72; Oct., 1969, 89; Dec. 1969, 106.

Freemasonry and the Entertainment World, Series of articles by Jerry Erikson, starting with 9 RAM 195 (1969) and running for several years.

James R. Case, *Freemasons Depicted in the National History Series of John Trumbull's Paintings.* MSA Digest.

Masons in Sports. Phil. Mag., Dec., 1971, 103.

Brothers of the Bat. Jerry R. Erikson. 7 RAM 48, 85, 182, 308 (1961). 8 RAM 177 (1963). 9 RAM 12 (1967). 10 RAM 209 (1971).

Fraternal Footballers, by Jerry R. Erikson. 7 RAM 103 (1961). 9 RAM 84 (1967).

Hiram Hoopsters, by Jerry R. Erikson. 10 RAM 239 (1971-1972).

Olympic Masons, by Jerry R. Erikson. 8 RAM 71 (1964).

The Husbands of Betsy Ross. K. T. Mag., June, 1976, 23.

CHAPTER THREE

Philosophy

3.01 EARLY WORKS

Wellins Calcott, *A Candid Disquisition of the Principles and Practices of the Most Ancient and Honorable Society of Free and Accepted Masons.* 1769. James Dixwell, publisher.
Comments: Henry W. Coil, Sr., "First book published attempting a general discussion of the subject, rather vapid. . . ." H. L. Haywood, "Before Calcott there had been no attempt to give that whole-of-interpretation that came to be called in aftertimes Masonic philosophy. No other attempt was undertaken a second time until William Hutchinson published his *The Spirit of Masonry* in 1774, 15 years later." William R. Denslow, "He has been called the father of the didactic school. . . . He twice visited America. On Jan. 20, 1779 he was made an honorary member of Apollo Lodge at York, England." See John Stokes, *Masonic Teachers of the 18th Century, 1928 Prestonian Lecture.* Reviewed: *The Essays of H. L. Haywood,* 86; Collected Prestonian Lectures 65. Libraries: 2, 3, 4, 7, 9, 10, 11, 12, 13, 14.

William Hutchinson, *The Spirit of Masonry.* 1903; 229 pp. (originally published in 1774); this edition published by Macoy Publishing Co.
Comments: William R. Denslow, "He is best known for his Spirit of Masonry, which did much to elevate the spirit and character of the Craft." Henry W. Coil, Sr., "The first book discussing Freemasonry from the standpoints of religion, philosophy, and spiritual value. Not particularly interesting or valuable as to modern Masonry." L. B. Blakemore, "One of the oldest and greatest books on the interpretation of Masonry. A Masonic classic." Reviewed: Carr, ed., Collected Prestonian Lectures, 73. Libraries: 2, 3, 7, 8, 9, 10, 11, 12, 14.

George Oliver, *The Symbol of Glory; The Object and End of Freemasonry.* 1870. 298 pp. Macoy Publishing Co., publisher.
Author: See 1980 book of the Masonic Book Club; introduction. Comments: L. B. Blakemore, "A personal and vivacious personal philosophy of Freemasonry in the terms of one Masonic Symbol." Libraries: 2, 3, 4, 5, 6, 7, 8, 9, 10, 11, 12, 13, 14.

Jonathan Ashe, *Masonic Manual.* 1843; First ed; 1843 ed., 311 pp. D. Deans, publisher.
Comments: William R. Denslow, "Author of Masonic Manual, 1814 which he copied from Hutchinson without giving credit." Silas H. Shepherd, "This work follows the ideas of Hutchinson. The author has been accused of plagiarism, although hardly with justice." Libraries: 3, 4, 8, 9, 11.

Cornelius Moore, *Outlines of the Temple.* 1858. J. Ernst, Cincinnati, publisher.
Contents: Discusses the moral aspects of the Craft. Libraries: 3, 9.

Jirah D. Buck, *Symbolism of Mystic Masonry.* 1896; 265.
Contents: An illustration of the use of a vivid imagination and making the Craft an occult organization. To be read with caution. Comments: Silas H. Shepherd, "Those desiring to study the connection between the occult philosophies and Freemasonry may read this work to advan-

tage.'' Reviewed: 12 Build. Mag. 158 (1926). Mast. Mas., Aug., 1926, 749.
Libraries: 1, 2, 3, 4, 5, 7, 8, 9, 10, 12, 13, 14.

Thaddeus M. Harris, *Discourses on Freemasonry.* 1801; 348 pp. Reproduced in Vol. 4, Universal Masonic Library.
Libraries: 3, 7, 10, 11, 12, 13, 14.

3.02 LATER WORKS

Roscoe Pound, *The Philosophy of Freemasonry.* Five lectures delivered under the auspices of the Grand Lodge of Massachusetts. Reproduced in 1 Build. Mag., as follows: William Preston, p. 7; Karl C. F. Krause, p. 31; George Oliver, p. 54; Albert Pike, p. 77; A 20th Century Masonic Philosophy, p. 106. Also reproduced in Roscoe Pound, *Masonic Addresses and Writings.*

Harry L. Haywood, *The Great Teachings of Masonry;* 1923; 188 pp. Southern Publishers, Kingsport, Tenn., publishers. Originally appeared as a series of articles in The Build. Mag., Volumes 7, 8, and 9.
Author: See Appendix No. 16. Comments: L. B. Blakemore, "A series of interpretative, modern chapters on each of the teachings of the Craft — and introduction to Masonic philosophy." Carl H. Claudy, "Haywood comes down to earth and cases and discusses his subject with neither glittering generalities nor vagueness of ideas. He discusses Freemasonry in relation to industry, liberty, democracy, religion, human nature, education. He makes the reader walk with him into 'the Masonic theory of the good life.' He brings some sound common sense to bear on the meaning of the initiation and secrecy. And finally he has a few vital pages on Masonic philosophy which will open, or forever close, the doors to that fascinating study according to whether the ears of the reader are acute or deaf." Libraries: 1, 2, 3, 4, 5, 6, 7, 8, 9, 10, 11, 12, 13, 14.

Akira Yamaya, *Masonic Charity.* New Age Mag., Aug., 1978. 43.

Otis V. Jones, Jr., *What Come Ye Here to Do?* Phil. Mag., Aug., 1979, 13.

The Story of Masonic Philosophy. Mast. Mas., July, 1928, 467.

H. L. Haywood, *The Philosophy of Freemasonry;* in his Masonic Essays, 418.

Douglas MacArthur, *Morality, The Basis of Masonry.* New Age Mag., Dec., 1937, 739.

James H. Begg, *Philosophy of Albert Pike.* New Age Mag., Feb., 1925, 81.

Approach to Morals and Dogma. New Age Mag., March, 1963, 21.

Roscoe Pound, *What Is Truth?* Phil. Mag., Aug., 1957, 52.

L. L. Walker, Jr., *If a Man Die.* A Study of Masonic Philosophy of Death and Immortality. 3 Trans. Tex. L. of Res. 470 (1965-1968).

Wallace E. Caldwell, *Spiritual Force of Freemasonry;* 1951 Proc. Grd. Mast. Conf., 19.

Harry E. Howard, *Philosophy of the First Degree.* 1953 Proc. Grd. Mast. Conf., 62.

Dudley Wright, *The Ethics of Freemasonry.* 1924; 88 pp. Reproduced in Vol. 4, Little Masonic Library, 255.
Libraries: 1, 2, 3, 5, 7, 9, 12, 14.

Ethos of Freemasonry. STB, June, 1952.

Personal Masonic Philosophy. STB, July, 1945.

Herman A. Sarachan, *Philosophy of Freemasonry.* 9 ALR 207 (1964).

Augustus C. L. Arnold, *Rationale and Ethics of Freemasonry.* 1914; 298 pp. Macoy Publishing Co., publisher.
Comments: L. B. Blakemore, "An essay treatment of the religion, philosophy and ethics of the Craft; fine in spirit; of the period dominated by George Oliver." Silas H. Shepherd, "This work, covering a wide range, affords splendid reading." Libraries: 2, 3, 4, 5, 6, 7, 8, 9, 10, 12, 13, 14.

George W. Steinmetz, *Freemasonry: Its*

Hidden Meaning. 1948; 215 pp. Macoy Publishing Co., publisher.

Contents: Listed here merely as an illustration of what constitutes a claimed Masonic book which is not worth reading. It contains chapters on such strange subjects as "mental science," "evolution," and "The Secret Doctrine." Reviewed: Phil. Mag., Oct.-Nov., 1948, 11. Libraries: 2, 3, 4, 5, 6, 7, 8, 9, 10, 11, 12, 13, 14.

The Story of Masonic Philosophy. Mast. Mason, July, 1928, 467.

Thomas S. Roy, *Ultimate Lessons of the First Degree*. Ind. Free., Jan., 1969, 12.

William M. Brown, *Dust, Sparks, Wind, and God*. Ind., Free., Nov., 1958, 8.

Malcolm W. Bingay, *The Spirit of Masonry*, Ind. Free., Aug, 1954, 7.

The Plan of Freemasonry, 5 Build. Mag. 266 (1919).

A Progressive Science. STB, Sept., 1963.

Joseph Fort Newton, *The Spirit of Masonry*. Ind. Free., Oct., 1959, 20.

Samuel Gompers, *Freemasonry in Industry*. Ind. Free., Sept., 1951, 14.

Alphonse Cerza, *The Attraction of Freemasonry*. No. Light, April, 1970, 7.

J. M. Horvarth, *The Meaning and Purpose of Masonry*. 84 AQC 285 (1971).

CHAPTER FOUR

Freemasonry and Religion

4.01 EARLY WORKS

Henry Josiah Whymper, *Religion of Freemasonry*. 1888; 260 pp. George Kenning, London, publisher. Introduction by W. J. Hughan; and edited by G. W. Speth.
Author: 6 AQC 94 (1893). Comments: The Introduction in this book was reproduced in 8 Build. Mag. 282. Silas H. Shepherd, "Brother Whymper took a decidedly Christian view of Freemasonry." Libraries: 1, 3, 4, 5, 6, 9, 11, 12, 14.

Chalmers I. Paton, *Freemasonry: Its Two Great Doctrines*. 1879; 163 pp. Reeves & Turner, London, publisher.
Comment: L. B. Blakemore, "A discussion of the religion and philosophy of the Craft." Libraries: 2, 3, 5, 7, 9, 11, 12, 13.

4.02 MODERN WORKS

Forrest D. Haggard, *The Clergy and the Craft*. 1970; 149 pp. MLR, publisher.
Author: Appendix No. 14. Contents: Examines the relationship and attitude between organized religion and Freemasonry. It considers such touchy subjects as the conflict between the funeral service of a minister and the Masonic ceremony, the opposition of some clergymen and some churches to Freemasonry, and other areas where the churches and Freemasonry touch each other. Comments: J. Fairbairn Smith, "One of the greatest books ever published . . . its pages provide the details of a growing conviction that its contents are actually monumental . . . treatise which is both illuminating and at the same time dispells much unwarranted criticism by some elements of the clergy. . . . Almost every phase of the dialogue of the clergy with Freemasonry has been faithfully recorded. . . . " Libraries: 2, 3, 7, 9, 10, 11, 12, 14.

Forrest D. Haggard, *The Man, the Church, and the Lodge*. Phil. Mag., Feb., 1965, 9.

L. L. Walker, Jr., *The Mason and His Church*. Tex. Free., Nov., 1972, 4.

W. M. Turner, *The Relationship of Masonry and Christianity*. Tex. Free., Nov., 1972, 17.

Elbert Bede, *Is Freemasonry a Religion?* Phil. Mag., June, 1956, 45.

Religion and Masonry. New Age Mag., Sept., 1971, 53.

Elbert Bede, *A Preacher Who Refused to Renounce Freemasonry*. Phil. Mag., April, 1955, 6.

Joseph Fort Newton, *Religion in Masonry*. Author: Appendix No. 26. Libraries: 1, 2, 3, 4, 5, 6, 7, 8, 9, 10, 11, 12, 13, 14, 15.

H. L. Haywood, *The Theology of Joseph Fort Newton*. Build. Mag., 362.

Forrest D. Haggard, *Religious Renewal, Its Impact on Freemasonry*. Phil. Mag., Dec., 1978, 10.

L. L. Walker, *"The Religion on Which All Men Agree,"* 12 Trans. Tex. L. of Res. 44 (1976-1977).

Julian M. Hodgskin, Jr., *The Religion of Freemasonry*. Phil. Mag., Dec., 1970, 108.

John A. Mirt, *Freemasonry Is Religious —*

Not a Religion. Ill. Enlight., Feb., 1953, 4.

Oscar A. Guinn, Jr., *Message of an Evangelist.* Ind. Free., Dec., 1976, 12.

Religious Universality: What Does It Mean? Ind. Free., June, 1977, 8.

Rev. Canon Richard Tydeman, *Freemasonry and the Church.* 1976 Trans. Leic. L. of Res., 8.

Lester C. Noerr, *Masonic Clergy Night.* 1975 Proc. Midw. Conf. Mas. Ed. 21.

Rev. H. G. M. Clarke, *Freemasonry and Religion.* 1972 Grd. L. of Scot. Yrbk. 57.

Alex Horne, *Buddhist Ideas Concerning God and Immortality.* 86 AQC 136 (1973).

Thomas S. Roy, *Is Masonry a Religion?* New Age Mag., June, 1959, 372.

Masonry and Religion. STB, Oct., 1934.

Is Freemasonry a Religion? A Debate. Phil. Mag., Feb., 1968, 20.

R. J. Meekren, *The Grand Architect of the Universe.* 13 Build. Mag. 304 (1927).

Freemasonry and Religion. 13 Build. Mag. 309 (1927).

The Religion of All Good Men. 14 Build. Mag. 203 (1928).

Joseph Fort Newton, *The Religion on Which All Men Agree.* Mast. Mas., Sept., 1928, 611.

The Religion of Freemasonry. Phil. Mag., Dec., 1970, 108.

Freemasonry and Its Relation to the Church. 1 RAM 372 (1945).

J. R. Clarke, *The Change From Christianity to Deism in Freemasonry.* 78 AQC 49 (1962).

Louis L. Williams, *The American Passion Play.* General presentation of passion plays with special reference to the Passion Play presented annually for many years by the Scottish Rite Bodies of Bloomington, Ill.

Louis L. Williams, *For the Lord God Omnipotent Reigneth.* 1966 Ill. Grd. L. Proc. 84.

Thomas S. Roy, *Hammer Away, Ye Hostile Hands.* Ind. Free., April, 1972, 6. Summary of a talk explaining that the Craft is religious and not a religion.

W. W. Covey-Crump, *The Freemason's Vision of God.* 13 Build. Mag. 139 (1927).

G. W. Daynes, *Belief in God: A Historical Tenet of Freemasonry.* 13 Build. Mag. 265 (1927).

Christian Nature of the Craft., Harry Carr, ed., The Collected Prestonian Lectures, 186.

W. W. Wescott, *The Religion of Freemasonry as Illustrated by the Kabbalah.* 1 AQC 55 (1886-1888).

Silas H. Shepherd, *The Spiritual Significance of Freemasonry.* 12 Build. Mag. 321 (1926).

Charles Harold Lyttle, *The Religion of Early Freemasonry.* 1939. University of Chicago Press.

H. L. Haywood, *Deism and Masonry.* 3 Mackey's Rev. Ency. of Free. 1213 (1946).

Mervin B. Hogan, *The Supreme Architect of the Space Age.* 9 RAM 259 (1969).

E. J. Castle, *Enquery Into the Charge of Gnosticism Brought Against Freemasons and Templars.* 19 AQC 209 (1906).

H. L. Haywood, *Is Freemasonry a Religion?* 9 Build. Mag. 233 (1923).

G. W. Warvelle, *The Ineffable Name.* 1 Build. Mag. 271 (1915).

Agnosticism Considered. Mast. Mas., March, 1925, 264.

Knoop and Jones, *Freemasonry and the Idea of Natural Religion.* 56 AQC 38 (1934).

4.03 THE HOLY BIBLE AND FREEMASONRY

Clarence H. Cohen, *The Books of the Book.* 1973; 142 pp. Originally published in 1970-1972, in installments, in the Mas. Mess., Ga. Published in book form by the Educational and Historical

Comm. of the Grd. L. of Ga. The author is a P.G.M. He presents the Masonic significance of most books of the Holy Bible.

Thomas S. Roy, *The Volume of the Sacred Law*. No. Light, Jan., 1974, 14.

Hebrew Names of God. 7 RAM 272 (1957).

Jeremiah the Prophet. 8 RAM 267 (1966).

Biblical and Other Ancient Names in Freemasonry. MSA Digest.

The Scriptures and the Royal Arch Ritual. 4 RAM 338 (1954).

L. L. Walker, Jr., *The Biblical Framework of Freemasonry;* with long bibliography. 3 Tex. L. of Res. 279 (1965-1968).

The Holy Bible in Masonic Literature and in the Lodge. 75 AQC 233 (1962).

Bible Openings. 77 AQC 199 (1964).

G. W. Daynes, *The Bible, Its Place and Use in Lodges*. 67 AQC 73 (1954).

Using the V.S.L. at Lodge Instruction. 80 AQC 337 (1967).

Hal Burnett, *A Masonic Interpretation of Ecclesiastes 12:1-7*. Cal. Free., Summer, 1974, 128. Also: Tex. Free., July, 1973 8; 7 RAM 8, 222, (1955); 8 RAM 32 (1964).

W. W. Covey-Crump, *The Allegory of Koheleth*. 39 AQC 163 (1926). 4 Build. Mag. 185 (1918).

An Interpretation of Ecclesiastes. New Age Mag., Aug., 1971, 52.

The Mas. J. of So. Africa. June, 1972, 25.

Melchizedek. 4 RAM 26 (1952).

The Bible, a Basis for Masonic Research. Phil. Mag., April, 1958, 28.

Thomas S. Roy, *Immortality*. MSA Digest.

Ten Masonic Prayers. STB, May, 1952.

Joseph Fort Newton, *The Great Light in Masonry*. Ind. Free., Oct., 1958, 11.

The Bible in Masonic Ritual. MSA Digest.

The Bible and Freemasonry. New Age Mag., Sept., 1972, 29.

Alex Horne, *The Bible in the Hiramic Tradition*. New Age Mag., Dec., 1960, 55.

A History of the English Bible. MSA Digest.

The Gutenberg Bible. MSA Digest.

George M. Cordner, *The Names of God*. Phil. Mag., Oct., 1958, 67; Dec., 1958, 86; Feb., 1959, 6.

Louis L. Williams, *Whence Came the Bible and Whither Is It Bound?* No. Light, Nov., 1970, 4; Jan., 1971, 8.

H. L. Haywood, *Freemasonry in the Bible*. (1947).

Bible Quotations for Masonic Speakers. MSA Digest.

W. W. Covey-Crump, *The Biblical References to Hiram*. 30 Man. Assn. for Mas. Res. 23 (1929-1930).

James E. Craig, *Masonry and the VSL*. N.Y. Mas. Outl., Nov., 1928, 67.

Thomas C. Ehlers, *Your Due is the Dew*. Interpretation of the Word "Dew" in Psalms 133. New Age Mag., June, 1978, 28.

Harry Carr, *Bible Openings*. 89 AQC 263 (1976).

Minister and Mason. New Age Mag., Oct., 1955, 603.

In the Beginning Was the Word. 83 AQC 301 (1970).

One Volume of the Sacred Law. STB, Feb., 1949.

Beatitudes of a Freemason. Ca. Free., Autumn, 1972, 170.

Three Scripture Readings. STB, Dec., 1931.

The Holy Bible. STB, March, 1924.

Masonry and the Great Light. STB, June, 1934.

Biblical References of Especial Interest to Freemasons. 3 Mackey's Rev. Ency. of Free., by H. L. Haywood, 1455 (1946).

H. L. Haywood, *How the Bible Came to Be the Great Light*. In Essays of H. L. Haywood, 439.

Alex Horne, *The Significance of Maundy Thursday*. New Age Mag., April, 1976, 8.

4.04 MASONIC EDITIONS OF THE HOLY BIBLE

Oxford Edition, 1953. Contains an article by Joseph Fort Newton, *The Great Light;* and a Bible Concordance for use by Masons.

The World Publishing Co. ed., 1948. Has Masonic Concordance by C. C. Hunt, the longest and most detailed on the subject.

A. J. Holman Co., 1935. Has an article on The Bible and Masonry; a picture of conceived idea of King Solomon's Temple; and an article by Joseph Fort Newton.

A. Lewis Ltd., 1976. Has 32 pp. of introduction with a résumé of the history of the Bible. Reviewed in 88 AQC 105 (1976).

John A. Hertel Co., Reviewed in Phil. Mag., June-July, 1950.

Harold V. B. Voorhis, *Unusual Lodge Bibles*. Phil. Mag., Aug., 1978, 17; Oct., 1978, 25; Dec., 1978, 5; Feb., 1979, 15.

4.05 PATRON SAINTS

G. P. Hills, *Patron Saints*. 31 AQC 172 (1918).

Masonic Hagiology; Saint Names in the Craft. MSA Digest.

Laurence Healey, *How the Holy Sts. John Became Freemasonry's Patron Saints*. Ind. Free., May, 1966, 6.

Oscar A. Guinn, Jr., *Why Are We Dedicated to the Holy Saints John?* No. Light, Jan., 1976, 6.

H. L. Haywood, *The Sts. John*. In Masonic Curiosa, 83, 128, 170.

Alex Horne, *The Saints John in the Masonic Tradition*. 75 AQC 76 (1962).

Willaim R. Deutsch, *Masonry and the Holy Sts. John*. Phil. Mag., June, 1965, 50.

J. O. Manton, *The St. Johns as Patron Saints of Freemasonry*. 8 Man. Assn. for Mas. Res. 17 (1917-1918).

St. John the Baptist. Ind. Free., June, 1971, 6.

Alex Horne, *The Masons and St. John*. Ore. Free., Oct., 1974, 4.

Oscar A. Guinn, *Crying in the Wilderness*. Ind. Free., June, 1976, 14.

St. John, 91 AQC 67 (1979).

St. Barbara as Patron Saint of Masons. Harry Carr, The Freemason at Work, 96.

W. J. Chetwode Crawley, *The Two Saints John Legend*. 8 AQC 156 (1895).

Jacob Morton, *The Two Saints John Legend*. 7 AQC 135 (1894); 8 AQC 33 (1895).

D. C. Smith, *St. John the Apostle – the Patron Saint of Freemasonry in Scotland*. 21 AQC 66 (1908).

The Holy Saints John. 8 Build. Mag. 170, 202 (1922).

Masonry's Patron Saints. Ind. Free., June, 1954, 4.

Wayne Guthre, *The Holy Saints John*. Ind. Free., Dec., 1970, 6.

CHAPTER FIVE

Masonic Jurisprudence and Law

5.01 MASONIC JURISPRUDENCE

Albert G. Mackey, *Jurisprudence of Freemasonry*. 1927; 395 pp. Macoy Publishing Co. This edition was preceded by many others over the years. Author: Appendix 23. Comments: Henry W. Coil, Sr., "The standard work on the subject but modified by statutes of numerous Grand Lodges." L. B. Blakemore, "A manual of Masonic law. More widely used as an authority by Grand Lodges than any other Masonic book. A Masonic classic." H. L. Haywood, "It has a quality uniquely its own of stating the general and abstract principles clearly, and in a form easy to carry into practice." Norman B. Hickox, "Mackey wrote on Masonic law in 1855, but he did not publish his work on Jurisprudence until 1859, following which it immediately ran into several editions — about one edition each year until after the Civil War. Previously there had been no standard work of authority, all Masonic law being scattered over thousands of pages of various Jurisdictions' Proceedings, and these were often in conflict as no one had drawn together any general deductions. . . . A standard work of reference on American law is essential to the American Masonic student. Clegg's latest revision of Mackey on this subject covers the field with breadth and comprehension." Libraries: 1, 2, 3, 4, 5, 6, 7, 8, 9, 10, 11, 12, 13, 14.

Roscoe Pound, *Masonic Jurisprudence.* Appeared in the Build. Mag., Volumes 3 and 4, in installments. Reproduced in the Little Masonic Library, Vol. 1, p. 275.
Comments: H. L. Haywood, "The most philosophical, and in a degree the weightiest and most learned work on the subject . . . who at the time of writing it was Dean of the Law School at Harvard University." Reviewed: Mast. Mas., Feb., 1925, 165.

John W. Simons, *Familiar Treatise on the Principles & Practice of Masonic Jurisprudence*. 1864; 319 pp. Macoy & Sickels, publisher. Has an appendix with forms.
Libraries: 3, 8, 9.

John Thomas Lawrence, *Masonic Jurisprudence*. 1908; 334. A. Lewis, London.
Comments: L. B. Blakemore, "A well-printed and written work on Masonic Jurisprudence as practiced in England." Silas H. Shepherd, "affords a comprehensive idea of the theory of English Masonic Jurisprudence. Good." Reviewed: 22 AQC 207 (1909); 25 AQC 335 (1912). Libraries: 1, 2, 3, 4, 5, 7, 8, 10, 11, 14, 15.

Wildey E. Atchison, *Jurisprudence Studies.* 3 Build. Mag. 9, 50, 70, 134, 273 (1917).

A. C. Fraser, *Some Aspects of Masonic Jurisprudence*. Trans. M. P. M. L., Nov., 1978, 215.

George Draffen, *Some Aspects of International Masonic Law and Custom*. 88 AQC 85 (1975).

Roscoe Pound, *What Is Law?* Phil. Mag., Oct., 1959, 67.

The Declaration of Principles: What Does It Mean Today? Ind. Free., May, 1976, 8.

The Law of Freemasonry. Mas. Mes., Ga., Oct., 1977, 11.

Masonic Law. 16 Build. Mag. 46 (1930).
Comments: H. L. Haywood: "The most acute, detailed, and analytical discussion of the subject ever made in the United States was carried on by Judge Josiah H. Drummond in the form of Foreign Correspondence Reports for the Grand Lodge of Maine over a period of 38 years (he died in 1902); they have never been collected or published in book form but are included in the published proceedings of the Grand Lodge of Maine."

5.02 THE OLD CHARGES OF FREEMASONRY

The Old Charges: What Are They? Ind. Free., Feb., 1976, 6.

Herbert Poole, *The Old Charges.* 1924; 57 pp. Masonic Record, London, publisher.
Author: 41 AQC 298 (1928); 64 AQC 61 (1951). Libraries: 1, 3, 5, 7, 8, 9, 11, 12, 13, 14, 15.

William J. Hughan, *Old Charges of the British Freemasons.* 1872; 91 pp. Simpkins, Marshall & Co., London, publisher.
Author: 24 AQC 148 (1911); Appendix No. 21. Comments: Silas H. Shepherd, "Brother Hughan has done more to bring the study of Freemasonry to a systematic and critical stage than any other writer. The study of the organization has been particular full of evidence and to this he has devoted an amount of research which cannot be over-estimated. The records of the Craft were his specialty and in this work we have the results." See Essays of H. L. Haywood, 262. Libraries: 2, 3, 5, 7, 8, 9, 10, 11, 12, 14, 15.

William J. Hughan, *Bibliography of the "Old Charges."* 9 AQC 85 (1896).

Alex Horne, *King Solomon's Temple in the Masonic Tradition,* pp. 122-124, has a list of the easily obtainable copies of the Old Charges.

Cornelius Moore, *The Ancient Charges and Regulations of Freemasonry.* 1855;

300 pp. Masonic Review Office, publisher.
Libraries: 3, 8, 9.

Knoop and Jones, *Handlist of Masonic Pamphlets.* 1942; 56 pp. Manchester University Press, publisher.
Libraries: 3, 4, 5, 6, 7, 8, 9, 10, 11, 12, 14.

William J. Hughan, *The Masonic "Old Charges."* New Age Mag.; Oct., 1904, 473; April, 1905, 361; Sept., 1905, 273. Has picture of the author.

The Charges and the Landmarks of the Craft. N.Y. Mas. Outl., Feb., 1925, 112.

Frederick H. Baxter, *The Old Charges and the Ritual.* 31 AQC 33 (1918).

Herbert Poole, *The Old Charges in the 18th Century.* Reproduced in Harry Carr, ed., Collected Prestonian Lectures, 155.

H. L. Haywood, *Masonic Old Charges From a Royal Library.* In his Masonic Essays, 290, 314.

Alfred Flint, *Anderson and the Old Charges.* 2 RAM 158, 280 (1947-1948).

Colin F. W. Dyer, *The Radford and Tunnah Mss. and Their Relationship With the Pre-Union Lectures.* 88 AQC 50 (1975).

The Lechmere Manuscript. 88 AQC Reprints in back part of this volume. (1975).

The Inigo Jones Manuscript. 88 AQC 111 (1975); facsimile.

C. F. W. Dyer, *The Shadbolt and Williams Manuscript.* 88 AQC 93 (1975).

The Clausen Manuscript. 88 AQC 297 (1975).

C. F. W. Dyer, *The Williams-Arden Manuscript of the Old Soul's Lodge at Weymouth.* 87 AQC 167 (1974).

The Kevan Manuscript. 1955 Grd. L. of Scotl. Yrbk. 118.

The Schaw Statutes. 1953 Grd. L. of Scotl. Yrbk. 91.

Julius F. Sachse, *Thos. Carmick Ms., A.D. 1727;* 1908; 47 pp. Grand Lodge of Pennsylvania, publisher.
Contents: Facsimile of the Constitutions of St. John's Lodge, being a facsimile of the Thos. Carmick Ms. as well as a transcription into Roman type for easy reading. Libraries: 3, 7, 9.

Rev. Herbert Poole & F. R. Worts, *The "Yorkshire" Old Charges of Masons.* 1935; 277 pp. Installed Masters' Assn. of Leeds, England, publisher.
Authors: 41 AQC 298 (1928); 64 AQC 61 (1951). 78 AQC 15 (1965); 78 AQC 16 (1965). Contents: The first three chapters discuss the subject of the Old Charges. Then 29 manuscripts are reproduced in modern English. Reviewed: 36 AQC 113 (1923). Libraries: 3, 9, 12, 14.

William J. Hughan, *Ancient Masonic Rolls of Constitutions.* 1894; 102 pp.
Contents: Reproduction of some of the Old Charges with comments by the author. Comments: L. B. Blakemore, "Contains a number of the Ancient Mss., with critical comments by the greatest authorities on early Masonic documents." Libraries: 2, 3, 5, 6, 7, 9, 10, 11, 12.

Ray Baker Harris, *The William L. Boyden Manuscript.* MSA Digest.

The Carmick Manuscript. MSA Digest.

Sadwell-Cameron Manuscript. MSA Digest.

William L. Boyden, *Mss. Roll of Old Charges Discovered.* New Age Mag., Feb., 1926, 77. Short introduction and reproduction of the manuscript.

William J. Hughan, *The "Tho. Carmick Ms." and the Introduction of Freemasonry in Pennsylvania.* New Age Mag., Sept., 1909, 761.

N. R. M. Weir, *Charges of a Freemason.* Trans. M. & P. M. L. Sept., 1979, 310.

The Indenture of an Apprentice; reproduced. 10 RAM 236 (1971-1972).

The Famous Graham Manuscript. 10 RAM 44 (1970), 158 (1971).

Knoop and Jones, *Nomenclature of Masonic Manuscripts.* 54 AQC 69 (1941).

R. H. Baxter, *The Old Charges and the Ritual.* 31 AQC 33 (1918); 33 AQC 78 (1920).

W. Begemann, *An Attempt to Classify the Old Charges of the British Masons.* 1 AQC 152 (1886-1888).

Harry Carr, *The Conjoint Theory.* 66 AC 42 (1933).

W. J. Chetwode Crawley, *The Old Charges and Papal Bulls.* 24 AQC 47, 107, 125, 251, 296 (1911).

William J. Hughan, *Bibliography of the Old Charges.* 9 AQC 85 (1896).

William J. Hughan, *Connecting Links Between Ancient and Modern Freemasonry From a Non-Masonic Standpoint.* 1 AQC 50 (1886-1888).

William J. Hughan, *Old Charges of British Freemasons.* 6 AQC 198 (1893).

F. L. Pick, *The Old Charges.* 70 AQC (Inset).

J. E. S. Tuckett, *The Old Charges and the Chief Master Mason.* 36 AQC 179, 281 (1923).

F. R. Worts, *The Old Charges and Their Transcripts.* 45 AQC 54 (1932).

G. W. Speth, *Two New Versions of the "Old Charges."* 1 AQC 127 (1886-1888).

H. L. Haywood, *The Old Charges and What They Mean to Me.* 9 Build. Mag. 280 (1923).

Classification of the Old Charges. 9 Build. Mag. 368 (1932).

William J. Hughan, *The Main Ms.,* 20 AQC 249 (1907).

R. H. Baxter, *The Beswicke-Royde Mss. of the Old Charges.* 28 AQC 189 (1915).

C. C. Howard, *Critical Examination of the Alban and Howard Athelstan Legends, and the Buchanan Mss.* 4 AQC 73 (1891).

E. B. Beeseley, *The "Colne" Manuscript of the "Old Charges."* 34 AQC 59 (1921).

A. L. Kress, *The Carmick Ms.* 11 Build. Mag. 203 (1925).

C. C. Howard, *The Evidential Value of the Regius, the Cooke, and the W. Watson Mss.* 6 AQC 21 (1893).

Herbert Poole, *Two Hitherto Unknown Old Charges, Devonshire Ms.* 69 AQC 100 (1947).

William Waples, *The Stalwell Lodge and Embleton Ms.* 62 AQC 80 (1949).

Herbert Poole, *The Fortitude Ms.* 44 AQC 254 (1931).

E. L. Hawkins, *The Henery Heade Ms.* 21 AQC 161 (1908).

A. E. Evans, *Wessel Linden and Holywell Ms.* 58 AQC 128 (1945).

William Waples, *Wesel de Finder and Holywell Ms.* 75 AQC 74 (1962); 77 AQC 212 (1964).

Herbert Poole, *The Huddlestone Ms.* 52 AQC 160 (1939).

Herbert Poole, *The Joseph Chadwicke Ms.* 61 AQC 260 (1948).

Herbert Poole, *The Classification of the Langdale Ms.* 35 AQC 76 (1922).

F. W. Levander, *A Newly Discovered Version of the Old Charges; the Levander-York Ms.* 18 AQC 161 (1905).

A. R. Hewitt, *Phillips No. 2 Ms.* 78 AQC 110 (1965).

G. W. Speth, *The Two Versions of the "Old Charges."* 1 AQC 127 (1886-1888).

Herbert Poole, *The Ralph Poole Ms. 1665.* 46 AQC 451 (1933).

W. Begemann, *The Assembly (Regius Poem).* 6 AQC 169 (1893).

G. W. Speth, *The Assembly,* 6 AQC 173 (1893).

R. F. Gould, *The Assembly.* 5 AQC 203 (1892).

A. J. B. Milborne, *The Regius Poem and Mirk's Instructions.* 76 AQC 33 (1963).

John Yarker, *The Regius Ms. and the Haliwerk-Folk Ms.* 4 AQC 243 (1891).

W. Begemann, *Remarks on the Sloane Family of the Old Charges of Freemason's Including the John T. Thorp and John Strachan Mss.* 14 AQC 153 (1901).

William Watson, *The Taylor Ms.* 21 AQC 211 (1908).

Herbert Poole, *The Thistle Ms.* 35 AQC 41 (1922).

David Flather, *The Wilson Ms.* 53 AQC 328 (1940).

F. J. Underwood, *The Woodstock Ms. and the Old Charges.* 56 AQC 308 (1943).

5.03 THE LANDMARKS OF FREEMASONRY

Landmarks: What Are They? Ind. Free., Sept., 1974, 14; Ind. Free., April, 1976, 8.

Roscoe Pound, *The Landmarks.* Reproduced in his Masonic Addresses and Writings, 1953; 384 pp. published by Macoy Publishing Co.

Elbert Bede, *The Landmarks of Freemasonry.* 1954; 56 pp. Macoy Publishing Co., publisher.
Author: Appendix No. 1. Libraries: 1, 2, 3, 5, 7, 8, 9, 10, 11, 12, 13, 14.

Charles C. Hunt, *The Landmarks of Freemasonry.* 1943; 129 pp. Laurelle Press, Cedar Rapids, Iowa, publisher. Reviewed: Ill. Enlight., 1949, 3. Libraries: 3, 5, 7, 9, 10, 12, 13, 14.

Silas H. Shepherd, *The Landmarks of Freemasonry.* 1924; 180 pp. Wisconsin Grand Lodge Committee on Masonic Research, publisher.
Author: Phil. Mag., May, 1946, 12. His picture appears in Phil. Mag., March, 1941 3. Comments: Henry W. Coil, Sr., "Not exhaustive but a hand list of over two dozen codes of Landmarks adopted by Grand Lodges or authors." Also appears in 1 Build. Mag. 183, 197 (1915). Libraries: 2, 3, 4, 5, 7, 8, 9, 11, 12, 13, 14.

Ancient Landmarks of Freemasonry. MSA Digest.

W. B. Hextall, *The Old Landmarks of the Craft.* 25 AQC 91 (1912).

George Oliver, *Historical Landmarks*. 2 vols., 1843. Reproduced in the Universal Masonic Library, Volumes 11 and 12.
Author: See Introduction in the 1980 Masonic Book Club edition of Revelations of a Square. Comments: Henry W. Coil, Sr., ''Not particularly reliable. . . . '' L. B. Blakemore, ''A volume, now long out of date, by a once-famous Masonic writer, in the Eighteenth Century tradition.'' Libraries: 1, 2, 3, 4, 5, 7, 8, 9, 10, 11, 12, 13, 14.

F. G. Fox, *The Ancient Landmarks*. Ind. Free., Feb., 1975; March, 1975, 14.

A. J. A. Poignant, *The Landmarks*. 24 AQC 151 (1911).

T. O. Haunch, *It is Not in the Power of Any Man* . . . 85 AQC 194 (1971).

Dwight L. Smith, *Of Landmarks and Cuspidors*. Discussion of landmarks and changes made over the years. Phil. Mag., Feb., 1973, 6.

Charles Howard, *Landmarks, Customs and Me*. Phil. Mag., Feb., 1977, 17. Also in 1976 Proc. Midw. Conf. Mas Ed. 47.

G. W. Daynes, *Two Ancient Landmarks of Freemasonry*. N.Y. Mas. Outl. April, 1925, 170.

Thomas S. Roy, *Our Ancient Landmarks*, 1965 New Hamp. Grd. L. Proc. 9.

Peter A. Cawsey, *The Ancient Landmarks*. 7 Trans. Phoen. Lodge, Paris, 82.

F. G. Fox, *The Ancient Landmarks*. Ind. Free., Feb., 1975, 13.

H. L. Haywood, *The Ancient Landmarks*. Ind. Free., March, 1954, 6; also in 3 Build. Mag. 21 (1917); 4 Build. Mag. 141 (1918).

Melvin M. Johnson, *The Determination of Masonic Landmarks*. 9 Build. Mag. 195 (1923). Has picture of author.

Franklin J. Anderson, *Masonic Landmarks*. 10 RAM 150 (1971).

J. R. Rylands, The Ancient Landmarks. 72 AQC inset (1959).

F. R. Worts, *The Use of the Word ''Landmarks'': Deductions*. 75 AQC 10 (1962).

Theodore S. Parvin, *Old Landmarks*. 1 Build. Mag. 38 (1915); has picture of author.

The Fifty-Four Landmarks of the Grand Lodge of Kentucky. 6 Build. Mag. 26 (1920).

Louis D. Potter, *Ancient Landmarks:* (1) What Are They? (2) Should a restatement of them be made, and, if so, what shall they include? 1944 Proc. Grd. Mast. Conf. 74.

Roscoe Pound, *Landmarks*. 1952 Proc. Grd. Mast. Conf. 37.

Harry L. Martyn and Charles H. Cover, *Are Ancient Landmarks Significant Today and Should There Be a Uniform List?* 1958 Proc. Grd. Mast. Conf., 41, 46.

5.04 THE CONSTITUTIONS OF FREEMASONRY

Roberts Constitution. 1922.
Libraries: A copy of the first edition is in the Iowa Masonic Library. Many years ago a facsimile of this book was published but it is not too clear and is hard to read.

Eric Ward, *The 1722 Constitutions*. 89 AQC 269 (1976).

W. J. Williams, *The Roberts Constitution*. 38 AQC 102 (1925).

J. Hugo Tatsch, *Further Notes on the Roberts Constitution*. 13 Build. Mag. 342 (1927).

Alfred Robbins, *The Newly Discovered Print of the Roberts Ms*. 22 AQC 185 (1909).

James Anderson, *The Constitutions of the Free-Masons*. 1723 and 1738 editions. These have been reproduced many times. A facsimile appears in the first volumes of the Little Masonic Library. In 1976 Quatuor Coronati Lodge published a facsimile of both editions in one volume, the first time this was ever done. The Masonic Book Club in 1978 published a facsimile of the 1738 edition with a detailed paper on the differences between the two editions which had been published in AQC

Anderson's Constitutions. STB, Oct., 1946. The first Masonic book to be published in the western hemisphere was a copy of Anderson's Constitutions, by Benjamin Franklin, in 1734. A facsimile of this volume was published in 1971 by the Masonic Book Club.

Harold V. B. Voorhis, *The First American Masonic Book.* 6 ALR 180 (1953-1954).

Harold V. B. Voorhis, *Benjamin Franklin's Reprint of Anderson's Constitutions of 1723;* a discussion of the extant original edition and where they are located. 84 AQC 69 (1971).

William J. Hughan, *Ancient Masonic Roll of Constitutions.* 1894; 102 pp. Reproduced some of the old documents. Libraries: 2, 3, 5, 6, 7, 9, 10, 11, 12.

Laurence Dermott, *Ahiman Rezon.* 1756. This was the book of Constitutions of the Ancient Grand Lodge; a facsimile edition was published in 1972 by the Masonic Book Club.

R. H. Baxter, *Peculiarities of the Book of Constitutions.* 32 AQC 97 (1919).

F. W. Lavendar, *A Comparison of the Regulations Laid Down in the Book of Constitutions From 1723 to 1819.* 38 AQC 57 (1917).

William H. Upton, *The True Text of the Book of Constitutions.* 7 AQC 119 (1894); 8 AQC 34 (1895).

Book of Constitutions. STB, Aug., 1923.

The Grand Constitutions of 1786 (Scottish Rite). New Age Mag., Nov., 1912, 491.

Grand Constitutions of Frederick. 12 Build. Mag. 159 (1926).

A. Holmes-Dallimore, *The Three Constitutions.* 1927; 114 pp. The Masonic Record, publisher.
Contents: A consideration of the Constitutions of England, Ireland, and Scotland together with other regulations and decisions. Libraries: 3, 5, 7, 9, 11, 12, 13.

5.05 MASONIC LAW

P. M. Hazlitt, *Unwritten Laws of Freemasonry;* 1925; 70 pp.
Libraries: 3, 9.

George W. Chase, *Digest of Masonic Laws;* many editions have been published.
Libraries: 1, 2, 3, 5, 7, 8, 9, 10, 11, 12, 14.

Outline of Masonic Law. Mast. Mas., June, 1928, 400.

Foundations of Masonic Law. STB, March, 1934.

Laws of Masonry. STB, Dec., 1929.

Rob Morris, *Code of Masonic Law.* 1856; 480 pp.
Author: Appendix No. 25. Comments: Silas H. Shepherd, "This work is particularly devoted to the full and lengthy discussion of what Bro. Morris considered to be the 17 'Landmarks.' " Libraries: 2, 3, 4, 5, 7, 10, 11, 12, 14.

Lewis Edwards, *Practical Handbook of Masonic Law and Custom.* 1928; 259 pp. A. Lewis, Ltd., London, publisher.
Reviewed: 42 AQC 125 (1929); 14 Build. Mag., 348 (1928). Libraries: 3, 5, 7, 8, 9.

Parliamentary Law in Freemasonry. STB, Feb., 1948.

Luke A. Lockwood, *Masonic Law and Practice;* with forms. 1921; 137 pp. Macoy Publishing Co., publisher.
Comments: L. B. Blakemore, "First published in 1867 it is not up-to-date, but is still valuable for its exposition of the permanent principles of Masonic jurisprudence." Libraries: 2, 3, 5, 7, 8, 9, 11, 12, 13.

Henry M. Look, *Masonic Trials.* 1902; 326 pp. Macoy Publishing Co., publisher.
Comments: Silas H. Shepherd, "Very concise, containing the essential principles." L. B. Blakemore, "A treatise on the principles and procedure of trials." H. L. Haywood, "There are few Masonic authors of whom so little is known." And in his Masonic Curiosa, he also says "Look was an attorney who was admitted

to the bar in 1859 and died in Greeley, Colorado, in 1894, at the age of 57. He was Grand Lecturer of Michigan from 1869 to 1875 inclusive." Libraries: 2, 3, 5, 7, 8, 9, 10, 11, 12, 13, 14, 15.

Trial Methods of 49 Grand Jurisdictions. MSA Digest.

Judge Newell A. Lamb, *Instructions Concerning Masonic Trials;* with forms 1976; 24 pp. Published by the Grand Lodge of Indiana.

Albert Pike, *Masonic Trials.* New Age Mag., Dec., 1908, 575.

Harry Gershenson, *Masonic Law.* The Freemason, Mo., Fall, 1971, 112.

G. W. Warvelle, *The Perfect Youth.* 2 Build. Mag. 17 (1916).

Ralph D. Coppock, *Masonic Offenses and Trials.* 3 Trans. Tex. L. of Res. 228 (1965-1968).

Powers of Grand Masters. MSA Digest.

Grand Masters Powers. STB, Oct., 1935.

The Powers of the Worshipful Master. STB, Aug., 1929.

Waiting Period Before Application of Other Degrees. MSA Digest.

Dual and Plural Membership. MSA Digest.

Incorporation of Grand Lodges and Lodges. MSA Digest.

Herschel H. Rose, *Should Grand Lodges Be Incorporated Under Civil Law?* 1938 Proc. Grd. Mast. Conf., 93.

Grand Lodge Proficiency Requirements. MSA Digest.

Grand Lodge Supervision of Lodge Building Programs and Suggested Plans for Masonic Temples. MSA Digest.

Norman T. Avard, *Discipline of Members Charged With Un-Masonic Conduct.* 1939 Proc. Grd Mast. Conf. 62.

John H. Anderson, *Expelled or Suspended Member and What the Procedure and Laws Are With Respect to the Claim of Jurisdiction Over Rejected Candidates and Those Elected Who Have Not Re-ceived the Degrees.* 1928 Proc. Grd. Mast. Conf. 13.

Virgil R. Johnson and E. M. Wilson, *Dimits.* 1935 Proc. Grd. Mast. Conf., 54.

Alex Horne, *The Doctrine of Perfect Youth.* Cal. Free., Autumn, 1978, 179; also in Phil. Mag., June, 1978, 3.

Perfect Youth. STB, Feb., 1938.

George Draffen, *Multiple Jurisdiction.* Phil. Mag., Oct., 1978, 22.

Oliver D. Street, *Physical Qualifications of a Candidate.* 3 Build. Mag. 310 (1917).

Alphonse Cerza, *Exclusive Jurisdiction.* Phil. Mag., April, 1978, 16.

Roger F. Callejas, *More About "Exclusive Jurisdiction."* Phil. Mag., Dec., 1978, 14.

D. Boardman Lee, *The Case of Dr. William D. Purple. vs. Phlegmency Horton.* 12 ALR 124 (1972).

Jean O. Heineman, *Right of Visitation.* 12 RAM 53 (1976).

J. Willison Smith, *New Organizations Predicating Their Membership on Freemasonry.* 1929 Proc. Grd. Mast. Conf. 44.

The Penalties. Phil. Mag., Oct., 1963, 85.

Physical Penalties in Freemasonry. 8 RAM 23 (1964).

J. R. Rylands, *The Masonic Penalties.* 77 AQC 21 (1964).

The Penalty of the Third Degree. 14 Build. Mag. 153 (1928).

Penalties. Cal. Free., Autumn, 1972, 164.

Ives, *Penal Methods Reviewed.* 4 Build. Mag. 62 (1918).

Lodge Summons. Phil. Mag., Aug.-Sept., 1950, 3.

Solicitation. 1 Build. Mag. 40 (1915).

Jerry Marsengill, *Legal and Lawful Age.* Ore. Free., May, 1972, 4.

The Secret Societies Act of 1789. 4 RAM 376 (1954).

Masonic Obligation. 12 Build. Mag. 269 (1926).

William L. Boyden, *Quaint By-Gone By-Laws.* New Age Mag., April, 1924, 229.

Prerogatives, Powers, and Duties of Masters Lodges. Mast. Mason., May, 1928, 294.

Smoking in Lodge, Prohibited in 1755. Harry Carr, ed., Collected Prestonian Lectures, 327.

John M. Sherman, *The Doctrine of Exclusive Jurisdiction.* 13 RAM 99 (1979).

Occasionally there arises the question of the powers possessed by a Grand Lodge over Appendant Bodies of the Craft. In 1935 such a question arose in Illinois when an appendant body announced it was going to engage in a lottery, which was a violation of state law, and the Grand Master ordered the project stopped. Grover C. Neimeyer, the Grand Master, was a distinguished lawyer, who later served as a Justice of the Appellate Court of Illinois, and he wrote a formal opinion on the matter which is set out in full in the 1935 Proceedings of the Grand Lodge of Illinois, on pages 19-33.

5.06 FREEMASONRY AND THE LAW COURTS

W. Irvine Wiest, *Freemasonry in the American Courts.* 1958; 162 pp. MLR, publisher.
Author: 1969 Supreme Council Proc., NMJ, 350; has his picture. Comments: Henry W. Coil, "A great help and important to the Masonic lawyer." Libraries: 1, 2, 3, 5, 6, 7, 9, 10, 11, 12, 13, 14.

Alphonse Cerza, *Masonic Questions Answered by the Courts.* 1972 MSA Digest.

W. Irvine Wiest, *Freemasonry and the Nuremberg Trials.* 1959; MLR.

Isaac Blair Evans, *The Thomson Masonic Fraud.* 1922; 261 pp.
Contents: Detailed explanation of the prosecution of several men for selling Masonic degrees using the mail. A transcript of what occurred at the trial is in the Iowa Masonic Library; also copies of some issues of the magazine published by the group from 1908 to 1922. Comments: Editorial in 9 Build. Mag. 23 (1923). Article by Elbert Bede in 5 RAM 21, 59, 94 (1955). Case discussed in detail in 8 Build. Mag. 270, 299, 327, 361 (1922). L. B. Blakemore, "A history of the fraudulent American Federation and of its trial in Salt Lake City, Utah." Reviewed: 9 Build. Mag. 311 (1923). New Age Mag., Feb., 1923, 117. Libraries: 1, 2, 3, 5, 7, 8, 9, 10, 11, 12, 14.

Alphonse Cerza, *"Women's Liberation" and Freemasonry;* Phil. Mag., August, 1977. In 1978 a full scale treatment of the subject was published by Iowa Lodge of Research No. 2.

Six Months in Jail for "False" Mason. New Age Mag., April, 1913, 386.

Clandestinism in Europe. New Age Mag., Oct., 1924, 621.

W. B. Hextall, *The Craft in the Law Courts.* 30 AQC 222 (117).

A Resurgence of Clandestinism. Successful case in Pennsylvania. New Age Mag., July, 1944, 271.

William Fooks, *Freemasons in Reference to the Law of the Realm.* 5 AQC 88 (1892).

Frauds Against Masonry. N.Y. Mas. Outl. Feb., 1930, 163.

A. Reuben, *First Sentenced to the Penitentiary for Advertising and Wearing a Masonic Pin.* N.Y. Mas. Outl., Nov., 1926, 89.

Alphonse Cerza, *Freemasonry in the Courts.* 11 RAM 136 (1977).

Alphonse Cerza, *Freemasonry and Civil Law.* MSA Digest.

Alphonse Cerza, *What Are Our Rights? Can an Association Restrict Its Members From Joining Other Groups?* Phil. Mag., Aug. 1977, 10.

CHAPTER SIX

Symbolism

6.01 MASONIC SYMBOLISM-GENERAL

Why Teach by Symbols. Phil. Mag., Aug., 1959; 57.

Albert G. Mackey, *Symbolism of Freemasonry*. 1945; 313; Masonic History Co., Chicago, Ill. Revised by Robert I. Clegg.
Author: Appendix No. 29. Comments: Silas H. Shepherd, "The most comprehensive text on the subject written during the 19th century. The matter does not admit of full explanation in language, as the symbols themselves are the best teachers." L. B. Blakemore, "Has been for a long period one of the Masonic classics. Learned and yet easy-to-read chapters on the most important symbols." Carl H. Claudy, "The average lodge member who wishes only a modest amount of information on the subject will choose Street. The student who must have a background before he paints his picture must have Mackey. Who studies both is well equipped indeed to read with critical eyes and an understanding heart those later writers who have so beautifully developed a spiritual content of symbols to supplement the teachings of the Ancient Craft." Reviewed: 6 Build. Mag. 226 (1920); 8 Build. Mag. 382 (1922). Libraries: 1, 2, 3, 4, 5, 7, 9, 10, 11, 12, 13, 14.

Oliver Day Street, *Symbolism of the Three Degrees*. 1922; 190. This book is a collection of articles which appeared originally in various volumes of the Builder Magazine, especially in Volumes 1, 4, and 6.
Author: See Gould's History, 1936 ed., Vol. 6, p. 484. Comments: Henry W. Coil, Sr., "A more restrained and practical presentation." Carl H. Claudy, "Generally considered the simplest of the many books dealing with this complicated subject. Most writers on the symbolism of Freemasonry inevitably give their personal slants in their interpretations, as indeed, no less an authority than Albert Pike said all should do. Street has in large measure skillfully avoided this in bringing together a consensus on the majority of Masonic symbols which is a sound basis from which to proceed to other and more personal interpretations." L. B. Blakemore, "A series of short chapters, first published in The Builder on the important symbols and ceremonies of the Three Degrees." Norman B. Hickox, "He has written on the principle that Masonic symbols should have a Masonic explanation and interpretation as determined by the history and teaching of the Craft. He gives us, in clear, understandable style the information every Mason seeks, and thus the work is invaluable to the newly raised brother, as it gives him a splendid introduction to Masonic symbolism." Reviewed: 6 Build. Mag. 50 (1920); 11 Build. Mag. 61 (1925). Libraries: 2, 3, 4, 5, 6, 7, 8, 9, 10, 11, 12, 13, 14, 15.

Charles Clyde Hunt, *Masonic Symbolism*. 1939; 508; Laurence Press, Cedar Rapids, Iowa, publisher.
Author: Gould's History. 1936 ed., Vol. 6, p. 471; Phil. Mag., Nov., 1948, p. 5. Contents: Fifty-nine short chapters dealing with various symbols and related subjects by a devoted member of the Craft. Comments: Henry W. Coil, Sr., "Plainly and simply presented." L. B. Blakemore, "A series of instructive essays on the more

101

important Symbolism in the Three Degrees by the Grand Secretary and Grand Historian of the Grand Lodge of Iowa.'' Reviewed: 42 AQC 311 (1932); 50 AQC 125 (1940). Libraries: 3, 4, 5, 7, 8, 9, 11, 12, 13, 14, 15.

Silas Shepherd, *Notes on Symbolism;* 1929; 23 pp. Wisconsin Committee on Masonic Research. Pamphlet No. 40. Libraries: 3, 7, 9, 12.

Allen E. Roberts, *The Craft and Its Symbols.* 1974; 92 pp. Macoy Publishing Co., publisher.
Author: Appendix No. 29. Reviewed: 89 AQC 187 (1976). Libraries: 2, 3, 11, 12.

H. L. Haywood, *Symbolical Masonry.* 1923; 352 pp. Southern Publishers, Inc., Kingsport, Tenn., publisher.
Author: Appendix No. 16. Comments: Henry W. Coil, Sr., ''Adds little to the subject and more likely to serve as an attempt to systematize the subject.'' L. B. Blakemore, ''An interesting presentation of the Three Degrees by an American writer in the American spirit who was Editor of The Builder for a period of years. Reviewed: 10 Build. Mag. 154 (1924); Mast. Mas., Feb., 1924, 72. Libraries: 1, 2, 3, 4, 5, 6, 7, 8, 9, 10, 11, 12, 13, 14, 15.

Wendell Carnahan, *Symbolism – Its Background, Literature and Appreciation.* Phil. Mag., Aug., 1956, 56.

George Oliver, *Signs and Symbols of Freemasonry.* 1906; 170 pp. Macoy Publishing Co., publisher.
Author: See Introduction in the 1980 volume of the Masonic Book Club which reproduces his Revelations of a Square. Contents: Twelve lectures on Masonic subjects; many of the subjects will seem strange to the modern day reader such as ''on the Cherubim,'' ''on the deluge,'' and ''on the serpent.'' Comments: L. B. Blakemore, ''One of the oldest and most important books on the subject. Now out of date in many essentials but still a 'must' for students of the ritual.'' Libraries: 1, 2, 3, 4, 5, 7, 8, 9, 10, 11, 12, 13, 14.

J. E. Cirlot, *A Dictionary of Symbols.* 1962; 305; Philosophical Library, publisher. Written for the general reader but still of some interest to Masons. Libraries: 3, 7.

Goblet D'Alviella, *The Migration of Symbols.* 1894; 277 pp. Archibald Constable & Co., Westminster, publisher. Reissued in 1956 by University Books, New York.
Author: 38 AQC 223 (1925). Comments: H. L. Haywood, ''He was a Belgian savant; member of the Senate. This is one of the masterpieces on the subject.'' Silas H. Shepherd, ''One of the best works on symbolism.'' Reviewed: 3 AQC 104 (1890). Libraries: 3, 9.

Donald A. Mackenzie, *Migration of Symbols.* 1926; 219 pp. K. Paul Trench, Tauber & Co., London, publisher. Libraries: 3, 9.

H. C. Barlow, Essays on Symbolism. 1886; 144 pp.
Comments: Silas H. Shepherd, ''The chapters on the history and fundamental principles of Symbolism are of great value.''

Arthur Ward, *Masonic Symbolism and the Mystic Way.* 1913; 164 pp. The Theosophical Publishing Society, London.
Contents: Collection of papers on the ''true secret'' and the ''lost word'' attempting to weave strange doctrines into the thoughts of the Craft. Must be read with caution. Libraries: 3, 7, 9, 10, 11, 14.

J. S. M. Ward, *The Sign Language of the Mysteries.* Two volumes; The Baskerville Press, London, publisher.
Contents: A beautiful book with a long list of signs, paintings, rocks, etc., with much fine art work. The material may have appeal for some of our members but most of the material has no direct Masonic significance. Libraries: 1, 3, 4, 5, 7, 9, 10, 12, 13, 14.

J. S. M. Ward, *An Interpretation of Our Masonic Symbols.* 1948; 158. pp. A. Lewis, London, publisher.
Libraries: 1, 3, 4, 5, 7, 8, 9, 10, 11, 12, 13, 14.

Albert Churchward, *Signs and Symbols of Primordial Man.* 1913; 491 pp., George Allen & Co., publisher; also published

by E. P. Dutton & Co., New York. Has many pictures.
Comments: L. B. Blakemore, "An occultistic interpretation of Masonic rites. Very readable but at variance with the findings of Masonic scholarship." Silas H. Shepherd, "This is Dr. Churchward's most pretentious work. The many illustrations are of importance in learning about symbolic teaching in general. Although most readers probably will not concede the antiquity of the signs and ceremonies described by Dr. Churchward, all will be enlightened by this book." Mas. Sq., Dec., 1976, 150: " . . . from a strict Masonic point of view, the writings of Dr. Albert Churchward should be treated with caution." See: H. L. Haywood, 6 Build. Mag. 257 (1920) — it states his works are not recommended. Libraries: 2, 3, 4, 5, 7, 9, 10, 11, 13, 14.

Manley P. Hall, *The Lost Keys of Freemasonry*. 1931; 128.
Author: A famous lecturer and writer emphasizing the influence of Egypt and its mysticism. He wrote this book before he became a Mason. Comments: Henry W. Coil, Sr., "A non-Mason mystic who lectured on such subjects." 14 Build. Mag. 283 (1928): "A suspicion arises that the author is a theosophist . . . the author allegorizes the legend of Hiram Abiff very beautifully. Whether his knowledge of mythology and the history and evolution of religion is as complete as might appear upon the surface is perhaps open to question. . . . To the Mason who delights in symbolic imagery, the author presents a feast, much of it of original conception; but it is to be feared that most of it will be above the heads of the great body of the Craft." Libraries: 1, 2, 3, 4, 5, 6, 7, 8, 9, 10, 11, 12, 13, 14.

T. M. Stewart, *Symbolism of the Gods of the Egyptians*. 1927; 120 pp. The Baskerville Press, publisher.
Contents: Sets forth an Egyptian ritual and discusses the symbols in the Book of the Dead. To be read with caution. Reviewed: 1 Build. Mag. 47 (1915). Libraries: 3, 5, 6, 9, 11, 12, 13, 14.

T. M. Stewart, *Symbolic Teachings: or, Masonry and Its Message*. 1917; 242

pp. Stewart & Kidd Co., Cincinnati, publisher.
Comment: L. B. Blakemore, "A collection of articles and essays with an underlying basis of occultism." To be read with caution. Libraries: 2, 3, 4, 5, 7, 8, 9, 10, 11, 12, 14.

Arthur Edward Waite, *Some Deeper Aspects of Masonic Symbolism;* reprinted from several articles appearing in the April-June issues, 1916 (vol. 2), The Builder Magazine.
Author: 2 Build. Mag. 105 has an article on him; his picture is on page 107. He was the leading mystic and occultist of his day. His material must be read with caution. Libraries: 3, 7, 9, 12.

J. Finlay Finlayson, *Symbols and Legends of Freemasonry*. 1910; 166 pp. George Kenning & Son, publisher.
Comments: L. B. Blakemore, "Like many of the older books this is out-moded, nevertheless it is still valuable for many pages of information about ancient rites and symbols." Silas H. Shepherd, "Too few of this class are available. The interpretation of symbols is necessarily an individual task; nevertheless guides that assist in the word are much needed." Reviewed: 2 AQC 79 (1889). Libraries: 2, 3, 4, 5, 7, 8, 9, 11, 12, 13, 14.

W. H. Rylands, *Notes on Some Masonic Symbols*. 8 AQC 84 (1895); discussed in 83 AQC 371 (1970).

Robert F. Gould, *The Antiquity of Masonic Symbolism*. 3 AQC 7 (1890).

Pocket Encyclopedia of Masonic Symbols. MSA Digest.

I. Inglis, *Some Aspects of Masonic Symbolism*. 83 AQC 357 (1970).

Willard G. Burris, *Some Notes on Ancient Geometricians*. No. Cal. Res. L. Quart., Sept., 1979, p. 1.

L. M. Sherwood, *Symbolatry*. 85 AQC 317 (1972).

Carl W. Hopp, *Are Working Tools Important?* Phil. Mag., Feb., 1974, 7.

The Symbols of the Entered Apprentice. Ind. Free., Oct., 1977, 8.

Symbols and Allegories of the Second Degree. Ind. Free., Feb., 1978, 14.

Walter Linton, *Examination of the Working Tools of the Craft Degrees*. 1974 Grd. L. of Scotl. Yrbk. 110.

Alex Horne, *Albert Pike in London*. Discusses unpublished book written by Pike on symbolism. New Age Mag., Oct., 1974, 24.

Colin F. W. Dyer, *Symbolism in Craft Freemasonry*. 1976; 178 pp. A. Lewis Ltd., publisher.
Reviewed: New Age Mag., April, 1977, 54; 88 AQC 175 (1975). Libraries: 2, 3, 12.

Alfred North Whitehead, *Symbolism: Its Meaning and Effect*. The Macmillan Co. Reviewed in 14 Build. Mag. 219 (1928). Written for the general reader. Also reviewed in 39 AQC 283 (1925).

Dr. George H. T. French, *The Symbol and the Symbolized*. 3 Trans. Tex. Res. L. 385 (1965-1968).

H. L. Haywood, *The Voice of the Symbol*. N.Y. Mas. Outl., Jan., 1929, 137.

H. L. Haywood, *On Certain Masonic Symbols*. N.Y. Mas. Outl., Sept., 1927, 5.

L. R. R. Denny, *Symbolism*. Trans. M. & P. M. L. May, 1979, 268. General presentation of the ethical and religious aspects of the subject.

E. T. Reid, *Symbolism and Wisdom From the Babylonian Talmud*. 3 RAM 24 (1949).

W. W. Covey-Crump, *Medieval Master Masons and Their Secrets*. Harry Carr, ed., Collected Prestonian Lectures, 141.

Alex Horne, *Religious Symbolism in the Middle Ages*. New Age Mag., May, 1969, 47.

Carl H. Claudy, *Behind the Symbol*. Ind. Free., Aug., 1954, 10.

Joseph Johnson, *The Inwardness of Masonic Symbolism in the Three Degrees*. Harry Carr, ed., Collected Prestonian Lectures, 229.

Harold V. B. Voorhis, *Notes on the History and Symbolism of the Royal Arch Degree*. 8 RAM 110 (1964).

List of Books on Symbolism. 3 Build. Mag. 381 (1917).

Roscoe Pound, *A Preface to Masonic Symbolism*. 5 Build. Mag. 99 (1919).

H. L. Haywood, *Studies in Blue Lodge Symbolism*. 5 Build. Mag. 135 (1909).

A Primer of Masonic Symbolism. Ind. Free., Oct., 1959, 4.

Origin of Symbolism. New Age Mag., April, 1958, 217.

Symbolism. STB, March, 1925.

Illustrated by Symbols. STB, March, 1941.

The Nature of Symbols. STB, July, 1957.

J. R. J. Meekren, *The Secondary Symbolism of Gothic Architecture*. 11 Build. Mag. 375 (1925).

Raymond W. Miller, *Symbolism*, New Age Mag., Aug., 1970, 4.

Silas H. Shepherd, *Some Notes on Symbolism*. 15 Build. Mag. 76, 99 (1929).

Freemasonry's Symbology. Mas. J. So. Africa, June, 1972, 7.

David R. Lane, *Why Masonry Must Teach by Symbols*. Phil. Mag., Aug., 1959, 57.

Some Notes on Symbolism. Ill. Enlight., Oct., 1964, 4.

When Did Symbolism Begin? 2 RAM 349 (1948).

R. J. Meekren, *The Symbolism of Medieval Architecture*. 11 Build. Mag. 344 (1925).

Charles G. Reigner, *Basic Principles of Masonic Symbolism*. 8 RAM 41, 73 (1964).

Arthur C. Parker, *The Meaning of Symbols*. Phil. Mag., Feb., 1955, 3.

G. R. Cobham, *Antiquity of Masonic Symbolism*. 4 AQC 176 (1891).

W. W. Covey-Crump, *Symbolism*. 39 AQC 273 (1926).

J. W. Horsley, *Masonic Symbolism.* 10 AQC 60 (1897).

S. T. Klein, *The Great Symbol.* 10 AQC 82 (1897).

W. E. Montgomery, *Symbolism.* 78 AQC 270 (1965).

Asahel W. Gage, *Symbolism of the First Degree.* 1 Build. Mag. 234 (1915).

C. T. Sego, *Symbolism in Mythology.* 1 Build. Mag. 296 (1915).

Evidences of Symbolism in the Land of the Incas. 2 Build. Mag. 361 (1916).

R. J. Meekren, *Craft Symbols.* 12 Build. Mag. 23 (1926).

R. J. Meekren, *What Is Symbolism?* 11 Build. Mag. 312 (1925).

R. J. Meekren, *The Symbolism of the Old Catechisms.* 12 Build. Mag. 55 (1926).

Masonic Symbols in American Decorative Art; 1975; 112 pp. Published jointly by the Masonic Book Club and the Scottish Rite Museum of Our National Heritage, Lexington, Mass. Has pictures of furniture and other objects having Masonic symbols displayed at the Museum with a word explanation of each item.

6.02 KING SOLOMON'S TEMPLE AND FREEMASONRY

Alex Horne, *King Solomon's Temple in the Masonic Tradition.* 1972; 352 pp. The Aquarian Press, publisher.
Author: Appendix No. 20. Picture of author in Tex. Free., March-April, 1977, 28. Comments: Louis L. Williams, "A magnificient well-researched study of this subject, by the California scholar." Reviews: No. Light, Nov., 1972, 13; Cal. Free., Autumn, 1972, 154; New Age Mag., Sept., 1972, 55; Ind. Free., Jan., 1973, 20; Ore. Free., Oct., 1977, 9; Ore. Free., Sept., 1972, 15. Libraries: 2, 3, 4, 5, 7, 9, 11, 12.

Charles A. Conover, *Treatise on the Construction of King Solomon's Temple.* 1921; 94 pp.
Libraries: 3, 5, 7, 9, 12, 14.

Pictures of the Temple as conceived by John Wesley Kelchner appear in the A. J. Holman Co. ed. of the Holy Bible.

King Solomon and His Temple; article in the World Publishing Co. Ed. of the Holy Bible; with pictures.

Dudley Wright, *Masonic Legends and Traditions.* pp. 36-131.

Books on King Solomon's Temple. 8 Build. Mag. 386 (1922).

R. A. Wells, *Jerusalem and the Successive Temples.* 81 AQC 335 (1968).

Lewis Edwards, *The Story of the Fourth Temple.* 69 AQC 32 (1956).

Two Ancient Legends of King Solomon's Temple. 21 AQC 264 (1908).

C. Mina and H. Arthur Klein, *Temple Beyond Time.* 1972; 191 pp.

Victor Sampson, *King Solomon's Temple and Its Relation to Freemasonry.* 3 Trans. Phoe. Lodge, Paris, 141 (1971-1972).

Carroll Baker & Dotson Kelchner Expect to Finish the Job Begun by King Solomon 3,000 Years Ago. N.Y. Mas. Outl., Sept., 1974, 48.

A. W. Monks, *The Background of Masonry:* Mas. J. of So. Africa, Jan., 1975, 19. Gives historical background of the events leading to the construction of the Temple.

R. W. J. Webb, *King Solomon's Temple.* Mas. Sq., Sept., 1977, 110.

J. R. Clarke, *A New Look at King Solomon's Temple and Its Connection with Masonic Ritual.* 88 AQC 184 (1975).

King Solomon's Temple. Ind. Free., May, 1977, 14.

Richard H. Curtis, *Solomon's Temple at Toledo.* No. Light, Nov., 1978, 4. Discusses plans and pictures by Clarence Shields, sponsored by E. Roger Kirk.

Fred Armitage, *The Origin of the Pillars to King Solomon's Temple.* 21 AQC 270 (1908).

H. Baxter, *The Architectural Style of King*

Solomon's Temple. 33 AQC 114 (1920).

S. P. Johnston, *17th Century Description of Solomon's Temple*. 12 AQC 135 (1899).

W. H. Rylands, *Schott's Model of Solomon's Temple*. 13 AQC 24. (1900).

F. J. Trumper, *Some Notes on the Building of King Solomon's Temple*. 78 AQC 226 (1965).

Our Friend, King Solomon. New Age Mag., Dec., 1972, 50.

Solomon. Phil. Mag., April, 1959, 25; June, 1955, 12.

King Solomon's Signet Ring. Phil. Mag., Dec., 1965, 97.

The Building of King Solomon's Temple. New Age Mag.: Sept., 1955, 527; Oct. 1955, 621; Nov., 1955, 671.

Alex Horne, *King Solomon and His Temple*. New Age Mag., Nov., 1959, 650.

Solomon's Temple. New Age Mag., May, 1968, 49.

King Solomon's Temple, New Age Mag., Dec., 1960, 39.

Where Is King Solomon's Temple? New Age Mag., June, 1959, 351.

Alex Horne, *King Herod's Temple*. 79 AQC 233 (1966).

Lewis Edwards, *The Story of the Fourth Temple*. 69 AQC 32 (1956); 70 AQC 54 (1957).

H. Baxter, *The Architecture of King Solomon's Temple*. 33 AQC 114 (1920).

Alex Horne, *King Solomon's Temple in the Masonic Tradition*. 75 AQC 221 (1962).

Alex Horne, *The Masonic Tradition of King Solomon's Temple*. 80 AQC 8 (1967).

Alex Horne, *King Solomon's Temple — Did It Ever Exist?* 82 AQC 156 (1969).

James B. Gale, *King Solomon and His Temple*. Ind. Free., Oct., 1968, 8.

Reconstruction of King Solomon's Temple. New Age Mag., Jan., 1967, 39.

Gerard Brett, *Solomon and the Temple*. 61 AQC 253 (1948).

Gerard Brett, *King Solomon*. 66 AQC 89 (1953); 67 AQC 53 (1954).

W. A. Paine, *Masonry and King Solomon's Temple*. 3 Build. Mag. 101, 137, 172 (1917).

George W. Warvelle, *Legends of King Solomon*. 2 Build. Mag. 85 (1916).

6.03 SPECIFIC SYMBOLS

Acacia: Clinton H. Brauer, *A Spring of Acacia,* 13 Trans. Tex. L. of Res. 106 (1978). Ill. Enlight., Feb., 1962, 261. New Age Mag., Nov., 1962, 48; Dec., 1960, 13; Jan., 1968, 23. STB, Dec., 1932. *Trees in Freemasonry*, Mas. Sq., June, 1977, 74. Leon Zeldis, *The Acacia,* 88 AQC 194 (1975).

All-Seeing Eye: STB, Dec., 1932.

Allegory: L. L. Walker, Jr., *The Veil of Allegory,* 11 Trans. Tex. L. of Res. 25 (1975-1976). G. E. W. Bridge, *Veiled in Allegory and Illustrated by Symbols;* reproduced in Harry Carr, ed., Collected Prestonian Lectures, 265. STB, Sept., 1949.

Altar: A. B. Leamer, 2 Build. Mag. 277 (1916). STB, Feb., 1924. STB, Jan., 1955.

Anchor and Ark: STB, June, 1949.

Angle: W. H. Barron, *An Angle of Ninety Degrees*. 26 Trans. Leic. L. of Res., 115 (1917-1918).

Animals and Plants: Mast. Mas., 1925, 137.

Apron: Plez A. Transou, *The Origin and Development of the Masonic Apron,* 10 Trans. Tex. L. of Res. 208 (1974-1975). *Past Master's Aprons,* MSA Digest. Dr. George H. T. French, *The Masonic Apron*, Tex. Free., June, 1977, 5. *Lambskin Apron,* STB, Nov., 1927. *Masonic Aprons,* Pa. Free., May, 1974, 7. *Some Aprons of the Royal Arch Mason,* 3 RAM 374 (1951). STB, June, 1932. Ill. Enlight., April, 1951, 4. Cal. Free., Summer, 1973, 123. Phil. Mag., June, 1957, 36. *Vermont Apron,* Phil. Mag., Feb.,

1971, 8. F. R. Worts, *Apron and Its Symbolism*, 74 AQC 133 (1961). D. R. Clark, *A Curious Masonic Apron*, 4 AQC 56 (1891). F. J. W. Crowe, *Masonic Clothing*, 5 AQC 29 (1892); 6 AQC 160 (1893). 7 AQC 51, 194 (1894); M. Doe, *Moira Apron*, 17 AQC 66 (1904). *Flap Up, Corner Up*, 77 AQC 303 (1964). J. E. Green, *Curious Hand-Painted Masonic Apron*, 4 AQC 108 (1891). W. H. Rylands, *The Masonic Apron*, 5 AQC 172 (1892). F. R. Worts, *The Apron and Its Symbolism*, 5 AQC 133 (1948). Sydney Pope, *An Old Irish Apron in Kent*, 61 AQC 114 (1948). 3 Build. Mag. 19, 74 (1917). R. J. Meekren, *The Apron*, 12 Build. Mag. 164 (1923). *Symbolism of the Apron*, 4 Build. Mag. 324 (1918). H. V. B. Voorhis, *Unusual Masonic Aprons Used in New York Lodges*, 8 ALR 196 (1961).

Ark of the Covenant: 3 RAM 360 (1951). 8 RAM 26 (1964). 12 Build. Mag. 45 (1926).

Ashlar: *The Ashlars: What Do They Mean Today?* Ind. Free., June, 1976, 8. John Thomas Lawrence, *Perfect Ashlar and Other Symbols*, 1937. STB, Aug., 1933. *The Perfect Ashlar*, 3 Build. Mag. 103 (1917). F. C. Higgins, *The Two Ashlars*, 2 Build Mag. 373 (1916). Phil. Mag., Feb., 1966, 23. 6 RAM 283 (1960).

Astronomy: *Astronomy and Freemasonry*, STB, June, 1953.

Attentive Ear: STB, March, 1964.

Banners: *The Tribal Banners*, 1 RAM 21, 132, 157, 185, 223, 249 (1944). *The Banners of the Twelve Tribes*, 5 RAM 181 (1956). 8 RAM 141 (1965).

Beehive: 76 AQC 228 (1963). G. W. Bullamore, *The Beehive and Freemasonry*, 36 AQC 219 (1923). STB, Sept., 1951.

Black Cube: STB, Nov., 1929.

Blazing Star: STB, March, 1965.

Brazen Serpent: New Age Mag., Sept., 1962, 31.

Breast Plate: G. W. Speth, *Master's Breast Plate*, 14 AQC 54 (1901). *Aaron's Breastplate*, Phil. Mag., Feb., 1961, 9.

Broken Column: 5 RAM 138 (1956). STB, Feb., 1956.

Broached Thurnel: G. W. Speth, *Broached Thurnel*, 12 AQC 205 (1899).

Burning Bush: Phil. Mag., April, 1960, 25.

Brotherhood: James E. Craig, *The Plane of Brotherhood*, N.Y. Mas. Outl., Feb., 1930, 173.

Cable Tow: *The Length of Our Cable Tow*, N.Y. Mas. Outl., Feb., 1929, 172. John A. Sherren, *The Cable-Tow*, 1 Trans. Author's Lodge No. 3456, 177 (1915). W. Graham Brown, *The Cable Tow*, 1965 Grd. L. of Scot. Yrbk. 57. Joseph Barrett, *The Square and Cabletow*, 3 Build. Mag. 341 (1917). 9 Build Mag. 332 (1932). Phil. Mag., Feb., 1949, 6. Aug., 1962, 50. Ind. Free., Aug., 1954, 13. STB, March, 1926. Mas. J. of So. Africa, Aug., 1972, 9.

Caduceus: New Age Mag., June, 1973, 15.

Candle Box: Percy Still, *A Masonic Candle-Box*, 72 AQC 60 (1959).

Candles: Ind. Freemason., Sept., 1954, 10. STB, Aug., 1945. *The Legends of the Candles*, Ind. Free., Oct., 1954, 13. *Lighting Candles*, STB, April, 1061. Elbert Bede, *Lighted Candles*, Phil. Mag., Feb., 1947, 6.

Candlesticks: Harry Carr, *Pillars and Globes, Columns and Candlesticks*, 75 AQC 204 (1962). C. C. Hunt, *The Seven-Branches Candlestick*, 10 Build. Mag. 44 (1924). Ray V. Denslow, *Candlesticks and Freemasonry*, 1 RAM 339 (1945).

Cedars of Lebanon: 8 Build. Mag. 385 (1922). 10 Build. Mag. 46 (1924).

Chalk, Charcoal, and Clay: STB, March, 1951.

Chart: *Symbolic Chart of 1789*. 3 AQC 36 (1890).

Chisel: *The Chisel and Its Symbolism*, 85 AQC 364 (1973).

Circle: STB, Feb., 1962. *Point Within a Circle*, Phil. Mag., Aug., 1947, 6. Mas. Sq., Dec., 1979, 156.

Color: Wallechensky and Wallace, *The People's Almanac No. 2*, 1006, has general discussion of the symbolism, use, and meaning of the color blue. Elmer Mantz, *The Symbolic Colors*, N.Y. Mas. Outl., March, 1926, 204. Fred J. W. Crowe, *Colour in Freemasonry*, 17 AQC 3 (1904); 18 AQC 148 (1905). W. J. Chewode Crawley, *Masonic Blue*, 23 AQC 309 (1910). 36 AQC 284 (1923). Cyril N. Batham, *Why Blue?* 3 Trans. Phoe. L., Paris, 138 (1971-1972). STB, July, 1934. *Why Do We Call Them Blue Lodges?* Phil. Mag., June, 1958, 41. Red, STB, Sept., 1926. *The Symbolism of the Color Blue*, 2 Build. Mag. 236 (1916). *The Use and Symbolism of Color in Masonry*, 2 Build. Mag. 270, (1916). *Significance of Masonic Color*, 5 Build. Mag. 178 (1919). *The Blue Lodge*, Phil. Mag., Feb., 1965, 20.

Columns: 11 Build. Mag. 287 (1925). STB, Nov., 1949.

Compasses: Harry Carr, *The Great Architect and the Compasses*, 75 AQC 108 (1962). R. J. Meekren, *Compasses: Singular or Plural?* 14 Build. Mag. 103 (1928). STB, May, 1924. *The Compasses*, 14 Build. Mag. 17 (1928).

Cord: Cord, Rope, and Cable-Tow, STB, Sept., 1950.

Corn, Wine and Oil: STB, Aug., 1930.

Cornerstone: STB, July, 1936.

Covering of a Lodge: STB, Oct., 1949.

Crosses: *The Cross in Freemasonry*, New Age Mag., Jan., 1907, 57. W. I. Grantham, *The Triple Tau*, 57 AQC 283 (1944). Norman Hackney, *The "Tau" in the Royal Arch*, 76 AQC 218 (1963). Mrs. H. G. M. Murray-Aynsley, *The Tau, or Cross: A Heathen and a Christian Symbol*, 5 AQC 81, 224 (1892). H. J. Whymper, *The Tau as a Keystone*, 6 AQC 92 (1893). *Tau Cross*, 7 RAM 11 (1961). *Triple Tau*, 2 RAM 222 (1947). Albert C. Hanson, *Crosses*, K. T. Mag., April, 1973, 7. W. J. Songhurst, *Templar Crosses*, 14 AQC 54 (1901). 3 Build. Mag. 355 (1917).

Destitution: *Rite of Destitution*, STB, 1949.

Dew Drop Lecture: STB, July, 1949.

Discalceation: STB, April, 1933.

Doors: *Masonic Doors*, Phil. Mag., April-May, 1948; 8. H. L. Haywood, *The Outer and Inner Door*, N.Y. Mas. Outl., March, 1929, 205.

Double-Headed Eagle: Arthur C. Parker, Ind. Free., Nov., 1954, 8. 9 Build. Mag. 138 (1923). New Age Mag., Feb., 1907, 176; Nov., 1919, 489; April, 1929, 245; Aug.-Sept., 1945, 339; March, 1946, 82; Feb., 1953, 82; June, 1958, 353; March, 1958, 181; July, 1960, 13.

Due Form: STB, Feb., 1928.

Entrance: *The Shock of Entrance*, Phil. Mag., April, 1975, 46. C. W. Coons, *Stand Erect*, Phil. Mag., Oct., 1977, 10.

Fire: Harry Carr, *Masonic Fire*, 79 AQC 273 (1966). *Craft Fire*, 77 AQC 301 (1964). *Royal Arch Toasts and Fire*, 79 AQC 300 (1966).

Five Points: STB, May, 1931.

Five Senses: STB, Feb., 1958.

Flags: C. S. Lobingier, *Some Sources of Symbolism in Old Glory*, 5 Build. Mag. 159 (1919). *Old Glory in Masonry*, 11 Norcalore 35. *Masonic Flags and Incidents*, 3 ALR 162, 637 (1938-1939). *Masonic Flags and Incidents*, 3 ALR 162, 637 (1938-1939). *Masonic Flags at Sea*, Phil. Mag., Oct., 1971, 92.

Foreign Countries: STB, Nov., 1928.

Forget Me Not: Phil. Mag., Dec., 1970, 113.

Forty-Seventh Problem: Thomas Greene, *Forty-Seventh Proposition of the First Book of Euclid as Part of the Jewel of a Past Master*, 14 AQC 27 (1901). 2 Build. Mag. 254 (1916). 4 Build. Mag. 309 (1918). *"Eureka" and the 47th Problem*, 7 Build. Mag. 332 (1921). 1 Build. Mag. 55 (1916); has picture of C. C. Hunt. Eureka, Phil. Mag., June, 1949, 6. *Pythagorus*, New Age Mag., March, 1954, 151. Mervin A. Hogan, *Euclid's Right-Angles Triangle*, No. Light, Sept.,

1979, 12. *The Forty-Seventh Problem: What Does It Mean Today?* Ind. Free., Aug., 1976, 8. Mervin B. Hogan, *Euclid's 47th Proposition,* 11 RAM 279 (1975). STB, Oct., 1930. New Age Mag., Aug., 1909, 153. Ind. Free., April, 1953, 10.

G: H. L. Haywood, *The Letter "G,"* N.Y. Mas. Outl., Dec., 1927, 101. Juston O. King, *The Letter G,* K. T. Mag., June, 1974, 28. Leszek Ochota, *The Letter "G,"* 13 RAM 14 (1979). Julien M. Hodgskin, Jr., *The Letter "G,"* Trans. Atlantic L. of Res., Jan 31, 1969. *Gemetria and the Letter G,* 14 Build. Mag. 225 (1928). J. A. Cockburn, *The Letter G,* 10 AQC 40, 158 (1897). 13 AQC 176 (1900). Harry Carr, *The Letter G,* 76 AQC 172 (1963). STB, July, 1927. Phil. Mag., Feb., 1972, 16. *Geometry and the Letter G in the East,* New Age Mag., Oct., 1972, 16.

Gavel: James E. Craig, *The Common Gavel,* N.Y. Mas. Outl., Nov., 1929, 75. William L. Boyden, *The Gavel and Its Antiquity,* New Age Mag., Feb., 1927, 101. STB, July, 1931.

Geometry: STB, May, 1934.

Glass: Phil. Mag., Dec., 1949, 9.

Globes: STB, July, 1967. Phil. Mag., Oct., 1970, 98. H. L. Haywood, *The Two Globes,* N.Y. Mas. Outl., Oct., 1928, 44. Harry Carr, *Pillars and Globes,* 75 AQC 204 (1962). *Globes and Pillars,* 82 AQC 322 (1969). 11 Build. Mag. 383 (1925).

Gloves: STB, Feb., 1940. New Age Mag., March, 1960, 32. Harry Carr, *Two Pair of White Gloves,* 75 AQC 117 (1962).

Golden Fleece: Matthew Hoath, *Golden Fleece, Roman Eagle, Star and Garter,* Ind. Free., July, 1960. 4. Mast. Mas., June, 1927, 512. Plez A. Transou, *The Fleece, The Eagle, The Star and Garter,* 11 Trans. Tex. L. of Res. 44 (1975-1976).

Hand: *The Significance of the Hand,* Mas. J. of So. Africa, April, 1972, 9. STB, Nov., 1946.

Hats: *Master's Hat,* 76 AQC 230 (1963). Eric Ward, *The Worshipful Master's Hat,* 74 AQC 154 (1961). STB,

Sept., 1934. Cal. Free., Summer, 1972, 122.

Heart: *Language of the Heart,* STB, March, 1929.

Hoodwink: 9 Build. Mag., 272 (1923). Ind. Free., Nov., 1954, 12. STB, Aug., 1957.

Horizontals: STB, Nov., 1966.

Horse: *The Horse in Freemasonry,* 8 Norcalore 9.

Hour Glass and Scythe: STB, June, 1935.

Illustrated by Symbols: STB, March, 1941.

Joachin and Boaz: New Age Mag., Oct., 1904, 398, 493.

Justice: New Age Mag., Jan., 1965, 13.

Key: STB, Oct., 1953.

Keystone: Phil. Mag., 1957, 93. 6 RAM 318 (1960). 3 RAM 278 (1951).

Knocks: Harry Carr, *The Knocks in the Craft Degrees,* 77 AQC 267 (1964). *Three Distinct Knocks,* STB, July, 1962.

Left to Right: STB, Feb., 1927.

Lesser Lights: STB, Feb., 1926.

Level and Plumb: STB, 1924.

Liberal Arts and Sciences: H. T. C. De Lafontaine, *The Seven Liberal Arts and Sciences,* 43 AQC 50 (1930). W. J. Williams, *The Seven Liberal Arts and Sciences,* 40 AQC 84 (1927). W. J. Bunney, *Freemasonry and the Contemplative Art,* in Harry Carr, ed., Collected Prestonian Lectures, 195. Series of articles by Frederick Parker in: Phil. Mag., June-July, 1950, 8; Oct.-Nov., 1950, 2; March, 1951, 11; Aug.-Sept., 7; Dec., 1951, 6.

Lights: *Lesser Lights,* STB, Feb., 1926. *Third Great Light,* STB, May, 1941. *More Light,* STB, April, 1927. Robert E. Anderson, *From Darkness to Light,* K. T. Mag., Aug., 1979, 28. Paul John Rich, *The Rediscovery of Light,* New Age Mag., March, 1976, 31. *Great Lights and Lesser Lights,* 80 AQC 331 (1967). *Master's Light,* 78 AQC 282 (1965). R. F.

Gould, *Three Great Lights*, 16 AQC 105 (1903). *The Symbolic Lights*, 4 Build. Mag. 269 (1918). *The Three Lesser Lights*, 4 Build. Mag. 274 (1918). *Lights Around the Altar*, Phil. Mag., Feb., 1969, 4. Reginald E. Dobson, *The Lesser Lights*, The Craftsmen (Mexico), March-April, 1974, 5.

Living Perpendicular: STB, Nov., 1958.

Lost Word: Alva Harry Sweet, *The Lost Word*, 3 Norcalore 22. William C. Blaine, New Age Mag., Oct., 1974, 44. STB, May, 1928. Alex Horne, *The Lost Word*, Ind. Free., July, 1956, 10. A. C. Parker, *The Lost Word*, 9 Build. Mag. 329 (1923); also: 7 RAM 345 (1963); 8 RAM 242 (1965). *Henry Pirtle, The Lost Word of Freemasonry*, 1951; 231. Tinted with occultism.

Manna: 10 RAM 15 (1970).

Marks: *Marks of the Operatives*, N.Y. Mas. Outl., April, 1930, 237.

Mason Word: G. S. Draffen, *The Mason Word*, 65 AQC 54 (1952). Douglas Knoop, *The Mason Word*, 51 AQC 194 (1938). Knoop and Jones, *Prolegomena of the Mason Word*, 52 AQC, 52 AQC 139 (1939). Charles A. Newman, *A Reference to the Mason Word in 1653*, 80 AQC 278 (1967). W. H. Rylands, *The Mason Word: The Earls of Roslin and Freemasonry*, 7 AQC 55 (1894). W. F. Shepherd, *The Mason-Word in Scotland*, 7 AQC 56 (1894). Edward M. Selby, *Early Masonry and the Mason Word*, 2 RAM 142 (1947). Knoop & Jones, *The Scottish Mason and the Mason Word*, 1939; 109.

Master's Carpet: Jay Finley Christ, *Whence Came the "Master's Carpet?,"* Ind. Free., Jan, 1957, 8.

Middle Chamber: W. W. Covey-Crump, *Symbolism of the Middle Chamber*, 39 AQC 273 (1926). Also in 2 Trans. Author's Lodge No. 3456 224 (1917) and Manchester Assn. of Mas. Res. 9 (1915-1916).

Mosaic Pavement: Phil. Mag., Aug., 1974, 79. STB, April, 1951

Movable and Immovable: STB, March, 1961.

Mystic Tie: John B. Davis, *The Mystic Tie*, Montana Mas. News, April, 1976; quoted in Mas. Mess., Ga., June, 1976, 7. STB, Oct., 1940.

North: Dr. George H. T. French, *The North*, Ind. Free., Dec., 1978, 10. *North as Applied to Freemasonry*, Phil. Mag., Aug., 1958, 59.

North East Corner: Charles C. Hunt, Phil. Mag., Aug.-Sept., 1951, 9. STB, Oct., 1927. New Age Mag., Nov., 1959, 663. J. W. Horsley, *The North East Corner of the Lodge*, 2 Trans. Author's Lodge No. 3456 92 (1917). Alex Horne, *The North-East Corner*, Mas. Sq., June, 1977, 62. *The North East Corner*, Ind. Free., Sept., 1976, 8.

Northwest Corner: 12 Build. Mag. 34 (1926).

Oblong Square: STB, Sept. 1953.

Pelican: No. Light, April, 1972, 16.

Phoenix-Sublime: Mervin B. Hogan, *The Phoenix-Sublime Symbol*, 10 RAM 244 (1971-1972). *Phoenix and the Pelican*, Phil. Mag., Feb., 1971, 20.

Pillars: Raymond J. Brown, *The Pillars*, Ore. Free., Oct., 1973, 19. *Two Pillars*, STB, Sept., 1935. *Crossed Pillars*, 12 Build. Mag. 31 (1926). H. L. Haywood, *Grand Pillars*, Phil. Mag., Oct.-Nov., 1947, 3. George L. Marshall, *A Tale of Two Pillars*, Phil. Mag., Oct., 1976, 92; also 12 RAM 99 (1976-1977). H. L. Haywood, *J and B Pillars of the Porch*, Ind. Free., April, 1960, 14. STB, Nov., 1949. Harry Carr, *Pillars and Globes*, 75 AQC 204 (1962). *The Broken Column*, 8 Build. Mag. 92 (1922). *The Column of Beauty*, 5 Build Mag. 135 (1919). Robert Kitchell, *Columns and Masonry*, Iowa Grd. L. Bulletin, May, 1972, 486. C. P. Harrington, *The Two Great Pillars*, 1977 Trans. Leic. L. of Res. 25. *Canopy over the Pillars*, Ind. Free., Aug., 1976, 15. *Pillar of Beauty*, N.Y. Mas. Outl., April, 1930, 232. *The Two Brazen Pillars*, Phil. Mag., Dec., 1957, 92. New Age Mag., Jan., 1955, 27. *Biblical References*, Ind. Free., April, 1972. Fred Armitage, *The Origin of the Pillars to King Solomon's Temple*, 21

AQC 270 (1908). *Left-Hand Pillar*, 77 AQC 320 (1964). *Network Over the Pillars*, 76 AQC 232 (1963).

Plumb Line: C. G. Lawrence, *An Interpretation of the Plumb Line*, 9 Build. Mag. 4 (1923). William F. Kuhn, *The Plumb-Line*, 1 Build. Mag. 289 (1915). *Amos and the Plumbline*, Ind. Free., July, 1976, 8. Dr. Edwin S. Malone III, *A Plumbline in Our Midst*, New Age Mag., Jan., 1979, 29.

Points of My Entrance: 85 AQC 367 (1972).

Points of Fellowship: H. L. Haywood, *The Five Points of Fellowship*, 6 Build. Mag. 335 (1920). Joseph Johnson, *The Five Points of Fellowship*, 4 Trans. Author's Lodge 288 (1928).

Point Within a Circle: STB, Aug., 1931. 7 Build. Mag. 172 (1921). 4 Build. Mag. 206 (1918). STB, April, 1953. New Age Mag., Jan., 1917, 15.

Pot of Incense: STB, May, 1935.

Rods: 2 Build. Mag. 367 (1916). STB, Sept., 1957. Sir Frederick Pollak, *Notes on Early History of Masonic Rods*, 6 Build. Mag. 145, 187, (1920). James E. Craig, *The Law of the Rod*, N.Y. Mas. Outl., Oct., 1929, 35. *Symbolism of the Steward Rods*, Ind. Free., March, 1954, 17.

Rough and Perfect: STB, Aug., 1933.

Ruffians: STB, Sept., 1927.

Sanctum Sanctorum: STB, July, 1914.

Seal: Julian H. Cambridge, *Symbols, Their Effects on Man;* being a far-out explanation of the Great Seal of the United States as a mystic and occult symbol with Kabbalistic overtones. *The Great Seal of the United States*, New Age Mag., Feb., 1971, 51. *Cal. Supreme Court Seal*, New Age Mag., Oct., 1970, 35.

Senses: Carleton F. Graham, *The Five Senses*, 3 Trans. Anniversary L. of Res., N. H., 30 (1978).

Shibboleth: 9 Build. Mag. 31 (1923).

Signs: STB, Aug., 1937.

Square: F. G. Kirkby, *The Square: Its History and Morals*, 23 Leic. L. of Res. 71 (1919-1920). James E. Craig, *Why By the Square?* N.Y. Mas. Out., Jan., 1930, 138. STB, March, 1935. *Oblong Square*, 10 RAM 185 (1971). 2 Build. Mag. 127 (1916). STB, Sept., 1953. Ill. Enlight., Jan., 1951, 2. STB, April, 1924. *Square, Level, and Plumb:* STB, Dec., 1943. W. H. Rylands, *Symbolism of the Square*, 13 AQC 28 (1900). G. W. Speth, *Squaring the Circle Geometrically*, 8 AQC 217 (1895). *Squaring the Lodge*, 80 AQC 335 (1967). Joseph Barrett, *The Square and the Cabletow*, 3 Build. Mag. 341 (1917). *The Return of the Square*, 7 RAM 372 (1963).

Square and Compasses: *Inverted Square and Compass*, Phil. Mag., Dec., 1971, 111. Elbert Bede, *Square and Compasses*, Phil. Mag., Dec., 1950, 5. W. R. Reed, *Square and Compass*, 2 Build. Mag. 179 (1916).

St. John: New Age Mag., Dec., 1968, 45.

Seven Cardinal Virtues: STB, Aug., 1950.

Shekel: Elmer T. Reid, *The Jewish Half Shekel*, 2 RAM 134 (1947). *The Law of the Shekel*, 10 RAM 67 (1970).

Shittim Wood: Phil. Mag., Jan., 1951, 11.

Signs: STB, Aug., 1937.

Stairs: *A Stairway and a Ladder*, STB, Nov., 1962.

Starry Decked Heaven: 8 Build. Mag. 385 (1921).

Steps: *Three Steps and the First Regular Step*, 76 AQC 225 (1963). *One Regular Upright Step*, Mas. J. of So. Africa, July, 1972, 23: copied from the New Age Mag. STB, June, 1925.

Stones: STB, Oct., 1948.

Sun, Moon and Stars: STB, March, 1930.

Swastika: Mrs. H. G. M. Murray-Aynsley, *The Swastika*, 4 AQC 26 (1891). 5 AQC 225 (1892). S. C. Pratt, *Notes on the Swastika*, 4 AQC 85 (1891). H. M. Temple, *Note on this subject in Indian*

Antiquary, 4 AQC 30 (1891). New Age Mag., June, 1908, 529. Thomas Carr, *The Swastika, Its History and Significance,* 2 Am. Free. 108, 168, 228, 337, 394 (1911). Joseph Fort Newton, *The Oldest Symbol of Man,* Mast. Mas., June, 1926, 467.

Sword: STB, Jan., 1930. Ralston J. James, *The Tyler's Sword,* Phil. Mag., Oct., 1977, 7.

Tabernacle: W. W. Westcott, *On the Symbolism of the Tabernacle,* 6 AQC 12 (1893).

Tetragrammaton: 8 RAM 15 (1964).

Three Distinct Knocks: STB, July, 1912.

Time: *Better to Observe the Time,* STB, Feb., 1959.

Tools: *No Tool of Iron Was Heard,* Phil. Mag., Feb., 1963, 19. STB, April, 1928. STB, Feb., 1952.

Trestleboard: STB, July, 1932.

Triangle: Arthur Bowes, *The Equilateral Triangle in Gothic Architecture,* 19 AQC 165 (1906). L. Vibert, *The Interlaced Triangle of the Royal Arch,* 80 AQC 328 (1967). Dudley Wright, *The Interlaced Triangle,* 9 Build. Mag. 9 (1923). 5 Build. Mag. 45 (1919). 4 RAM 104 (1952). *The Equilateral Triangle,* Phil. Mag., Oct., 1956, 75.

Trowel: W. W. T. Sharpe, *Trowel Jewels,* 17 AQC 64 (1904). 2 Build. Mag. 35 (1916). 4 Build. Mag. 38 (1918). 9 ALR 406 (1965). STB, Oct., 1960.

Truth: Raymond W. Miller, *Truth, What Is It?* New Age Mag., Jan., 1968, 19.

Twenty-Four Inch Gauge: New Age Mag., May, 1922, 276. *A Perfect Day,* Mas. J. of So. Africa, April, 1972, 27. STB, Sept., 1933.

Tubal Cain: W. W. Covey-Crump, *Symbolism of Tubal Cain,* 39 AQC 373 (1926). *Tubal Cain,* 78 AQC 280 (1965). 3 Build Mag. 64 (1917). Ill. Enlight., April, 1952, 2.

Stone: *A White Stone,* Phil. Mag, April, 1969, 41.

Veiled in Allegory: STB, Sept., 1944. STB, Nov., 1974.

Veils: *Allegories and Symbols of the Veils,* 9 RAM 57 (1967).

Virtue: *The Four Cardinal Virtues,* New Age Mag., Dec., 1962, 14.

Wages: C. B. Antonio, *The Wages of Masons, the Cabletow,* Nov.; 1970, 8. *The Wages of a Mason,* 4 Build. Mag. 255 (1918).

Warden's Columns: STB, Aug., 1973.

Wayfaring Man: 9 Build. Mag. 95 (1923).

Weeping Virgin: James R. Case, *A Bit of Puzzling Symbolism,* Ind. Free., Oct., 1978.

Winding Stairs: 1972 Grd. L. of Scotl. Yrbk 69. John R. Nocas, *The Beautiful Symbolism of the Winding Stairs,* New Age Mag., Sept., 1975, 27. Phil. Mag., Dec., 1966, 101. STB, Jan., 1932. A. L. Shane, *The Mystery of the Winding Stairs,* New Age Mag., Sept., 1975, 27. Phil. Mag., Dec., 1966, 101. STB, Jan., 1932. A. L. Shane, *The Mystery of the Winding Staircase,* 81 AQC 340 (1968). Phil. Mag., Oct., 1971, 90. 2 Build. Mag. 237 (1916). Clarence E. Rose, *The Winding Stairs,* New Age Mag., June, 1977, 50.

Windlass and Rope: STB, May, 1942.

The Word: *An Historical and Masonic Explanation,* 10 RAM 195 (1971). 5 RAM 243 (1956). Edward M. Selby, *The Word in Masonic Ritual,* Phil. Mag., June, 1975, 61.

Working Tools: *Working Tools,* 78 AQC 278 (1965). F. J. Underwood, *The Common Judge (a tool),* 54 AQC 111 (1941). Phil. Mag., Feb., 1956, 8. Ross Hepburn, *The Working Tools,* Trans. M. & P. M. L., Sept., 1979, 319. Carl W. Hopp, *Are Working Tools Important?* Ore. Free., August, 1973, 7.

CHAPTER SEVEN

Masonic Ritual and Ceremonies

7.01 HISTORY OF THE MASONIC RITUAL

Harry Carr, *600 Years of Craft Ritual*. 81 AQC 153 (1968). Also in 12 ALR 344 (1974). The author has delivered a talk on this subject in many places. The talk has been printed by the Committee on Masonic Education of the Grand Lodge of Missouri.

Joseph Fort Newton, *Whence Came the Ritual?* Ind. Free., March, 1952, 17.

Origin of the Degrees. 11 Norcalore 22.

Diagram of the History of the Standard Work. Phil. Mag., Oct., 1956, 69. Also has biographical sketches of the creators of the Standard Work.

Lionel Vibert, *The Development of the Trigradal System*. In Harry Carr, ed., Collected Prestonian Lectures, 31.

Lionel Vibert, *The Evolution of the Second Degree*. In Harry Carr, ed., Collected Prestonian Lectures, 47.

Roderick H. Baxter, *The Antiquity of Our Masonic Legends Especially in Relation to the Legend of the Third Degree*. In Harry Carr, ed., Collected Prestonian Lectures, 95.

Colin F. W. Dyer, *Emulation, A Ritual to Remember*. History of the Emulation Lodge of Improvement, 1823-1973. 405 pp.
Reviewed: 86 AQC 292 (1973). Libraries: 2, 3, 11, 12.

Louis L. Williams, *Masonry's Modern Mystery: The Origin of Its Ritual*. 1967 Proc. Grd. L. of Ill. 87.

J. E. S. Tuckett, *The Origin of the Addi- tional Degrees*. 32 AQC 5 (1920); 33 AQC 78 (1921).

Henry C. Chiles, *From Mouth to Ear*. 1936; 70 pp. Grand Lodge of Mo., publisher.
Contents: General history of the ritual with biographical sketches of leading ritualists. Libraries: 1, 3, 4, 5, 9, 10, 11, 12.

Freemasonry and the Evolution of Ritualism. New Age Mag., June, 1912, 584; Aug., 1912, 184; Sept., 1912, 293; Oct., 1912, 394.

R. V. Carleson, *Evidence of Antiquity in the Ritual*. Phil. Mag., Aug., 1956, 58.

Henry W. Coil, Sr., *How the Ritual Grew*. Phil. Mag., Oct., 1957, 67.

Richard Tydeman, *Masters and Master Masons; a Theory of the Third Degree*. 84 AQC 187 (1971).

Where Virginia Got Her Ritual. Mast. Mas., May, 1927, 366.

W. Ivor Grantham, *Lodges of Instruction, Their Origin and Development*. In Harry Carr, ed., Collected Prestonian Lectures, 331.

J. M. Harvey, *Initiation Two Hundred Years Ago*. 75 AQC 212 (1962).

William Simpson, *An Ancient Rite*. 79 AQC 292 (1966).

R. J. Meekren, *The Origin of the Third Degree Legend*. Ind. Free., April, 1953, 14.

Colin F. W. Dyer, *William Sadbolt, and His Papers on the Craft Ritual of the*

Lodge of Reconciliation. 87 AQC 137 (1974).

Allen E. Roberts, *The Convention That Changed the Face of Freemasonry* (The Baltimore Convention). Mas. Res. L. No. 104, Atlanta, Ga., 1973.

The Baltimore Convention. STB, Jan., 1936.

C. Ellwood Smyrk, *Baltimore Convention Centennial.* 1 RAM 143 (1944).

Masonic Conservators. STB, Jan., 1946.

Ray V. Denslow, *The Masonic Conservators.* 1931; Grand Lodge of Mo.
Contents: Gives the details of the movement started by Rob Morris to bring about a uniformity of the ritual. Libraries: 1, 2, 3, 4, 5, 6, 10, 11, 12, 14.

Harold V. B. Voorhis, *The "Mnemonics" of Rob Morris.* 11 ALR 85 (1969).

R. V. Carleson, *Conservators of Symbolic Freemasonry.* Phil. Mag., Feb., 1956, 4.

Their Work is Different. Discussion of the differences in the ritual. Ind. Free., April, 1977, 4.

Colin F. W. Dyer, *The Official 1816 Ritual?* 88 AQC 211 (1975).

Will Read, *The Eighteenth Century French Degree of Chevalier De L'Epee.* 87 AQC 235 (1974).

Colin F. W. Dyer, *The Work of Waller Rodwell Wright on the Craft Ritual and Lectures.* 89 AQC 197 (1976).

Erwin L. Hippe, *Enigma of the Third Degree.* A study of the various authors who have written about the history of the ritual. 5 Mas. Papers of the Walter F. Meier L. of Res., Washington, June, 1976.

E. L. Hawkins, *The Evolution of the Masonic Ritual.* 26 AQC 6 (1913).

J. H. Lepper, *The Traditioners.* A Study of the Masonic Ritual in England in the 18th Century. 56 AQC 138 (1943); 57 AQC 264 (1944).

James E. Craig, *Whence Came Our Standard Ritual?* N.Y. Mas. Outl., April, 1929, 237.

John R. Nocas, *Musical Society Confers Third Degree.* Phil. Mag., Dec., 1973, 111.

R. H. Baxter, *The Third Degree: An Attempt to Establish Its Antiquity and to Find Evidence of Its Legend in Holy Writ.* 10 Installed Masters Assn. of Leeds 77 (1913-1914).

H. G. Rosedale, *The Evolution of Our Ritual Before the Union.* 10 Manchester Assn. for Mas. Res. 9 (1919-1920).

R. H. Baxter, *The Number of Degrees in 1723.* 16 Manchester Assn. for Mas. Res. 11 (1925-1926).

A. L. Kress and R. J. Meekren, *The Degrees of Masonry; Their Origin and History.* 14 Build. Mag. 131, 170, 196, 240, 269, 299, 332, 356 (1928); 15 Build. Mag. 18, 35, 67, 107, 138, 164, 195, 232, 267, 294, (1929).

Ward K. St. Clair, *A Background of Masonic Ritual.* Phil. Mag., April, 1958, 25.

George Oliver, *History of Initiation.* 1866; 218 pp.
Comments: L. B. Blakemore, "A work, extraordinarily learned for its period, which tries to show that Freemasonry is a link in a long chain of various forms of initiation. Needed for reference, and because of its author's fame as one of the first Masonic historians." Libraries: 1, 3, 4, 5, 6, 7, 8, 9, 10, 11, 12, 13, 14.

Henry Sadler, *Illustrated History of the Emulation Lodge of Improvement.* 1904; 217 pp.
Comments: Silas H. Shepherd, "This work contains all that the sublibrarian of the Grand Lodge of England was able to learn regarding the transmission of the ritual as it was authorized at the Union of 1813 by the Lodge of Reconciliation." L. B. Blakemore, "By the author of the epoch-making Masonic Facts and Fictions, this is a book needful to any study of the history of the ritual." Libraries: 7, 8, 9, 14.

F. W. Golby, *Century of Masonic Working, Being a History of Stability Lodge of Instruction.* 1921.
Comments: L. B. Blakemore, "A study

of the 'standard workings,' or versions of the ritual, used in lodges in England. Required reading for students of the Ritual.'' Libraries: 1, 3, 4, 5, 6, 7, 11, 14.

R. J. Meekren, *Historical Notes on the Masonic Ritual*. Phil. Mag., Aug.-Sept., 1949, 10; Dec., 1949, 3; Jan. 1950, 3; April-May, 1950, 3; Oct.-Nov., 1950, 6; April-May, 1951, 2; Oct.-Nov., 1951, 6.

R. H. Baxter, *The Old Charges and the Ritual*. 31 AQC 33 (1918): 33 AQC 78 (1920).

Harry Carr, *The Conjoint Theory*. 66 AQC 42 (1953).

Harry Carr, *The Obligation and Its Place in the Ritual*. 74 AQC 130 (1961).

Masonic Ritual in England and the United States. 75 AQC 231 (1962).

E. H. Cartwright, *The Lodge of Reconciliation and the Ritual*. 54 AQC 115 (1941).

Herbert Poole, *Masonic Ritual and Secrets Before 1717*. 37 AQC 4 (1924).

A. C. Powell, *French Rituals*. 30 AQC 246 (1917).

E. L. Hawkins, *The Evolution of the Masonic Ritual*. 26 AQC 6 (1913).

W. I. Grantham, *An Operative Mason's Ritual*. 63 AQC 307 (1950).

Silas H. Shepherd, *The Webb Ritual in the United States*. 2 Build. Mag. 166 (1916). Has picture of the author.

A. L. Kress, *The Masonic Ritual in the United States*. 9 Build. Mag. 291 (1923).

The Egyptian Influence on Our Ceremonial and Ritual. 8 Build. Mag. 265, 307 (1922).

History of the Masonic Ritual. 1 Build. Mag. 291 (1915).

William J. Hughan, *The Three Degrees of Freemasonry*. 10 AQC 127 (1897).

G. W. Bullamore, *The Antiquity of the Third Degree*. 38 AQC 68 (1925).

Age of the Third Degree. 75 AQC 236 (1962).

Harry Carr, *Three Phases of Masonic History*. 77 AQC 256 (1964).

R. F. Gould, *The Degrees of Pure and Ancient Freemasonry*. 16 AQC 28 (1903).

R. F. Gould, *The Grand Lodge of the Schismatics or Ancients*. 6 AQC 44 (1893).

R. F. Gould, *The Antiquity of Masonic Symbolism*. 3 AQC 7 (1890).

Herbert Poole, *The Substance of Pre-Grand Lodge Freemasonry*. 61 AQC 7 (1948).

G. W. Speth, *The Two Degree Theory*. 11 AQC 47 (1898).

Eric Ward, *Early Master's Lodges and Their Relations to Degrees*. 75 AQC 125, 155 (1962).

John Yarker, *The Unrecognized Lodges and Degrees of Freemasonry Before and After 1717*. 1 AQC 107, 150 (1886-1888).

William F. Kuhn, *The Fourth Degree*. 1 Build. Mag. 44 (1915).

C. C. Adams, *Masonic Degrees in England*. 3 Build. Mag. 44, 67 (1917).

Antiquity of the Third Degree. 9 Build. Mag. 127 (1923).

Anyone making a study of the history of the Masonic ritual cannot ignore the exposures printed over the years. When a ritual is transmitted orally from generation to generation, these exposures sometimes can shed light on what may have been taking place in our lodges.

7.02 ANALYSIS OF THE MASONIC RITUAL

E. H. Cartwright, *Commentary on the Freemasonic Ritual*. 1947; 235 pp. A second edition was published in 1973 by Penrose, Tunbridge Wells, Kent, England, with a complete introduction by Harry Carr who also made some additions to the text.
Author: 66 AQC 49 (1953); also good sketch in the second edition, page 229. Reviewed: 59 AQC 84 (1948). Libraries: 2, 3, 4, 5, 7, 9, 11, 12.

J. Walter Hobbs, *The Masonic Ritual, Described, Compared, Explained.* 1923. Author: 42 AQC 69 (1929). Contents: Described in 10 Build. Mag. 127 (1924). Reviewed: 10 Build. Mag. 29 (1924). Libraries: 9, 15.

Meredith Sanderson, *An Examination of the Masonic Ritual.* 1923; 105 pp. The Baskerville Press, London, publisher. Contents: Part of the Ritual is in cypher form and the author tries to connect some parts of the ceremony with the rites of primitive tribes and relies too much on imagination. To be read with caution. Libraries: 3, 5, 6, 12, 14.

Our Ritual Differences. STB, Jan., 1934.

Materials of the Ritual. STB, March, 1955.

Presenting of the Working Tools. STB, Aug., 1961.

The Why of Initiation. STB, April, 1940.

Silas H. Shepherd, *Notes on the Ritual.* 1954; 54 pp. Wisconsin Committee on Masonic Research; pamphlet No. 19. Libraries: 2, 3, 7, 9, 12, 14.

James Stevens, *Chips From a Rough Ashlar.* 1885; 133 pp. Richard Tilling, London, publisher. Contents: Discusses ritual and ceremonies and differences. Libraries: 3, 9.

Who May Confer Degrees? MSA Digest.

J. S. M. Ward, *Studies in the Meaning of Our Ritual.* 254 pp. The Baskerville Press, London, publisher. Contents: Consists of three small booklets weaving into the story the Ancient Mysteries and occult subjects. To be read with caution. Libraries: 3, 4, 5, 9, 13.

Poetry of the Ritual. STB, Aug., 1947.

Debate on the Value of the Ritual. 7 Trans. Phoenix L. No. 30, Paris, 36.

Henry Sadler, *Notes on the Ceremony of Installation.* 1889; 57 pp. George Kenning, London, publisher. Author: 23 AQC 328 (1910); 24 AQC 277 (1911). Comments: Silas H. Shepherd, "This little book is valuable both from an historical and from a ritualistic standpoint." Libraries: 3, 7, 9, 12, 14.

Arthur E. Powell, *Magic of Freemasonry.* 1924; 136 pp. The Baskerville Press, London, publisher. Comments: L. B. Blakemore, "An inspiring book on the meaning and teaching of the Fraternity." Analyzes the ritual with emphasis on its spiritual appeal. Libraries: 3, 5, 6, 9, 11, 12, 14, 15.

Charles W. Moore, *The New Masonic Trestle-Board.* 1856. Explains the ritual as discussed at the Baltimore Convention. Reproduced by the Masonic Book Club in 1978 together with a rare pamphlet on the subject.

Alphonse Cerza, *Is Ritualistic Work Enough?* Phil. Mag., June, 1964, 44.

Norman C. Dutt, *Ceremonials and Degrees.* Phil. Mag., Aug., 1967, 77.

Allen Cabaniss, *Importance of the Fellow Craft's Degree.* Phil. Mag., April, 1957, 20.

William H. Knutz, *Interpretation of the Master Mason Degree.* Phil. Mag., Dec., 1947, 5.

P. R. James, *The Lectures of English Craft Freemasonry.* 79 AQC 140 (1966).

Two English Mark Rituals. 19 Norcalore 174 (1949).

The Ragon Mark Rituals. 17 Norcalore 123 (1947).

The French Mark Ritual. 17 Norcalore 94 (1947).

E. H. Cartwright, *A Note on Brown's Master-Key.* A discussion of an early cypher book. 45 AQC 90 (1935).

R. J. Meekren, *The Entered and Accepted Mason.* 64 AQC 140 (1951).

Wait With Patience, Tex. Free., May, 1973; Ind. Free., Sept., 1973, 9.

E. Van Krugel, *The Hidden Meaning of the Opening and Closing Ritual in Masonry.* New Age Mag., July, 1973, 10.

Many U.S.A. Lodges Work in Foreign Languages. 6 RAM 77 (1958).

The "Why" of Initiation. STB, April, 1940.

Dr. William L. Cummings, *The Psychology of Ritual.* Ind. Free., Dec., 1978, 8.

Albert L. Woody, *Ritual, The Skeleton of Freemasonry.* Phil. Mag., June, 1977, 6.

A. L. Vibert, *The Second Degree: A Theory.* 39 AQC 208 (1937).

Lewis Edwards, *Freemasonry, Ritual and Ceremonial.* 49 AQC 142 (1936).

R. Tydeman, *A Theory of the Third Degree.* 84 AQC 187 (1971).

Estel Brooks, *Solomon – The Copper King.* Phil. Mag., Dec., 1977, 4.

James Endell Tyler, *Oaths; Their Origin, Nature and History.* 1834; 320 pp. Written for the general reader. A good presentation of the subject also appears in James Hastings' Encyclopedia of Religion and Ethics found in most public libraries.

Robert J. Meekren, *The Lodge and Essay Method.* 61 AQC 3 (1948).

Colin F. W. Dyer, *In Search of Ritual Uniformity.* 86 AQC 143 (1973).

Colin F. W. Dyer, *Some Notes on the Deptford Rituals.* 91 AQC 156 (1979).

N. Katkolff and C. N. Batham, *An Initiation Ceremony in a Modern Russian Lodge.* 88 AQC 189 (1975).

Dennis A. Leventhal, *A Confucian View of Ritual.* New Age Mag., March, 1979, 30.

Albert L. Woody, *Masonic Rods.* 1955, published by the Illinois Grand Lodge Committee on Masonic Education. Author: See 1980 volume of the Masonic Book Club; the introduction has his biographical sketch. Libraries: 1, 2, 3, 4, 5, 7, 9, 11, 12, 13, 15.

George Oliver, *Discrepancies of Freemasonry.* 336 pp. John Hogg & Co., London, publisher. Contents: Presents some contradictions in the ritual, analyzes the lectures, spurious rituals, etc. Comments: L. B. Blakemore, "A philosophical discussion of what appears to be paradoxes, self-contradictions, etc., of Masonry." Libraries: 1, 2, 3, 5, 7, 9, 10, 11, 12, 14.

Harry B. Wrights, *Are Printed Rituals Advisable?* 1938 Proc. Grd. Mast. Conf. 18.

Ward K. St. Clair, *The Background of Masonic Ritual.* Phil. Mag., April, 1958, 25.

The American Masonic Ritual. Mast. Mas., May, 1927, 361.

The Hidden Meaning of the Opening and Closing Ritual. New Age Mag., July, 1973, 10.

H. L. Haywood, *The Rite of Circumambulation.* 4 Build. Mag. 79 (1918); 9 Build. Mag. 265 (1923).

G. W. Speth, *Squaring the Circle Geometrically.* 8 AQC 217 (1895).

Ross Hepburn, *Notes on the Tracing Board Lectures.* Trans. M. & P. M. L., Nov., 1972, 340.

R. H. Brown, *A Charge at the Closing of the Lodge.* 83 AQC 369 (1970).

Fellow Crafts and the Middle Chamber. 76 AQC 229 (1963).

Instruction and Improvement of Craftsmen; Why Only Craftsmen? 80 AQC 334 (1967).

Scotland, Grand Lodge, *The Candidate: The E.A.; the F.C.; the M.M.* 76 AQC 121 (1963).

Ward St. Clair, *Notes on Craft Ritual.* 7 ALR 74 (1957); Phil. Mag., March, 1949, 8.

William L. Cummings, *The Genesis of the Third Degree.* Phil. Mag., Aug., 1961, 51.

G. M. Does, *Oaths in the Last Century.* 24 AQC 296 (1911).

Harry Carr, *The Obligation and Its Place in the Ritual.* 74 AQC 130 (1961).

H. H. Partlow, *Obligations and Oaths.* 7 Build. Mag. 47 (1921).

"Often Tried, Never Denied, and Willing to Be Tried Again." 4 Build. Mag. 309 (1918).

Uniformity of the Work. 9 Build. Mag. 126 (1923).

High Twelve and Low Twelve. 6 RAM 209 (1959).

A. L. Kress and R. J. Meekren, *The Form of the Lodge.* 12 Build. Mag. 119, 151, 183, 215, 248 (1926).

Could a Freemason Forget His Initiation? 13 Build. Mag. 298 (1927).

Destitution. Ill. Enlight., Jan., 1951, 4.

What's My Line? Do's and Don'ts for Ritualists. 7 RAM 242 (1962).

Entered Apprentice Degree With Its Groups of Three. 10 Build. Mag. 16 (1924).

L. A. Holland, *Some Thoughts on the Ritual.* Trans. M. & P. M. L., Nov., 1972, 329.

William E. Yeager, *Characteristics Peculiar to Penn. Free.* Trans. No. Cal. Res. L., March, 1972.

William R. Deutsch, *Why We Should Revise Our Ritual.* 10 RAM 12 (1970).

The late William L. Cummings, of New York, spent over 50 years collecting Masonic rituals. They are in many languages. Before he departed this life the presented them to the Library of the Scottish Rite, NMJ, and they are now located at Lexington, Mass.

7.03 MASONIC CATECHISMS

Knoop, Jones, and Hamer, *The Early Masonic Catechisms.* 1963; 242 pp. Quatuor Coronati Lodge, publisher.
Authors: 48 AQC 301 (1935); 62 AQC 2 (1949). Comments: Louis L. Williams, "An interesting study of the origin of the early ritual." Reviewed: Trans. United Master's Lodge No. 167, July, 1972, 221. Libraries: 1, 2, 3, 4, 5, 7, 8, 9, 10, 11, 12, 14.

John T. Thorp, *Bibliography of Masonic Catechisms and Exposures.* Trans. Leic. L. of Res., 1929.

R. F. Gould, *Early Masonic Catechisms.* 3 AQC 186 (1890).

Harry Carr, *An Examination of Early Masonic Catechisms.* 83 AQC 377 (1970); 84 AQC 294 (1971); 85 AQC 331 (1972).

P. R. James, *The Lectures of English Craft Freemasonry.* 79 AQC 140 (1966).

Herbert Poole, *The Masonic Catechisms.* 60 AQC 27 (1947).

How Do You Know Yourself to Be a Mason? Mas. J. of So. Africa, June, 1972, 13.

7.04 MASONIC MONITORS

William Preston, *Illustrations of Masonry.* 1772. Printed in many editions. A facsimile of the second ed. (the best) was published by the Masonic Book Club, in 1973, with commentary.
Comments: Henry W. Coil, Sr., "The first finished lectures and ritual; one of the most influential Masonic books." L. B. Blakemore, "A Masonic classic; an interpretation of the Ritual by one of the authors of the Webb-Preston versions of the Ritual, which is everywhere used in America." Norman B. Hickox, "Essential to any study of the ritual of Freemasonry is the Monitor of Preston, who so elaborated and improved the lectures that his work has formed the basis of the present American ceremonies. . . . Although the later editions of his work were revised by many different Masons, many original parts are still used in some form. His 'Illustrations' had run through 17 editions by 1861; his own personal work being current until 1813, and having a great influence long after that time." Libraries: 1, 2, 3, 4, 5, 6, 7, 8, 9, 10, 11, 12, 13, 14.

Preston's Illustrations: Sources of the first American edition. 24 AQC 71 (1911).

P. R. James, *William Preston's First Lecture of Free Masonry.* 82 AQC 104 (1969).

P. R. James, *William Preston's Second Lecture.* 83 AQC 193 (1970).

P. R. James, *William Preston's Third Lecture.* 85 AQC 69 (1972).

Colin F. W. Dyer, *The Various Editions of William Preston's Lectures.* 89 AQC 1 (1976).

A. C. F. Jackson, *Preston's England.* 89 AQC 97 (1976).

T. O. Haunch, *Preston's Lectures in Manuscript.* 85 AQC 124 (1972).

G. P. G. Hills, *William Preston: The Man, His Methods, and His Work.* 41 AQC 163 (1928).

J. B. Saul, *Preston's Illustration of Masonry.* 24 AQC 71 (1911).

F. W. Worts, *Preston's Use of Leslie's Work.* 73 AQC 120 (1960).

F. L. Pick, *Preston – The Guild and the Craft.* 59 AQC 90 (1946).

Alex Horne, *Preston as Preceptor and Ritualist.* 81 AQC 129 (1968).

William Preston and the Prestonian Lectures. 10 Build. Mag. 101 (1924).

Alex Horne, *William Preston's Lecture on the Five Orders of Architecture: Its Origin and Development.* 77 AQC 105, 143 (1964).

P. R. James, *The Lectures of English Craft Masonry.* 79 AQC 140 (1966).

Thomas Smith Webb, *Freemason's Monitor.* 1860; 350 pp. John Sherer, Cincinnati, Ohio, publisher. Has gone through many editions.
Author: Herbert T. Leyland, Freemason-Musician-Entrepreneur; 1965; 462; the Chapter of Research of Ohio, publisher. A full scale biography of Thomas Smith Webb. Comments: Silas H. Shepherd, "Many editions and reprints have appeared and the work has been standard for over a century. An excellent bibliography of 'Early Editions of Webb's Freemason's Monitor' is contained in Vol. 1, No. 9, of the Masonic Bibliophile, for December, 1912." L. B. Blakemore, "The most famous Masonic book by an American. Monitorial. It is an adaptation for American use of Preston's Illustrations of Masonry." Alex Horne, "Webb's work, in its first edition, was in turn based upon William Preston's still more famous 'Illustrations of Masonry.' This first edition of Webb is in somewhat less elaborate form than his later ones, and its first 64 pages of the 1797 edition is actually a reprint, almost verbatim, of a part of the work of Preston, probably of the 1792 edition. But subsequent editions of Webb were recast to some extent in Webb's own words." Libraries: 1, 2, 3, 4, 5, 6, 7, 8, 9, 10, 11, 12, 13, 14.

Jeremy L. Cross, *True Masonic Chart or Hieroglyphic Monitor.* 1846; 343. Huntington & Savage and A. S. Barnes, New York, publishers. Went through many editions.
Comments: Described in 7 Build. Mag. 109 (1921). L. B. Blakemore, "Once a very popular Monitor, based on Webb's Freemason's Monitor, but with variations of its own. Its illustrations made it popular." Libraries: 1, 2, 3, 4, 5, 6, 7, 8, 9, 10, 11, 12, 13, 14.

Z. A. Davis, *The Freemason's Monitor.* 1843; 312 pp. Desilver & Muir, Philadelphia, publisher.
Contents: Brief history of the Craft, quotations from various regulations, and constitutions, with a monitor of the three degrees and of several appendant bodies. Libraries: 1, 3, 4, 5, 6, 7, 12, 14, 15.

Daniel Sickles, *The General Ahiman Rezon.* 1882; 407 pp. Macoy Publishing Co., publisher.
Author: Coil, Mas. Ency., 623; Baynard, History of the Scottish Rite, NMJ, Vol. 1, 263; has picture of Sickles. Contents: Monitor with songs, odes, and ceremonies of various kinds. Comments: Silas H. Shepherd, "A useful monitor, well compiled." Libraries: 2, 3, 4, 7, 8, 9, 10, 11, 12, 13, 14.

George E. Simons, *Standard Masonic Monitor.* 1948; 248 pp. Macoy Publishing Co., publisher. Originally published in 1878, and republished in 1891 and in 1899, with revisions. Designed primarily for use in New York. Libraries: 3, 7, 8, 9, 11, 12, 13, 14.

Monitorial Symbolism of the Third Degree. 7 Build Mag. 349 (1921).

Cipher Rituals, STB, May, 1956.

Cyphers, 8 Build. Mag. 30 (1922).

Myron K. Lingle, *The Word;* 1969; 118 pp. Being an arrangement in chronological order of the York Rite degrees. Author: 1 Trans. Ill. of Res. 186; Ill.

Scottish Rite History, p. 173. The author tells how he wrote this book in: K. T. Mag., March, 1973, 13. Libraries: 2, 3, 7, 9, 11.

7.05 MASONIC CEREMONIES

Ceremonies of Freemasonry. STB, May, 1948.

Ballots and Balloting Practices of the 49 Grand Lodges of the U.S. MSA Digest.

M. A. Howard, *The Ceremonies of Freemasonry.* 3 Walter F. Meier L. of Res., Wash., 302.

Hugh A. Cole, *Attentive Ears, Instructive Tongues, and Faithful Breasts.* 1979; 15 pp. Iowa Lodge of Research No. 2. A brief history of Masonic ceremonies with a chapter relating to Illinois.

A. C. F. Jackson, *Masonic Passwords; Their Development and Use in the Early 18th Century.* 87 AQC 106 (1974).

Plez A. Transou, *The Sound of the Gavel.* Tex. Free., March, 1977, 12.

J. W. Stubbs, *Due Examination of Visitors.* 80 AQC 327 (1967).

Harold V. B. Voorhis, *Examining Visiting Masons.* Phil. Mag., Feb., 1955, 13.

Visitors and Visitors' Committee. STB, Jan., 1977.

Lodge Visitation. Ill. Enlight., April, 1951, 7.

The Examination of Visitors. Mas. Sq., Dec., 1978, 154.

R. J. Meekren, *Points of Entrance.* Phil. Mag., Dec., 1978, 91.

William L. Boyden, *Behavior in the Lodge.* New Age Mag., Nov., 1924, 665.

Courtesy Degrees. 19 Build. Mag. 256 (1924).

William L. Boyden, *Curiosities of the Ballot.* New Age Mag., May, 1925, 269.

W. B. Hextall, *Adjournment of a Lodge.* 23 AQC 203 (1910).

Masonic Baptism of the Young. 3 Build. Mag. 287 (1917).

Robert H. Gollmar, *Masonic Baptism.* Phil. Mag., Feb., 1957, 3; April, 1957, 26.

Lewis Edwards, *Freemasonry, Ritual and Ceremonial.* In Harry Carr, ed., Collected Prestonian Lectures, 213.

Presenting the Working Tools. STB, Aug., 1961.

W. W. Wescott, *The Rite of Circumambulation.* 2 Trans. Author's Lodge No. 3456 345 (1917).

H. G. Meachem, *Duly and Truly Prepared.* N.Y. Mas. Outl., Dec., 1928, 107.

Look Well to the West. N.Y. Mas. Outl., April, 1929., 236.

Richardson Wright, *The Rise and Fall of Masonic Drinking.* 4 ALR 13 (1942-1943).

Frederick H. Smyth, *The Highways and Byways of American Freemasonry.* 10 ALR 126 (1966).

When Refreshment Was Liquid. 5 ALR 282 (1947-1948).

Latin Language in Lodges. 12 Build. Mag. 275 (1926).

The VSL in Our Ceremonies. 83 AQC 377 (1970).

T. O. Haunch, *The Constitution and Consecration of New Lodges Under the Grand Lodge of England.* 83 AQC 1 (1970).

Signs of Recognition. 8 RAM 122 (1964).

Sketches of Some of the Characters in the Royal and Select. 6 RAM 185 (1949).

English Freemasonry as Seen by Argentine Member. 4 RAM 203 (1953).

Art of Presiding. STB, Oct., 1939.

Cup of Brotherly Love, No. Light, Sept., 1972. Also MSA Digest by John B. Vrooman.

Irish Masonic Customs. Phil. Mag., June, 1955, 3.

H. L. Haywood, *Drama of the Third Degree.* N.Y. Mas. Outl., May, 1929, 263.

Harry Carr, *Freemasonry in the United States*. 1977 Grd. L. of Scotl. Yrbk. 100. Impressions of a trip he took in the United States.

Ritual, Paraphernalia, and Rehearsals. 4 RAM 342, 370 (1954).

A. T. Brand, *The Opening and Closing of the Lodge and the Use of Knocks in Craft Masonry*. 8 Installed. Mast. Assn., Leeds, 73 (1911-1912).

The World's Largest Breakfast. 7 RAM 131 (1962).

William L. Boyden, *The Goat in Freemasonry*. New Age Mag., April, 1925, 207.

William L. Boyden, *Ye Olde Refreshment Days*. 12 Build. Mag. 265 (1926).

Summons. STB, March, 1931.

Truly Prepared. STB, May, 1926.

William L. Cummings, *Rites and Ritual*. 1 RAM 178, 215, 270, 302, 357 (1944).

William L. Boyden, *Lodges and Lotteries*. New Age Mag., Dec., 1924, 741.

Outdoor Degree Conferred in Illinois. No. Light., Sept., 1972, 18.

R. R. Clemons, *Masonic Notebook: Texas Compares English and Texas Ceremonies*. Mas. Sq., Sept., 1979, 116.

Edward F. Fowler, Jr., *Passing to the Chair in Pennsylvania*. 85 AQC 312 (1972).

Colin F. W. Dyer, *The Women Have Their Way; a Ladies Night of the 1790's*. 88 AQC 193 (1975).

M. G. Davies, *Firing Glasses*. 89 AQC 274 (1976).

How to Kill a Banquet. K. T. Mag., March, 1974, 25.

Toast to Absent Brethren. 85 AQC 367 (1972).

John D. Hamilton, *Ceremonial Swords in Masonry*. No. Light, Jan., 1979, 10.

Correct Titles, Mas. Mess., Ga., July, 1974, 20.

Ernest Henry Cook, *Origin of the Ceremony Known as ''Passing of the Veils'' as Practiced in Bristol Province*. 85 AQC 325 (1972).

Alphonse Cerza, *A Successful Lodge Year*. Lodge programs presented during bicentennial year by Saugatuck Lodge No. 328, of Michigan. Phil. Mag., Aug., 1977, 14.

J. T. Thorp, *Masonic ''Fire'' and ''Firing.''* 35 Trans. Leic. L. of Res. 134 (1926-1927).

Leonard Langeneckert, *Dedication of the George Washington National Memorial*. The Freemason, Mo., Spring, 1977, 42.

G. W. Speth, *Builders' Rites and Ceremonies; The Folk-Lore of Masonry*. 89 AQC 139 (1976). Reprint of a paper written in 1894.

Harry Carr, *The Obligation and Its Place in the Ritual*. 1963 Grd. L. of Scotl. Yrbk. 99.

Will Read, *The Final Toast*. 91 AQC 198 (1979).

Alphonse Cerza, *Travel in Foreign Countries*. Suggestions on what to do in visiting foreign lodges. Phil. Mag., April, 1975, 46.

Stewart M. L. Pollard, *Visiting a German Lodge*. Phil. Mag., Aug., 1970, 76.

Masonic Funeral Service. MSA Digest.

7.06 CORNERSTONE LAYING CEREMONY

Yancey L. Russell, *Origins of the Cornerstone Ceremony*. 3 Trans. Tex. L. of Res. 335, 408 (1965-1968).

Cornerstone Customs. Phil. Mag., June, 1956, 47.

Famous American Cornerstones. STB, June, 1951.

Ray Baker Harris, *The Laying of Cornerstone*. 1961; 54 pp. Supreme Council, 33°, S.J.
Author: Phil. Mag., June, 1964, 50.
Libraries: 3, 7, 9, 11, 12, 14.

Ray Baker Harris, *The Two Cornerstones*

of the U.S. Capitol. New Age Mag., Jan., 1943, 343.

Alex Horne, *The Foundation and Cornerstone.* Mas. Sq., March, 1977, 26. Has picture of the author.

Builder Laid the Foundation. MSA Digest.

A. Byron Croop, *Stone Laying Ceremonies and Traditions.* 5 Mas. Papers, Walter F. Meier L. of Res., Wash., June, 1976.

Truman Library Cornerstone Laid. Mas. World of Ray V. Denslow, 148.

Clarence D. Philips, *The First Stone.* Ore. Free., June, 1974, 5.

Corner-Stone. STB, July, 1936.

Alphonse Cerza, *A Cornerstone and Independence.* Phil. Mag., Dec., 1959, 86.

Knights of Columbus Object. 7 RAM 90 (1961).

Warren F. Mellny, *Cornerstone Customs.* Phil. Mag., June, 1956, 46.

Bruce Hunt, *Why Freemasons Lay Cornerstones.* Phil. Mag., Feb., 1968, 18.

Joseph Fort Newton, *Great Corner Stone.* STB, Sept., 1925.

Norman C. Dutt, *On Cornerstones.* Phil. Mag., Dec., 1963, 93.

David Flather, *The Foundation Stone.* 48 AQC 212 (1935).

G. W. Daynes, *A Masonic Foundation Stone at the Bank of England.* 41 AQC 160 (1928).

W. J. Chetwode Crawley, *Two Cornerstones Laid in the Olden Times.* 24 AQC 21 (1911).

Famous Cornerstone Laid by American Masons. New Age Mag., Nov., 1911, 483; Dec., 1911, 598; Feb., 1912, 186.

Capitol Ceremony. Phil. Mag., Oct., 1959, 71.

R. Baker Harris, *Laying the Cornerstone of Public Buildings.* New Age Mag., Oct., 1955, 591.

Smithsonian Institution. 5 RAM 214 (1956).

B. & O. Cornerstone. 5 RAM 179 (1956).

Bunker Hill. 5 RAM 227 (1956).

National Capitol. 7 RAM 163, 235 (1962).

John A. Mirt, *Are Masonic Cornerstone Laying Ceremonies Relics of the Past?* 3 RAM 339 (1951).

Capitol Cornerstone Laid by President With Masonic Ceremony. 6 RAM 195 (1959).

7.07 MAKING A MASON AT SIGHT

STB, March, 1937.

Cal. Free., Autumn, 1979, 155.

Phil. Mag., April, 1964, 35.

89 AQC 262 (1976).

New Age Mag., March, 1925, 143.

2 Build. Mag. 47 (1916).

Prerogatives "At Sight." 2 Build. Mag. 274 (1916).

7.08 MASONIC FUNERAL SERVICE

Robert L. Dillard, Jr., *Masonic Funeral and Burial Ceremonies.* 11 Trans. Tex. L. of Res. 132 (1975-1976).

J. Thomas Middleton, *Masonic Funerals at Graveside and Memorial Service at Funeral Homes.* 1975 Proc. Grd. Mast. Conf., 115.

Robert Henderson and Thomas W. Hooper, *Masonic Funerals.* 1935 Proc. Grd. Mast. Conf. 72.

Aubry L. Burbank and Elmer I. Gibson, *Masonic Funeral Service.* 1957 Proc. Grd. Mast. Conf. 120.

Silas E. Ross, *Funeral Customs Through the Ages.* New Age Mag., June, 1968, 48.

Masonic Funeral Service. MSA Digest.

John B. Vrooman comments on this subject: Phil. Mag., Dec., 1962, 93. Responses appear in: Phil. Mag., June, 1963, 43; Aug., 1963, 62; Oct., 1963, 77; and Dec., 1963, 96.

The subject is discussed in depth in Forrest D. Haggard, *The Clergy and the Craft,* 73-83 (1970); MLR, publisher.

7.09 TABLE LODGE

Masonic Feasts. MSA Digest.

The Table Lodge. STB, Aug., 1951.

How to Conduct a Table Lodge. 1978; 12 pp. Lodge Service Committee of the Grand Lodge of Iowa.

History of the Table Lodge. 13 Trans. Tex. L. of Res. 178 (1977-1978).

Table Lodge Demonstration. 1955 Proc. Mdw. Conf. on Mas. Ed. 115.

Dr. George H. T. French, *Ancient Masonic Conviviality.* Tex. Free., Sept., 1972, 19.

M. Henderson, *Planning the Masonic Dinner.* N.Y. Mas. Outl., Oct., 1927, 41; Dec., 1927, 110; 1928, 173; May, 1928, 267; Jan., 1929, 133.

Having a Lodge Picnic. N.Y. Mas. Outl., May, 1930, 269.

R. J. Meekren, *Breaking Bread.* N.Y. Mas. Outl., Aug., 1925, 265.

William L. Boyden, *Convivial Lodge Customs.* 12 Build. Mag. 360 (1926).

Masonic Toasts. 82 AQC 332 (1969).

7.10 MASONIC HONORS AND AWARDS

Public Grand Honors. 75 AQC 239 (1962).

Grand Lodge Honors and Distinctions. MSA Digest.

Distinguished Achievement Award. No. Light., June, 1971, 12.

Empire State's Distinguished Achievement Award. Phil. Mag., Aug., 1960, 61; 3 RAM 295 (1951); Ind. Free, May, 1957, 10.

Jeremy Cross Medal of New Hampshire. 2 RAM 360 (1948).

Josiah Drummond Medal. 2 RAM 304 (1948).

The Gold Jordan Medal. 2 RAM 270 (1948).

The Pierpont Edwards Medal. 2 RAM 231 (1948).

Maryland Medal. 10 RAM 253 (1971-1972).

General Grand Chapter Awards. 4 RAM 79 (1952).

The KCCH. New Age Mag., Sept., 1962, 28.

Distinguished Achievement Award. No. Light, June, 1971, 12.

Dewey H. Wollstein Award. Mas. Mess., Ga., Dec., 1974, 7.

London Rank. 86 AQC 101 (1973).

T. O. Haunch, *Arms of the United Grand Lodge of England.* 89 AQC 266 (1976).

Certificate of Literature of the Philalethes Society. Phil. Mag., Feb., 1956, 14; April, 1958, 30.

T. O. Haunch, *English Craft Certificates.* 82 AQC 169 (1969).

Henry Price Medal of Massachusetts. Phil. Mag., Aug., 1960, 61; 3 RAM 295 (1951).

Heraldry. 6 RAM 121 (1958) R. V. Harris, *The Heraldry of Freemasonry.* 15 Build. Mag. 224 (1929).

7.11 MASONIC OFFICES AND OFFICERS

Grand Lodge Officers. MSA Digest.

Grand Representatives. STB, Jan., 1963.

Advisory and Executive Boards. MSA Digest.

The Lodge Secretary, A Balance Wheel. Cal. Free., Autumn, 1972, 172.

Grand Pursuivant. 83 AQC 374 (1970); Phil. Mag., Feb., 1972, 9; So. Dakota Mas. Mess., Nov., 1972, 3; Phil. Mag., Feb., 1975, 11.

District Deputy Grand Master System in the U.S. Grand Lodges. MSA Digest.

Assistant Grand Lecturers in New York. 7 ALR 178 (1958).

Tylers: Henry Sadler, *Tylers and Tyling.* 82 AQC 309 (1969). Roy A. Wells, *The Tyler or Outer Guard,* 90 AQC 194 (1978). Eric Ward, *The Tylers,* 74 AQC 73 (1961). William L. Boyden, *The Tyler and Ye Olden Days.* New Age Mag.. Oct..

1924, 599. Arthur J. Votava, *The Tiler, Past and Present,* 1 Trans. Ill. L. of Res. 100.

Grand Stewards: P. J. Dawson, *Grand Stewards of the Premier Grand Lodge,* 5 Trans. Phoenix L., Paris, 79. J. M. Hamill, *The Country Feast and Their Stewards,* 89 AQC 222 (1976). *Grand Stewards,* 1728-1978, 91 AQC 168 (1979); Edmund Poole, *A History of the Grand Stewards,* 2 Trans. Author's L. No. 3456 412 (1917). *Grand Stewards and Other English Masonic Lodge Notices,* 9 ALR 75 (1963).

E. R. Turnbull, *The Dispensing Power.* 5 Norcalore 70 (1935).

J. W. Horsley, *Masonic Titles Compared With Those of the Church.* 23 AQC 98 (1910).

Titles of the United Grand Lodge of England, the "Antients" and the "Moderns." 64 AQC 76 (1951).

7.12 THE FEAST OF TISHRI

This feast is observed annually by the Scottish Rite, S.J., and a great deal has been written about it over the years. Here are some illustrative articles in the New Age Mag., Sept., 1962, 52; Sept., 1964, 25; Sept., 1965, 44; Sept., 1969, 12; Sept., 1970, 11; Oct., 1972, 42.

7.13 MASONIC CLOTHING AND LODGE FURNITURE

F. J. W. Crowe, *Masonic Clothing.* 5 AQC 29 (1892); 6 AQC 160 (1893); 7 AQC 52, 194 (1894).

G. S. Knocker, *The Use of Pre-Union "Atholl" Regalia 28 Years After the Union.* 53 AQC 339 (1963).

J. A. Cockburn, *Masonic Furniture.* 4 Trans. Author's L. No. 3456 44 (1928).

Tracing Boards: C. P. Clarke, *Tracing Boards in Modern Oriental and Medieval Operative Masonry,* 6 AQC 99, 124 (1893). E. H. Dring, *The Evolution and Development of the Tracing Board,* 29 AQC 243, 275 (1916). David Flather, *The Tracing Boards of Britannia Lodge No. 139,* 54 AQC 228 (1941). T. O. Haunch, *Arthur L. Thiselton: A Little Known Paint-*er *of Tracing Boards,* 76 AQC 144 (1963). T. O. Haunch, *Tracing Boards, Their Development and Designers,* 75 AQC 182 (1962); 77 AQC 255 (1964). W. H. Rylands, *Remarks on Bro. Purdon Clarke's Paper on the Tracing Board,* 6 AQC 124 (1893). O. N. Wyatt, *Some Notes on the Tracing Boards of the Lodge of Union No. 38,* Chichester. 3 AQC 191 (1910). 11 Build. Mag. 151 (1925). Norman B. Spencer, *The Evolution of Our Modern Tracing Board,* Phil. Mag., Dec., 1949, 6. *Trestleboard and Tracing Board,* STB, July, 1932. G. E. W. Bridge, *A Study of the Tracing Board of the First Prestonian Lecture for 1939,* reproduced in Harry Carr, ed., Collected Prestonian Lectures, 265. G. E. W. Bridge, *A Study of Tracing Boards,* 1962 Gr. L. of Scotl. Yrbk. 81. Prince Alexander of Yugoslavia, *An Appraisal of the Second Degree Tracing Board,* 7 Trans. of Phoenix L., Paris, 86.

Alex Horne, *The Masonic Gloves.* New Age Mag., Sept., 1953, 545.

Arthur Heiron, *The Craft in the 18th Century. Old Time Manners and Customs.* 37 AQC 52 (1924).

William L. Boyden, *Old Smoking Customs of the Craft.* 13 Build. Mag. 140 (1927).

Smoking Customs of the Craft. Ind. Free., July, 1954, 14.

A. C. F. Jackson, *Why a Black Tie?* Mas. Sq., Sept., 1977, 107.

William L. Boyden, *What They Wore of Yore.* New Age Mag. Feb., 1925, 83.

Your Masonic Ring and Its Ancestors. Ind. Free., Oct., 1953, 8.

The Master's Hat. 76 AQC 230 (1963).

Eric Ward, *The Master's Hat,* 74 AQC 154 (1961). Cal. Free., Summer, 1973, 124.

The Use of Costume in Conferring the Chapter Degrees. 3 RAM 83 (1949).

A. F. Calvert, *Uniforms in Lodges.* 29 AQC 388 (1916); 30 AQC 121 (1917).

R. Kenneth Miller, *Aprons – Let's Wear 'Em.* Iowa Grd. L. Bull., March, 1972, 60.

Furniture: W. G. Ibberson, *Curious Masonic Furniture*, 72 AQC 126 (1959). B. W. Oliver, *The Bath Furniture*, 57 AQC 109 (1944). C. M. Rose, *18th Century Lodge Inventories*, 62 AQC 204 (1949). C. M. Rose, *The Irish Lodge: Its Furniture and Properties*, 63 AQC 163 (1950). C. M. Rose, *The Scottish Lodges — Its Inventories, Furniture and Regalia*, 64 AQC 98 (1951). Edward Conder, *The Chairs of Bowyer Lodge*, 10 AQC 63 (1897). J. Jerman, *Old Lodge Chairs in Freemasons Hall, Exeter*, 6 AQC 146 (1893). E. T. Joy and A. R. Hewitt, *Some Unrecorded Masonic Ceremonial Chairs of the Georgian Period*, 80 AQC 123 (1967). W. F. Lamonby, *Old Chairs, Lodge 254, Coventry*, 6 AQC 147 (1893). H. R. Evans, *Lodge Furniture and Degrees*, 2 Build. Mag. 207 (1916).

7.14 MASONIC INSTALLATION CEREMONY

Installation. STB, Feb., 1945.

Henry Sadler, *Notes on the Ceremony of Installation* (1899).

Alex Horne, *"Open" and "Closed" Installations in U.S.A.* 83 AQC 65 (1970).

N. B. Spencer, *The Installation Ceremony.* 72 AQC 100 (1959).

The Installation Ceremony and Rites. 4 Build. Mag. 131 (1918).

Eric Ward, *The Development of Installation at Bristol.* 71 AQC 85 (1958).

A. L. Kress, *The Ceremony of Installing a Grand Master in 1768.* 12 Build. Mag. 49 (1926).

H. C. Booth, *The Ceremony of Installation.* 89 AQC 244 (1976).

William Reed, *The Ceremony of Installation.* 5 Trans. Phoenix L., Paris, 1.

Harry Carr, *The Evolution of the Installed Ceremony and Ritual.* 89 AQC 32 (1976).

W. Reed, *The Extended Working in the Board of Installed Master.* 84 AQC 26 (1971).

CHAPTER EIGHT

The Fine Arts

8.01 MASONRY IN GENERAL LITERATURE

Dr. Larry C. Helms, *Masonry and Literature*. New Age Mag., Aug., 1978, 11.

William H. Knutz, *Literature of Masonry*. Phil. Mag., March, 1947, 2; April, 1972, 45.

Thomas S. Roy, *Freemasonry and Literature*. Ind. Free., Jan., 1971, 6.

William L. Cummings, *Freemasonry in Fiction*. 3 Norcalore 219 (1933).

J. T. Thorp, *References to Freemasonry in Early Printed Books*. 9 Trans. Leic. L. of Res. 20 (1900-1901).

Freemasons: Early Printed References. New Age Mag., Dec., 1933, 735.

Heinrich Schneider, *Quest for Mysteries*. 1947; 137 pp. Cornell University Press. Contents: Masonic background for literature in 18th century Germany. Reviewed: New Age Mag., Feb., 1948, 114; Dec., 1948, 695. Libraries: 1, 3, 5, 7, 10, 11, 12, 14.

H. W. Loewe, *Masonry in Hebrew Literature*. Mast. Mas., April, 1924, 253.

Omar Khayyamm the Mason. New Age Mag., July, 1923, 387.

Alfred Dodd, *Shakespeare, Creator of Freemasonry*. 1936; 276 pp. Rider & Co., London, publisher. Comments: H. L. Haywood, "There is no obvious connection between Masonic research and Shakespeare research. Freemasonry as a Fraternity does not appear in any of the plays, and there is no indication that Shakespeare belonged to any one of the Time Immemorial Lodges. But out of Shakespearean research and theory arose two or three theories which became connected with the Craft, and Masonic research was thereby drawn into 'the Shakespearean question.' " Reviewed: 2 Build. Mag. 125 (1916). Libraries: 1, 2, 3, 5, 9, 12, 14.

F. G. Palmer, *Shakespeare and Freemasonry*. 32 AQC 142 (1919).

Raymond B. Pease, *Masonic Parallels in Shakespeare*. MSA Digest.

Newcomb Condee, *Shakespeare and Freemasonry*. New Age Mag., April, 1951, 215.

Alphonse Cerza, *William Shakespeare and Freemasonry*. New Age Mag., Nov., 1973, 8.

Alphonse Cerza, *Freemasonry and Shakespeare*. Phil. Mag., Aug., 1964, 60.

Hamlet and Masonry. New Age Mag., Sept., 1970, 30.

Robert I. Clegg, *Was William Shakespeare a Freemason?* 5 Build. Mag. 32 (1919).

Dr. Raymond W. Miller, *Masonry Recorded in History and Literature*. New Age Mag., May, 1978, 6.

Richard H. Brown, *An Old Masonic Commonplace Book*. 13 ALR 8 (1975).

Life Magazine, Oct., 1956, p. 104, had a long illustrated article about Freemasonry. Editorial about this article: 5 RAM 280 (1957).

J. M. Watkins, *Some Allegories Between the Teachings of Dante and That of*

Freemasonry. 3 Trans. Author's L. No. 3456 415.

F. W. Billson, *Freemasonry and Bacon's New Atlantis.* 15 Trans. Leic. L. of Res. 87 (1906).

Masonic Symbolism in Chinese Literature. New Age Mag., Jan., 1928, 35.

Bedford Village and Hervey Allen. 4 ALR 341 (1944-1945).

Robinson Crusoe and Freemasonry. New Age Mag., Oct., 1958, 599.

Sherlock Holmes a Mason? 8 RAM 248, 317 (1963-1968).

K. F. Langford, *Was Sherlock Holmes a Mason?* Mas. Sq., Dec., 1977, 159.

H. L. Haywood, *Masonic Curiosa,* 108: "In his famous story 'The Red-Headed League' Conan Doyle has Sherlock Holmes use a half page deducing the fact that a visitor is a Freemason."

A. L. Mclead, *Masonic Allusions in Kipling's Works.* 8 Trans. Leic. L. of Res. 65 (1929-1930).

Kipling, *In the Interest of the Brethren.* 8 Build. Mag. 67 (1922).

Spenceley Walker, *Kipling as a Freemason.* Trans. M. & P. M. L., May, 1979, 274. Detailed presentation of Kipling's works with Masonic references.

Edgar Allen Poe and Freemasonry. Mast. Mas., May, 1928, 385.

Alphonse Cerza, *Edgar Allen Poe and Freemasonry.* Description of "The Cask of Amontillado" and its Masonic implications. 12 RAM 62 (1979).

War and Peace, by Leo Tolstoy. New Age Mag., May, 1957, 299.

Richard H. Brown, *The Masonic Observations in George Crabbe's "The Borough."* 12 ALR 126 (1972).

Allen Cabaniss, *Casanova and Freemasonry.* Phil. Mag., Oct., 1975, 98.

Kenneth D. Gemmell, *Conversations of Ernest and Falk.* 3 Trans. Tex. L. of Res. 417 (1965-1968).

Gotthold Ephraim Lessing. New Age Mag., 1933, 663.

Ernest and Falk, by Lessing. 1 Build. Mag. 20, 59 (1915); 2 Build. Mag. 201 (1916). 15 Build. Mag. 321, 354 (1929).

Comments on Lessing: L. B. Blakemore, "This masterpiece of one of the greatest German Masons has been widely read in the Craft as a fictional presentation of Masonic tolerance" (Nathan the Wise). See also: Katz, *Jews and Freemasons, 1723-1939,* pp. 24-25.

Daniel Pearce Thompson, *Adventures of Timothy Peacock, Esq.* 1835; 218 pp., anti-Masonic fiction. A copy of this book is in the Chicago Historical Society Library.

Harry Carr, *A Russian Initiatory Ceremony.* 89 AQC 268 (1976). Comment on the ceremony in War and Peace by Leo Tolstoy.

Henry Fielding's Tom Jones Has Reference to Freemasonry. 8 RAM 59 (1964).

Mervin B. Hogan, *There's Masonic Significance in Rudyard Kipling's Tale.* No. Light, Jan., 1972, 4.

Deacon Brodie, respected citizen by day and a burglar by night; inspired Robert Louis Stevenson's novel *Dr. Jekyll and Mr. Hyde.* Mas. Mess., Ga., Aug., 1972, 9.

Albert Schweitzer's *The Philosophy of Civilization* mentions the Craft in 1717. New Age Mag., May, 1955, 296.

Douglas, *Old Calabria,* has Masonic significance. See H. L. Haywood, Masonic Curiosa, 166.

Arthur Barnett, *The Masonic Inspiration of the Augustans.* Trans. Phoen. Lodge, Paris, 37 (1971-1972).

Currier and Ives, *Masonic Chart.* 7 RAM 263 (1963).

Masonic Folklore – A Plea for Its Cultivation. 9 ALR 334 (1965).

Alex Horne, *Fichte on Freemasonry.* New Age Mag., Feb., 1955, 97.

The Craft Mentioned in Wilder's "The Eighth Day." Phil. Mag., June, 1970, 67.

8.02 MASONIC WORDS

GENERAL

Pocket Dictionary. MSA Digest.

Masonic Vocabulary. STB, July, 1958.

One Hundred "Lost Words." STB, Feb., 1947.

Some Curious Masonic Words. STB, Aug., 1953.

Raymond B. Pease, *Language Landmarks.* MSA Digest.

Raymond B. Pease, *The Richness of Masonic Language.* 1951, MSA Digest.

Masonic Words. 2 RAM 370 (1948); 3 RAM 347, 370 (1951); 5 RAM 76 (1955).

R. H. Baxter, *Masonic Words and Their Meaning.* 23 Trans. Manch. Assn. for Mas. Res. 203 (1933).

Charles King, *So Spake the Master.* 1967; 92 pp. Scottish Rite Bodies of Helena, Montana. A pronouncing dictionary of Masonic words.

B. H. B. Pinfold, *New Zealand Ritual Pronouncing Dictionary.* 44 pp. published by Research Lodge of Otago No. 161, Dunedin, New Zealand. A copy is in the Scottish Rite Library in Washington, D.C.

Masonic Mispronunciation. STB, April, 1948.

Harry C. Bauer, *Masonic Editorial Acuity Test.* 5 Mas. Papers, Walter F. Meier L. of Res., June, 1976.

K. E. Keith, *Hebrew Words Used in Craft Masonry.* 21 Proc. Manch. of Res. 33 (1931).

Words, Words, Words. STB, Jan., 1963.

H. L. Haywood, *On Certain Words in Freemasonry.* Ill. Enlight., Feb., 1956, 70.

C. J. Ball, *The Proper Names of Masonic Tradition: A Philological Study.* 5 AQC 136 (1892).

SPECIFIED WORDS

Accepted Masons: Harry Carr, ed., Collected Prestonian Lectures, 429.

Ancient, Free and Accepted: Phil. Mag., Aug., 1956, 57; Ill. Enlight., Jan., 1949, 1; Phil. Mag., April, 1950, 9; Phil. Mag., Aug., 1959, 51; 9 Build. Mag. 285 (1923).

Antients: Alex Horne, *"Antients" and "Moderns" in American Masonry.* New Age Mag., June, 1954, 367.

Assembly: 5 AQC 203 (1892); 6 AQC 169 (1893); 6 AQC 173 (1893).

Blue Lodge: C. F. Willard, New Age Mag., July, 1926, 413.

Clichés: Cal. Free., Autumn, 1972, 171.

Cleft of the Rocks: Cal. Free., Winter, 1974, 19.

Common Gavel: Mas. Mess., Ga., Aug., 1974, 11.

Compasses: R. J. Meekren, *Compasses: Singular or Plural?* 14 Build. Mag. 103 (1928).

Cowans and Eavesdroppers: New Age Mag., June, 1956, 353; Phil. Mag., Oct., 1963, 104; 8 RAM 254 (1965); Mas. J. of So. Africa, Aug., 1972, 31.

Curious: Cal. Free., Winter, 1974, 20.

Demit or Dimit: Sandusky Mas. Bull. and Phil. Mag., April, 1952; 12; 5 Build. Mag. 308 (1919); 6 Build. Mag 28 (1920); Ill. Enlight., Dec., 1952, 8; Feb., 1953, 8.

Due Guard: 8 Build. Mag. 6 (1922).

Entered Apprentice: Ill. Enlight., Feb., 1950, 4.

F. & A.M. vs. A.F. & A.M.: Cal. Free., Autumn, 1975, 177.

Fraternity: Cal. Free., Winter, 1974, 19.

Fellow Craft: Ind. Free., Dec., 1977, 12.

Free: Phil. Mag., Jan., 1952, 5.

Free and Accepted: STB, Nov., 1931. New Age Mag., Dec., 1953, 747.

Free Born: Phil. Mag., Oct., 1954, 7. Harry Carr, ed., Collected Prestonian Lectures, 375.

Freemason: B. E. Jones, *"Free" in "Freemasons"*, in Collected Prestonian Lectures, 363. F. F. Schitger, *Free and Freemasons*, 2 AQC 141 (1889). G. W. Speth, *Free and Freemasonry*, 10 AQC 10 (1898). STB, Feb., 1953. 8 RAM 113 (1964). The Craftsman (Mex.), Nov.-Dec., 1974, 28. *Earliest Use of the Word "Freemasons,"* 7 RAM 381 (1963). *Freemason Used in Deed Dated September 20, 1502*, New Age Mag., Dec., 1972, 32. *"Freemason" Found in Book Published in 1526;* New Age Mag., Oct., 1954, 616. 91 AQC 81 (1979). *The Crisp English Word Freemason*, 68 AQC 58 (1956). Eric Ward, *The Word Freemason*, 91 AQC 78 (1979).

Hele: Origin of the Word "Hele," 7 Build. Mag. 208 (1921). Ill. Enlight., March, 1949, 2. New Age Mag., Feb., 1910, 165. 6 RAM 153 (1959). 10 Build. Mag. 127 (1924).

Irreligious Libertine: A. Cerza, Phil. Mag., June, 1955, 11.

"It Rains": Cal. Free., Winter, 1974, 19.

Lewis: 10 AQC 210 (1897); 70 AQC 121 (1957); Phil. Mag., Oct., 1962, 67; 8 Build. Mag. 335 (1922); Ind. Free., Aug., 1954, 7; STB, Feb., 1935.

Lodge: 3 Trans. Tex L. of Res. 125 (1965-1968).

Mason: Walter M. Callaway, Jr., *Mason or Freemason; Masonry or Freemasonry*, Trans. Res. L. No. 104, Atlanta, Ga., Nov., 29, 1968.

Mason Word: Douglas Knoop, *The Mason Word*, in Harry Carr, ed., Collected Prestonian Lectures, 243. Ross Hebburn, Trans. M. & P. M. L., Sept., 1970, 162. Harry Carr, *A Collection of Early References to the Mason Word*, 85 AQC 217 (1972). Knoop and Jones, *The Scottish Mason and the Mason Word*, 1939; 109 pp., Manchester University Press, publisher.

Mote: 10 Build. Mag. 127 (1924).

Mystery: 9 Build. Mag. 254 (1923).

Neighbor: Ind. Free., Dec., 1973, 10.

Passed or Past Master: New Age Mag., Jan., 1979, 42.

Peculiar System: No. Cal. Res. L. Quart. J., March, 1974.

Philalethes: Phil. Mag., Aug., 1972, 77.

Profane: Cal. Free., Winter, 1974, 19, Spring, 1973, 70; Iowa Grand L. Bulletin, March, 1974, 75.

Pure Ancient Masonry: Ill. Enlight., Feb., 1954, 8.

Rabboni: *Masonic Implications of the Word*, 9 RAM 110 (1967).

Rank or Office: 56 AQC 350 (1973).

Ritual: In Collected Prestonian Lectures, 414.

Silver Cord: Phil. Mag., Aug., 1967, 76; Dec., 1967, 110.

So Mote it Be: STB, June, 1927.

Speculative: STB, Feb., 1964. Ill. Enlight., Oct., 1953, 8.

"Stupid Atheist": STB, April, 1932.

"System of Morality": Mas. Mess., Ga., Sept., 1977, 7.

Veiled in Allegory: 1962 Grd. L. of Scotl. Yrbk. 81.

Warden: STB, April, 1931.

Whence and Whither: Mas. J. of So. Africa, May, 1974, 21.

Word: Edward M. Selby, *The Word in Masonic Ritual*, Phil. Mag., June, 1975, 61.

Word-Pairs: Phil. Mag., July, 1968, 76. Phil. Mag., Aug., 1968, 76. *Half Letters or Split-Letter System*, 80 AQC 337 (1967). Phil. Mag., June, 1973, 56.

Worthy? Well Qualified: Ind. Free., Feb., 1978, 16.

Worshipful: 10 Build. Mag. 287 (1924). Cal. Free., Autumn, 1972, 168. Phil. Mag., Feb., 1973, 20.

Worshipful Master: Norman Rogers, *The Principal Officer*, 68 AQC 3 (1955).

8.03 MASONIC ESSAYS

Robert Freke Gould, *Collected Essays and*

Papers Relating to Freemasonry, 1913; 302 pp. William Tait, Belfast & Spencer & Co., London, publisher.

Author: Appendix No. 12. Comments: Silas H. Shepherd, "The contents of this volume are well selected and are valuable to the student. The essays on 'English Freemasonry Before the Era of Grand Lodges,' and 'On the Antiquity of Masonic Symbolism,' will save the student a vast amount of time. They place in concise form a view of both the physical organization and its inner spirit, which makes intelligible many otherwise obscure points." Reviewed: 4 Build. Mag. 93 (1918); 26 AQC 209 (1913); Am. Free., July, 1913, 445. Libraries: 1, 2, 3, 5, 7, 8, 9, 10, 11, 12, 15.

Roscoe Pound, *Masonic Addresses and Writings*. 384 pp.

Author: Phil. Mag., Oct., 1964, 78. Libraries: 1, 2, 3, 4, 5, 6, 7, 8, 9, 10, 11, 12, 13, 14.

Carl H. Claudy, *Masonic Harvest*. 1948; 376 pp. Temple Publishing Co., publisher.

Author: Appendix No. 6. Contents: A collection of Short Talk Bulletins. Libraries: 1, 2, 3, 4, 5, 7, 9, 10, 11, 12, 13, 14.

Carl H. Claudy, *Old Tiler Talks*. 1949; 251 pp. Temple Publishing Co., publisher.

Author: Appendix No. 6. Contents: The Fellowship Forum originally published Old Tiler Talks; 414 in all were published. In 1925 a few were selected and printed in book form. These talks or essays have been popular and deal with a variety of subjects of Masonic interest presented in a unique form. Reviewed: Mast. Mas., June, 1925, 519. Libraries: 1, 2, 3, 4, 5, 7, 8, 9, 10, 11, 12, 13, 14, 15.

Carl H. Claudy, *The Old Past Master*.

Author: Appendix No. 6. Libraries: 1, 2, 3, 4, 5, 7, 9, 10, 11, 12, 13, 14.

Wes Cook, Ed., *The Masonic World of Ray V. Denslow*. 1964; 312 pp.

William J. Hughan, *Masonic Sketches and Reprints*. 1871; 224 pp. Masonic Publishing Co., New York, publisher.
Author: Appendix No. 21. Comments:

L. B. Blakemore, "Very important. Contains a history of Masonry in York, one of the oldest Craft centers, with much material on the old MSS." Silas H. Shepherd, "Until Gould wrote his history, this work contained the only authentic records of York Masonry." Libraries: 2, 3, 7, 8, 9, 10, 11, 12, 14, 15.

Carl H. Claudy, *Foreign Countries*. 1925; 160 pp. Masonic Service Association, publisher.

Author: Appendix No. 6. Contents: Collection of essays keyed to the progress being made by a candidate from degree to degree intending to make the ceremonies clearer to him. Reviewed: Mast. Mas., Jan., 1926, 79; 12 Build. Mag. 92 (1926). Libraries: 1, 2, 3, 4, 5, 6, 7, 8, 9, 10, 11, 12, 13, 14, 15.

Joseph Fort Newton, *The Men's House*. 1923; 262 pp. Southern Publishers, Inc., Kingsport, Tenn., publisher.

Author: Appendix No. 26. Comments: L. B. Blakemore, "A collection of essays and addresses by the author of, The Builders, famous for the beauty of his English style. The title essay is a brief history of Freemasonry." Reviewed: Mast. Mas., Feb., 1924, 78; 10 Build. Mag. 121 (1924); New Age Mag., Feb., 1924, 123; Phil. Mag., Feb., 1958, 9. Libraries: 1, 2, 3, 4, 5, 6, 7, 8, 9, 10, 11, 12, 13, 14.

Joseph Fort Newton, *Brothers and Builders*. 65 pp. Masonic Record, Ltd., London, publisher.

Author: Appendix No. 26. Contents: Has eight short chapters dealing with basic Masonic subjects. Reviewed: Mast. Mason., Jan., 1925, 81; June, 1925, 521. Libraries: 3, 5, 6, 7, 8, 9, 10, 11, 12, 13, 14, 15.

Joseph Fort Newton, *Short Talks on Masonry*. 1928; Macoy Publishing Co., publisher.

Author: Appendix No. 26. Contents: Collection of Short Talk Bulletins written by him. Libraries: 1, 2, 3, 4, 5, 6, 7, 8, 9, 10, 11, 12, 13, 14.

H. L. Haywood, *Masonic Curiosa*. 1968; 316 pp. MLR. Edited by Wes Cook.

Author: Appendix No. 16. This volume has his picture and a biographical sketch.

Dewey H. Wollstein, *Rays of Masonry.* 1953; 150 pp. Macoy Publishing Co., publisher.
Author: Appendix No. 35. Contents: Collection of inspirational editorials written by him. Libraries: 1, 2, 3, 5, 7, 9, 10, 12, 13, 14.

J. S. M. Ward, *Freemasonry, Its Aims and Ideals.* 1923; 232 pp. William Rider & Son, Ltd., London, publisher.
Reviewed: Mast. Mas., March, 1924, 197. Libraries: 1, 3, 4, 5, 6, 7, 8, 9, 10, 11, 12, 13, 14.

The Masonic Philosophy of Ken Shumaker. 1972; 65 pp. Research Lodge No. 2, Iowa, publisher.
Contents: Compilation made by Jerry Marsengill of editorials and articles written by the author over a period of years. Libraries: 2, 3.

Charles Van Cott, *Freemasonry, A Sleeping Giant.* 1959; 353 pp. The author for a number of years published a periodical which made many sensational statements. This book is a collection of articles from that paper.
Libraries: 2, 3, 4, 5, 7, 8, 9, 11, 12, 15.

John T. Thorp, *Masonic Papers.* 1901. Printed by George Gibbons, Leicester.
Author: 21 AQC 261 (1908); 45 AQC 114 (1932). Libraries: 3, 7, 9, 11, 12.

Thomas Sherrard Roy, *Dare We Be Masons.* 1966; 111 pp. Grand Lodge of Massachusetts, publisher.
Author: See his Stalwart Builders, 1971, p. 411. Contents: Collection of 15 of his best talks and writings. Libraries: 2, 3, 5, 7, 11, 14, 15.

James K. Remick, *Altar Lights.* 1952; 118 pp. Published by his wife after his passing.
Contents: Reproduces 42 articles written by the author. Libraries: 3.

A. S. MacBride, *Speculative Freemasonry.* 1924; 256 pp. Southern Publishers, Kingsport, Tenn., publisher.
Author: 2 Build. Mag. 52; (1916) 3 Build. Mag. 6 (1917). Comments: L. B. Blakemore, "A wise and beautiful book by a master of lodge practice. The chapters cover a wide range of subjects." Silas H.

Shepherd, "The work deals with the philosophical principles of Freemasonry and its symbolism." Reviewed: 2 Build. Mag. 27 (1916); 10 Build. Mag. 218 (1924); Mast. Mas., June, 1924, 406. Libraries: 1, 2, 3, 4, 5, 7, 8, 9, 10, 11, 14.

J. T. Lawrence, *The Keystone and Other Essays.* 1913; 321 pp. A. Lewis Ltd., London, publisher.
Comments: L. B. Blakemore, "A collection of essays on a variety of Masonic topics in the graceful style which made its author famous." See: H. L. Haywood, *Masonic Essays,* 407: "He has given us a long series of 100 and 200 delightful pieces . . . themes of which you have never heard . . . written in a facile style. . . ." Libraries: 3, 4, 5, 7, 8, 9, 10, 11, 13, 14.

The Masonic Essays of H. L. Haywood. 1963; 491 pp. MLR, publisher.
Author: Appendix No. 16.

John Thomas Lawrence, *Sidelights of Freemasonry.* 1924; 263 pp. A. Lewis, London, publisher.
Comments: Silas H. Shepherd, "Good; containing general information in readable style." Reviewed: 22 AQC 210 (1909). Libraries: 3, 4, 5, 7, 8, 9, 10, 11, 14.

J. T. Lawrence, *By-Ways of Freemasonry.* 1911; 312 pp. A. Lewis, Ltd., London, publisher.
Comments: L. B. Blakemore, "Delightfully written essays on a group of Masonic topics, of literary value, and very informative." Reviewed: 25 AQC 126 (1912); Mast. Mas., June, 1924, 408. Libraries: 1, 3, 4, 5, 8, 9, 10, 11, 12, 14, 15.

John A. Nocas, *Short Talks for Lodges and Trestleboard Gems.* 1972; So. Calif. Res. L.

A. Holmes-Dallimore, *Masonic Side-Lines.* 135 pp. William Reeves, London, publisher.
Libraries: 3, 4, 5, 9, 12.

Norman B. Hickox, *The Master's Lectures.* 1923; 96 pp. Beautifully printed book reproducing the 12 lectures delivered in Evans Lodge, of Illinois, during the year the author was Master. Tinged with mysticism. Reprinted

around the year 1975 by Paul E. Rudbeck, of South Bend, Indiana.
Reviewed: 10 Build. Mag. 284 (1924).
Libraries: 1, 2, 3, 4, 5, 7, 8, 9, 12, 14.

R. E. Hedblom, *A Medley of Masonic Miscellanea*. 1955; 122 pp.
Libraries: 5, 8, 12.

H. L. Haywood, *Masonic Curiosa*. 1968; 301; MLR, publisher.
Author: Appendix No. 16.

Edwin Du Laurens, *Masonic Sketch Book*. 1905; 345 pp. Macoy Publishing Co., publisher. Originally published in 1877.
Contents: Collection of articles by various authors on Masonic subjects. Libraries: 2, 3, 4, 7, 9, 11, 12, 13.

Robert Glenn Cole, *Masonic Gleanings*. 1954; collection of essays.
Reviewed: 6 RAM 20 (1958); New Age Mag., Dec., 1954, 763. Libraries: 2, 3, 5, 7, 8, 9, 12, 13, 14.

Bascom B. Clarke, *The Gospel of Freemasonry*. 1920; 60 pp. Clark Publishing Co., Madison, Wis., publisher.
Comments: L. B. Blakemore, ''A series of chapters on Masonic topics in a homespun, person-to-person style; wise and kindly.'' Silas H. Shepherd, ''Uncle Silas' commonsense philosophy appeals to every Mason.'' 15 Build. Mag. 118: ''One of the best books of its kinds, and one that has had a deservedly wide circulation.'' Libraries: 3, 4, 5, 9, 11, 13, 14.

John H. Brownell, *Gems From the Quarries*. 1893; three vols.
Comments: Silas H. Shepherd, ''One of the best collections of this kind ever compiled. The selections are well arranged and indexed. Libraries: 1, 2, 3, 4, 5, 7, 8, 9, 10, 11, 12, 14.

William Adrian Brown, *Fact, Fables, and Fantasies of Freemasonry*. 1968; 185 pp. It would have been well if the author had labelled which of the items are ''fact'' and which are the ''fables.''
Libraries: 3, 5, 7, 11, 12.

Robert J. Blackham, *Apron Men; The Romance of Freemasonry*. 1933; 275 pp. Rider & Co., London, publisher.
Comments: L. B. Blakemore, ''A loosely sketchy volume on a variety of topics, but valuable for its chapters on lodges in the British Empire.'' Libraries: 3, 5, 7, 8, 11, 12, 14.

J. S. M. Ward, *Labour and Refreshment*. 1926; 210 pp. The Baskerville Press, Ltd., London, publisher.
Contents: Collection of 21 essays or talks on a variety of subjects. Reviewed: 14 Build. Mag. 29, 159 (1928). Libraries: 3, 5, 7, 9, 12, 13, 14.

Arthur F. Bloomer, *Ante-Room Talks*. 1907; 107 pp. Tyler Publishing Co., Ann Arbor, Mich., publisher.
Comments: Silas H. Shepherd, ''Imaginary chats on Masonic topics . . . good.'' L. B. Blakemore, ''A collection of short, pithy talks on a varied list of Masonic topics.'' Libraries: 3, 7, 9, 12, 14, 15.

8.04 MASONIC SPEECHES

Ten Minute Masonic Addresses. MSA Digest.

Dress Up Your Speech. MSA Digest.

So You're Going to Make a Speech. STB, Dec., 1959.

Orators in Freemasonry. 83 AQC 377 (1970).

Elbert Bede, *3-5-7 Minute Talks on Masonry*. 1945; 112 pp. Macoy Publishing Co., publisher.
Author: Appendix No. 1. Reviewed: New Age Mag., June, 1946, 370; Phil. Mag., July, 1946, 11. Libraries: 1, 2, 3, 4, 5, 7, 8, 9, 10, 11, 12, 13, 14.

Elbert Bede, *5-15 Minute Talks*. 1972; 132 pp. Macoy Publishing Co., publisher.
Author: Appendix No. 1. Libraries: 2, 4, 12.

Samuel Lawrence, *Practical Masonic Lectures*. 1874; 407 pp.
Contents: Collection of 19 Masonic talks. Libraries: 9.

E. B. Riegel, *Gems of Thought for Fraternal Speakers*. 1932; 136 pp. Macoy Publishing Co., publisher.
Contents: Useful primarily for Eastern Star talks. Libraries: 3, 5, 7, 9, 12, 14.

John L. Sanford, *Studies in Freemasonry.* 1924; 110 pp. Collection of Masonic talks.
Libraries: 3, 8, 9.

Alice C. Edgerton, *Speech for Every Occasion.* 1936; 461; Noble and Noble, New York, publisher.
Comments: L. B. Blakemore, "A collection of short addresses, a few of them on Masonic subjects, most of them on subjects appropriate for lodge programs."
Libraries: 3, 5, 7, 9, 12, 14.

J. Walter Hobbs, *Masonic Speech Making.* 1929; Masonic Record, Ltd., London, publisher. Reissued in 1975 by A. Lewis Ltd.
Reviewed: 15 Build. Mag. 28.

Alfred A. Montapert, *Distilled Wisdom.* Material for speakers in alphabetical order.
Libraries: 7, 10.

L. S. Myler, *Jewels of Masonic Oratory* 1930; 672 pp. Originally published in 1898.
Contents: Collection of famous orations with pictures of the speakers. Described in The Essays of H. L. Haywood, 351. Libraries: 1, 2, 3, 4, 5, 7, 8, 9, 10, 11, 12, 14.

Charles J. Johnson, *One Common Purpose.* 1937; 315 pp. Gettinger Press, New York, publisher.
Comments: L. B. Blakemore, "A collection of 44 addresses by the Grand Secretary of New York, one of the modern Masters of Masonic oratory." Libraries: 3, 5, 7, 8, 9, 11, 14.

Brother P.M., After the Lodge Is Closed. 1934; 72 pp. Masonic Record Co., London, publisher. After-dinner speech helper.
Libraries: 2, 3, 7, 9, 12, 13.

A Collection of Addresses by South Carolina Masons, 1800-1900. 1977; 278 pp. Grand Lodge of South Carolina.
Libraries: 2, 3, 12.

Salem Town, *A System of Speculative Masonry.* 1818; 283 pp. Dodd and Stevenson, publisher.
Author: *Salem Town,* by Temple R. Hollcroft, 5 ALR 240 (1951). Comments: Vol. 2, p. 1045, Mackey's Ency. of Free.:

"This work is of course tinged with all the lengendary ideas of the origin of the Institution which prevailed at that period, and which would not now be accepted as authoritative; but it contains, outside of its historical errors, many valuable and suggestive thoughts." Libraries: 3, 7, 9, 11.

See: *Master Masons* (believed to have been written by Henry Dana Ward), Freemasonry, 1828; 396, in which the author reviews Town's book and quotes extensively from the fairy tales of Barruel and Robison. Found in the following libraries: 3, 5, 7, 9, 12, 14.

Joseph E. Perry, *The Masonic Way of Life.* 1968; 209 pp. Grand Lodge of Massachusetts, publisher.
Contents: Collection of talks given by a Past Grand Master of Massachusetts. Libraries: 3, 5, 7, 9.

John L. Sanford, *Studies in Freemasonry.* 1924; 110 pp. Collection of speeches.
Libraries: 3, 8, 9.

The Joseph Robbins Oration. 11 Build. Mag. 239 (1925). 1869 Proc. of Grand Lodge of Illinois.

H. L. Haywood, *Masonic Curiosa,* 138. Discusses Masonic orations.

J. R. Lestee, *Correct Speech – With Special Reference to the Delivery of Ritual.* 12 Trans. M. & P. M. L. 147.

Henry Drewes, *Brother Toastmaster.* N.Y. Mas. Outl., July, 1925, 247.

The Making of a Speech. Mas. J. of So. Africa, Sept., 1953, 17.

8.05 MASONIC FICTION — NOVELS

Clarence M. Boutelle, *The Man of Mount Moriah.* 1893; 298 pp. J. W. Brown, Chicago, publisher.
Comments: Silas H. Shepherd, "The first edition was published in 1893. This story has been read with delight by thousands of Masons." Libraries: 2, 3, 4, 5, 6, 7, 8, 9, 10, 11, 12, 13, 14.

Carl H. Claudy, *The Lion's Paw.* 1944; 218 pp. Temple Publishing Co., Washington, D.C., publishers. A delightful novel with a Masonic background.

Libraries: 1, 2, 3, 4, 5, 7, 8, 9, 10, 11, 12, 13, 14.

Sylvanus Cobb, Jr., *The Caliph of Bagdad*. 1868; 224 pp. George H. Doran Co., New York, publisher.
Author: 2 Build. Mag. 351 (1916): 16 Build. Mag. 32 (1929). Comments: Silas H. Shepherd, "The semi-Masonic tales of the writer have afforded pleasant hours for many readers. They are filled with high ideals and afford interesting and inspiring reading." Libraries: 3, 5, 7, 9, 11, 14.

Robert S. Easter, *The Sword of Solomon*. 1962; 256 pp. Macoy Publishing Co., publisher.
Reviewed: 76 AQC 167 (1963). Libraries: 2, 3, 5, 7, 9, 11, 12, 13, 14.

Augustus C. L. Arnold, *Signet of King Solomon or the Freemason's Daughter*. 1903; 288 pp. Originally published in 1860.
Comments: Silas H. Shepherd, "Masonic literature has few works of fiction. This is a delightful story with a high moral purpose." L. B. Blakemore, "One of the very few Masonic novels; old-fashioned, but still interesting." Libraries: 1, 2, 3, 4, 9, 10, 11, 12.

Harlan H. Ballard, *Tiler's Jewel*. 1921; 134 pp. The Stratford Co., Boston, Mass. Masonic novel in a humorous vein. Libraries: 3, 5, 7, 9, 10, 11, 12, 13, 14.

Robert A. Heinlein, *Revolt in 2100*. 1955; 188 pp. Signet, publisher. Written by a non-Mason, a popular science fiction writer. The book has as its theme a "secret society" involved in a series of experiences.
Libraries: 3, 7.

F. J. Smith, *Amy Lawrence; or the Freemason's Daughter*. 1840; 169 pp.
Comments: Silas H. Shepherd, "This is one of the earliest works of Masonic fiction." Reviewed: 32 AQC 79 (1917). Libraries: 11.

W. I. Grantham, *The Knight and a Mason; A Masonic Novel*. 76 AQC 143 (1903).

Henry Lovegrove, *Three Masonic Novels*.

32 AQC 79 (1919); 33 AQC 79, 185 (1920).

Roger Peyrefitte, *Sons of Light*. 1961; 426 pp. (In French.) Highly imaginative novel about the Craft woven with a complicated set of problems with the Roman Catholic Church.
Reviewed: 91 AQC 113 (1979).

8.06 MASONIC FICTION — SHORT STORIES

William M. Stuart, *Masonic Soldiers of Fortune*. 1928; 276 pp.
Reviewed: New Age Mag., May, 1929, 285. Libraries: 2, 3, 4, 5, 7, 8, 9, 10, 11, 12, 13.

William M. Stuart, *Hand to Back*. 1926; 264 pp.
Reviewed: N.Y. Mas. Outl., July, 1927, 323. Libraries: 2, 3, 4, 5, 7, 8, 9, 10, 11, 12, 14.

P. W. George, *The Lodge in Friendship Village*. 1927; 256 pp.
Author: P. W. George was the pen name of Douglas D. Martin, managing editor of the Masonic News, of Detroit, Michigan (Phil. Mag., Feb., 1975, 24; Empire State Mason, June, 1976, 47; 12 ALR 245 [1973]). Libraries: 1, 3, 5, 7, 8, 9, 11, 12.

Carl H. Claudy, *These Were Brethren*. 1947; 277 pp.
Author: Appendix No. 6. Libraries: 1, 2, 3, 4, 7, 9, 10, 11, 12, 13, 14.

Edward S. Ellis, *Low Twelve*. 1928; 247 pp. Macoy Publishing Co., publisher.
Comment: Silas H. Shepherd, "Masonic fiction is not common. This will fill a need during leisure moments." Libraries: 1, 2, 3, 4, 5, 6, 7, 8, 9, 10, 11, 12, 13, 14.

Edward S. Ellis, *High Twelve*. 1920; 268 pp. Macoy Publishing Co., publisher.
Libraries: 1, 2, 3, 4, 5, 6, 7, 8, 9, 10, 11, 12, 13, 14.

Rob Morris, *The Lights and Shadows of Freemasonry*. 1853; 390 pp. Reproduced in vol. 23 of the Universal Masonic Library.
Author: Appendix 25. Libraries: 1, 2, 3, 4, 5, 6, 7, 8, 9, 11, 12, 14.

Catherine W. Towle, *Stories for the Amer-*

ican Freemason's Fireside. 1868; 408 pp.
Comment: Silas H. Shepherd, "Old-fashioned stories."

J. S. M. Ward, *Told Through the Ages*. 1926; 238 pp. The Baskerville Press, London, publisher.
Reviewed: 13 Build. Mag. 59 (1927).
Libraries: 1, 2, 3, 5, 7, 8, 9, 11, 13, 14.

The Pawnbroker and a Customer. Ind. Freemason, April, 1979. Story of how a Masonic pin, worn by a pawnbroker who was a nonmember, caused the young man as well as the pawnbroker to join the Craft.

Alphonse Cerza, *The Three Lights*. Ill. Enlight., May, 1957.

8.07 MASONIC PLAYS

Archibald H. Allen, *The Lost Ashlar*. 1952; 24 pp. Macoy Publishing Co., publisher.
Libraries: 9, 12, 14.

Carl H. Claudy, *Masonic Plays*. 1950 Proc. Midw. Conf. on Mas. Ed. 43.

Harry L. Baum, *John Brent*. 1934; 102 pp.
Libraries: 3, 5, 7, 9, 14.

Harry L. Baum, *Prelude to Victory*. 1928; 46 pp.
Libraries: 3, 5, 7, 12, 14.

F. T. Campbell, *Initiation of Philander McNutt*. Comedy for presentation before Masonic groups.
Libraries: 7, 14.

Carl H. Claudy, *Where Your Treasure Is*. 1946; 271 pp. Twelve Masonic plays.
Author: Appendix No. 6. Libraries: 1, 2, 3, 4, 5, 7, 8, 9, 10, 11, 12, 13, 14.

John J. Lanier, *The Daughter of Hiram Abif*. 1922; 87 pp. Macoy Publishing Co., publisher.
Libraries: 2, 3, 4, 5, 7, 9, 10, 11, 12, 14.

Hugh A. Cole, *May Brotherly Love Prevail*. 1974; 36 pp. Published by the Illinois Grand Lodge Bicentennial Committee.
Libraries: 2, 3, 10, 11.

Rex Hunter, *Putting on the Lodge Play*. N.Y. Mas. Outl., Feb., 1929, 171.

N. B. Cryer, *Drama and the Craft*. 87 AQC 74 (1974).

The Hiramic Legend as a Drama. 85 AQC 370 (1972).

Archbald H. Allen, *The Second Crucifixion*. 1952; 24 pp. A three-act play: The struggle between the principles of the Craft and totalitarianism.
Libraries: 9, 12, 14.

Edward Conder, *The Miracle Play*. 14 AQC 60, 138 (1901).

W. B. Hextall, *The Man of Taste, a Satire of 1733*. 21 AQC 230 (1908); 23 AQC 334 (1910).

W. B. Hextall, *A Masonic Pantomime and Some Other Plays*. 21 AQC 138 (1908); 24 AQC 180 (1911).

G. W. Speth, *The Generous Freemason* (a play). 7 AQC 87 (1894).

8.08 MASONIC POETRY

Rob Morris, *Poetry of Freemasonry*. 1894; 399 pp. Macoy Publishing Co., publisher. A collection of his poems and a few by others.
Author: Appendix No. 25. Libraries: 1, 2, 3, 4, 5, 6, 7, 8, 9, 10, 11, 12, 13, 14.

Rob Morris, *Masonic Odes and Poems*. 1875; 94 pp. Masonic Publishing Co., New York. A collection of 300 poems and odes.
Author: Appendix No. 25. Libraries: 2, 3, 5, 7, 9, 10, 11, 12, 13, 14.

Fay Hempstead, *Poems*. 1922; 461 pp. Designated as the Poet Laureate of Freemasonry in a Chicago ceremony.
Libraries: 2, 3, 5, 7, 9, 12.

Dewey H. Wollstein, *From You to Me*. 1973; 173 pp.
Author: Appendix No. 35. Reviewed: New Age Mag., April, 1974, 55. Libraries: 3, 4, 12.

The Lodge Room Over Simpkin's Store. Ore. Free., Oct., 1974, 24. Picture and article about the lodge room erected in memory of L. N. Greenleaf and his famous poem.

The Poetry of H. L. Haywood. 1972. Published by Iowa Lodge of Research No. 2.
Reviewed: New Age Mag., Feb., 1973, 54.

The Little Masonic Library, Vol. 5 (1946 ed.) has a collection of Masonic poems.

The Poetry of Masonry and Masonic Poems. New Age Mag., Feb., 1914, 164.

Walter K. Belt, *Poems on the Trestleboard.* 1965; plus a later second volume. Collection of poems originally published in various issues of the Oregon Freemason.
Libraries: 3, 4, 11.

J. Walter Brown, *Masonic Musings.* 1928; 181 pp. The Upland Publishing Co., Sussex, publisher. Collection of Masonic poems.
Libraries: 3.

Dudley Wright, *Ancient Masonic Poet.* New Age Mag., Nov., 1924, 673; 5 ALR 272 (1947-1948).

H. L. Haywood, *Masonic Curiosa,* pp. 133-134, has a list of books with Masonic poems.

Charles G. Reigner, *The Poetry of Freemasonry.* Phil. Mag., Dec., 1954, 41; Feb., 1955, 11.

Aiken McClelland, *Nineteenth Century Ulster Masonic Poets.* 13 ALR 44 (1969).

Knife and Fork Degree, a poem. 5 RAM 220 (1956).

8.09 MASONIC STAMPS

R. J. G. *Freemasonry and Philately.* 13 Trans. M. & P. M. L. 103.

John A. Mirt, *Masonic Education Through Postage Stamps.* 1953 Proc. Midw. Conf. on Mas. Ed. 94.

John A. Mirt, *The Story of Masonry on Postage Stamps.* New Age Mag., Nov., 1949, 663.

Gregory R. Lucy, *Freemasons of Many Nations.* 1963; 180 pp.
Libraries: 2, 3, 7, 9, 10, 12.

Gregory R. Lucy, *Freemasonry in the Making of a Nation.* 1963; 66 pp.
Libraries: 2, 3, 7, 9, 10, 12, 14.

George B. Clark, *A Masonic Stamp Collection.* Two MSA Digests.

George B. Clark, *A Masonic Stamp Collection as a Hobby.* Phil. Mag., April-May, 1946, 2. Has picture of the author.

Masonic Postage Stamps. New Age Mag., June, 1961, 27.

Masonic Stamp Collection. New Age Mag., Oct., 1943, 533.

Harry L. Steinberg, *An Introduction to Masonic Philately.* 3 Trans. Walter F. Meier L. of Res. 289.

R.O.S. *First Day Covers.* 12 RAM 339 (1978).

S. A. White, *Masonic Stamp Collecting.* 10 Trans. Tex. L. of Res. 171.

Trevor J. Fray, *Masonic Philately.* Mas. Sq., March, 1976, 9.

John R. Allen, *The First "Truly Masonic" U.S. Postage Stamp.* K. T. Mag., June, 1979, 9.

Masonic Philately, Mas. Sq., Dec., 1976, 133.

Richard Needham, *Yankee Doodle Dandy Saluted on Postage Stamp.* Cal. Free., Autumn, 1978, 176.

Masonic Postage Stamps. STB, Jan., 1949.

Norman Thomas, *Anti-Masonic Postage Stamps.* 60 AQC 99 (1947).

J. W. Smith, *Masonic Philately — A Guide for Beginners.* 78 AQC 265 (1965).

John M. Cunningham, *Masonry on Postage Stamps.* 12 RAM 77 (1976).

Freemasonry on Postage Stamps. 2 RAM 115 (1946); reproduced anti-Masonic stamps of Serbia and Honduras.

Cuban Masonic Stamps. 5 RAM 213 (1956).

Three Royal Arch Stamps. 5 RAM 158 (1956).

8.10 MASONIC COINS, MEDALS, ETC.

R. G. Ball, *Masonic Coins.* 13 Trans. M. & P. M. L. 26.

Numismatics. Phil. Mag., April, 1958, 32.

Masonic Honor Medals. MSA Digest.

Medals. Phil. Mag., Feb., 1959, 9.

Dr. William G. Peacher, *The Evolution of Chapter Pennies.* 8 RAM 259 (1956).

John W. Kloss, *The Master's Jewel.* Ind. Free., Jan., 1957, 6.

Two Medals of Masonic Interest. 7 ALR 364 (1959).

Name, Origin, and Hobbies Shown in Book Mark. 6 RAM 79 (1958).

Herbert Poole, *The Sketchley Masonic Token.* 46 AQC 320 (1933); 47 AQC 259 (1934).

The Sketchley Half Penny. New Age Mag., Nov., 1968, 42.

J. Joseph Hersh, *German Masonic Steins.* No. Light., Nov., 1972, 14.

Judson L. Parker, *Masonic Coin That Became Coin of the Realm.* 8 RAM 145 (1965).

Dr. Benjamin Luntz, *Masonic Numismatics.* 12 RAM 35 (1976).

Masonic Symbols in American Decorative Art. 1976. Published jointly by the Masonic Book Club and the Supreme Council, NMJ.

Alphonse Cerza, *Masonic Coin as Money.* Ind. Free., Nov., 1976, 14.

T. O. Haunch, *Freemasons' Hall Committee Token, 1778.* 89 AQC 206 (1976).

Harold V. B. Voorhis, *Washington Memorial Medals.* K. T. Mag., Aug., 1977, 13.

E. A. King, *Masonic Chapter Pennies.* 1926; 465 pp.
Reviewed: Masonic World, Detroit, Sept., 1972, 2. Libraries: 3, 5, 7, 9, 10, 11, 12.

William T. R. Marvin, *The Medals of the Masonic Fraternity.* 1880; 301 pp.
Libraries: 2, 3, 5, 7, 9, 12, 14.

George L. Shackles, *The Medals of British Freemasonry.* 1901; 99 pp. Quatuor Coronati Lodge, publisher.
Libraries: 2, 3, 7, 12.

William Hammond, *Masonic Emblems and Jewels.* 1917; 86 pp. George Philip & Son, London, publisher.
Reviewed: 30 AQC 213 (1917). 3 Build. Mag. 187 (1917). Libraries: 1, 3, 4, 7, 8, 9, 10, 11, 12, 14.

William T. R. Marvin, *The Medals of the Masonic Fraternity.* 1880; 301 pp. A supplement of 257 pages was published later.
Libraries: 2, 3, 5, 7, 9, 12, 14.

George M. Garfitt, *English Masonic Pottery.* 4 Trans. Manch. Assn. of Mas. Res. 55 (1913-1914); 13 Trans. Manch Assn. of Mas. Res. 19 (1922-1923).

Andrew Hope, *Masonic Teapots.* 5 AQC 227 (1892).

E. Winterburgh, *Masonic Ceramics.* 70 AQC 101 (1957).

An Old Masonic Pitcher. 9 Build. Mag. 25 (1923).

The Famous "Hummelwek" Creates Masonic Figurines. 7 RAM 269 (1930).

The Movable and Immovable Jewels. 6 Build. Mag. 286, 343 (1920).

Masonic Jewels, 3 Build. Mag. 111 (1917).

Kress and Meekren, *The Precious Jewels,* 12 Build. Mag. 312, 344, 374 (1926); Vol. 13, 24, 54, 87, 120, 153, 183 (1927).

Masonic Charms and Fobs. 10 RAM 134 (1971).

W. Begemann, *The Sackville Medal.* 12 AQC 204 (1899).

J. Campbell, *Some Old Jewels.* 7 AQC 86 (1894).

F. J. W. Crowe, *Continental Lodge Jewels and Medals.* 7 AQC 25 (1894).

Gotthelf Greiner, *German Masonic Charms.* 9 AQC 178 (1896).

W. E. Heaton, *Masonic Jewels.* 60 AQC 201 (1947).

W. J. Hughan, *The "Lambton" Lodge Medals.* 8 AQC 50 (1895).

Herbert Poole, *The Royal Medal of the Lodge of Antiquity.* 61 AQC 261 (1948).

W. H. Rylands, *Dagger Jewels*. 16 AQC 157 (1903); 17 AQC 233 (1904).

W. T. Sharpe, *Trowel Jewels*. 17 AQC 64 (1904).

A Masonic Medallion of 1516. 8 Build. Mag. 107 (1922).

Notes on the Dome Medallion. 8 Build. Mag. 342 (1922).

8.11 MASONIC BOOKPLATES

J. Fairbairn Smith, *Masonic Bookplate Lore*. Masonic World, Detroit, Sept., 1973, 10. Also: Cal. Free., Summer, 1974, 132.

J. Hugo Tatsch, *Have You a Masonic Book Plate?* N.Y. Mas. Outl., Feb., 1929, 173.

Tatsch & Prescott, *Masonic Book Plates*. 1928; 153 pp. The Masonic Bibliophiles, Cedar Rapids, Iowa, publisher.
Contents: Discussion of bookplates; reproduction of some bookplates; selected bibliography of bookplate literature. Comment: The Iowa Masonic Library has a scrapbook which contains a collection of Masonic bookplates. Review: 14 Build. Mag. 314 (1928). Libraries: 3, 5, 9, 12.

8.12 MASONIC HUMOR

Stewart M. L. Pollard, *Tied to Masonic Apron Strings*. 1969; 126 pp. MLR, publisher.
Author: Appendix No. 27. Reviewed: No. Light, Nov., 1970. Libraries: 2, 3, 5, 7, 11.

George W. Martin, *Fun Among Masons*. 1931; 127 pp. David Winter & Son, Dundee.
Libraries: 3, 5, 7, 9, 11, 12.

James Pettibone, *The Lodge Goat and Goat Riders*. 1903; 600 pp.
Libraries: 2.

8.13 MASONIC MUSIC

David Vinton, *Masonick Minstrel*. 1816; 463 pp.
Comment: Silas H. Shepherd, "David Vinton wrote the dirge, 'Solemn Strikes the Funeral Chime,' which was first printed in this book, 12,000 were sold on subscription." Libraries: 3, 4, 9.

Vincent Stevens, *A Guide to Lodge Music for Use of Organists*. 1926; 26 pp. A. Lewis, Ltd., London, publisher. Also had an edition in 1964.
Libraries: 3, 5, 7, 11, 12.

Carl F. Price, ed., *Sing Brothers, Sing*. 1940; 16 pp.
Contents: Collection of the words of 152 popular songs. Libraries: 3, 7, 9, 12, 13.

Thomas Powers, *Masonic Melodies*. 1844; 105. O. Ditson, Boston, publisher.
Libraries: 3, 4, 9, 11.

Robert Macoy, *Masonic Vocal Manual*. 1864.

William H. James, *Masonic Musical Manual*. 1909. Macoy Publishing Co., publisher.
Libraries: 1, 3, 5, 7, 9, 10, 12, 13, 14.

Jacob Ernst, *Melodies of the Craft*. 1852; 151 pp.
Libraries: 3.

Luke Eastman, *Masonic Melodies*. 1818; 204 pp.
Comments: Silas H. Shepherd, "A Masonic songbook that was popular for nearly half a century." Libraries: 3, 9.

George W. Chase, *The Masonic Harp*. 1858; 160 pp. Ditson & Co., Boston.
Contents: Collection of Masonic odes, hymns, songs, for private and public ceremonies. Libraries: 3, 9, 11.

Loyal A. Alford, *Masonic Gems*. 1868; 48 pp. Masonic Publishing Co., publisher.
Contents: Collection of odes and poems with Masonic significance. Libraries: 3, 4, 5, 7, 9, 11, 12, 14.

For Variety in Lodge Music. N.Y. Mas. Outl., Feb., 1928, 169; April, 1928, 239; Oct., 1929, 45.

Geoffrey O'Hare, *Set the Whole Craft Singing*. N.Y. Mas. Outl., May, 1926, 273.

W. Barrett, *Masonic Musicians*. 4 AQC 90 (1891).

W. B. Hextall, *Some Old-Time Clubs and Societies*. 27 AQC 25 (1914).

American Masonic Music. 5 ALR 47 (1947-1948).

Richardson Wright, *Our Singing Craft. Notes on American Masonic Music with a Bibliography.* 5 ALR 39 (1947-1948).

Old Freemasons Music. 3 ALR 406 (1939-1940).

Frederick Smyth, *The Singing Masons.* 10 ALR 443 (1968).

Masonry and Music. STB, Sept., 1947.

Great Songs. STB, Sept., 1946.

Small Songs. STB, Aug., 1941.

Appropriate Odes to Be Used in Masonic Work; 1915; Published by the Grand Lodge of Illinois. Copies are in many Masonic libraries.

August Comba, *Masonic Music.* Phil. Mag., Aug., 1969, 69.

Arthur Sharp, *Sibelius' Masonic Ritual Music.* 75 AQC 1 (1962).

Herbert Poole, *Masonic Songs and Verse of the 18th Century.* 40 AQC 7, 268 (1927).

R. F. Gould, *The Entered Apprentice's Song.* 4 AQC 169, 245 (1891).

"In the Sweet By and By." 6 RAM 134 (1959).

"Little Brown Church in the Vale." 6 RAM 201 (1959).

Paul Nettl, *Early Masonic Composers.* 6 RAM 305 (1960).

Masonic Music. Phil. Mag., Aug., 1969, 79.

Jan Sibelius. 3 RAM 13 (1949).

Proper Music an Essential in Conferring Degrees. 2 RAM 237 (1947).

L. B. Blakemore, *Masonic Lodge Methods.* Chapter 4 is entitled "Music" and pages 257-263 present a list of books dealing with this subject.

"Solemn Strikes the Funeral Chime." 4 RAM 295 (1954).

Ignaz Pleyel and the Pleyel Hymn. 5 RAM 174 (1956).

C. P. Peeler, *Masonry and the Great Operas of the World.* N.Y. Mas. Out., May, 1927, 276.

J. T. Thorp, *Freemasonry in Gounod's Opera "Irene, the Queen of Sheba."* 16 AQC 193 (1903).

L. Rabes, *Beethoven and His Masonic Music.* 80 AQC 144 (1967).

Gerald D. Foss, *A Masonic Musicale.* 3 Trans. Anniversary Res. L. No. 175, N.H., 68 (1978).

Music and Degree Presentation. New Age Mag., Nov. 1962, 26.

Ancient Masonic Music. 3 RAM 87 (1949).

Songs of Liberty. 10 RAM 3 (1970).

W. B. Hextall, *Catnach's Masonic Music.* 27 AQC 234 (1914).

G. W. Speth, *Catnach's Masonic Hymn.* 7 AQC 84 (1894).

F. C. Price, *Hymns of Dunckerley.* 7 AQC 52 (1894).

Wagner and Freemasonry. New Age Mag., Dec., 1937, 719.

J. M. Hamill, *Vocal Music in Craft Ceremonies and After Proceedings.* 88 AQC 187 (1975).

J. H. Morehan, *Patriotic Songs and Masonry.* Mas. Sq., June, 1976, 54.

John Morehan, *Early American Masonic Music.* Mas. Sq., March, 1976, 14.

J. A. Jowett, *Goethe and Freemasonry.* 87 AQC 255 (1974).

Dr. Irving I. Lasky, *Military Music and the March King.* K. T. Mag., Nov., 1975, 21.

Dr. Irving I. Lasky, *The Masonic Music of John Julius Christian Sibelius.* New Age Mag., March, 1975, 48.

John Morehan, *18th Century Masonic Music.* Mas. Sq., Sept., 1975, 92.

John Morehan, *Masonic Instrumental Music of the 18th Century: A Survey,* 89 AQC 176 (1976).

Carols From the Royal Masonic Hospital. A record described in 89 AQC 194 (1976).

C. L. Rothwell, *The U.S. Army Band and Chorus*. K. T. Mag., Oct., 1974, 25.

Opening and Closing Odes. 79 AQC 295 (1966).

J. F. Newton, *"Solemn Strikes the Funeral Chime."* 1 Build. Mag. 62 (1915).

8.14 MOZART AND HIS MASONIC MUSIC

Paul Nettl, *Mozart and Masonry*. 1957; 150 pp. Philosophical Library, New York, publisher.
Contents: Describes Mozart's interest in the Craft, how he became a Mason, a short biographical sketch, with his Masonic association. There is then a discussion of his Masonic music with emphasis on The Magic Flute. Reviewed: New Age Mag., Dec., 1977, 748. 6 RAM 19, 89 (1958). Libraries: 1, 3, 5, 7, 8, 9, 10, 11, 12, 14.

Mozart's Masonic Music Now Available to the Craft. 6 RAM 216 (1959).

The Masonic Music of Mozart. New Age Mag., Dec., 1971, 54.

Mozart's Masonic Opera. Mast. Mas., May, 1926, 406.

Paul Nettl, *Masonic Fountains of Music*. Ind. Free., Dec., 1956, 14; has picture of Paul Nettl.

The Mozarteum of Salzburg. New Age Mag., June, 1973, 50.

Jacques Chailley, *The Magic Flute*. 1971; 336 pp. Alfred A. Knopf, New York, publisher. Translated from the French; for general readers.
Contents: This book presents a detailed interpretation of the libretto and music of the opera. Some debatable views are expressed in the book. Reviewed: No. Light, Jan., 1973, 13; 84 AQC 231 (1971). Libraries: 1, 2, 3, 7, 10, 11, 12.

Herbert Bradley, *Bro. Mozart and Some of His Masonic Friends*. 26 AQC 241 (1913).

Frederick Smyth, *Brother Mozart of Vienna*. 87 AQC 37 (1974).

Arthur Sharp, *Mozart's Masonic Music*. 69 AQC 15 (1956).

Dr. L. C. Helms, *Mozart and Freemasonry*. 12 RAM 343 (1978).

David O. Johnson, *Mozart, Masonry and The Magic Flute*. New Age Mag., Sept., 1979, 17.

Spike Hughes, *Notes on "The Magic Flute."* 11 RAM 195 (1977).

Newcomb Condee, *Brother Mozart and "The Magic Flute."* New Age Mag., May, 1950, 273.

8.15 COLLECTED ITEMS

Ray V. Denslow, *Masonic Portraits*. 1973; 322 pp. Edited by Wes Cook. MLR, publisher.
Contents: Twenty-one chapters presenting a variety of items written by Ray V. Denslow over a period of many years.

Alphonse Cerza, *A Masonic Thought for Each Day of the Year*. 1972; 228 pp. MLR, publisher.
Contents: Collection of a variety of items from many sources, both Masonic and non-Masonic, expressing Masonic ideals, arranged under appropriate days with additional information on items of Masonic interest. Reviewed: New Age Mag., April, 1973, 56.

Carl Glick, *A Treasury of Masonic Thoughts*. 1953; 325 pp. Thomas Y. Crowell Co., publisher.
Reviewed: New Age Mag., Nov., 1953, 700. Libraries: 1, 3, 5, 6, 7, 9, 10, 11, 13, 14.

H. L. Haywood, *Masonic Curiosa*. 1968; 316 pp. Edited by Wes Cook. MLR, publisher.
Contents: Collection of essays and articles written by him over the years and arranged under 12 chapters. Contains Haywood's picture and a biographical sketch.

The Masonic Essays of H. L. Haywood. 1963; 459 pp. Edited by William R. Denslow. MLR, publisher.
Contents: Collection of articles written by H. L. Haywood and published over the years in the Iowa Grand Lodge Bulletin. Arranged under seven chapter headings

and covers a large number of items of interest generally.

William T. Anderson, *The Masonic Token*. 1868.
Libraries: 1, 2, 3, 4, 5, 7, 8, 11, 12, 14.

George M. Martin & John W. Callaghan, *The Treasury of Masonic Thought*. 1924; 315 pp. David Winter & Son, London, publisher.
Comments: H. L. Haywood. "One of the most valuable collections of Masonic essays and articles in existence." Reviewed: 11 Build. Mag. 285 (1925). Mast. Mas., March, 1925, 259. Libraries: 1, 3, 5, 7, 9, 12.

8.16 POCKET COMPANIONS

C. C. Adams, *Freemasons' Pocket Companions of the 18th Century*. 45 AQC 165 (1932); 46 AQC 222 (1933).

C. C. Adams, *Notes on Some 18th Century Masonic Handbooks*. 50 AQC 145 (1937).

J. H. Lepper, *Smith's Pocket Companion*, Dublin, 1735. 56 AQC 300 (1943).

The Pocket Companion and History of Freemasonry of 1764. 7 Build. Mag. 26 (1921).

Discussed in H. L. Haywood, Masonic Curiosa, pp. 126-127. Also in his vol. 3 of Mackey's Rev. Ency. of Freemasonry, p. 1337 (1946).

8.17 MASONIC LEGENDS

Alex Horne, *The York Legend in the Old Charges*. 1978; 152 pp. A. Lewis, Ltd., London, publisher.
Contents: Considers the legend in depth with the views expressed by authors in the past on the subject. Libraries: 2, 3, 11, 12.

Dudley Wright, *Masonic Legends and Traditions*. 1921; 152 pp. William Rider & Son, publisher.
Comments: Silas H. Shepherd, "This work deals chiefly with the traditions respecting the Temple and its architecture." Reviewed: 8 Build. Mag. 221 (1922) reproduces a review of this book written by Waite and published in The Occult Review, hardly a recommendation for the book. Libraries: 1, 3, 4, 5, 6, 7, 8, 9, 11, 12, 14.

John Yarker, *Two Ancient Legends Concerning the First Temple, Termed King Solomon's Temple*. 21 AQC 264 (1908).

Alex Mellor, *Masonic Myths*. 1974; Ed Payot, Paris, publisher. In French. Discusses the myths of the ancient Templars and Masonry and the Compagnonnage, states that the Craft did not cause the French Revolution.

C. C. Howard, *A Critical Examination of the Alban and Athelstan Legends*. 4 AQC 73 (1891).

The Prince Edwin Legend. 22 AQC 6 (1909).

Edmund H. Dring, *The "Naimus Grecus" Legend*. 18 AQC 179 (1905); 19 AQC 45 (1906); 21 AQC 68 (1908); 63 AQC 7 (1972).

W. H. Rylands, *Some Notes on Legends in Masonry*. 16 AQC 4 (1913).

Alex Horne, *The Legend of Osiris*. New Age Mag., Jan., 1968, 48.

Dr. W. Begemann, *The Craft Legends of the Old British Masons*. 5 AQC 37 (1892).

Roman Legends of the Quatuor Coronati. 1 AQC 149 (1886-1888)

Legend of the Quatuor Coronati. 27 AQC 60 (1914).

Gordon P. G. Hills, *Some Usages and Legends of Crafts Kindred to Masonry*. 28 AQC 115 (1915).

W. H. Rylands, *A Word on the Legends of the Compagnonnage*. 1 AQC 116 (1886-1888); 2 AQC 52 (1889).

W. J. Chetwode Crawley, *The Two Saints John Legends*. 8 AQC 156 (1895).

W. J. Chetwode Crawley, *Templar Legends of Freemasonry*. 26 AQC 45, 146, 221 (1913).

W. W. Covey-Crump, *The Hiramic Tradition*. 115 pp., Masonic Record, Ltd., publisher.

Contents: Twelve chapters devoted to the possible sources of the ritual: The Holy Bible, the Ancient Mysteries; etc. Libraries: 3, 5, 7, 8, 9, 12, 14.

James E. Craig, *The Meaning of Hiram Abif.* N.Y. Mas. Outl., March, 1926, 201.

George S. Draffen, *The Hiramic Legend.* Ind. Free., Feb., 1976, 14. Also in Phil. Mag., Dec., 1955, 6; has picture of author.

Hiram, King of Tyre. New Age Mag., Sept., 1951, 545.

Hiramic Legend. 2 RAM 31 (1946). 5 RAM 88, 110 (1955).

Early Versions of the Hiramic Legend. 1 AQC 25 (1886-1888).

Hiram Abif, STB, Feb., 1934.

Harold V. B. Voorhis, *The Hiramic Legend.* Phil. Mag., June, 1956, 38.

Easter Lore and Legend. 10 RAM 131 (1971).

Malcolm H. Van Dyke, II, *Hiram, King of Tyre.* K. T. Mag., March, 1974, 19.

L. M. Sherwood, *Hiram Abif.* 1977 Trans. Leic. L. of Res. 59. Covers Biblical sources, how the legend came into the Craft and its survival.

The Labyrinth and Its Legend. 13 Build. Mag. 271, 294 (1927).

The Legend of the Secret Vault. 8 RAM 174 (1965); 69 AQC 43 (1956).

Ross Hepburn, *The Third Degree,* M. & P. M. L., Nov., 1979, 347.

The Hiramic Legend. No. Light, Jan., 1970, 14.

The Legendary Origin of Freemasonry. 5 Build. Mag. 297 (1919).

A. S. Macbride, *The Four Hirams of Tyre.* 3 Build. Mag. 81, 113 (1917).

George Oliver, *Revelations of a Square.* This is a controversial book. Some members believe it deals with Masonic legends; others that the author is reporting traditions he had heard over the years. At any rate, it makes interesting reading. An edition of this book has been published in 1980 by the Masonic Book Club with a commentary on Oliver's life and work by Albert L. Woody.

8.18 NUMBERS AND THE CRAFT

A great deal of pompous nonsense has been written about the symbolism of numbers and the Craft. The subject is partially covered here as a matter of interest by some of our members.

H. P. H. Bromwell, *Restoration of Masonic Geometry and Symbolry.* 1905; 559 pp. The Henry P. H. Bromwell Publishing Co., Denver, Colo., publisher.

Author: The book contains his biographical sketch and his picture. Comments: The subheading of the title is "Being a Dissertation on the Lost Knowledge of the Lodge." Silas H. Shepherd, "A remarkable book dealing with geometrical symbolism." L. B. Blakemore, "A work of little value to scholarship, enthusiastic, amateurish, and occultistic, yet full of out-of-the-way information about symbolism." Libraries: 1, 2, 3, 4, 5, 7, 8, 9, 11, 12, 14, 15.

The Golden Section. MSA Digest.

Numerology of Masonry. STB, June, 1946.

The Symbolism of Numbers. 3 Build. Mag. 232 (1917).

Roger E. Hopkins, *Symbols and Numerology in Freemasonry.* 3 Trans. Ann. Lodge of Res. No. 175, N. H., 25 (1978).

Robert D. Thayer, *The Geometric Road to Discovery.* Cal. Free., Autumn, 1975, 163.

Franklin J. Anderson. *A Study in Triads.* 9 RAM 209 (1968).

The Number "7." 4 RAM 250 (1953).

Sacred Triads in Masonry. Ind. Free., July, 1972, 16.

The Mystic Number (Three). Mas. J. of So. Africa, June, 1972, 32.

Number Three. Phil. Mag., Feb., 1967, 21.

M. Melville Richards, *The Mystic Number 3*. New Age Mag., May, 1973, 26.

Some Triads Often Overlooked. Phil. Mag., Feb., 1969, 20.

Ossian Lang, *The Triads in Religions*. New Age Mag., Dec., 1908, 569.

3-5-7. STB, June, 1925.

The Number Seven. 6 Build. Mag. 168 (1920).

Mathematics and Masonry. New Age Mag., Jan., 1958, 29.

8.19 MASONIC ALMANACS

Masonic Almanacs. 4 ALR 128 (1942-1944).

Many years ago Masonic Almanacs as well as Anti-Masonic Almanacs were published. A brief description of these appear in Coil's Masonic Encyclopedia, p. 27.

8.20 ARCHITECTURE

Architecture in Masonry. 75 AQC 238 (1962).

Arthur Bowes, *The Equilateral Triangle in Gothic Architecture*. 19 AQC 165 (1906).

William Wonnacott, *Architecture and Freemasonry*. 28 AQC 200 (1915).

H. Kent Atkins, *The Five Noble Orders of Architecture*. 82 AQC 35 (1979).

Alex Horne, *William Preston's Lecture on the Five Orders of Architecture: Its Origin and Development*. 77 AQC 105 (1964).

Edward Conder, *William of Wykeham*. 16 AQC 94 (1903).

S. T. Klein, *Magister-Mathesios*, 23 AQC 107, 334 (1910); 24 AQC 68 (1911).

CHAPTER NINE

Organizations

9.01 GENERAL WORKS

Harold Van Buren Voorhis, *Masonic Organizations and Allied Orders and Degrees*. 1952; 146 pp. Press of Henry Emmerson, New York, publisher.
Author: Appendix No. 33. Contents: Presents basic information about the Grand Lodges and many appendant bodies in the United States. Libraries: 1, 2, 3, 5, 7, 9, 11, 12, 13, 14.

Ray V. Denslow, *Masonic Rites and Degrees*. 1955; 261 pp. MLR, publisher.
Author: Appendix No. 10. Contents: Presents in alphabetical order a brief explanation of each Masonic group in the United States.

Allied Masonic Groups and Rites. MSA Digest reissued from time to time.

Organizations Predicating Membership Upon Masonic Membership. MSA Digest.

Earl W. Snell, *Organizations Whose Membership Is Based on Blue Lodge Membership*. 1941 Proc. Grd. Mast. Conf. 94.

Silas H. Shepherd, *Masonic Homes*. 1 Build. Mag. 75, 117 (1915).

Masonic Homes, Hospitals, and Charity Foundations of 49 Grand Jurisdictions of the United States 6th ed. 1979; MSA Digest.

The Structure of Freemasonry. Chart showing various groups. MSA.

Knoop and Jones, *The Evolution of Masonic Organization*. 45 AQC 267 (1932).

The Influence of Masonry in the Founding of the Phi Beta Kappa Society. 10 ALR 86 (1966).

Jerry Marsengill, *Unions and Masonry*. 9 RAM 212 (1968).

Members of the Movie Industry Formed the World's Largest Masonic Club. 9 RAM 163 (1968).

Superior Masonic Groups. 3 ALR 258 (1939-1940).

Congressional Effort of 1822. 3 ALR 264 (1939-1940).

General Grand Lodge. 11 Build. Mag. 319 (1925).

J. E. Morcombe, *General Grand Lodge*. 1 Am. Free. 1, 49, 97, 104, 145, 195, 243, 341, 393, 563 (1910).

R. Bruce Brannon, *A Brief Sketch of Ancient Craft Masonry and Other Rites Often Called Higher Degrees*. Phil. Mag., Feb., 1973, 8.

J. L. Carson, *The Rites of Freemasonry*. 2 Build. Mag. 209 (1916).

Lionel A. Seemungal, *The Rise of the Additional Degrees*. 84 AQC 307 (1971).

9.02 THE STRUCTURE OF FREEMASONRY

Roy A. Wells, *An Introduction to the Structure of Freemasonry*. 12 RAM 118 (1976-1977).

C. C. Falkner, Jr., *Grand Lodge: What Is It; What It Is Not*. Ind. Free., May, 1969, 9.

Grand Lodge. STB, Sept., 1948.

Grand Lodge Seals. STB, Nov., 1951. Also MSA Digest.

Grand Lodges Are Different. STB, Dec., 1956.

Incorporation of Grand Lodges. MSA Digest.

Charter-Warrants. STB, Sept., 1948.

Lodge Is Born. STB, June, 1948.

Lodge Name. MSA Digest.

Lodge Organization. STB, May, 1966.

Master Mason Certificates. MSA Digest.

Dual and Plural Membership. MSA Digest.

Forty-Nine Petitions. MSA Digest.

Jurisdiction Contrasts. STB, July, 1935.

Honorary and Life Memberships. MSA Digest.

Class Lodges in the U.S. Grand Lodges. MSA Digest.

Pension Plans of U.S. Grand Lodges. MSA Digest.

Masonic Shrines. MSA Digest.

Masonic Treasures. MSA Digest.

European Grand Lodges. STB, May, 1960.

Universal Masonry. STB, Nov., 1963.

Classification of Degrees. Coil's Masonic Ency., 163-199.

Masonic Calendars. STB, Nov., 1947; Ill. Enlight., Nov., 1957, 128; May, 1962, 276; Nov., 1964, 380.

W. F. Mellny, *Moon Lodges.* MSA Digest.

Reuben Perry and Clark D. Chapman, *Places of the Social Club in the Lodge.* 1963 Proc. Grd. Mast. Conf. 60.

Harold J. Richardson, *Endowment Funds.* 1937 Proc. Grd. Mast. Conf. 93.

Jesse Clark and Innes B. Ross, *How Can Endowment and Other Grand Lodge Funds Be Best Promoted to Supplement Per Capita Tax Income?* 1937 Proc. Grd. Mast. Conf. 130.

William R. Gentry, *Organizations of Commercial Character Which Limit Their Activities to Freemasons.* 1931 Proc. Grd. Mast. Conf. 33.

Arthur P. Johnson and Frank C. Barnhill, *Employment and Service Bureau.* 1934 Proc. Grd. Mast. Conf. 16.

John Lane, *Masonic Records.* 1717-1894; 1893; 397 pp.
Contents: Lists all lodges warranted by the Grand Lodge of England from 1717 to 1886. Comments: Silas H. Shepherd, "A most exhaustive accomplishment giving statistical information in compact and available form." L. B. Blakemore, "A masterpiece of its kind." Libraries: 2, 3, 5, 7, 9, 11, 12, 14.

Alphonse Cerza, *Are Appendant Bodies Beneficial?* 12 RAM 271 (1978).

9.03 SECRET SOCIETIES

Norman Ian Mackenzie, *Secret Societies.* 1967; 350 pp.
Libraries: 1, 3, 5, 7, 9, 11, 12.

John H. Lepper, *Famous Secret Societies.* 1933; 344 pp. Sampson, Low, Marston & Co., London.
Author: 37 AQC 303 (1924); 66 AQC 9 (1953). Contents: Describes the Ancient Mysteries, Carbonari, Orange Society, and other secret societies in history. Libraries: 3, 9, 11.

C. W. Heckethorn, *Secret Societies of All Ages and Countries.* 1897; 2 vols.; New Amsterdam Book Co., London, publisher. Found in many public libraries.
Comments: L. B. Blakemore, "A loosely-written book of no great scholarship and unsound in fundamentals, but covering a number of topics not often found in more authentic treatises." Silas H. Shepherd, "The author is opposed to secret societies and is considerably biased in his judgement but he has searched the records of history diligently to find facts, the result being of great historical value to the student conversant with Masonic history, the book is a delight." Libraries: 9.

Arkon Daraul, *A History of Secret Societies.* 1961; 251. The Citadel Press.
Contents: Describes various secret societies; Chapters 3 and 4 deal with the

rise and fall of the Knights Templar. Libraries: 2, 3, 7.

Una Birch, *Secret Societies and the French Revolution*. 1911; 261.
Comments: L. B. Blakemore, "A collection of essays. One of a large number of books on the possible connection between Masonry and the French Revolution. Very informative." Silas H. Shepherd, "The title essay is well worth the price of this book and it contains other studies of much importance. This is especially true of the studies of St. Germania and on Religious Liberty." Libraries: 3, 4, 9, 12.

Hutton Webster, *Primitive Secret Societies*. 1908; 221 pp. The Macmillan Co., publisher. Designed for the general reader.
Comments: L. B. Blakemore, "A brilliant, learned and fascinating work on rites, symbols, and religions of primitive people; extraordinarily useful to a student of the Ritual of the Three Degrees." Libraries: 2, 3, 5, 7, 9, 10, 11, 12, 13, 14.

Nesta Webster, *Secret Societies and Subversive Movements*. 1924; 414 pp. Boswell Printing & Publishing Co., London.
Contents: The first part of the book deals with organizations of the past and covers such diverse subjects as the revolt against Islam, occultism, the Illuminati, and the Cabalist. The balance of the book deals with Freemasonry and other "secret" societies and weaves in the "Jewish" peril and "Germanism." Can be classified as an anti-Masonic book. Reviewed: 36 AQC 110 (1923); Mast. Mas., May, 1925, 429. Libraries: 1, 3, 5, 7, 9, 12.

William J. Whalen, *A Handbook of Secret Societies*. 1967; Bruce Publishing Co., Milwaukee, Wis.
Author: A Roman Catholic teacher who, before 1974, wrote extensively about the Craft in its relationship with the Roman Catholic Church; critical of Freemasonry.
Contents: This book lists and describes many associations but its emphasis is in its opposition to Freemasonry. Libraries: 3, 7, 11, 12.

H. P. Marriott, *The Secret Tribal Societies of West Africa*. 12 AQC 66 (1899).

Arthur Preuss, *A Dictionary of Secret and Other Societies*. 1924; 520 pp. B. Herder Book Co., St. Louis, Mo. Reprinted in 1966 by Gale & Co.
Contents: Presents brief explanation of many organizations which the author classified as "secret." Freemasonry is covered on pages 137-144. The author was an ardent anti-Mason. Libraries: 3.

Carl Glick and Sheng-Hwa, *Swords of Silence*. 1947; 292 pp. Whittlesey House, of McGraw-Hill Book Co., publisher.
Contents: Interesting description of various secret societies of China. Libraries: 3, 7, 8.

Ward and Stirling, *The Hung Society*, 3 vols. beautifully printed. The Baskerville Press, publisher. Re-issued in 1975 by A. Lewis, Ltd, London.
Contents: A complete historical and operational description of the Hung or Triad Society, its offshoots, its ritual and its ceremonies. Reviewed: 12 Build. Mag. 284 (1927). Libraries: 1, 3, 5, 7, 9, 10, 12, 15.

John Levington, *The Essential Oneness of All Secret Societies*. 1890; 222 pp. Wesleyan Methodist Publishing Association, publisher.
Contents: The author has a strong aversion to any organization with a so-called secret ritual. He even attacks the Grand Army of the Republic, a patriotic association, because of its ritual. Libraries: 9, 12, 14.

Noel Gist, *Secret Societies: A Cultural Study of Fraternalism in the United States*. 1940; 172 pp.
Libraries: 3.

Charles A. Blanchard, *Modern Secret Societies*. 1915; 310. National Christian Association, publisher. The association was formed primarily to combat the "evils of secret societies."
Author: He was the son of Jonathan Blanchard. Both were antimasons. Libraries: 2, 4, 5, 7, 9, 10, 11, 12, 14.

E. J. Castle, *Secret Societies*. 15 AQC 179 (1902).

J. M. Campbell, *Chinese Secret Societies.* 6 AQC 193 (1893).

J. C. Moyle, *Chinese Secret Societies.* 7 AQC 131 (1894).

William Simpson, *Secret Societies in China.* 2 AQC 117 (1899).

Dudley Wright, *Secret Societies of the Roman Catholic Church.* 7 Build. Mag. 99 (1921); 9 Build. Mag. 39, 74 (1923).

John M. Roberts, *The Mythology of the Secret Societies.* Anti-Masonic.
Reviewed: 85 AQC 372 (1972); Phil. Mag., Aug., 1973, 71; Phil. Mag., Feb., 1976, 22.

9.04 RECOGNITION

Thomas S. Roy, *Information for Recognition.* 1958; 159 pp. Macoy Publishing Co., publisher.
Contents: Reports on some Grand Lodges of other lands.

Thomas S. Roy, ed., *Grand Lodge Recognition.* 1956; 76 pp. Macoy Publishing Co., publisher.
Contents: Five chapters, each written by an authority on the subject discussing the elements of securing recognition. The appendix has the standards of recognition set forth.

Standards of Recognition. MSA Digest.

Ray V. Denslow, *Regular, Irregular, and Clandestine Lodges.* 1956. MSA, publisher.
Author: Appendix No. 11. Libraries: 3, 10, 11.

Alphonse Cerza, *Masonic Recognition.* New Age Mag., April, 1979, 24.

The Masonic World of Ray V. Denslow. 3.

Foreign Recognition Chart. Issued annually by the MSA.

Fraternal Recognition. STB, Aug., 1948.

Melvin M. Johnson, *Recognition of Rehabilitated Grand Lodges.* Phil. Mag., June, 1948, 5.

The Number of Lodges Needed to Form a Grand Lodge. 91 AQC 222 (1979).

Clandestine. STB, Dec. 1935.

John M. Sherman, *Exclusive Jurisdiction.* 13 RAM 99 (1979).

Alphonse Cerza, *Exclusive Jurisdiction.* Phil. Mag., April, 1978, 16.

Roger Fernandez Callejas, *More on "Exclusive Jurisdiction."* Phil. Mag., Dec., 1978, 14.

Alec Mellor, *The Great Problem of French Freemasonry Today.* Written in French. Reviewed in 89 AQC 190 (1976).

Harry W. Bundy, *What Yardstick Should We Use in Determining Regularity?* Phil. Mag., Oct., 1958, 72.

Principles of Grand Lodge Recognition. Cal. Free., Summer, 1973, 102.

H. L. Haywood, *Comity.* Phil. Mag., Jan., 1951, 4.

Alfred Robbins, *Spurious Freemasonry.* 18 AQC 270 (1923); 10 Build. Mag. 4 (1924).

Henry Sadler, *Spurious Freemasonry.* 23 AQC 324 (1910).

Einar W. Johnson, *Legitimacy of Origin.* 1953 Proc. Grd. Mast. Conf. 99.

Irregular Bodies. 1968 Proc. Grd. Mast. Conf. 75.

Louis Block, *Clandestine and Irregular.* New Age Mag., Oct., 1926, 591.

Is French Masonry Authentic? N.Y. Mas. Outl., Jan., 1925, 93.

9.05 THE SCOTTISH RITE

Harold V. B. Voorhis, *The Story of the Scottish Rite.* 1955; 66.
Contents: Brief history of how it started, the Grand Constitutions, how the Mother Supreme Council was formed, the Cerneau problem, and how the Northern Jurisdiction was formed. With list of officers and other pertinent information. Libraries: 1, 2, 3, 5, 7, 9, 11, 12, 15.

J. Fairbairn Smith, *The Rise of the Ecossais Degrees.* 1965; 112 pp. Chapter of Research of the Grand Chapter, RAM, of Ohio, publisher.
Reviewed: 79 AQC 250 (1966). Libraries: 2, 7, 9, 11, 14.

Charles S. Lobingier, *The Supreme Council, 33°*. 1931; 1004 pp. Supreme Council, 33°, S.J., publisher.
Contents: Excellent history of the Scottish Rite with a great deal of biographical material. Author: 1 Build Mag. 302 (1915) has his picture. Carter, *Supreme Council*, Vol. 3, 656, 660; has his picture. Reviewed: New Age Mag., April, 1927, 225; 15 Build. Mag. 157 (1929). Libraries: 3, 4, 6, 7, 8, 9, 10, 11, 12.

Charles T. McClenachan, *The Book of the Ancient & Accepted Scottish Rite*. 1899; 622 pp. 1867 and 1885 eds.
Comment: L. B. Blakemore, "Though first published in 1867 this monitorial work of the Scottish Rite is still a standard work." Libraries: 2, 3, 4, 5, 7, 9, 11, 12.

Ray Baker Harris, *Eleven Gentlemen of Charleston*.
Contents: Biographical sketches of the men who formed the Mother Supreme Council of the Scottish Rite. Libraries: 3, 7, 9, 10, 11, 12.

William L. Boyden, *Chronology of the Supreme Council, 1801-1859*. 1960; 60 pp.
Libraries: 3, 5, 9, 12.

Charles S. Lobingier, *Chronology of the Scottish Rite*. 21 AQC 67 (1908).

Ancient Documents Relating to the Scottish Rite. 1915; 310 pp. Grand Lodge of Pennsylvania, publisher.
Contents: Reproduces all old documents on the subject in the Pennsylvania Grand Lodge Library. Annotated by Julius F. Sachse. Reviewed: 2 Build. Mag. 219 (1916). Libraries: 2, 3, 5, 7, 8, 9, 14.

Ray Baker Harris & James D. Carter, *History of the Supreme Council, 33°*. 1964; 415 pp. Published by the Supreme Council, 33°, S. J. Covers the years 1801-1861.

James D. Carter, Volume 2 of above, 1967, covering the years 1861 to 1891, 496 pp. Volume 3, 1971, covering the years 1891 to 1921, 611 pp.
Authors: Harris: Phil. Mag., June, 1964, 50; New Age Mag., June, 1963, 21. Carter: Appendix No. 4.

Samuel Harrison Baynard, *History of the Supreme Council, 33°, NMJ*. 1938; 2 Vols. Supreme Council, 33°, NMJ, publisher. Libraries: 1, 2, 3, 4, 5, 7, 8, 9, 10, 11, 12.

R. S. Lindsay, *The Scottish Rite for Scotland*. 1958.
Comments: Henry W. Coil, Sr., "Theorizing of doubtful validity." Reviewed: New Age Mag., July, 1958, 407. 90 AQC 266 (1977). Libraries: 1, 2, 3, 5, 7, 9, 11, 12, 14.

Henry C. Clausen, *Authentics of Fundamentals for Scottish Rite Masonry*. 1979; 104 pp.
Contents: States how the Grand Constitutions were adopted and the foundation laid for the formation of the Scottish Rite. Author: Appendix No. 7. Reviewed: 91 AQC 217 (1979). Libraries: 2, 3, 10, 11, 12.

William Nash, *The Rite*. Historical background and description of the workings of the Scottish Rite. New Age Mag., Feb. 1979, 16.

Henry C. Clausen, *Our Historical Roots*. Brief statement of the beginning of the Scottish Rite. New Age Mag., June, 1973, 2.

Albert Pike, *Morals and Dogma*. 1906; 861 pp. Supreme Council, 33°, publisher. Published in many editions. For many years a copy was presented to each new member in the Southern Jurisdiction. Some editions have an elaborate index.
Comments: Silas H. Shepherd, "Albert Pike was one of the great thinkers of the age, and this is one of his deepest philosophical works." L. B. Blakemore, "The Bible of the Scottish Rite. The famous interpretation of the Scottish Rite Degrees by the man who did more than any other before or since to build and to propagate the Scottish Rite in America." Norman B. Hickox, " . . . is a huge manual for the instruction of the Scottish Rite, able but ill-arranged, and is to this day a monument of learning. It contains the lectures of the Rite, carefully hidden within its various chapters, and is intended for use in connection with the ritual of the Rite. It was

first printed in 1872, and has been reissued in several later editions. No one is ever solicited to buy it, Pike never having written any book for sale. . . . It is an amazing book — alike for the wealth of its learning, the breadth and sanity of its teachings, and the lucidity and beauty of its style, which not even Ruskin could excel. It rivals in its grace and ease the noblest pages of man. No one can lay aside this volume without feeling that he has visited the high places of wisdom and of truth, led by a Master of those who know." Libraries: 1, 2, 3, 4, 5, 7, 9, 10, 11, 12, 14.

T. W. Hugo, *Digest of Morals and Dogma.* 1909; 219 pp.

Robert M. Walker, *Approach to Morals and Dogma.* New Age Mag., March 1963, 21.

Walter M. Callaway, Jr., *Pike and Morals and Dogma.* New Age Mag., May, 1966, 19.

Frank W. Ells, *Reflections on the Philosophy of Albert Pike.* 2 Build. Mag. 9 (1916).

Joseph Fort Newton, *Albert Pike: A Master Genius of Freemasonry.* 3 Build. Mag. 301 (1917).

Outline of Morals and Dogma. New Age Mag., Aug., 1962, 47.

Where Albert Pike Wrote Morals and Dogma. New Age Mag., June, 1935, 345.

Charles S. Lobingier, *The Great Work of Morals and Dogma.* New Age Mag., May, 1928, 257.

Henry C. Clausen, *Commentaries on Morals and Dogma.*
Author: Appendix No. 7. Contents: Distilled wisdom and thoughts of Morals and Dogma in a beautifully illustrated book. Reviewed: New Age Mag., Nov., 1974, 54; Ind. Free., May, 1975, 22; New Age Mag., July, 1975, 17; New Age Mag., Dec., 1978, 11.

Albert Pike, compiler, *Grand Constitutions.* 1863; 467 pp. Masonic Publishing Co., New York, publisher.
Libraries: 2, 3, 4, 5, 7, 9, 10, 11, 12, 14.

James R. Case, *A History of the Ancient Accepted Scottish Rite in Connecticut.* 1967; 195 pp. Conn. Council of Deliberation, publisher.

Steiner and Skelly, *History of the Scottish Rite, Valley of St. Louis.* 1950; 390 pp. Libraries: 3, 10, 12.

Alphonse Cerza, compiler and ed., *Scottish Rite History of Illinois.* 1966; 352 pp. Illinois Council of Deliberation, publisher.

Henry C. Clausen, *Our Historical Roots.* New Age Mag., June, 1973, 2.

James R. Case, *Scottish Rite and Freemasonry.* No. Light, April, 1973, 6.

George W. Warvelle, *History of Scottish Rite in Chicago.* 1907; 264 pp.

Anderson and Whitsell, *California's First Century of Scottish Rite Masonry.* 1962; 346 pp.
Reviewed: New Age Mag., March, 1964, 51.

Lionel A. Seemungal, *Supreme Council French West Indies.* Phil. Mag., Oct., 1978, 16.

Edson W. Card, *The Sign of the Good Shepherd.* New Age Mag., Oct., 1976, 44.

Scottish Rite in Cal. Cal. Free., Autumn, 1974, 161.

A History of the Supreme Council of Canada. 1874-1974.

Laurence E. Eaton, *Early Signs of Scottish Rite in Martha's Vineyard.* No. Light., June, 1974, 16.

Manlio Cecovini, *Historical Notes on the Age of the Scottish Rite in Italy.* Proc. of XI International Conf. of Sup. Councils, held in Indianapolis, Indiana, June 1 to 5, 1975, 90.

A. R. Hewitt, *The Ancient Accepted Scottish Rite.* Another Francken mss. rediscovered. 89 AQC 209 (1976).

George Draffen, *A Register of Supreme Councils Active and Extinct;* 1972; 29 pp. MSA.
Reviewed: 87 AQC 215 (1974).

James R. Case, *Washington's "Scottish Rite" Apron.* No. Light, April, 1975, 8.

Norman D. Peterson, *A Documentary Notebook on the Latin Craft*. Discusses the first three Scottish Rite Degrees. 1975; 139 pp.

Reviewed: 89 AQC 186 (1976); Mas. Sq., Sept., 1975, 98.

James R. Case, *Scottish Rite and the Presidency*. No. Light, April, 1973, 6.

Carl M. Wilensky, *Music of the Supreme Council*. New Age Mag., May, 1978, 47.

Jean Five, *Scottish Rite in Belgium*. No. Light, Nov., 1974, 16.

A Concise History of the Scottish Rite in Pennsylvania, 1867-1967. 1967; 140 pp. Pa. Council of Deliberation, publisher.

Charles S. Lobingier, *Stephen Morin and His Patent*. New Age Mag., Sept. 1926, 536.

The Pike Rituals. New Age Mag., 1947, 300.

The Renaissance of the Scottish Rite. 4 Build. Mag. 13 (1918).

Story of the Scottish Rite. 4 Build. Mag. 79 (1918).

Ramsay's Oration. 13 Build. Mag. 229 (1927).

Secret Constitutions of the Scottish Rite. 10 Build. Mag. 350 (1924).

Van Rensselaer's Role in the Union of 1867. No. Light, June, 1973, 4.

Charles S. Lobingier, *The Anti-Cerneau Movement in the American Grand Bodies*. 13 Build. Mag. 130, 164 (1927).

9.06 THE YORK RITE

C. C. Hunt, *Why the York Rite Is So-Called*. Phil. Mag., Oct., 1972, 90.

A. W. Gage, *The Chapter: What It Stands for*. 3 Build. Mag. 95 (1917). 2 RAM 169 (1947).

Kenneth Culver Johnson, *The York Rite of Freemasonry*. K.T. Mag., Feb., 1978, 11.

G. Wilbur Bell, *The York Rite Story*. Ben-
efits to be received from the York Rite. K. T. Mag., Nov., 1977, 19.

Frederick G. Spiedel, *The York Rite of Freemasonry*. 1978; 78 pp. General description of the York Rite, its history and how organized.
Reviewed: K. T. Mag., April, 1979, 15.

W. F. Kuhn, *The York Rite*. 2 Build. Mag. 327 (1916).

9.07 THE ROYAL ARCH

Fifield D'Assigny, *A Serious and Impartial Inquiry Into the Causes of the Present Decay of Freemasonry*. 1974. The Masonic Book Club. This was the first book which had a reference to the Royal Arch.

Alex Horne, *The Royal Arch and Its Origin, Development, and Ritual*. Phil. Mag., Oct., 1978, 20.

Ray V. Denslow, *Handbook for Royal Arch Masonry*.
Author: Appendix No. 20. Libraries: 1, 2, 7, 9, 10, 12, 14.

Ray V. Denslow and Everette Turnbull, *History of Royal Arch Masonry*. 1956; 3 vols. General Grand Chapter, publisher.
Author: Appendix No. 10. Libraries: 1, 2, 3, 4, 5, 7, 9, 10, 11, 12, 14.

E. T. Reid, *Practical Guide for Royal Arch Chapter Officers and Companions*. 1950; 92 pp.
Libraries: 3, 7, 9, 11, 12, 14.

Aubrey J. B. Thomas, *A Brief History of the Royal Arch in England*. 85 AQC 349 (1972).

Ray V. Denslow, *A Royal Arch Encyclopedia*. 1951. Published by the Grand Chapter of Missouri.

Harry Carr, *The Relationship Between the Third Degree and the Royal Arch*. 86 AQC 35 (1973).

Bernard E. Jones, *Freemasons' Book of the Royal Arch*. 1957; 275 pp.
Author: 74 AQC 9 (1961); 78 AQC 146 (1965). Contents: Presents the early history of the Royal Arch with a discussion of

the traditions, ritual and its development, and its symbols. Reviewed: 70 AQC 124 (1957). Libraries: 3, 4, 5, 7, 9, 10, 13, 14.

Roy A. Wells, *Some Royal Arch Terms Examined*. 1978; 64. A. Lewis, Ltd., London, publisher.
Contents: Scholarly explanation of 16 Hebrew words and phrases used in the Craft. Reviewed: 12 RAM 337 (1978). New Age Mag., Sept., 1978, 52; 18 Trans. M. & P. M. L. May, 1979, 266. Libraries: 2, 3, 11, 12.

Roy A. Wells, *Why the Royal Arch?* An Introduction to the Supreme Degree. 78 AQC 216 (1965).

Roy A. Wells, *The Royal Arch as the Perfection of the Master's Degree*. 12 RAM 149 (1977).

"Essex Master" (believed to be George E. Roebuck), *An Introduction to Royal Arch Masonry*. 1930; 111 pp. Rider & Co., London, publisher.
Comment: "Taking the book as a whole it may be stated that it is a valuable contribution to the literature of Masonic symbolism, but the history must not be considered either as authoritative or accurate." 15 Build. Mag. 92 (1929). Reviewed: New Age Mag., May, 1929, 286. Libraries: 3, 8, 9.

Roy A. Wells, *The Royal Arch Degree in England*. 12 RAM 23 (1979).

E. E. Ogilvie, *Freemasons' Royal Arch Guide*. 1978; 247 pp. A. Lewis, Ltd., London, Publisher.
Reviewed: 91 AQC 215 (1979).

H. H. C. Prestige, *Secrets Communicated to a Past Z*. 89 AQC 271 (1976).

W. R. Kelly, *The Advent of Royal Arch Masonry*. 30 AQC 7 (1917).

J. Cooper Malcolm, *The "Tau"; its Origin and Use in Royal Arch Masonry*. 4 Trans. Install. Mast. Assn., Leeds, 171 (1907-1908).

Wylie B. Wendt, *Philosophy and Symbolism of the Royal Arch Degree*. 9 RAM 115 (1967).

Jesse E. Ames, *The Beginning of the Order of High Priesthood*. 1 RAM 332 (1945).

Symbolism of the Royal Arch. 2 RAM 116 (1946).

A Royal Arch Quiz. 2 RAM 13 (1946).

Link Between the Lodge and Chapter. 11 Build. Mag. 300 (1925).

Lewis J. Birt, *Influence of Royal Arch Masonry on Grand Lodge Seals*. 11 RAM 163 (1974).

Mordant Cohen, *Hebrew and the Royal Arch*. Mas. Sq., March, 1978, 22.

C. N. Batham, *Chagall's Windows and Their Royal Arch Significance*. 89 AQC 226 (1976).

John M. Sherman, *Early Royal Arch Masonry in Boston*. 9 RAM 299 (1969).

James R. Case, *History of Royal Arch Masonry in Connecticut, 1783-1972*. 1973; 41 pp. Grand Royal Arch Chapter of Conn., publisher.

T. O. Haunch, *The Royal Arch in England and Ireland, and Scotland – Apparent Differences Within Basic Identity*. 86 AQC 326 (1973).

Harry Mendoza, George Adams Browne, *The 1834/5 Reunion of the Royal Arch Ritual*. 88 AQC 32 (1975).

C. Leigh Kingford, *Formation of the General Grand Chapter RAM of the USA*. 11 RAM 88 (1973).

Mark W. Baum, *Origin of Royal Arch Masonry*. New Age Mag., April, 1947, 229.

Cyril N. Batham, *Why the Royal Arch?* 4 Trans. Phoen. L., Paris, 74.

G. Wilbur Bell, *York Rite Masonry*. Phil. Mag., Aug., 1973, 70.

George Oliver, *Origin of the Royal Arch*. Libraries: 1, 3, 4, 5, 7, 9, 12, 13, 14.

W. J. Hughan, *English Royal Arch Masonry, 1744-1765*. 4 AQC 220 (1891).

Knoop and Jones, *Pure Antient Masonry*. 53 AQC 4 (1940).

William Adrian Brown, *The History of*

Royal Arch Masonry in Alexandria, Virginia. 1965.

History of the Grand Royal Arch Chapter of Illinois. 1900.

John Stokes, *Royal Arch Masonry.* 1924; 60 pp. Masonic Record, London, publisher.
Libraries: 3, 5, 7, 8, 9, 11, 12, 13, 14.

C. A. Snodgrass, *Light From the Sanctuary of the Royal Arch.* 1947; 225 pp. Masonic History Agency, Chattanooga, Tenn., publisher.
Comments: L. B. Blakemore, "A series of chapters on symbolism and teachings of Ancient Craft Masonry including the Royal Arch." Reviewed: New Age Mag., Dec., 1947, 761; April, 1952, 247. Libraries: 2, 3, 5, 7, 8, 9, 10, 11, 12, 13.

Selby and Walker, *History of Royal Arch Masonry in Ohio.* 1965; 2 Vols. Grand Chapter of Ohio, publisher.

A. R. Hewitt, *The Supreme Grand Chapter of England.* 1966.
Libraries: 1.

9.08 THE CRYPTIC RITE

J. H. Chase, *Textbook of Cryptic Rite.* 1875; 94 pp. Masonic Publishing Co., New York, publisher.
Contents: Ritual instruction; monitorial; with installation ceremony. Libraries: 2, 3, 7, 9, 12, 14.

Ray V. Denslow, *An Encyclopedia of Cryptic Rite.* 1950. Grand Council, R. & S.M., of Missouri.

Hinman, Denslow, and Hunt, *History of the Cryptic Rite.* 1931; 2 Vols. General Grand Council, R. & S.M., USA, publisher.
Libraries: 3, 5, 6, 7, 8, 9, 10, 11, 12, 14.

One Hundred Years of Cryptic Rite in Illinois. 1953.

The Cryptic Rite. 6 Build. Mag. 63, 101, 120 (1920).

A. W. Gage, *The Capitular Rite.* 2 Build. Mag. 244 (1916).

George W. Warvelle, *A Review of Cryptic Masonry.* 10 Build. 139, 173 (1924).

9.09 THE KNIGHTS TEMPLAR

C. C. Addison, *Knights Templar.* 1873; 631 pp. Macoy Publishing Co., publisher.
Comment: L. B. Blakemore, "The old standby of the Orders of Masonic Templarism." Libraries: 2, 4, 7, 8, 9, 10, 11, 12, 13, 14.

Archer and Kingsford, *The Crusades.* 1895; 467 pp. G. P. Putnam Sons, publishers. Written for the general reader.
Comment: L. B. Blakemore, "One of the best works on the Crusades, Templarism, etc." Good background material for a study of Templarism.

Harold V. B. Voorhis, *Thumb-Nail Sketches on Medieval Knighthood.* 1945.
Author: Appendix No. 33. Libraries: 3, 4, 7, 9, 11, 12, 14.

Ray V. Denslow, *A Knight Templar Encyclopedia.* 1951. Grand Commandery, K.T. of Missouri, publisher.
Author: Appendix 11.

Chalmers L. Pancost, *The Modern Templar.* 1932; 173 pp.
Comment: L. B. Blakemore, "A compilation of addresses, sermons, and editorials especially useful for Knights Templar purposes." Libraries: 3, 5, 7, 9, 10, 14.

Dr. Francis J. Scully, *History of the Grand Encampment of Knights Templar.* 1952; 583 pp. William Mitchell Printing Co., publisher. Long out-of-print but plans are under way to reprint with the guidance of the General Grand Chapter.
Author: 8 RAM 308 (1966). Libraries: 2, 3, 5, 7, 9, 10, 11.

Julius F. Sachse, *History of Masonic Knights Templar.*
Libraries: 3, 5, 9.

Edith Simon, *The Piebald Standard.* 1959. Little, Brown & Co., publisher, for the general reader.
Libraries: 2, 4, 11.

John B. Vrooman, *Vistas in Templary.* 1967; 39 pp.

Jewel T. Lightfoot, *Digest of the Approved Decisions of the Grand Masters of the Grand Encampment.* 1946; 88 pp.

James R. Case, *History of the Grand Commandery of Knights Templar of Connecticut.* 1977; 31 pp.

Form of Reception for Ancient Knights Templar. K. T. Mag., Aug., 1979, 11.

Knight Templar Eye Foundation. K. T. Mag., Feb., 1974; 19.

Wylie B. Wendt, *The Order of Knights Templar.* K. T. Mag., March, 1974, 21.

Jean O. Heineman, *Templar Legends.* K. T. Mag., July, 1978, 23.

William H. Stemper, *Knight Templar and the Church.* Phil. Mag., Aug., 1977, 4.

Joel W. and Karl J. Krauer, *Foundation of Templary in the Old World.* K. T. Mag., Jan., 1978, 19.

Herbert W. Sumner, *The Seal of the Grand Encampment.* K. T. Mag., Dec., 1975, 13.

Robert J. Russell, *Templar March.* K. T. Mag., Oct., 1974, 19.

A. C. F. Jackson, *Early Statutes of the Knights Templar.* 89 AQC 214 (1976).

Theo. J. Jena, *Rise and Fall of the Teutonic Knights.* No. Light Mag., Sept., 1975, 12.

W. J. Chetwode Crawley, *The Templar Legends in Freemasonry.* 26 AQC 45, 146, 221 (1913).

John Yarker, *The Order of the Temple.* 11 AQC 97 (1898).

F. H. Goldney, *Knights Templar.* 16 AQC 203 (1903).

Roland J. Maddox, *The Islands of Templar Masonry.* 14 Trans. Tex. L. of Res. 87 (1978-1979).

Thomas E. Dabney, *Marching Down the Years.* 1963; 54 pp. Contents: History of the Grand Commandery of Louisiana.
Libraries: 7.

9.10 THE ROYAL ORDER OF SCOTLAND

Harold V. B. Voorhis, *The Royal Order of Scotland.* 1960; 54 pp. Henry Emmerson Press, New York, publisher.

Author: Appendix No. 33. Libraries: 3, 5, 7, 9, 11, 12, 13, 14.

R. S. Lindsay, *A History of the Royal Order of Scotland.* 1971; 116 pp. Brings the history to 1843. A second volume brings it up to date.
Reviewed: 83 AQC 329 (1970).

George S. Draffen, *The Royal Order of Scotland.* Mas. Sq., March, 1978, 20.

Jean O. Heineman, *The Royal Order of Scotland.* K. T. Mag., May, 1978, 11.

George S. Draffen, *Early Charters of the Royal Order of Scotland.* 62 AQC 325 (1949).

A. M. Mackey, *Notes on the Royal Order of Scotland.* 22 AQC 59 (1909).

Charles S. Lobingier, *The Royal Order of Scotland.* 6 Build. Mag. 183 (1920).

9.11 THE RED CROSS OF CONSTANTINE

Harold V. B. Voorhis, *The Order of the Red Cross of Constantine.* 1963; 103 pp.
Author: Appendix 33. Libraries: 2, 3, 5, 7, 9, 11, 12, 14.

Ward K. St. Clair, *Notes on the Red Cross of Constantine in the U.S.A.* 13 Norcalore 38 (1944).

L. E. C. Peckover, *The Red Cross of Constantine.* 76 AQC 75 (1963).

9.12 THE SHRINE

Fred Van Deventer, *Parade to Glory.* 1959; 304 pp. William Morrow & Co., New York, publisher. A revised paperback edition was published in 1967.
Libraries: 1, 2, 3, 5, 6, 7, 11, 12, 14.

William B. Melish, *The History of the Imperial Council AAONMS of North America.* 1921; 282 pp. Abingdon Press.
Reviewed: 6 Build. Mag. 285 (1920).
Libraries: 2, 3, 5, 7, 8, 9, 11, 13.

George M. Saunders, *The Mystic Shrine and Its Hospitals for Crippled Children.* MSA Digest.

Harry H. Beall, *The Ancient Accepted Order of the Nobles of the Mystic Shrine.* Phil. Mag, April, 1950, 6.

Shriners' Burns Institutes. No. Light, Sept., 1972, 6.

George L. Root, *History of the A.A.O.N.M.S.* 1903. Nicely printed and bound with many pictures, but it expounds the theory of the ancient Arabian origin of the Shrine; hard to believe.

9.13 MILITARY LODGES

Robert Freke Gould, *Military Lodges, 1732-1899.* 1899; 223 pp. Gale and Polden, publisher.
Author: Appendix No. 12. Comments: H. L. Haywood, "The first full-size book on the subject of lodges warranted expressly for the use of soldiers and men in the Navy." Silas H. Shepherd, "One of the most readable books this gifted author has written. The military lodges were of sufficient importance to make a knowledge of their history necessary for those who wish to be well informed on the subject of transmission of the ritual and on many phases of our present jurisprudence." L. B. Blakemore, "This history of Army and Navy lodges is studded with sketches of famous men in them; throws light on the general history of Masonry, especially on the beginnings of American Masonry." Reviewed: 12 AQC 182 (1899); 14 AQC 32 (1901); Mast. Mason, Jan., 1925, 81. Libraries: 3, 4, 5, 6, 7, 9, 10, 11, 12, 14.

J. L. Carson, *Regimental Lodges.* Mast. Mas., Jan., 1928, 47.

Stories From a Travelling Military Lodge. 6 RAM 51 (1958).

Military Lodges. 14 Build. Mag., 325 (1928).

William E. S. Jarrett, *Field Lodges of the Revolutionary War.* New Age Mag., March, 1960, 23.

American Union Lodge. Phil. Mag., June, 1967, 59.

A Delaware Military Lodge, Baron De Kalb, and the American Revolution. Phil. Mag., Oct., 1957, 74.

G. Alfred Lawrence, *Military Lodges.* 1918; 45 pp. Articles which originally appeared in the Builder Magazine. Libraries: 3, 7, 10, 12, 14.

John T. Thorp, *French Prisoners' Lodges.* 1900; 304 pp.
Author: 21 AQC 261 (1908); 45 AQC 114 (1932); 1 Build. Mag. 73 (1916). Contents: Brief history of 50 lodges and chapters conducted by French prisoners of war; reproduces jewels, certificates, collars, etc. Reviewed: 46 AQC 230 (1937); 15 AQC 45 (1902); 13 AQC 129 (1900). Libraries: 3, 5, 7, 9, 11, 12, 14.

John B. Vrooman and Allen E. Roberts, *Sword and Trowel.* 1964; 169 pp. MLR, publisher.

A. J. B. Milborne, *Overseas Development and Military Lodges (1917-1967).* United Grand Lodge of England, publisher.

R. R. Walker, *Military Masonry.* Mas. Sq., June, 1976, 59.

C. N. Batham, *The First Overseas Lodge.* 88 AQC 206 (1975).

Norman Rogers, *Lancashire Military Lodges.* 76 AQC 101 (1963).

Deed L. Vest, *Texas Military Lodges in the Confederate Army.* 13 Trans. Tex. L. of Res. 129 (1978).

Military Lodge Formed on Old Ironside. Mo. Light, June, 1976, 6.

James R. Case, *The Story of Military Lodges.* Ind. Free., Sept., 1976, 6.

C. N. Batham, *A French Prisoner-of-War Lodge.* 7 Trans. Phoenix. L., Paris, 2.

Warren H. Deck, *Colonial Military Lodges of the American Revolution.* K. T. Mag., July, 1979, 19.

Irish Military Lodge Regalia Returned by General Washington. No. Light, Sept., 1973, 10.

C. R. Martin, *Traveling Military Lodges.* New Age Mag., Instalments starting with July, 1943 issue and continuing each month to April, 1944.

J. Ray Shute, *Six North Carolina Army Lodges.* 5 Norcalore 10 (1935).

John Goddard, *A Brief Sketch of the Campaigns of the 47th Foot; 1750-1763.* Trans. L. of Res. No. 209, Dublin, 39 (1922).

The Royal American Regiment. New Age Mag., April, 1950, 221.

Freemasonry as Prisoner of War. New Age Mag., series of articles starting with Nov., 1948, issue and continuing each issue until Oct., 1949.

Maurice Guimelchain, *French Prisoner-of-War Lodges in England During the Napoleonic Wars.* 4 Trans. Phoenix L., Paris, 89.

Story of Military Lodge No. 93. N.Y. Mas. Outl., Oct., 1928, 39.

George N. Cole, *America's Most Remarkable Lodge. American Union Lodge.* N.Y. Mas. Outl., April, 1927, 233.

Charles F. Irwin, *Masonic Clubs in the A. E. F. in the Great War* (World War I). 16 Build. Mag. 105, 141, 116, 141 (1930).

American Army Lodge in the World War (World War I). 14 Build. Mag. 228, 264, 304, 325, 359 (1928); 15 Build. Mag. 13, 39, 71, 103, 143, 172, 207, 237, 261, 299 (1929).

Archie D. Gibbs, *A Military Lodge at Labor and Refreshment.* N.Y. Mas. Outl., July, 1925, 242.

Emergency Lodge in the State of Indiana. 14 Build. Mag. 325 (1928).

History of No. Dakota Military Lodge No. 2 UD. 14 Build. Mag. 304 (1928).

History of Montana Army Lodge No. 1 UD. 14 Build. Mag. 228 (1928).

Charles E. Green, *A Regimental Lodge in His Britannic Majesty's 17th Regiment of Foot.* Phil. Mag., Aug., 1958, 54.

Charles E. Green, *A Delaware Military Lodge.* Phil. Mag., Oct., 1957, 74.

British Military Lodges in the American Revolution. 10 ALR 22 (1970).

Dr. Stephen R. Greenberg, *Masonic Activity in War: The Revolutionary War.* Phil. Mag., June, 1968, 56. *2. The War of 1860.* Phil. Mag., Aug., 1968, 70. *3. Spanish-American War.* Phil. Mag., Oct., 1968, 109. *4. World War I.* Phil. Mag., Dec., 1968, 128. *5. World War II.* Phil. Mag., April, 1969, 36.

Masonry and the Military. 12 RAM 23 (1976).

James R. Case, *American Union Lodge.* No. Light, Jan., 1976, 8. Ind. Free., Feb., 1976, 8.

Leon C. W. Kettring, *The Lodge at Fort Meigs in 1813.* Ohio Lodge of Research Newsletter, Aug., 24, 1974.

Field Lodges in the Revolutionary War. New Age Mag., March, 1960, 23.

French Masons Meet Masonically in Nazi Concentration Camp. Phil. Mag., Jan., 1947, 3.

Keith Arrington, *Parfit Peace and Harmonie in Lodge.* 13 RAM 106 (1979).

9.14 WOMEN AND FREEMASONRY

Dudley Wright, *Women and Masonry.* 1925; 194 pp. David McKay & Co., Philadelphia, publisher. Appeared originally in The Builder Mag., Vols. 6 and 7.
Comments: L. B. Blakemore, "Of special usefulness to students of the Eastern Star and Co-Masonry." Reviewed: 6 Build. Mag. 204 (1920); N.Y. Mas. Outl., Aug., 1925, 278; New Age Mag., Oct., 1922, 621. Libraries: 1, 3, 4, 5, 7, 8, 9, 11, 12, 14, 15.

Women Freemasons. STB, Nov., 1933.

Woman Tyler. 8 RAM 62 (1964).

Women Governors. 9 RAM 29 (1967).

Harry Carr, *Women and Freemasonry.* Cal. Free., Autumn, 1978, 157. Copy of talk given on one of his tours.

Harold V. B. Voorhis, *Masonic Ladies.* 12 RAM 239 (1978).

Charles Garvice, *Why Women Are Not Freemasons.* 2 Author's L. No. 3456 1 (1917).

Charles Holmes, *Should Women Be Admitted to Masonry?* Phil. Mag., April-May, 1949, 4.

Edward Conder, *The Hon. Miss St. Leger and Freemasonry.* 8 AQC 16 (1895).

Jerry Marsengill, *The Making a Woman a Mason.* Iowa Grand Lodge Bulletin. Jan., 1974, 9 and the next two issues.

Also in Paper No. 86, Educational L. No. 1002, Minn. (1974). 12 RAM 3 (1976).

Christopher Haffner, *Women in the Craft.* 1976 Grd. L. of Scotl. Yrbk. 62.

Gordon P. G. Hills, *Women and Freemasonry.* 33 AQC 63 (1920).

W. J. Chetwode Crawley, *Notes on Irish Freemasonry.* 8 AQC 53 (1895). Being a supplemental note on the Lady Freemason.

R. J. Fynmore, *The Hon. Mrs. Aldsworth and the Castle Lodge No. 1436, Sandgate.* 18 AQC 46 (1905).

James H. Davis, *Was Catherine (Sweet) Babington a Mason?* 3 Norcalore 75 (1933).

Clara Barton, *Friend of Rob Morris.* In H. L. Haywood, Masonic Curiosa, pp. 159-161.

When the Freemasons Aided Mary Baker Eddy. 8 RAM 239 (1965).

Catherine Babington. 3 Build. Mag. 157 (1917).

Robert I. Clegg, *Marie Antoinette on Freemasonry.* New Age Mag., Sept., 1923, 517.

Alphonse Cerza, *Women's Liberation and Freemasonry.* Iowa Res. L. No. 2. Discusses the historical background and legal aspects of the subject.

9.15 WOMEN GROUPS RELATED TO FREEMASONRY

Harold V. B. Voorhis, *The Eastern Star: The Evolution From a Rite to an Order.* 1938; 133. Macoy Publishing Co., publisher. New ed. issued in 1976; 138 pp. Author: Appendix No. 33. Comments: L. B. Blakemore, "Brief, scholarly, easy to read, this volume covers the important points in the origin and development of the Order." Reviewed: New Age Mag., Oct., 1954, 631. Libraries: 1, 3, 4, 5, 7, 9, 10, 11, 12, 13, 14.

Willis D. Engle, *History of the Order of the Eastern Star.* 1912; 296 pp. W. D. Lyle, Indianapolis, Ind., publisher. Comments: L. B. Blakemore, "A standard work by one of the foremost modern writers in Eastern Star activities." Libraries: 2, 3, 5, 7, 9, 11, 12.

Jean M'Kee Kenaston, *History of the Order of the Eastern Star.* 1917; 198 pp. The Torch Press, Cedar Rapids, Iowa, publisher. Comment: L. B. Blakemore, "A capable and reliable book more modern and more comprehensive than Engle's book by the same name." Reviewed: 3 Build. Mag. 124 (1916). Libraries: 2, 3, 5, 7, 9, 11, 12.

John Kennedy Lacock, *History of the Star Points, Order of Eastern Star.* 1930; 78 pp. Sampson Publishers, Inc., Boston, publisher. A reprint of articles written by the author starting in 1928 and published in the Eastern Star Magazine. Comment: L. B. Blakemore, "An inspiring, useful interpretation of Eastern Star symbolism." Libraries: 3, 9.

Alphonse Cerza, *The Eastern Star.* New Age Mag., Oct., 1961, 46.

The Pennsylvania Edict Concerning the Eastern Star. 8 Build. Mag. 222 (1923).

Vera Sappington, *The Centennial Book.* A history of the Eastern Star in Missouri; 1975; 425; has 200 pictures.

Fred H. Kruger, *A History of the White Shrine of Jerusalem.* 1939; 94 pp. A copy is in the Chicago Scottish Rite Library.

White Shrine of Jerusalem. 8 Build. Mag. 60 (1922).

History of the International Order of Job's Daughters. 1966.

9.16 CO-MASONRY

E. L. Hawkins, *Adoptive Masonry and the Order of Mopses.* 24 AQC 6 (1911).

Adoptive Masonry. 5 RAM 153 (1956).

Jerry Marsengill, three articles starting with the January, 1974, issue of the Iowa Grand Lodge Bulletin.

Jerry Marsengill, *The Grand Secretary Was Embarrassed.* 11 RAM 143 (1974).

Joseph H. Fussell, *Co-Masonry.* 7 Build. Mag. 224 (1921).

A. E. Waite, *Notes on the Origin of Co-Masonry*. 3 Build. Mag. 112 (1917).

The Iowa Masonic Library has some copies of The American Co-Mason and of Universal Masonry, two magazines published by co-masonic groups.

9.17 YOUTH GROUPS RELATED TO FREEMASONRY

Freemasonry and Youth. MSA Digest.

Official History of the International Order of Job's Daughters. 1967; 202 pp.

Youth Programs for Boys and Girls. STB, Dec., 1961.

Herbert Ewing Duncan, *Hi, Dad!* 1970; 174 pp. MLR, publisher. A biography of Frank S. Land, founder of the Order of DeMolay.

William S. Dye, Jr., *The First Half Century of the Acacia Fraternity*.

Order of DeMolay. New Age Mag., June, 1969.

Jephthah's Daughter. 15 Build. Mag. 333 (1929).

Job's Daughters. New Age Mag., March, 1964, 29.

Order of Rainbow. New Age Mag., June, 1958, 369; 10 Build. Mag. 209 (1924).

Order of the Builders, for boys. 7 Build. Mag. 363 (1921).

9.18 THE NEGRO GROUP KNOWN AS THE PRINCE HALL ORGANIZATION

W. H. Grimshaw, *Official History of Freemasonry Among the Colored People of North America*. 1903; 392 pp. Macoy Publishing Co., New York, publisher.
Contents: Covers the claimed origin of Freemasonry, the Landmarks, how the Craft came to the United States. Chapter 8 starts with Prince Hall and recites how Freemasonry is claimed to have started among blacks in the Boston area. The book was influential in that generations of students relied on its contents. But research in recent years have shown that he had a vivid imagination when he stated the "facts." He was the doorkeeper of one of

the reading rooms of the Library of Congress, but this did not stop him from sending a letter to England in which the letterhead was changed to show that he was the Assistant Librarian. This book should be read with caution in the light of more recent books on the subject, some of which are listed below. Reviewed: 36 AQC 108 (1936). New Age Mag., Oct., 1904, 409. Libraries: 2, 3, 4, 5, 7, 12, 13, 14.

Harry E. Davis, *History of Freemasonry Among Negroes in America*. 1946; 305 pp.
Author: An Ohio attorney active in the Prince Hall Organization. He added a few more details to the Grimshaw fairy tales but relied on many of the "facts" stated in the Grimshaw book. Reviewed: Phil. Mag., March, 1947, 4; 4 ALR 619 (1946-1947). Libraries: 1, 2, 3, 7, 9, 10, 13, 14, 15.

Amos T. Hall, *The Prince Hall Counsellor*. 1965.
Contents: Designed as a guide for Prince Hall groups in combating bogus negro groups. Libraries: 3, 9.

William H. Upton, *Light on a Dark Subject*. 1899; 137 pp. Later republished under the title "Negro Masonry."
Author: He was a lawyer and a Past Grand Master of the State of Washington. He made a study of the subject and became a warm advocate of the view that the Prince Hall Organization should be recognized. His obituary by J. H. Tatsch is in the 1907 Proc. of the Grd. L. of Washington. Contents: The book sets out the purported points urged against the regularity of the Prince Hall Organization and sets forth what the author believes to be the answers to these various points. Libraries: 3, 4, 9.

Harold V. B. Voorhis, *Negro Masonry in the United States*. 1949; 125 pp. Originally published in 1940; Henry Emmerson Press, New York.
Author: Appendix No. 33. Contents: This widely-read book was prepared by the author relying on the statements made in the Grimshaw book. When he learned from other sources that the basic facts were not correct he withdrew the balance of the

books on hand from circulation. Libraries:
1, 3, 5, 7, 8, 9, 10, 11, 12, 14.

Harry A. Williamson, *Prince Hall Primer*.
1925. Macoy Publishing Co., issued in
many editions and states the traditional
and customary Prince Hall Organization
point of view as to the facts and conclusions.
Author: The author of this widely read
booklet was a gentleman and scholar who
did much with his literary efforts and personal contacts to create good will for his
race and the Prince Hall Organization.
Libraries: 1, 3, 7, 9, 11, 12, 13, 14.

Harry A. Williamson, *Negro in Masonic
Literature*. 1922; 30 pp. Lists 500 refer-
ences to books, proceedings, etc.
Libraries: 3, 9.

Dr. Charles H. Wesley, *Prince Hall Life
and Legacy*. 1977; 237 pp. Joint publication of The United Supreme Council, J.J., Prince Hall Aff. of Washington, D.C. and the Afro-American Historical and Cultural Museum, of Philadelphia, Pa.
Author: Prominent educator, who lived
in Ohio for many years. He wrote a history
of the Prince Hall Organization in Ohio
while living there and has been active in
the affairs of the group for many years.
When he discovered the need for bringing
the subject up-to-date he made several
trips to the Boston area to check the available records there and he also took a trip to
the West Indies to check if there was any
light on the claimed birth of Prince Hall
there. He wrote this book and corrects
most of the glaring mistatements made by
Grimshaw and is mildly critical of the
Grimshaw work. Contents: The book re-
states the facts as the author sees them in
the light of the records he examined in the
Boston area. He had several interviews
with John M. Sherman of the Grand Lodge
Library at which he was given leads to
material to be located in the area. Reviewed: This book has been covered in
detail in 90 AQC 306 (1977), by John M.
Sherman, of Massachusetts. The Prince
Hall Organization in recent years has been
publishing a magazine called *The Phylaxis
Magazine*, which is an imitation of *The
Philalethes Magazine*, and in a number of
issues published in 1979-1980 there
appear a series of articles purporting to
analyze the review in 90 AQC 306 and to
answer the points brought out by the reviewer.

Clyde G. Townsend, *Negro Freemasonry*.
1960 Proc. Midw. Conf. Mas. Ed. 98.
The speaker relied heavily on the Grimshaw ''facts.''

Harold V. B. Voorhis, *Our Colored
Brethren*. The Story of Alpha Lodge of
New Jersey, a lodge chartered by the
Grand Lodge of New Jersey and has a
membership consisting of all colored
men.

John M. Sherman, *More About Prince
Hall: Notes and Documents*. Phil.
Mag., June, 1962, 42.

John M. Sherman, *More Data on Prince
Hall Brought to Light*. A copy of No-
tarial Certificate releasing Prince Hall
from his status as a slave. Phil. Mag.,
May, 1963, 32.

George Draffen, *Prince Hall Freemasonry*. 89 AQC 92 (1976).

The United Grand Lodge of England for
many years has taken the view that the
Prince Hall Organization is irregular
and is not entitled to recognition.

Joseph A. Walkes, Jr., *Black Square and
Compass, 200 Years of Prince Hall
Freemasonry*. 1979; 163 pp. The author
has been an officer and editor of The
Phylaxis Society since its inception.
The book is reviewed in Phil. Mag.,
Aug., 1979, p. 16.

William Alan Muraskin, *Middle-Class
Blacks in a White Society*. 1975; 317 pp.
University of California Press. The author is a white man who purports to
describe what he believes to be the nature and the working of the Prince Hall
Organization expressing opinions on a
variety of aspects of the group.

Prince Hall's Letter Book. 13 AQC 54
(1900).

Raymond H. Dragat, *Prince Hall Freema-
sonry in the United States*. 1959; 39 pp.
Re-issued in 1978. Published by the
Philosophical Lodge of Hartford, Conn.

Expounds the view that the Prince Hall Organization is legitimate and repeats some of the errors of the Grimshaw book although in the bibliography he lists the Wesley book.

George W. Crawford, *Prince Hall and his Followers.* 1965; 95 pp. The Crisis, New York, publisher.
Comments: Silas H. Shepherd, "One of the few available works that treats of this subject. The book is written by a leader of the Prince Hall Organization who enjoyed a fine reputation as a gentleman and as a scholar as well as a leader of his race. The book deals partly with the history of the subject and then considers the sensitive subjects of recognition and its elements. Libraries: 3, 5, 9, 12, 13, 14.

Donn A. Cass, *Negro Freemasonry and Segregation.* 1957; 149 pp. Ezra A. Cook Publications, Inc., publisher. The publisher of this book for years has been publishing exposés of all the "secret" organizations.
Author: He was an employee of the publisher at the time. Contents: The book does not deal with the subject in its title. It has a brief history of what the author assumed were the facts and has a brief discussion of the subject of exclusive jurisdiction. It then has an appendix which reproduces material from a number of sources. The book contains nothing new or of value and was clearly a money-making project. Libraries: 3, 4, 5, 7, 9, 11, 12.

John A Cowles, *Negroes and Freemasonry.* New Age Mag., March, 1947, 145.

Negro Freemasonry. New Age Mag., 1948, 471.

Thomas J. Harkins, *Symbolic Freemasonry Among the Negroes of America.* This is a printed copy of a talk presented on a number of occasions by the author, a Past Grand Commander of the Scottish Rite, S.J. It presents the view that the Prince Hall Organization is not legitimate and states a few reasons to sustain this view. It was not intended to be a complete or exhaustive treatment of the subject. This booklet was later reviewed in a long, rambling, disorganized and repetitious booklet written by Harvey Newton Brown in 1965, entitled *"Freemasonry Among Negroes and Whites in America."*

Anyone making a study of this subject should read the 1897, 1898, and 1899 Proceedings of the Grand Lodge of Washington which deal with this subject. Also, one should read the 1947 and subsequent Proceedings of the Grand Lodge of Massachusetts and the Correspondence Reports written during this period to note the heat that was generated by the discussion of this subject. In recent years the matter has been under consideration by the Grand Lodge of Wisconsin and its Proceedings should be read; it is to be noted, however, that the Wisconsin committee relied heavily on the Davis book and accepted some of the statements made therein as true while they are debatable.

It is to be noted that a few years ago several lodges chartered by the Prince Hall Organization working in South Africa surrendered their charters and joined the regular white Masonic Grand Lodge there. This subject is discussed briefly in the 1978 Proceedings of the Conference of Grand Masters, pages 120-121.

Unfortunately, this is a subject that generates considerable enmity in many places while we need more light on the subject. Too often when one assumes the position that the facts do not support recognition of the Prince Hall Organization, that person is accused of being a racist and being prejudiced against blacks because of the color of their skin.

Anyone making a study of this subject cannot overlook material that may be on file in the Iowa Masonic library, or records on the subject by John M. Sherman, which may be in the Massachusetts Grand Lodge Library, or files of the late Brother Edward Cusick, of New York, which may be in the library of the Grand Lodge of New York.

The New York Public Library Branch at 103 W. 135th St., New York, has what is known as the Schomburg Collection, material relating to Negro culture; among this material is the valuable Harry A. Williamson collection of Prince Hall Material.

9.19 MISCELLANEOUS GROUPS RELATED TO FREEMASONRY

Acacia Fraternity: W. S. Dye, Jr., *Acacia Fraternity, the First Half Century.* Edwin S. Malone, III, *Acacia – A Masonic University Fraternity.* 9 Trans. Tex. L. of Res. 230 (1973-1974). New Age Mag., Jan., 1961, 23.

Adelphes: F. R. Radice, 55 AQC 66 (1942).

Allied Masonic Degrees: *A Century of the Allied Masonic Degrees,* 1979, 86 pp.; reviewed: 91 AQC 218 (1979). *Introduction to the Allied Masonic Degrees,* 80 AQC 233 (1967). 8 Build Mag. 60 (1922).

American Eagle Mark Lodge: 18 Norcalore 139 (1948).

American Philosophical Society: Richardson Wright, *Masonic Strains in the American Philosophical Society,* 2 ALR 437 (1936-1937).

Bibliophiles, Masonic: 4 ALR 344 (1944-1945).

Blue Friars: Harold V. B. Voorhis, *The Society of Blue Friars,* 2 RAM 307 (1948). 4 ALR 344 (1944-1945).

Bucks: J. C. Brookhouse, *The Antient and Honorable Order of Bucks,* 20 AQC 369 (1907); 21 AQC 66 (1908). W. B. Hextall, *Bucks,* 19 AQC 244 (1905); 20 AQC 367 (1907). W. H. Rylands, *A Forgotten Rival of Masonry: The Noble Order of Bucks,* 3 AQC 140, 194 (1890); 4 AQC 64 (1891).

Ark Masons: 24 AQC 81 (1911).

Baldwyn Rite: 71 AQC 28 (1958).

Carbonari: F. R. Radice, *An Introduction to the History of the Carbonari,* 51 AQC 37 (1938); 52 AQC 63 (1939); 53 AQC 48 (1940); 54 AQC 122 (1941).

Collectors: *The Masonic Collectors Association.* Phil. Mag., Feb., 1966, 11.

Colleges, Masonic: 7 Norcalore 66. 2 ALR 188 (1936). *College Fraternities,* Phil. Mag., Aug., 1964, 61. Henry C. Chiles, *Masonic College of Missouri,* (1935). *Collegiate Freemasons,* Phil. Mag., Aug., 1964, 61. J. C. Mitchell, *The Society of College Youths,* 29 AQC 386 (1916). *Coming Men of America,* 13 Build. Mag., 137 (1927).

Congresses: *Historic Masonic Congresses,* 5 RAM 170 (1956).

Constantinian Orders of Knighthood: G. W. Warvelle, *A Sketch of the Constantinian Order of Knighthood,* 9 Build. Mag. 364 (1923).

Constructors Masons Order: 4 RAM 115 (1952).

Council of Knight Masons: K. T. Mag., Dec., 1978, 11.

Druses: Haskett Smith, *The Druses of Syria in Their Relation to Freemasonry.* 4 AQC 7, 63 (1891).

Essenes: W. W. Wescott, *Freemasonry and Its Relations With the Essenes.* 28 AQC 67 (1915).

Friendly Society: William Wonnacott, *The Friendly Society of Free and Accepted Masons,* 29 AQC 107 (1916).

Hermeticism: A. F. A. Woodford, *Freemasonry and Hermeticism.* 1 AQC 28 (1886-1888).

Forget Me Not: Ore. Free., April, 1975, 28.

George Washington Masonic National Memorial: MSA Digest. Bruce H. Hunt, *The George Washington Masonic National Memorial Association,* Free. Mo., Spring, 1977, 40. 9 RAM 291 (1969); has picture of building.

Geometric Masons: G. W. Speth, *The Order of Geometric Masons.* 12 AQC 205 (1899).

Golden Fleece: New Age Mag., March, 1961, 21. 6 RAM 309 (1960).

Gormogons: R. F. Gould, *History of the Gormogons.* 8 AQC 114 (1895); 11 AQC 86 (1898); 12 AQC 106 (1899). W. B. Hextalls, *The Gormogons,* 18 AQC 45, 243 (1905). Herbert Poole, *A Hitherto Unknown Gormogon Medal,* 48 AQC 203 (1935). G. L. Schackles, *The Gormogon Medal,* 15 AQC 65 (1902).

Grand College of Rites: 3 Norcalore 84. 3 RAM 267 (1948).

Grand Council: 7 RAM 168 (1962).

Grand Masters Conference: Conrad Hahn, *A Short History of the Conference of Grand Masters.* MSA Digest, 1963.

Grangers: *Freemasonry and the Grangers.* 11 ALR 364 (1971).

Grotto: 9 Build. Mag. 319 (1923).

Harodim: William Waples, *An Introduction to the Harodim,* 60 AQC 118 (1947). John Yarker, *The Old Awalwell and the Harodim,* 15 AQC 184 (1902). N. Barker Cryer, *A Fresh Look at the Hardim,* 91 AQC 116 (1979).

Hermetic Order of Egypt: 85 AQC 263 (1972).

High Twelve International: Phil Mag., Feb., 1963, 16.

Illuminati: Reginald W. Wing, Sr., *Adam Weishaupt & the Illuminati,* Maine Mason, Fall, 1979, 6. 85 AQC 375 (1972). 4 RAM 365 (1954). 11 Build. Mag. 198 (1925). Vernon Stauffer, *New England and the Bavarian Illuminati, 1918.*

International League: Dr. J. S. Von Solkema, *The International League of Freemasons.* Phil. Mag., June-July, 1947, 6. Leo Fischer, *Congress of International League of Freemasons,* Phil. Mag., Dec., 1947, 4.

Ishmael, Order of: 85 AQC 264 (1972).

Kabala: L. F. Strauss, *The Kabala and Freemasonry,* 14 Build. Mag. 136 (1928).

Key Square Club: Mas. Mess., Ga., Sept., 1973, 11.

Knight of the Red Branch: 85 AQC 271 (1972).

Knights Beneficent: 3 RAM 381 (1951).

Knights of Malta: 14 Build. Mag. 230 (1928). 83 AQC 71 (1970).

Knight Masons: Otis V. Jones, Jr., *Knight Masons, A History,* 1979, 16 pp. Iowa Res. L. No. 2.

Knights of the York Cross of Honour: 2 RAM 227 (1947).

Ku Klux Klan: Donovan Duncan Tidwell, *The Ku Klux Klan and Texas Masonry.* 14 Trans. Tex. L. of Res. 160 (1978-1979).

Macoy Publishing Co.: Allen E. Roberts, *History of the Company,* Phil. Mag., Feb., 1975, 14.

Mark Masonry: John A. Grantham, *An Introduction to Mark Masonry,* 1934, 63 pp. C. A. Conover, *A Treatise on the Registration of the Masons' Marks,* 1920, 66 pp. 4 RAM 310 (1954). 77 AQC 287 (1964). 70 AQC 120 (1957). 73 AQC 37 (1960). 74 AQC 104 (1961). 6 Build. Mag. 303, 328 (1920). 7 Build. Mag. 7, 15, 60 (1921). 1 RAM 152 (1943). 3 RAM 371 (1951). 3 RAM 47 (1949). 5 RAM 105 (1955). Phil. Mag., Dec., 1961, 104. 73 AQC 37 (1960). 74 AQC 104 (1961). Bernard H. Springett, *The Mark Degree,* 1946.

Masonic Orders of Chivalry: Wylie B. Wendt, K. T. Mag., March, 1976, 23.

Masonic Relief Association: History of, New Age Mag., April, 1949, 207.

Masonic Service Association: Allen E. Roberts, *Freemasonry's Servant,* 1969. Richard H. Curtis, *MSA – Its Yours to Use.* No. Light, Dec., 1979, 10; has picture of Stewart M. L. Pollard. See: Phil. Mag., Feb., 1969, 7; April, 1969, 30. No. Light, Sept., 1972, 12. STB, Aug., 1962.

Memphis, Rite of: J. A. Gottlieb, *The Ancient and Primitive Rite of Memphis,* 1899. 2 Build. Mag., 255 (1916). 85 AQC 244 (1972).

Mizraim, Rite of: William L. Cummings, *Rites of Mizraim and Memphis.* 2 RAM 6 (1946). 85 AQC 246 (1972).

Modern Operatives: 11 Build. Mag. 332 (1925). 12 Build. Mag. 33 (1926).

Moon Lodges: Warren Fowler Mellny, *Moon Lodges,* MSA Digest. James R. Case, *Moon Lodges,* 11 ALR 277 (1970).

Mopses: 24 AQC 6 (1911).

Oriental Order of the Sat B'hai: 85 AQC 266 (1972).

National Sojourners: Lavon Parker Linn, *Fifty Years of National Sojourners* (1970); reviewed: New Age Mag., Sept., 1971, 57; K. T. Mag., April, 1978, 15. Elmo C. Correll, *National Sojourners*, 9 Trans. Tex. L. of Res. 87 (1974).

National Masonic Research Society: H. L. Haywood, Vol. 3 of Mackey's Rev. Ency. of Free., 1316 (1946).

Orange, Order of: 86 AQC 302 (1973); reviews a book on this subject.

Order of Malta: K. T. Mag., Aug., 1972, 7. Wylie B. Wendt, *The Order of Knights of Malta*, K. T. Mag., Jan., 1975, 21.

Past Master Degree: 5 RAM 47 (1955). 2 RAM 219 (1947).

Philalethes Society: 50th Anniversary issue of the *Philalethes Magazine*, Oct., 1978. Also see: Phil. Mag., Oct., 1968 and June, 1978.

Philadelphia: 55 AQC 66 (1942).

Priestly Order of the Temple: 2 RAM 357 (1948).

Red Cross: Wylie B. Wendt, *The Illustrious Order of the Red Cross*, K. T. Mag., May, 1974, 19.

Rosicrucians: W. J. Hughan, *A Curious Old Illuminate MS Roll*, 16 AQC 65, 132, 254 (1903). W. W. Westcott, *The Magic Roll*, 16 AQC 254 (1903). W. W. Westcott, *Rosicrucians, Their History and Aims*, 7 AQC 36, 83 (1894). A. F. A. Woodford, *Freemasonry and Hermeticism*, 1 AQC 28 (1886-1888). A. B. J. Milborne, *The Rosicrucians*, 14 Build. Mag. 129 (1930). *Rosicruciana and Freemasons*, 4 Build. Mag. 16 (1918). Harold V. B. Voorhis, *Rosicrucianism in Freemasonry*, 16 Build. Mag. 129 (1930).

Royal Ark Mariner: C. N. Batham, *The Legend of the Royal Ark Mariner*, 8 Trans. Phoe. L. No. 30, Paris, 33 (1977).

Royal Masonic Hospital: Mas. Sq., June, 1977, 60.

St. John, Order of: 91 AQC 47 (1979).

Sarastro Club of Vienna: Phil. Mag., Dec., 1962, 87.

Sciots, Ancient Egyptian Order of: 10 Build. Mag. 136 (1924).

Sea Captain Lodge: 9 ALR 288 (1964).

Secret Monitor: R. J. Wilkinson, *History of the Order of the Secret Monitor*, 1964, 54 pp.

Sigma Mu Sigma: 11 Build. Mag. 190 (1925).

Societas Rosicruciana in Civitiatibus Foederatis: Ore. Free., Sept., 1973, 15. 2 RAM 339 (1948).

Society of the Cincinnati: 5 RAM 248 (1956).

St. John of Jerusalem, Order of: 14 Build. Mag. 193 (1928).

Strict Observance: 12 Build. Mag. 267 (1926).

Swedenbourg Rite: New Age Mag., June, 1924, 341. 85 AQC 271 (1972).

Swedish Rite: 6 Build. Mag. 262 (1920). Mast. Mas., Jan., 1926, 27. 6 Norcalore 35. 9 Build. Mag. 259 (1920).

Thistle, Order of: K. T. Mag., Sept., 1974, 23.

Virginia Craftsmen: Allen E. Roberts, *Brotherhood in Action*, 1968. Degree team and its work.

Zionism: *Zionism and Its Relation to the Sacred History of Masonry*, 4 Build. Mag. 52 (1918).

CHAPTER TEN

Anti-Masonry

10.01 GENERAL WORKS

Alphonse Cerza, *Anti-Masonry*. 1962; 362 pp. MLR, publisher.
Contents: Covers the history of the subject, describes the opponents of Freemasonry, and then lists the objections usually urged against the Craft by these opponents and answers each point. Many items in the appendix. Comment: Louis L. Williams, "A splendid account of Masonry's enemies through the years." Henry W. Coil, "Recent, authoritative and complete." Libraries: 1, 2, 3, 4, 5, 6, 7, 8, 9, 10, 11, 12, 13, 14.

W. W. Redding, *The Scarlet Book of Freemasonry*. 1888; 544 pp. Redding & Co. New York, publisher.
Comments: L. B. Blakemore, "Complete accounts of the persecutions of Masons by the Roman Catholic Church." Henry W. Coil, "details of repeated persecutions." Libraries: 1, 2, 3, 4, 5, 7, 8, 9, 10, 11, 12, 13, 14.

A. Lloyd Collins, *Anti-Masonry in Missouri*. 1950; MLR, publisher.
Libraries: 7, 12.

Alphonse Cerza, *Let There Be Light*. 1954; MSA Digest. A summary of the subject of anti-Masonry.

Why Freemasons Have Enemies. STB, May, 1949.

Reply to Opponents. Did you know this about Freemasonry? 8 RAM 373 (1966).

Alphonse Cerza, *Anti-Masonry*. 80 AQC 241 (1967).

Alphonse Cerza, *The Opponents of Freemasonry*. New Age Mag., April, 1976, 13.

Church Opposition. STB, Oct., 1955.

John Robison, *Proof of a Conspiracy Against All Religions and Governments, etc.* 1797; 391 pp. This imaginative accusation by a prominent Scottish professor had an enormous influence in creating opposition towards Freemasonry. Today no one who is familiar with history takes his book seriously.
Libraries: 2, 5, 7, 9, 12, 13.

Abbee Barruel, *The Anti Christian and Antisocial Conspiracy*. 1812; 438 pp. Many editions of this book have been issued; it has had a wide readership, and has created a great deal of antagonism towards the Craft.
Libraries: 3.

William Preston, *The Misinformation of Barruel and Robison Exposed*. Reproduced in Oliver's Golden Remains, vol. 3, pp. 274-300.

The Jesuits Who Discovered Our Secrets. 7 ALR 370 (1959).

Abbee Barruel, *Memoirs Illustrating the History of Jacobism*. 1798; 4 Vols.
Comment: L. B. Blakemore, "By an exiled priest of the period of the French Revolution; pure trash; yet a required item, because Roman Catholics have made so much use of it." Silas H. Shepherd, "The work was written by a French Clerical who was exiled to England during the revolution and who advocated many theories regarding Freemasonry which were purely imaginary. The work, however, contains

much that is valuable. Libraries: 3, 4, 7, 9, 10, 12.

W. K. Firminger, *The Romances of Robison and Barruel*. 50 AQC 31 (1937).

Arthur Preuss, *A Study in American Freemasonry*. 1914; 426 pp. B. Herder, publisher.
Libraries: 2, 3, 7, 9, 11, 12, 14.

Bernard Fay, *Revolution and Freemasonry*. 1935; 349. Little, Brown & Co., publisher.
Author: He was an anti-Mason and during the Vichy regime in France was the head of the Anti-Masonic Bureau of the government and was responsible for the death and imprisonment of many Masons. He was tried for these crimes after the war and was found guilty and sentenced to a long prison term, but he escaped to Switzerland. Contents: Presents the thesis that Freemasonry has been a conspiratorial society everywhere. Comments: L. B. Blakemore, "Not reliable. It is one of a number of books of the same type which, under a veneer of impartial statements of facts, are in reality anti-Masonic." Lorman Ratner, in his book "Anti-Masonry" states "Fay's claim as to the influence of the Fraternity in causing both the American and the French Revolution seem much exaggerated, and in any case, they are not substantiated." Reviewed: New Age Mag., Jan., 1936, 57. Libraries: 1, 3, 4, 7, 9, 12, 14.

E. Cahill, *Freemasonry and the Anti-Christian Movement*. 1930; 255 pp. M. G. Gill & Son, Dublin, publisher.
Libraries: 1, 3, 5, 9, 12.

Stephen Knight, *Jack the Ripper, the Final Solution*. 1976; 284 pp. David McKay, publisher.
Reviewed in the Washington Post, July 8, 1976. Contents: Presents the theory that Masons were responsible for the Jack the Ripper killings as they were protecting one of their members, a grandson of Queen Victoria, from being blackmailed. A movie, "Murder by Degree," resulted from this book (See 13 RAM 59 [1979]). Libraries: 12. It is likely to be found in many public libraries, however.

John Morris Roberts, *The Mythology of the Secret Societies*. 1972; 370 pp. Scribner, publisher.
The Preface states: "This book is intended to be about what has been believed and said about secret societies, not about secret societies." The author relies primarily on books such as Barruel and concludes that Freemasonry is subversive and seeks to destroy religion, the family, morals, and property by covert means. Libraries: 12. Probably in many public libraries.

William P. Vaughn, *Thaddeus Stevens: High Priest of Antimasonic Vindictiveness*. 12 Trans. Tex. L. of Res. 62 (1976-1977).

Norman Rogers, *Anti-Masonic Postage Stamps*. 60 AQC 99 (1947).

A. C. F. Jackson, *Freemasonry in Jersey*. 86 AQC 177 (1973). Tells the story of how the Nazis in World War II mutilated the Masonic Temple when they invaded the Island of Jersey.

D. Hamer and J. R. Clarke, *An Anti-Masonic "Deliberation" by Six Doctors of the Sorbonne in 1745*. 86 AQC 29 (1973).

Elbert Bede, *A Preacher Who Refused to Renounce Freemasonry*. Phil. Mag., April, 1955, 7.

David Brion Davis, *Some Themes of Counter-Subversion: An Analysis of Anti-Masonic, Anti-Catholic, Anti-Mormon Literature*. 47 The Mississippi Valley Historical Review, Sept. 1960, 205.

Ex-Presidents of the U.S. Who Were Anti-Masonic. Mas. Mess., Ga., July, 1974, 8.

Albert Van Damm, *Swiss Plebiscite on the Banning of Freemasonry*. Phil. Mag., June, 1976, 61.

Pierre Lutrec, *Spanish Freemasonry in the 18th Century*. Trans. Phoe. Lodge No. 30, Paris, 40 (1974-1975). Of special interest as there is reproduced actual examination of witnesses at the trial of a Mason by the Inquisition.

Gen. Erich Ludendorf, *Destruction of Freemasonry*. 142 pp. Translated into

English by J. Elizabeth Koester. Published by the Noontide Press, Los Angeles, Cal. A good illustration of the ravings of an anti-Mason who wrote and spoke extensively against the Craft for years after World War I. He may have been the one to influence Hitler against the Craft. See: 14 Build. Mag. 93 (1928).

Freemasonry, Judaism, and General Erich Ludendorf. 15 Build. Mag. 205, 230 (1929).

Christian Convention, Aurora, Illinois. 1867; Printed proceedings of the meeting which laid the foundation for creation of the National Christian Association whose chief aim was to combat the "evils" of secret societies. A copy is in the library of the Chicago Historical Society.

Knoop and Jones, *Anti-Masonic Leaflet of 1698.* 55 AQC 152 (1942).

Keith Arrington, *Jefferson Davis Speaks Out.* 12 RAM 72 (1979). An anti-Masonic periodical stated that Jefferson Davis had been pardoned for his activities for the Confederacy as the result of his Masonic influence. He wrote a letter to the editor stating that he had never been a Mason nor had he been pardoned. He also stated that his father had been a Mason and that he had a high opinion of the Fraternity.

John G. Stearns, *An Inquiry Into the Nature and Tendency of Speculative Freemasonry.* 1869; 338 pp. The original ed. had been published in 1829. Libraries: 2.

The Anti-Masonic Movement. 4 Build. Mag. 341 (1919).

D. H. Botha, *South Africa Commission on Enquery Into Secret Organizations.* 78 AQC 74 (1965).

The Kals Letters: The Anti-Masonic Documents of 1761. 2 ALR 498 (1936-1938). More on Kals. 3 ALR 177 (1938-1939).

Arthur E. Waite, *London Morning Post's Attack on Freemasonry.* 6 Build. Mag. 333 (1920).

Some Anti-Masonic Almanacs. 12 ALR 34 (1972).

Prosecution of Freemasons in France and Germany. 3 RAM 46 (1949). Phil. Mag., May, 1947, 14.

10.02 BIBLIOGRAPHY

Dr. William L. Cummings, *A Bibliography of Anti-Masonry.* Second ed.; 1963; 79 pp. (Originally published in Norcalore). This ed. was published by the Henry Emmerson Press, New York.

Stevenson, *Catalog of Anti Masonic Books.*

James C. Odiorne, *A Compilation of Anti-Masonic Documents.* 1830.

Alfred Creigh, *Masonry and Anti-Masonry.* 1854; covers Pennsylvania items primarily. Reproduced in Vol. 25 of the Universal Masonic Library. Libraries: 1, 2, 3, 4, 5, 7, 9, 12, 14, 15.

10.03 DEFENSE OF FREEMASONRY

Martin Clare, *Defence of Masonry.* 1730. This was the answer to Prichard's Masonry Dissected, the first full-scale exposure of the ritual. Reproduced in Anderson's 1738 Constitutions.

William Wonnacott, *Martin Clare and the "Defence of Masonry"* (1730). 28 AQC 80 (1915).

Maria Elizabeth De Greer. *The Defence of Freemasonry.* 1884. Debate conducted in Lisle, Illinois, with Charles A. Blanchard, an anti-Mason.
Reproduced in A. Cerza, Anti-Masonry. Libraries: 2, 3.

J. L. C. Dart, *Christianity and Freemasonry.* Published in Theology, April, 1951, as a reply to an article by Walton Hannah, on Jan., 1951. This item was reproduced in 12 Trans. M. & P. M. L. 72.

Vindex Light Visible: 1952. Result of the Hannah book.
Libraries: 3, 5, 7.

Puerilities. STB, Jan., 1953. Reproduction of the article in the Christian Science Monitor; Ill. Enlightener, May, 1956, 73.

10.04 THE WILLIAM MORGAN AFFAIR

Rob Morris, *William Morgan or Political Anti-Masonry*. 1883; 388 pp. Robert Macoy, Masonic Publisher, New York, publisher.
Author: Appendix No. 25. Comments: L. B. Blakemore, "A lengthy account of the revival of anti-Masonry in 1882 as well as of the original movement in 1832." Silas H. Shepherd, "A lengthy review of the anti-Masonic wave of 1832 and its revival in 1882. This has claimed the attention of many writers, but probably no Mason has given such thorough attention to all the details as Robert Morris." Libraries: 2, 3, 4, 5, 7, 11, 12, 14, 15.

John Quincy Adams, *Letters and Opinions of the Masonic Institution*. 1851; 276 pp. Lorenzo Stratton, Cincinnati, Ohio, publisher.
Contents: Has an anonymous, lengthy preface followed by a collection of letters and a talk given during the anti-Masonic storm following the disappearance of William Morgan. Comments: L. B. Blakemore, "A bitter attack on Freemasonry in the form of letters by a former President of the United States, written during the period of the Morgan affair." Libraries: 2, 3, 4, 5, 7, 9, 10, 11, 12, 13, 14, 15.

W. L. Stone, *Letters on Masonry and Anti-Masonry Addressed to the Honorable John Quincy Adams*. 1832; 566 pp.
Comments: Silas H. Shepherd, "One of the prominent anti-Masonic books of its period." Libraries: 2, 3, 7, 9, 12, 13, 14, 15.

Charles McCarthy, *The Anti-Masonic Party: A Study of Political Anti-Masonry in the United States, 1827-1840*. 1903; 194 pp. Government Printing Office, publisher. This item was part of the Annual Report of the American Historical Association for the year 1902, Vol. 1, pp. 365-547.
Contents: The author, a professional historian and professor at the University of Wisconsin, studied the social, religious, and political events of the period and presents a good impartial view of the subject. He covers specific items in the various states. Comments: Ratner, in his book *Anti-Masonry*, states "McCarthy is obviously influenced by the Turnerian explanation of the rise of democracy on the frontier and the conflict of frontier democrats with Eastern urban elements. Though not accepting the frontier part of the theory, Lee Benson has accepted McCarthy's conclusion that anti-Masonry, at least in New York, was an egalitarian movement." Libraries: 2, 5, 7, 9, 10, 11, 12.

Stanley Upton Mock, *The Morgan Episode in American Free Masonry*. 1930; 152. The Roycrofters, East Aurora, New York, publisher.
Contents: Designed to be a vindication of the accusations made against the Craft a hundred years before. Comments: Henry W. Coil, Sr., "Possibly as a recognition of the centennial of the excitement of 1826-1840, there seems to have been renewed interest in this matter, in the 1930s." Reviewed: New Age Mag., July, 1933, 437. Libraries: 1, 3, 4, 5, 7, 9, 11, 12.

Harold V. B. Voorhis, *"The Morgan Affair" of 1826 in the USA*. 7 AQC 197 (1963).

J. Hugo Tatsch, *An American Crisis*. 34 AQC 196 (1921).

P. C. Huntington, *The True History Regarding the Abduction of William Morgan*. 1880; 151 pp. C. H. Shaver, Chicago, publisher.
Contents: Intended to correct erroneous statements on the subject. Many original documents are reproduced. Libraries: 2, 3, 4, 5, 7, 9, 12, 13, 15.

Thomas A. Knight, *The Strange Disappearance of William Morgan*. 1932; 266 pp. With introduction by J. Hugo Tatsch.
Contents: A good presentation of the facts; has claimed picture of Morgan plus a picture of the Morgan monument in the Batavia cemetery described by Rob Morris as the "lie in granite." Libraries: 3, 5, 7, 8, 9, 10, 11, 13, 14, 15.

C. C. Finney, *The Character, Claims, and Practical Workings of Freemasonry*. 1879; 272 pp. Ezra A. Cook, Chicago, publisher.

Contents: This is a violent attack against the Craft by a clergyman and teacher who wrote and lectured extensively on the subject. Libraries: 2, 3, 4, 5, 9, 11, 12, 13, 14.

John G. Stearns, *Inquiry Into the Nature and Tendency of Speculative Freemasonry.* 1829; 211 pp.
Comments: Silas H. Shepherd, "One of the many tirades of the political anti-Masonic period." Libraries: 9.

Samuel D. Greene, *The Broken Seal.* 1870; 304 pp.
Contents: Purports to be a recitation of personal observations on the Morgan affair by one who, in old age, remembers that he was a neighbor of Morgan, how the author became a Mason, and presents some facts about Morgan. There is an extensive appendix reproducing many documents. Libraries: 2, 5, 7, 9, 12, 14.

Lorman Ratner, *Anti-Masonry, The Crusade of a Party.* 1969; 100 pp. Prentice-Hall, Inc., publisher.
Contents: This book is designed for the general reader and is a valuable addition to the literature on the Morgan affair. It has comments by the author and reproduces the following items: A sermon of Jedidiah Morse; a John Adams letter; a report of a Committee; a clerical appeal to quit Masonry; a political committee resolution; a report of Thurlow Weed; a speech of William H. Seward; excerpts of a convention resolution; and an article of Jabbez Hammond.

William Preston Vaughn, *The Boston Advocate: Chronicle of Antimasonic Extremism.* 19 Trans. Tex. L. of Res. 198 (1974-1975). Description of an anti-Masonic newspaper and its editor, Benjamin Franklin Hallett.

William P. Vaughn, *William Wirt: Antimasonic Enigma.* 9 Trans. Tex. L. of Res. 235 (1974).

J. Hugo Tatsch and Erik Erikson. *The Rise and Development of Anti-Masonry in America, 1737-1826.* 12 Build. Mag. 232, 257, 298 353, (1926); 13 Build. Mag. 33, 72, 100 (1927).

Erik Erikson, *The Anti-Masonic Party.* 7 Build. Mag. 71 (1921).

Rob Morris, *A Tale of Anti-Masonry.* Ind. Free., July, 1952, 12.

The Morgan Affair. STB, March, 1933.

Some Unique Morgan Documents. 6 Norcalore 25.

Harold V. B. Voorhis, *What? William Morgan Again!* 4 RAM 335 (1954).

Impact of Morgan Episode on Masonry in Indiana. Ind. Free., March, 1957, 6.

Edward Harter, *The Morgan Affair – The Local Tradition.* 12 ALR 438 (1974).

The Rise and Fall of the Anti-Masonic Party. STB, July, 1977.

Sherry Penney, *Patrician in Politics.* 1974; 206 pp. A Biography of Daniel Dewey Barnard, prominent attorney and political leader in the area of the Morgan storm who refused to join the witch hunt.

William P. Vaughn, *Legislative Proscription of Freemasonry, 1830-1840.* 13 Trans. Tex. L. of Res. 152 (1977-1978).

Rob Morris, *The Biography of Eli Bruce, Sheriff of Niagara County, N.Y.* 1861; 313 pp. Morris and Monsarratt, Louisville, Ky. The story of the persecution of a public official during the Morgan storm.

Dorthy A. Lipson, *Freemasonry in Federalist Connecticut, 1789-1835.* 1977; 380 pp. Princeton University Press. Has an excellent background of the anti-Masonic climate in the area culminating with the Morgan affair. It clearly shows that the plan of Morgan to publish the exposure of the ritual in itself would never have resulted in the public excitement that resulted from his disappearance.

Herman A. Sarachan, *History of Masonry in Monroe County, 1840-1870.* 1971. Chapter 4 deals with the Morgan period and contains a good brief statement; this part of the book was reviewed by Dr. William J. Cummings, a longtime student of the Morgan affair.

Paul Jones, *The Protest of Certain Masons in Ulster County, New York.* 12 ALR 35

(1972). Protest made to an anti-Masonic publication in 1829.

Myron H. Luke, *Some Anti-Masonic Almanacs*. 12 ALR 35 (1972).

William R. Phinney, *Opposition to Masonry in the New York Annual Conference of the Methodist Episcopal Church*. 11 ALR 426 (1971).

Glen Buzzell, *Masonry in Vermont During and After the Morgan Affair and You Are There*. Unpublished skit on file in the Grand Lodge Library, Burlington, Vermont.

Dr. James D. Carter, *The Truth About William Morgan*. Tex. Grd. L. Mag., Dec., 1972. Expresses view that Morgan ended his days in Central America.

J. Fairbairn Smith, *Dateline 1764*. 1979; Volume 2 of the history of the Craft in Michigan. Pages 76-93 covers the Morgan affair and presents an investigation made by Past Master Smead who expresses the belief that Morgan ended his days in Central America.

Dr. Donovan D. Tidwell, *Rev. David Barnard – Anti-Mason*. 9 Trans. Tex. L. of Res. 203 (1974).

William Morgan Affair in New York. N.Y. Mas. Outl., Sept., 1925, 18.

James E. Craig, *Morgan and Anti-Masonry*. N.Y. Mas. Outl., Jan., 1929, 131.

J. C. Palmer, *The Morgan Affair and Anti-Masonry*. Reproduced in Vol. 2 of the Little Masonic Library. Reviewed in Mast. Mas., Feb., 1925, 163.

Thomas C. O'Donell, *Outline of a New Approach to the "Morgan Mystery."* 3 ALR 72 (1938-1939).

William Morgan's Wife. Ind. Free., July, 1956, 12.

Richardson Wright, *William Morgan's Press*. 4 ALR 389 (1946-1947).

The Causus Belli of the Anti-Masonic Crusade in New York. 2 ALR 545 (1936-1938).

Paul F. Ela, *The Morgan Affair, After 100 Years*. Mast. Mas., May, 1926, 417.

Southwick, *A Solemn Warning Against Free-Masonry*. 1827.
Comment: H. L. Haywood, "That labored pamphlet is familiar to students of the anti-Masonic movement. Not so well known to them is the fact that in 1828 Luther Pratt, also of New York, pulverized it with a well-reasoned and dignified reply, in the form of a 216-page book, entitled 'A Defense of Freemasonry.'"

For many years Dr. William L. Cummings and Dr. William G. Peacher collected books on the Morgan affair. These volumes are now in the Scottish Rite Library, located at Lexington, Massachusetts. This is the largest collection of such material in one place.

10.05 FREEMASONRY AND THE ROMAN CATHOLIC CHURCH

H. L. Haywood, *Freemasonry and Roman Catholicism*. 1943; 216 pp. Masonic History Co., Chicago, publisher.
Author: Appendix No. 16. Contents: Presents a general consideration of the subject with the list of the Papal Bulls issued against the Craft plus reproduction of Humanum Genus and the Reply of Albert Pike. One chapter is devoted to the subject "What and How to Read on Freemasonry and Roman Catholicism." Comments: Henry W. Coil, Sr., "Clear and authentic." L. B. Blakemore, "A fair, up-to-date, straightforward history of Roman Catholic anti-Masonry; contains Leo XIII's Bull and Albert Pike's Reply." Reviewed: New Age Mag., Feb.-March, 1944, 115. The Freemason, of Canada, Dec., 1978-Jan., 1979, 7 stated: "After 35 years, his presentation seems polemic, bigoted, intolerant, and rather out-of-step with the present climate of reconciliation. But it does serve to remind us of a significant chapter in Masonic history." Libraries: 1, 2, 3, 4, 5, 6, 7, 8, 9, 10, 11, 12, 13, 14.

Dudley Wright, *Roman Catholicism and Freemasonry*. 1922; 247 pp. Some of the material in this book was originally published in The Builder Magazine. Volume 7.
Comments: L. B. Blakemore, "Con-

tains an account of the Papal Bulls against Freemasonry, instances of persecutions, etc." Reviewed: New Age Mag., Feb., 1923, 115. Libraries: 2, 3, 4, 5, 6, 7, 8, 9, 10, 11, 12, 14, 15.

Alphonse Cerza, *Freemasonry and the Roman Catholic Church*. Phil., Mag., March, 1950, 2. Reprinted in the New Age Mag., June, 1953, 355.

Count Goblet D'Alviela, *The Papal Bulls and Freemasonry in Belgium*. 25 AQC 81 (1912).

Henry Charles Lea, *An Anti-Masonic Mystification*. New Age Mag., July, 1916. Article from Lippincott's Mag., referring to the Leo Taxil fiasco.

Alphonse Cerza, *The Lively Adventures of Leo Taxil*. Phil. Mag., Aug., 1958, 57. Also see: 14 Build. Mag. 182 (1928).

Alvah T. Westdahl, *The Curious Career of Leo Taxil*. Phil. Mag., April, 1970, 61.

The Roman Catholic Viewpoint. New Age Mag., May, 1925, 294.

Charles W. Frossel, *Freemasonry and the Roman Catholic Church*. 12 RAM 360 (1978).

Jean O. Heineman, *An Early Pronouncement of the Church, A.D. 1326?* 87 AQC 239 (1974). Also in Phil. Mag., Aug., 1971, 67.

William J. Whalen, *Christianity and American Freemasonry*. 1958; 184. Bruce Publishing Co., Milwaukee, Wis., publisher.
Analyzed: Phil. Mag., Feb., 1960, 7.
Libraries: 2, 3, 5, 7, 11, 12, 14.

Palladism and the Papacy. New Age Mag., Aug., 1971, 10.

Alphonse Cerza, *Forgotten Reason*. New Age, Oct., 1954. *Another Forgotten Reason*, Phil. Mag., Dec., 1954, 14.

George Oliver, *Papal Teachings in Freemasonry*. 1866; 38 pp. The subtitle is "Being a rectification of the errors and misrepresentations contained in recent allocutions promulgated from the secret consistory at Rome, by Pius IX."

In a clear style he answers the points raised.
Libraries: 3, 4, 7, 9, 12.

Leon de Poncin, *Freemasonry and the Vatican*. 1968.
Reviewed: 81 AQC 235 (1968). Libraries: 2, 3, 12.

J. J. Knowles, *Some Papal Pronouncements*. 9 Trans. Leic. L. of Res. 106 (1900-1901). Also in 11 British Misc. 112.

Bernard P. Magnan died; he was a prominent Frenchman, a Roman Catholic and a Mason. When he died, he was given a Masonic funeral. New Age Mag., July, 1939, 421.

Catholics and Freemasons in Quebec. 12 RAM 107 (1976-1977).

Joseph McCabe, *A History of Freemasonry*. Subtitle: "The Story of Its Relations With Satan and the Popes." 1949; 31 pp. Haldeman-Julius, Girard, Kansas.

Alex Horne, *A Pontiff Freemason*. New Age Mag., April, 1962, 17.

Was Pope Pius IX a Freemason? 26 AQC 218 (1913).

Translation of the First Papal Bull. 24 AQC 47 (1911). Also see a newer translation in the 1979 volume of the Masonic Book Club, which reproduces *The Sufferings of John Coustos* with an excellent commentary by Wallace McLeod.

Louis L. Williams, *Persecuted by the Inquisition, How John Coustos Suffered*. No. Light, Sept., 1979. 4.

Catholic Encyclopedia. 1913; has an article entitled *Freemasonry* which later was reproduced in 5 Build. Mag. 18, 210, 347, 272 (1919). A later edition has an item written by William J. Whalen.

A Roman Catholic Grand Master. 15 Build. Mag. 161 (1929).

Can a Roman Catholic Become a Freemason? A Debate. Phil. Mag., Feb., 1972, 3.

Leo Fischer, *The Inquisition*. 3 Build. Mag. 264 (1917).

Claim of Infallibility. 9 Build. Mag. 345 (1923).

Catholic Freemasons in Germany. New Age Mag., March, 1933, 159.

The Papal Warning Against Non-Roman Catholic Organizations. 7 Build. Mag. 107 (1921).

Humanum Genus, the Papal Bull of Leo XIII and Albert Pike's Reply; reproduced in 5 Build. Mag. 287, 314 (1920); 6 Build. Mag. 13, 35 (1924).

John Coustos, Unparalleled Sufferings. 1797. Reproduced by the Masonic Book Club in 1979 with an outstanding commentary by Wallace McLeod, of Canada.

Dr. S. Vatcher, *John Coustos and the Portuguese Inquisition*. 81 AQC 9 (1968).

Dr. S. Vatcher, *An Early Record of Inquisition Proceedings*. 84 AQC 74 (1971).

Alphonse Cerza, *The Vatican Council and Religious Liberty*. Phil. Mag., April, 1966, 2.

Alphonse Cerza, *The Reasonableness of Pope John*. Phil. Mag., June, 1962, 44.

10.06 FREEMASONRY AND THE ECUMENICAL MOVEMENT

Father Berteloot's Book Reviewed by Leo Fischer. Phil. Mag., June-July, 1948, 8.

Albert Lantoine, *Letter to the Sovereign Pontiff*. 1937; written in French; translated into Italian in 1977.

Riquet and Baylot, *The Freemasons; a Dialogue Between Michael Riquet, S.J., and Jean Baylot*. 1968; Ed. Beauchesne, Paris; 100 pp.

Father John A. O'Brien, *Can a Roman Catholic Become a Freemason?* Phil. Mag., June, 1973, 62.

Alphonse Cerza, *Freemasonry and the Ecumenical Movement*. Phil. Mag., Oct., 1965, 76. Also in 9 RAM 73 (1967).

Alec Mellor, *Our Separated Brethren: The Freemasons*. 1964; 224 pp.
Reviewed: 1965 Grd. L. of Scotl. Yrbk. 105; 74 AQC 51 (1964); 77 AQC 187 (1967). Libraries: 2, 3, 5, 7, 9, 10, 11, 12, 14.

Alec Mellor, *Contemporary French Freemasonry*. 76 AQC 208 (1966).

Alec Mellor, *The Roman Catholic Freemason*. 10 RAM 259 (1972).

Catholic Word Book, reprinted from the 1973 Catholic Almanac: "Present relations between the Catholic Church and Freemasonry in the United States are marked by greater circularity and mutual understanding than in the past, but the prohibition against Catholic membership still stands." But the rule was interpreted to the contrary in 1974.

Alec Mellor, *The Roman Catholic Church and the Craft*. 89 AQC 60 (1976).

Father J. A. Ferrer Benimeli, *La Masoneria Despue Del Concilio*. 1968; 331 pp.; in Spanish. Father Benimeli in the years that followed continued his study of Freemasonry and has written numerous other books on the subject. Included in his work are two extensive bibliographies on the subject of Freemasonry.

Historia, a Spanish Magazine, devoted its Nov., 1977, issue to the subject of Freemasonry; had many pictures.

Alphonse Cerza, *The Announcement of the Change Made in 1974*, with a translation of the pertinent parts of the letter sent to the Catholic Bishops. Chicago Scottish Rite Mag., Jan., 1975, 3.

Father Rosario F. Esposito, *La Reconciliazione Tra La Chiesa e la Masoneria*. 1979; 146 pp. Pleiadi, Longo Editore, Ravenna, Italy. In Italian. Detailed presentation of the conferences, debates, and exchanges in Italy between the leaders of the Craft and of the Roman Catholic Church designed to create a climate of understanding.

Is Catholic Attitude Towards Freemasonry Changing? 8 RAM 20 (1964). Answer by Emmett McLoughlin. 8 RAM 46 (1964).

Alec Mellor, *The Roman Catholic Freemason.* 10 RAM 259 (1972). Has picture of the author.

Giordano Gamberini, *The Excommunication of the 20th Century.* Phil. Mag., April, 1979, 16.

Terence Cardinal Cooke, *On the Road to Friendship.* Ind. Free., April, 1978, 8. Reproduces talk given by the Archbishop of New York at a dedication breakfast in 1976.

Let Bishops Decide. Reprint of article from the Catholic Herald Citizen. In the Mas. J. of So. Africa, May, 1974, 20.

P. Giovanni Caprile, S.J., *Massoneria e Chiesa Cattolica.* 1973.
Reviewed: Rivista Massonica, Feb., 1974, 124.

C. C. Falkner, Jr., *Behold, How Pleasant.* Ind. Free., April, 1974, 10.

Dr. Leszek Ochista, *Roman Catholic Church and Freemasonry.* Dialogue in German between 1968 and 1973. 12 RAM 348 (1978).

Alex Horne, *Freemasonry and the Vatican.* Phil. Mag., April, 1979, 7, and for the next two issues.

Priest Praises Freemasons. Phil. Mag., Oct., 1973, 95.

Nathan Greenstein, *The Spanish Saga.* 8 Trans. Phoe. L. No. 10, Paris, 54 (1977).

Dr. Jose Roberto Levi-Castillo, *The Other Side of the Coin.* Expresses the view that the so-called reconciliation is a ruse designed to lull the Craft into closing its eyes in an attempt to destroy liberty and the public schools. 13 RAM 74 (1979).

Time Magazine Reported on Recent Joint Mason-Knights of Columbus Activities. 8 RAM 334 (1966).

Masons and Knights of Columbus Sponsor Joint Projects in Iowa. 8 RAM 367 (1966).

Notre Dame Priest Speaks. 8 RAM 253 (1965).

Priest Greets Masons at Mass. 8 RAM 189 (1965).

Roman Catholics Aid Shriner Hospital. 8 RAM 176 (1965).

Catholic Bishop Addresses Grand Lodge Banquet. 8 RAM 168 (1965).

Knights of Columbus Withdraw Anti-Masonic Publication. 8 RAM 381 (1956).

John A. O'Brien, *Encouraging Words From a Noted Catholic Theologian.* 9 RAM 145 (1968). Has picture of Father O'Brien.

Dwight L. Smith, *The Recent "Vatican Announcement."* 9 RAM 173 (1968).

Cardinal Cody Addresses Ecumenical Group. 10 RAM 168 (1971). Also see: Phil. Mag., Aug., 1971, 72.

New Era for Catholics and Masons? 10 RAM 250 (1971-1972).

John A. O'Brien, *The Walls Are Crumbling.* Talk presented before the Illinois Scottish Rite Council of Deliberation, in 1965 (reproduced in the 1965 Proc. of the Council, pp. 39-42; also has a picture of Father O'Brien).

10.07 FREEMASONRY AND THE MORMONS

Samuel H. Goodwin, *Mormonism and Masonry.*
Author: Was Grand Secretary of the Grand Lodge of Utah for many years. He wrote many articles and booklets on the subject of Freemasonry and the Mormon Church; many of his articles appeared in the Build. Mag.: Vol., 7, 8, 10, and 13. His material has also been reproduced in the early editions of the Little Masonic Library. In the current edition of this set the material has been replaced by an article written by Dr. Mervin B. Hogan. Libraries with the Goodwin booklet: 1, 2, 3, 5, 7, 9, 12, 13, 14, 15.

Anthony W. Ivins, *The Relationship of "Mormonism" and Freemasonry.* 1934; 254 pp. Presents the Mormon point of view.
Libraries: 1, 3, 5, 7, 11, 12, 14, 15.

E. Cecil McGavin, *Mormonism and Masonry.* 1947; 200 pp. Presents the Mormon point of view.

Reviewed: New Age Mag., July, 1947. Libraries: 5, 7, 9, 11, 12, 14.

Mervin B. Hogan, *Founding Minutes of Nauvoo Lodge, U.D.* 1971; 103 pp. Iowa Research Lodge No. 2, publisher.

Mervin B. Hogan, *The Official Minutes of Nauvoo Lodge, U.D.* 1975; 103 pp. Iowa Res. L. No. 2, publisher.

Mervin B. Hogan, *Vital Statistics of Nauvoo Lodge.* 1975; 114 pp. Iowa Res. L. No. 2, publisher.

Mervin B. Hogan, *The Confrontation of Grand Master Abraham Jonas and John Cook Bennett at Nauvoo.* Phil. Mag., June, 1976, 54 and Aug., 1976, 76. A talk given at the Blue Friar meeting, in Washington, D.C., held on Feb. 22, 1976.

Mervin B. Hogan, *The Impact of Mormonism on the Founding of the Grand Lodge of Utah.* 11 Proc. Chap. of Res. of Ohio 80 (1965-1967).

Mervin B. Hogan, *The Cryptic Tow Between Mormonism and Freemasonry.* Arizona Res. L. No. 1, Paper No. 22, presented on Feb. 24, 1970.

Mervin B. Hogan, *Utah's Memorial to Freemasonry.* 11 RAM 199 (1974).

Mervin B. Hogan, *Mormonism and the Grand Lodge of Arizona.* 11 ALR 287 (1970)

Mervin B. Hogan, *The Milieu of Mormonism and Freemasonry at Nauvoo: An Interpretation.* 13 ALR 188 (1976).

Mervin B. Hogan has deposited in the Archives of the University of Utah, located at Salt Lake City, a number of unpublished papers on the subject of the relationship between Mormonism and Freemasonry. One such paper is a long and detailed bibliography on the subject.

Mervin B. Hogan, *The Origin and Growth of Utah Masonry and Its Conflict With Mormonism.* 1978; 120 pp. Presents the view that the rule in Utah preventing Mormons from filing petitions in the local lodges is contrary to established Masonic law.

William J. Whalen, *The Latter Day Saints in the Modern World,* has a chapter entitled "Mormonism and Freemasonry." The author is a Roman Catholic teacher who has written extensively on the subject of Freemasonry prior to the change of climate in 1974.

Robert Bruce Flanders, *Nauvoo, Kingdom on the Mississippi.* 1965; 341 pp. University of Illinois, publisher. Libraries: 3, 11, 14.

10.08 EXPOSÉS OF THE MASONIC RITUAL

Samuel Prichard, *Masonry Dissected.* 1730.
Contents: This was the first complete exposé of the Masonic ritual. Reproduced by the Masonic Book Club, in 1977, with a detailed and definitive commentary by Harry Carr. Reviewed: 90 AQC 250 (1977).

S. N. Smith, *Prichard's "Masonry Dissected."* 51 AQC 138 (1938).

Harry Carr, ed., *The Early French Exposures, 1737-1751.* 1971; 488 pp. Quatuor Coronati Lodge, publisher.
Contents: Reproduces in English 12 of the exposures that were published in French.

To what extent do the early French exposures throw light on our present-day ritual? This question has been answered by Dr. Ross Hepburn in the Trans. of M. & P. M. L. Jan., 1973, 14.

James Dewar, *The Unlocked Secret, Freemasonry Examined.* 1966; 272 pp. William Kimber, London, publisher. The author prepared a television program on Freemasonry for the British Broadcasting Co. in 1965. This project led him to write this book.
Reviewed: The Freemason, Canada, Dec., 1977, 7. Libraries: 3, 5, 7, 11.

P. A. Tunbridge, *Emanuel Zimmerman, Freemason, and His Annotated Copy of J & B.* 79 AQC 94 (1966).

Ross Hepburn, *Attacks on the Craft and Exposures of the Ritual.* 15 Trans. M. & P. M. L. 155.

Richard Carlisle, *Manual of Freemasonry.*
1867; 311 pp.
Comment: Silas H. Shepherd, "Carlisle
claims more knowledge than we are willing to concede." Libraries: 1, 2, 3, 7, 12,
14.

S. J. Fenton, *Richard Carlisle, His Life
and Masonic Writings.* 39 AQC 83
(1936); 55 AQC 155 (1942).

N. B. Spencer, *Exposures and Their
Effect on Freemasonry.* 74 AQC 142
(1961).

S. N. Smith, *The So-Called "Exposures"
of Freemasonry of the Mid-Eighteenth
Century.* 56 AQC 4 (1943).

Those Terrible Exposés. STB, Dec.,
1938.

A. C. F. Jackson, *The English Exposures
of 1760/62.* 84 AQC 146 (1971).

Walton Hannah, *Darkness Visible.* 1952;
228 pp. Augustine Press, London, publisher.
Libraries: 2, 3, 5, 7, 9, 11, 12.

Walton Hannah, *Christians by Degrees.*
1954; 215 pp. Augustine Press, London, publisher. A supplement to Darkness Visible.
Libraries: 3, 5, 11, 12.

Hubert S. Box, *The Nature of Freemasonry.* 1952; 93 pp. Augustine Press, London, publisher. A partial exposure. Part
of the Hannah storm.
Libraries: 3, 5, 7, 9, 10, 11, 14.

A Gentleman, Jachin and Boaz. 1815;
104.
Contents: Claimed to be "An authentic
key to the door of Freemasonry." Libraries: 2, 9, 11.

J. T. Thorp, *Freemasonry Parodied in
1754.* By Slade's "Freemason Examined." 20 AQC 93 (1907).

Avery Allyn, *A Ritual of Freemasonry.*
1931; 302 pp. Had appeared in many
editions before this time. Author and his
work: Phil. Mag., Dec., 1961, 99; Feb.,
1962, 8.
Libraries: 1, 3, 9, 14.

Enoch T. Carson, *Archeological Curiosity
of the Ritual.*
Contents: Reproduces a number of exposures of the ritual. Comments: Silas H.
Shepherd, "Brother Carson limited the
edition of these reprints to 125 copies.
They are very scarce, but when obtainable
are a source of delight." Libraries: 10.

William Morgan, *Illustrations of Freemasonry.* 1827; 84 pp.
Libraries: 1, 2, 3, 5, 7, 8, 9, 12.

A. J. B. Milborne, *The Early Continental
Exposures and Their Relationship to
Contemporary English Texts.* 78 AQC
172 (1965); 83 AQC 177 (1970).

BBC Attempts an "Exposé" of Freemasonry – Church of Scotland "Investigates" the Fraternity. 8 RAM 187
(1965).

Harry Carr, *Some Foreign Masonic Documents.* 72 AQC 3 (1959).

Herbert Poole, *Masonic Ritual and Secrets
Before 1717.* 37 AQC 4 (1924).

Coil, *Masonic Encyclopedia,* 567; list of
exposés.

10.09 MISCELLANEOUS

*Crusade Against Secret Societies and the
National Christian Association.* Journal
of the Ill. St. Hist. Soc., Winter, 1971.

William T. Hastings, *Phi Beta Kappa as a
Secret Society and Its Relations to
Freemasonry and Anti-Masonry.* 1965.

Claude McClung, *Why I Left Masonry.*
National Christian Association, publisher.

George F. Dillon, *Grand Orient of
Freemasonry Unmasked.* 1888; 144 pp.
Libraries: 1, 5, 7, 11.

Arthur A. Weiss, S. J., *Freemasonry and
Communism.*

J. Edgar Hoover, Freemasonry and Communism. 6 RAM 384 (1960); and in
New Age Mag., Jan., 1958, 40.

Mervin A. Hogan, *Communism as a Religion.* New Age Mag., Sept., 1963, 23.

Can a Mason Be a Communist? New Age
Mag., Aug., 1963, 27.

Alphonse Cerza, *Bolshevism and Freemasonry*. Phil. Mag., Oct., 1975, 90.

Guy Vinatrell, *Communisme et Franc-Maconnerie*. 1961; in French.

Ainsley Sahai, *A Role to Play*. Anti-Masonic activity of the Greek Orthodox Church. 7 Trans. Phoe. Lodge No. 30, Paris, 90.

Jess Minton, *Equal (?) Opportunity; Anti-Masonic Activity of Army Bases*. 11 RAM 150 (1974).

Albert Van Damm, *Is Islam Forbidding Freemasonry?* Phil. Mag., April, 1974, 41.

Italian Freemasonry in Crisis. N.Y. Mas. Outlook, June, 1927, 303.

Declaration Issued by Mussolini Against Masons. N.Y. Mas. Outl., Sept., 1926, 75.

Mussolini and Masonry, New Age Mag., May, 1925, 281.

Thomas M. Stewart, *A Lutheran Minister's "Misinterpretation of Freemasonry."* New Age Mag., May, 1914, 483; June, 1914, 511.

William M. Stuart, *The Anti-Masonic Phase of Johnson's Impeachment*. 2 ALR 146 (1936).

The Order of Jacques-Cartier, French Canada's Powerful Super-Secret Society. 7 RAM 329 (1963).

Mob Violence Halts Chapter Degrees in Ancon Temple. 8 RAM 13 (1964).

Leo Mufflemann, *Ludendorf's War on Freemasonry*. Mast. Mas. Nov., 1927, 853.

Freemasonry and the Salvation Army. 3 RAM 8 (1949).

Quakers and Masonry. 7 Build. Mag. 366 (1921); 8 Build. Mag. 356 (1922).

Biographical Sketches of Selected Masonic Authors

1. ELBERT BEDE

Elbert Bede was born on June 28, 1881, at Randolph, Iowa. He was baptized with the full name Benjamin Elbert Bede but later dropped his first name and became known as Elbert Bede. On one occasion I asked him if he was a descendant of the Venerable Bede, of early English history, and he said that many years before he had explored the subject but gave up when he discovered that the Venerable Bede never married and did not want to discover that an early ancestor was a bastard. Early in life he moved to North Branch, Minnesota, where he learned the newspaper and publishing business. About 1911 he moved to Cottage Grove, Oregon, and became the owner and publisher of the *Cottage Grove Sentinel*. During this period he served for years as Clerk of the House of Representatives of the Oregon Legislature. In 1936 he moved to Portland, Oregon, and purchased the *Masonic Analyst*. Several years later he changed the name of the magazine to *The Oregon Mason*, and still later to *The Oregon Freemason*. From then on he spent all his time on Masonic activities. The magazine is still being published by his successors.

He became a Mason in Chicago Lodge No. 271 of North Branch, Minnesota, and when he moved to Cottage Grove, Oregon, he transferred his membership to Cottage Grove Lodge No. 51, and served that lodge as Worshipful Master. For years he served on the Jurisprudence Committee of the Grand Lodge of Oregon. In 1933 Research Lodge of Oregon No. 198 was chartered and Bede became a charter member. He also helped organize Ashlar Lodge No. 209 of Portalnd, Oregon. He joined the Scottish Rite in Duluth Minnesota, and received the Thirty-Third Degree of the Rite in 1935. He was also a member of the York Rite Bodies. Bede became a Shriner in Hillah Temple, Ashland, Oregon, and later transferred to Al Kader Temple, Portland. For many years he was a Fellow of the Philalethes Society, and served this Society as president from 1961 to 1963.

His funeral service was held on October 28, 1967, in the Caldwell Colonial Mortuary at Portland, Oregon.

REFERENCES

W. R. Denslow, *10,000 Famous Freemasons*, Vol. 1, p. 74. Phil. Mag., Feb., 1968, 81.

2. WILLIAM MOSELEY BROWN

William Moseley Brown was born on February 27, 1894, at Lynchburg, Virginia. He received his formal education in the public schools of Virginia and then attended Washington and Lee University, receiving the Bachelor of Arts Degree in 1914; he later received the Master of Arts Degree from the same school. He then attended Columbia University and received the Doctor of Philosophy Degree. Brown was professor of language, biology, and psychology at Washington and Lee University from 1913 to 1929. He was president of Atlantic University from 1929 to 1932, and between 1937 and 1942 he was personnel director of the Vick Chemical Company. In 1947 he became the personnel consultant for the company and served in that capacity for many years. He served in World War I and advanced from the rank of private to second lieutenant. He served in World War II as a major and later as a lieutenant colonel between 1942 and 1947. He was the independent Republican candidate for Governor of Virginia in 1929 and a candidate for Congress in 1932. In the years 1931-1932 he was the United States representative in the Ulrich expedition to the interior of Brazil, and the Rio Brown discovered at that time was named after him by the government of Brazil. He engaged in a similar expedition in 1933 and 1934.

Brown was a member of all the appendant bodies of the Craft and served as Grand Master as well as the head of all the other Grand Bodies of the State of Virginia. He received the Thirty-Third Degree of the Scottish Rite and served as president of the National Sojourners. As a result of his Masonic affiliations his name was placed on the Black List of the Vichy Government during World War II and if he had been captured by the Nazis he would have been executed promptly.

He was a Fellow of the Philalethes Society and served as president of this Society between 1957 and 1960.

He was an able Masonic researcher and wrote the history of many Virginia lodges, a complete biography of George Washington as a Mason for the Grand Lodge of Virginia, several Digests of the Masonic Service Association, a full-scale biography of Rennie Arnold, Imperial Potentate of the Shrine, and many Masonic articles for magazines.

Brown departed this life on January 8, 1966, at St. Petersburg, Florida, where he had lived as a retiree for a number of years.

REFERENCES

W. R. Denslow, *10,000 Famous Freemasons*, Vol. 1, p. 143. Phil. Mag., Feb., 1966, 4; April, 1966, 29.

3. HARRY CARR

Harry Carr was born on October 19, 1900, at London, England, and received his formal education at the Whitechapel Foundation School, a secondary school. Early in life he went into business and was successful at the venture. On the death of the secretary and editor of Quatuor Coronati Lodge, J. R. Dashwood, in May 1961, he retired from business at a financial sacrifice and became the secretary-editor of Quatuor Coronati Lodge. With his usual energy and vision he went to work to strengthen the lodge. When he was appointed to the job, the Correspondence Circle membership was around 3,900; in 1973 the membership had been increased to 12,000. He brought this about by soliciting Masonic writers to prepare papers on subjects of current interest beyond the provincial English material that had dominated the *Transactions* up to that time. With a larger membership the *Transactions* of the lodge could be issued with much more material; for example, the 1961 volume of the *Transactions* had 172 pages, but when his final volume as editor was published (Volume 85) the *Transactions* had over 400 pages.

He became a Mason in Barnato Lodge No. 2265 in 1929, and served the lodge as Worshipful Master in 1943. In 1946 he was the founder of Noble Brotherhood Lodge No. 6226 and was its first Master. He also has served as Worshipful Master of the following lodges: No. 2429 in 1963-1964; and No. 2076 in 1958-1959. He has served as secretary of the following lodges: Barnato No. 2265, from 1947 to 1970; Noble Brotherhood No. 6226, from 1947 to 1963; and Quatuor Coronati No. 2076, from 1961 to 1972.

Carr was Exalted in Barnato R.A. Chapter No. 2265 in 1935, and served at M.E.Z. in 1945. He served as Preceptor in several Lodges of Instruction between 1944 and 1967.

He has served the United Grand Lodge of England and other Masonic groups in many ways, including the following offices: Promoted to London Rank in 1953; Past Assistant Grand Director of Ceremonies in 1960; Past Junior Grand Deacon, Supreme Grand Chapter, in 1969; Past Assistant Grand Standard Bearer (R.A.), in 1960; Grand Lodge of Iran; elected to Board of General Purposes in 1965, and re-elected in 1968, 1971, 1974, 1977, 1980, serving as vice president in 1978-1979. He holds honorary membership in eight lodges. In 1973 he was presented with the James R. Case Medal of Excellence of the Research Lodge of Connecticut.

In 1968 Carr contacted Cardinal Heenan and discussed with him leaflets being distributed in some of the churches of London incorrectly describing Freemasonry. As a result of several meetings with the Cardinal, the leaflets were removed from circulation and on a visit to Rome Cardinal Heenan conferred with the committee studying the possibility of changing the view of the Roman Catholic Church towards Freemasonry; his interest no doubt contributed to the change that came about in 1974.

Harry Carr's outstanding work has been primarily in the educational quarries of the Craft. Between 1961 and 1973 he rendered outstanding service to Quatuor Coronati Lodge as secretary and editor. He had joined the lodge's correspondence in 1938, and was elected to full membership in 1953; he served the lodge as Worshipful Master in 1958. He has done a great deal of literary work for the Craft in editing a number of important volumes such as the *Minutes of Kilwinning Lodge*, of Edinburgh, the *Collected Prestonian Lectures*, the *French Exposés*, and the *Cartwright Book on the Ritual*. He has researched many vital subjects and has written many outstanding articles that have appeared in the transactions of many Masonic research lodges and other periodicals. In addition to this large amount of work he has found time to go on a number of extended lecture tours to Canada, the United States, and to other parts of the world. In 1976 he had published *The Freemason at Work*, a collection of the most popular 200 questions sent to Quatuor Coronati Lodge during the time that he was editor together with the answers; it has proved to be a popular book because it deals with basic questions relating to the Craft that are always being raised by thinking and interested Masons.

REFERENCES

72 AQC 7 (1959). 12 AQC 285 (1973). Preface in the 1977 volume of the Masonic Book Club, in which he wrote the analysis and commentary on *Prichard's Masonry Dissected*, where his picture appears.

4. JAMES DAVID CARTER

James D. Carter was born on January 27, 1907, at Evant, Coryell County, Texas. His formal education was at the following schools: Evant, Texas, public schools; John Tarleton College, Stephenville, Texas; North Texas Teachers College, Denton, Texas, which conferred the Bachelor of Arts Degree on him; North Texas State College, Denton, Texas, which conferred the Master of Arts Degree on him; and the University of Texas, Austin, Texas, where he specialized in American history, which conferred the Doctor of Philosophy Degree on him.

After completing his formal education he served as a teacher as follows: Eleven years in the Texas public schools; one year at North Texas State College, and two years at the University of Texas.

On June 30, 1927, he was married to Miss Lowell Lona Burney and three daughters have blessed this union.

For three years (1924-1927) Carter served in the Armed Forces of the United States, and in 1925 he received a commission from the Reserve Corps. He was the eighth successive generation in his family to serve in the armed forces of our country.

He is a member of two national academic honor societies. Pi Gamma Mu, which he served as secretary, and Phi Alpha Theta, which he served as president. He is also a member of the following civic groups: Sons of the American Revolution, Society of Colonial Wars, Civil War Round Table and Texas State Historical Society.

His Masonic career started as a member of the Order of DeMolay in 1922, and he received his Masonic degrees in Bee House Lodge No. 550 of Evant, Texas, with his father officiating in the East in each degree. He later served as secretary of the lodge and then served the lodge as Worshipful Master. Upon completing his term as Worshipful Master he served two years as a District Deputy Grand Master and then on various Grand Lodge Committees.

He was the leader who brought about the formation of the Texas Lodge of Research and was its first Master. The excellence of the work set by him for this lodge has continued to the present time.

Carter is a member of the York Rite. He

received the Scottish Rite degrees in San Antonio, Texas; received the Rank and Decoration of Knight Commander of the Court of Honour in 1957; and later received the Thirty-Third Degree and the Grand Cross of the Rite. In 1973 he was named the Librarian of the Library of the Supreme Council, S.J., in Washington, D.C. He holds membership in the Order of the Eastern Star, the National Sojourners, the Shrine, the Royal Order of Scotland, and many other Masonic organizations, and has served as an officer in many of them. He is a Blue Friar and a Fellow of the Philalethes Society.

He has been a prolific Masonic researcher, having written four outstanding books about the Craft in Texas, the multivolume *History of the Scottish Rite, S.J.,* as well as many magazine articles.

At present he is researching and writing, by assignment, a *History of the Scottish Rite, Northern Masonic Jurisdiction.*

REFERENCES

1 Trans. Tex. L. of Res. 383-387 (1959-1961).

5. JAMES R. CASE

James Royal Case was born on November 28, 1894, at Colchester, Connecticut, and traces his ancestry back to the Mayflower. He was educated at the Bacon Academy, Colchester, Connecticut, the Connecticut Agricultural College, Teacher's College of Columbia University, and Northwestern University. He was a teacher for many years, a 4-H Club Agent, County Agricultural Extension worker, administrative officer of the University of Connecticut, plus many other public service positions. He had extensive military service from 1912 to 1956 with 12 of these years on active duty. He retired from the service as a colonel.

On March 16, 1918, he was married to Miss Bessie Hall Randall, a high school classmate, and two daughters were born of this union. His wife passed away some years ago. He remarried but his second wife passed away after a few years.

Case became a Mason in Uriel Lodge No. 24, of Merrow, Connecticut, in 1916. He was Exalted in St. John's Chapter No. 57, of Virginia, in 1917, and in 1951 affiliated with Trinity Chapter No. 9, of Connecticut. He became a member of Virginia Council No. 28, R. & S.M. (now Wooster Council) of Connecticut, in 1954, and joined Hampton Commandery No. 5, K.T., of Virginia, in 1917. He has been Grand Historian of the Grand Lodge of Connecticut since 1953, and has held similar positions in all the state bodies for many years. He is a member of the National Sojourners, the Red Cross of Constantine, the Order of the Eastern Star, many research lodges, and is a Fellow of the Philalethes Society.

He joined the Scottish Rite in Washington, D.C., in 1949; he affiliated with the Connecticut Bodies in 1963. In 1965 he received the Thirty-Third Degree of the Scottish Rite, Northern Masonic Jurisdiction.

He has been a Blue Friar for many years and has written finely-researched articles which have appeared in Masonic magazines over the years. Named in his honor is the annual award known as the James R. Case Medal of Excellence presented by the Research Lodge of Connecticut. He served as the tenth Master of the American Lodge of Research, of New York.

REFERENCES

W. R. Denslow, *10,000 Famous Freemasons,* Vol. 4, p. 379.

6. CARL H. CLAUDY

Carl H. Claudy was born on January 13, 1879 at Washington, D.C. His father was Frank Claudy, a graduate of Heidelberg University, a Civil War soldier, an author, poet and lecturer. His mother was a member of the Mayflower Catlin family and an accomplished musician. He had little formal education and quit school to go to Alaska in the Valdez Gold Rush. He became a press photographer, reporter and editor. He was editor of the *American Inventor,* 1900-1904; *Prism,* 1908-1909; *Cathedral Calendar,* 1921-1927. For years he was the aviation correspondent of the *New York Herald* at Washington, D.C. For years he wrote a monthly column for *Adam's Impressions,* and some years later a large volume was printed with samples of this column. He wrote many books for general readers.

In 1902 Claudy was married to Clara Fitch Duvall, and two children were born of the marriage. He received an honorary degree of Doctor of Literature from Wake Forest College.

He became a Mason in Harmony Lodge No. 17, of Washington, D.C., in 1908, and served the lodge as Worshipful Master in 1932. He served as Grand Master of the Grand Lodge of the District of Columbia in 1943.

He was a member of many appendant bodies and the recipient of many honorary memberships, medals, certificates, and other honors from various Masonic groups. He was editor of the *Master Mason*, 1924-1930. In 1929 he became executive secretary of the Masonic Service Association and continued in that position until his passing on May 27, 1957.

He was a prolific writer on Masonic subjects, and wrote hundreds of the *Short Talk Bulletins* published monthly by the Masonic Service Association as well as *The Lion's Paw*, a novel, an *Introduction to Freemasonry*, *The Master's Book*, many Masonic books, and many other books. He collected the material for the *Little Masonic Library*. Many of his books are still available from the Temple Publishing Co. of Washington, D.C.

REFERENCES

Laurence R. Taylor, *Carl H. Claudy: In Memoriam*, MSA Digest (1958). Phil. Mag., Aug., 1957, 63. Ind. Free., Sept., 1952 issue. W. R. Denslow, *10,000 Famous Freemasons*, Vol. 1, p. 220. 6 ALR 276 (1954-1955).

7. HENRY C. CLAUSEN

Henry C. Clausen was born on June 30, 1905, at San Francisco, California and received his formal education in the public schools of San Francisco. The death of his father interrupted his high school education and he went to work to support his mother and sisters. But he continued his education by going to night school, attending the San Francisco Law School and receiving the J.D. Degree in 1927. He then took postgraduate work at the University of California, in San Francisco, from 1927-1932. Later he attended the University of Michigan, 1942-1943.

He was admitted to the California Bar in 1927 and started the practice of law in San Francisco, continuing in this work to the present time. He served one term as United States Attorney for the Northern District of California. From 1946-1967 he was associated with Judge George E. Crothers. He was chief counsel for the chief engineer during the construction of the Golden Gate Bridge. He volunteered in World War II and was assigned to the Judge Advocate General's Office as captain. He served on the Pearl Harbor Board of Inquiry and later conducted a supplemental investigation which resulted in military improvements. By the end of his career he was a lieutenant colonel. For his outstanding service he received the Legion of Merit Award, plus other honors.

Clausen was married to Miss Virginia Palmer and four children have been born of this union: Henry, Jr., Florian, Donald, and Karen.

He has been active in many civic, charitable, and patriotic organizations and is listed in Who's Who in America.

He became a Mason in Engleside Lodge No. 630, of San Francisco, in 1935, and served this lodge as Worshipful Master in 1940. He served the Grand Lodge of California as Grand Master in 1954; was Exalted in San Francisco Chapter No. 1, R.A.M., in 1956; and was Greeted in California Council No. 2, R. & S.M., in 1956. He was Knighted in California Commandery No. 1, K.T., in 1956, and received the Scottish Rite degrees in the San Francisco Scottish Rite Bodies. In 1947 he was honored with the Rank and Decoration of Knight Commander of the Court of Honour; he was Coroneted an Inspector General of the Thirty-Third Degree in 1951; and several months later was appointed Deputy of the Supreme Council in California. He was Crowned Sovereign Grand Inspector General in 1955, served the Supreme Council in many ways and became Deputy Grand Commander in 1967. Upon the retirement of Grand Commander Luther A. Smith in 1969, he became Sovereign Grand Commander of the

Scottish Rite, Southern Jurisdiction.

He has been a prolific writer of short messages, editorials in the *New Age Magazine*, and many books of outstanding value on various Masonic, civic, and patriotic subjects.

REFERENCES

Who's Who in America. Mimeographed material on file in the House of the Temple, Scottish Rite Library, in Washington, D.C.

8. HENRY WILSON COIL, SR.

Henry Wilson Coil, Sr., was born on December 12, 1885, at Denison, Texas. He received his formal education at Colorado College, Colorado Springs, Colorado, receiving the Bachelor of Arts Degree in 1910. He then attended the University of Denver and received the Bachelor of Law Degree. He joined many college fraternities and was a Phi Beta Kappa. He became a lawyer and started practice in Trinidad, Colorado. In 1918 he moved to Riverside, California. Between 1926 and 1955 he was general counsel for the California Electric Power Company, and afterward was engaged in private practice.

Coil became a Mason in 1916 in Las Animas Lodge No. 28, of Colorado, and later affiliated with Riverside Lodge No. 635, of California, serving this lodge as the second Worshipful Master. For years he was a member of the Grand Lodge Committee on Masonic Information. He was a member of the following appendant bodies: Riverside Chapter No. 67, R.A.M., having joined in 1917; Valley Council No. 27, R. & S.M., having joined in 1917; Riverside Commandery, K.T., having joined in 1922 and served as E.C. in 1929; the Long Beach Scottish Rite Bodies, having joined in 1926. He received the Thirty-Third Degree in 1957, and was a Fellow of the Philalethes Society.

He was the author of many articles on Masonic subjects plus a number of Masonic books. He is best remembered today for his monumental *Masonic Encyclopedia*. He departed this life on January 29, 1974.

REFERENCES

Phil. Mag., June, 1974, 63. *Coil's Masonic Encyclopedia,* p. X. 7 ALR 415 (1959).

9. LEWIS C. WES COOK

Lewis C. Wes Cook was born on May 20, 1929, at Weston, Missouri. He was given the name Lewis Calvert Cook, but later changed it officially to Lewis C. Wes Cook. The "Wes" was adopted by him for his radio and professional entertainment work. He was married to Miss Victoria Stevens, of Brattleboro, Vermont, and three children have blessed this union: Robert, Edwina, and Cathy.

Cook was formally educated in the public schools of Weston and North Kansas City, the Juilliard School of Music in New York, the Chicago Conservatory of Music, and the Kansas City Conservatory of Music. He studied musical composition under Dr. France Buebendorf and Dr. Roger Sessions. He did graduate work in English and history at the University of California at Los Angeles, Bockhurst College, and the University of Missouri at Kansas City.

He embarked on a musical career by playing piano with seven famous bands and the United States Marine Corps Band. He has also written and arranged music for these bands, and has written a number of serious musical compositions, one of which was performed by the Los Angeles Symphony Orchestra. In 1950 he started doing radio work as an announcer and later as a newscaster, branching out into the writing field and the teaching of writing and journalism at schools and special seminars. He has also had experience as an actor with the Pasadena California Playhouse and other places.

In 1953 Cook became a news writer and editorial supervisor with the Associated Press in Kansas City. He has been accredited as a science writer for the Associated Press because of his special studies in aerospace, nuclear physics, cloud physics, radio astronomy, quasi-stellar radio sources, cosmology, chemistry, and scientific investigation. He is a member of Sigma Delta Chi, a professional journalism fraternity.

He became a Master Mason on July 18, 1957, in Weston Lodge No. 53, and served the lodge as Worshipful Master in 1961. Between 1964 and 1972 he was a member of the Grand Lodge Committee on Masonic Education, and served as chairman of this committee between 1967 and 1971. As a member of this committee he was active in the work of the Midwest Conference on Masonic Education. He served as a member of the board of directors of the Masonic Home of Missouri, and for years was the Grand Representative of the Grand Lodge of New Hampshire. In 1970 he was appointed editor of *The Missouri Freemason*, the official publication of the Grand Lodge of Missouri. He served as Grand Master of the Grand Lodge of Missouri in 1975-1976.

He did outstanding work with the Midwest Conference on Masonic Education, and attended the conference for the first time in 1963 at Cedar Rapids, Iowa. The following year he served as chairman of the program committee and presided at the conference when it met in St. Louis. In 1965 he was elected vice president of the conference and presented a talk entitled "Masonic Education for the Candidate." In 1966 he was president of the conference and gave a demonstration with other members on presenting a book review at a lodge meeting. Each year thereafter, until 1975, he attended the conference and took an active part in programs.

In 1964 he was appointed editor of the Missouri Lodge of Research and served until 1979. In 1970 he was elected a Fellow of the lodge, one of four members so honored. In 1973-1974 he served the lodge as Worshipful Master. During the years he was editor of the lodge he supervised the publication of many fine volumes until he became burdened with the duties of an officer of the Grand Lodge.

Cook is a member of many appendant bodies of the Craft. Among them are the following: He was Exalted in Weston Chapter No. 4, R.A.M.; he served this Chapter as High Priest in 1963-1964, and served as Grand High Priest in 1973-1974.

In 1971 he wrote a booklet entitled *"York Rite Public Relations Guide"* for the Grand Chapter. In 1963 he joined Liberty Council No. 50, R. & S.M., and served as I.M. in 1970. He joined Weston Commandery No. 2 in 1962, and was Eminent Commander in 1968-1969. He was elected a Fellow of the Philalethes Society, and holds membership in the following groups: Order of High Priesthood; Order of the Silver Trowel; Past Commanders Association; Knights York Cross of Honour; Mary Conclave, Red Cross of Constantine; Lord of Lord Tabernacle, K.T.P.; the Scottish Rite; the Shrine; Weston Chapter No. 197, Order of the Eastern Star, serving as Patron; Advisory Board of the Order of DeMolay, 1965-1968, and Chapter Dad, 1965-1967. In 1973 he was elected an honorary member of Kansas City Chapter No. 63, National Sojourners.

REFERENCES

Missouri Grand Lodge Proceedings, 1976, pp. i-ii (has his picture). Proceedings of Grand Chapter, R.A.M., of Missouri, 1974, pp. i-iii (has his picture).

10. RAY V. DENSLOW

Ray V. Denslow was born on March 6, 1885, at Spickard, Missouri, the son of William Marvin Denslow and Malinda Schooler Denslow. He attended the local public schools and, after graduating from high school, attended the University of Missouri between 1903 and 1907. Upon graduating from that school he married Clara Alice Marrifield, in Columbia, and one son was born of the marriage, William R. The new family lived in Trenton, Macon, and St. Louis, and then returned to Trenton to make it their permanent home. In 1909 he entered the photography and newspaper business with his father, publishing the *Trenton Daily News*. But he left that business to become assistant postmaster at Trenton, serving until 1921. After that time he devoted his entire time to Masonic work.

He was raised in Twilight Lodge No. 114, at the request of Censer Lodge No. 172, on his twenty-first birthday. Soon thereafter he joined the York Rite Bodies. He served as the presiding officer of all the Masonic Bodies of Trenton and became qualified for membership in Missouri Priory No. 17, Knights of the York Cross of Honour. He joined the Scottish Rite, receiving the Thirty-Third Degree in 1935, and was a member of Moila Shrine Temple. He served as Grand Master of the Grand Lodge of Missouri in 1931.

Denslow served in the highest office of practically all Masonic Bodies of Missouri. He was Grand High Priest of Missouri in 1919-1920; General Grand High Priest of the General Grand Chapter, 1942-1946; Grand Sovereign of the Grand Imperial Council of the Red Cross of Constantine of the United States 1943-1944. He received the Legion of Honor Award of the Order of DeMolay in 1927, and was an early Fellow of the Philalethes Society. He has received many Masonic honors, medals, and certificates.

He was active as an unofficial ambassador of good will in creating communications between Grand Lodges all over the world. He took an active part after World War II to investigate various reactivated Grand Lodges and helped establish their regularity.

His permanent contribution to the Masonic world was the creation of *The Royal Arch Mason Magazine* when he was General Grand High Priest in 1942. He was the editor of this fine magazine from the beginning until 1946 when his son, William R. Denslow, became the business manager and increased the number of subscribers. He wrote the correspondence reports for the Grand Lodge of Missouri for many years, and has written many articles, booklets, and books on Masonic subjects. He was one of the early workers in the Missouri Lodge of Research and was the author of many of the early volumes published by this lodge.

He departed this life on September 10, 1960.

REFERENCES

14 Build. Mag., 44; has his picture. W. R. Denslow, *10,000 Famous Freemasons*, Vol. 1, p. 306, and Vol. 4, 386. Phil. Mag., Oct., 1960, 67; Oct., 1960, 67, 96; Dec., 1958, 91. *Masonic World of R. V. Denslow*, 212. *Through Masonic Windows*, STB, Feb., 1961.

11. WILLIAM R. DENSLOW

William R. Denslow was born on May 2, 1916, the only child of Ray V. Denslow. His formal education was received in the public schools of Kansas City and St. Louis, and he was graduated from Trenton High School in 1933. In 1930-1935 he attended Kemper Military Academy at Boonville. In the summer of 1934 he attended Universitad National de Mexico and then attended the University of Missouri in 1936-1938, receiving the Bachelor of Arts Degree in 1937 and the Bachelor of Journalism Degree in 1938. He engaged in various types of work including that of news writing for Radio Station WGN, in Chicago, 1941-1948. In 1948 he returned to Trenton, Missouri. He was married to Juanita Margaret Daly, in Chicago, on November 18, 1939. During World War II he served in the United States Army. He has been active in many civic organizations.

He became a Mason in Trenton Lodge No. 111, in 1937, and served the lodge as Worshipful Master in 1955-1958. He was Grand Master of Missouri in 1967. He was Exalted in Trenton Chapter No. 66, R.A.M., in 1938, and was High Priest in 1949; he served as Grand High Priest in 1961. He was greeted in Trenton Council No. 37, R. & S.M., in 1939; was Knighted in Godfrey de Bouillon Commandery No. 24, K.T., in 1939, and was Commander in 1950. He became a member of St. John's Conclave No. 1, Red Cross of Constantine, and in 1949 affiliated with St. Chrysostom Conclave No. 36, of Columbia, serving as Missouri Sovereign in 1961-1962. He was elected to Missouri Priory No. 17, K.Y.C.H., in 1950. He received the Scottish Rite degrees in the Valley of Kansas City in 1938; he then transferred to the Valley of Chicago in 1944, and in 1959 affiliated with the Valley of St. Louis. He joined Moila Temple of the Shrine in 1949, and is a member of many other Masonic organizations and holds many honorary memberships.

He is a Blue Friar and a Fellow of the

Philalethes Society, and was president of the Society between 1970 and 1973.

REFERENCES

The Royal Arch Mason, Summer, 1978 issue, page 292 et seq. has a full scale biography with many pictures taken of him at various times of his life.

12. ROBERT FREKE GOULD

Robert Freke Gould was born in 1836, at Ilfracombe, Devon, England. In 1854 he joined the British Army and later that year was comissioned as a lieutenant; he served with distinction in North China in 1860-1862. On his return to England he studied law and became a barrister in 1868.

He became a Mason in Royal Naval Lodge No. 429, in 1854, joined Friendship Lodge at Gibraltar in 1857, and served as Worshipful Master of Inhabitan's Lodge at Gibraltar. He was the founder and first Master of Meriden Lodge No. 743, a military lodge attached to his regiment, the First East Surrey, then in Poona. He was also the founder and first Master of King Solomon's Temple Lodge No. 3464. In 1863 he was Master of Northern Lodge No. 570, in China, and in 1875 became a member of Moira Lodge of London. He served on the Board of General Purposes, and became Past Grand Warden in 1913. He was a member of Melita Chapter No. 349, R.A.M., of Gibraltar, and served as First Principal of Moira Chapter in London. Gould was one of the founders of Quatuor Coronati Lodge, and was the second Master of the lodge in 1887.

He was one of the pioneers in modern Masonic research and wrote many good Masonic books which have been reprinted over the years.

He departed this life on March 25, 1915.

REFERENCES

1 Build. Mag. 124 (1915). 1 AQC 73 (1886-1888). 28 AQC 111 (1915). W. R. Denslow, *10,000 Famous Freemasons,* Vol. 2, p. 132.

13. DR. STEPHEN R. GREENBERG

Stephen R. Greenberg was born on May 27, 1927, at Omaha, Nebraska. He received his professional education at St. Louis University, in St. Louis. He is a physician and for many years has been Associate Professor of Pathology at the Chicago Medical School. He and his wife Connie have two sons.

He is a member of the following professional associations: Fellow of the American Association for the Advancement of Science, New York Academy of Science, American Association of Clinical Scientists, International Academy of Pathology, Chicago Pathological Society, American Medical Association, and the American Society of Clinical Pathology. He has written many articles in medical journals on the subject of pathology and is recognized in the medical profession as a leader in this field of medicine.

Greenberg joined the Craft and many of the appendant bodies while living in Omaha, Nebraska. He is now a member of the following Masonic groups: Lawn Lodge No. 815; The Scottish Rite Bodies of Chicago, being a recipient of the Meritorious Service Award for his degree work and as a member of the Speaker's Bureau; Logan Chapter No. 196, R.A.M., having served as Excellent High Priest; Temple Council No. 65, R. & S.M., having served as Thrice Illustrious Master; he received the honorary degree of Super Excellent Master in Decatur, Illinois; Mizpah Commandery No. 73, K.T. El Jaala Grotto; Medinah Temple Shrine; Maple Chapter No. 90, Order of the Eastern Star; Wilmington Court No. 13, Order of the Amaranthe; Elmhurst Conclave No. 41, Order of True Kindred; York Rite College No. 15; The Philalethes Society, and The Illinois Lodge of Research.

At present he is a member of the Illinois Grand Lodge Committee on Masonic Education.

He has written extensively on Masonic subjects with his articles appearing in many Masonic periodicals. He has also developed a large number of audio-visual programs which he has been presenting to Masonic audiences for many years.

14. FORREST D. HAGGARD

Forrest D. Haggard was born on April

21, 1925, at Trumbull, Nebraska, the son of Arthur M. Haggard and Grace Hadley Haggard. He received his formal education in the public schools of Trumbull and Cozad, Nebraska, and Sterling, Colorado, and was graduated from Scottsbluff, Nebraska, High School in 1941. He then attended pre-engineering courses, but in 1944 entered Phillips University, a Christian Church school, enrolling in the College of the Bible. He received the following degrees from that University: Bachelor of Arts, Master of Divinity, and Doctor of Divinity. He has done work in the following schools: University of Nebraska, Lexington Theological Seminary in Kentucky, and received a Master's Degree in Psychology from the University of Missouri in Kansas City. In 1946 he was married to Miss Eleanor V. Evans and they are the parents of three children: Warren A., William Dean, and Katherine Ann. He began his work as a minister in 1945 when he became pastor of the Church of Christ at Lyman, Nebraska. He served a number of other churches and was formally ordained in 1948 at Central Church, Enid, Oklahoma. In 1953 he became pastor of the Overland Park, Kansas, Christian Church, which consisted of a congregation of 30 persons meeting in a downtown theater, and under his skilled leadership the church has grown in number and in services rendered to people in the community.

He became a Mason in 1946, in Keiffer Lodge No. 488, of Oklahoma. He dimitted and affiliated with other lodges as he moved from place to place in connection with his work. In 1966 he became a charter member of Ancient Form Lodge No. 34 of Kansas. He served as Grand Master of the Grand Lodge of Kansas in 1974, and is a member of the York Rite, the Scottish Rite, the Shrine, the Order of the Eastern Star, the Philalethes Society, the Missouri Lodge of Research, and other Masonic groups.

He has presented papers before the Midwest Conference on Masonic Education and has written an outstanding book, *The Clergy and the Craft,* which was published by the Missouri Lodge of Research in 1970.

REFERENCES

The Clergy and the Craft, pp. ix to xii. Ben W. Graybill, *History of Kansas Masonry,* p. 103 (1975). Grand Lodge Proceedings of Kansas, 1974-1975, pp. 224-225. The Freemason (Canada), July-August, 1974, p. 9.

15. CONRAD HAHN

Conrad Hahn was born on December 12, 1906, at Fuerte, Sinaloa, Mexico, of missionary parents. He received his formal education at the Scranton, Pennsylvania, Central High School: Yale University, where he received a Bachelor of Arts Degree in 1928; and Columbia University, where he received a Master of Arts Degree in 1933. While at Yale University he received the Phi Beta Kappa Key. He started work as a teacher of Latin in Suffield Academy in Connecticut and served the school as head master for 11 years. He became editor of the Masonic Service Association in 1958, and a few years later became executive secretary, a position he occupied until his sudden passing.

He became a Mason in Apollo Lodge No. 59 and served this lodge as Worshipful Master in 1944. Later he acquired dual membership in Bethesda Lodge No. 204, Maryland. He was made an Honorary Life Member of Leonard Wood Lodge No. 105 of the Philippines. He served the Grand Lodge of Connecticut as Grand Master in 1957-1958. He joined the following appendant bodies, all of Bridgeport, Connecticut: Jerusalem Chapter No. 13 in 1957; Jerusalem Council No. 16 in 1957; Hamilton Commandery No. 5, K.T., in 1958; and Lafayette Scottish Rite Bodies in 1958. He received the Thirty-Third degree in 1962, and belonged to many Masonic groups including the following: Red Cross of Constantine, Royal Order of Scotland, Fellow of the Philalethes Society, Blue Friars, and the National Sojourners.

He was the author of many *Short Talk Bulletins* and Digests of the Masonic Service Association. He was an accomplished public speaker and presented many outstanding talks throughout the country.

184

He departed this life quietly in his sleep on December 15, 1977.

REFERENCES

Phil. Mag., April, 1978, 14, has his picture. Dwight L. Smith, Ind. Free., Feb., 1978, 8. K.T. Mag., Feb., 1978, 27. STB, Feb., 1978.

16. HARRY L. HAYWOOD

Harry L. Haywood was born on November 1, 1886, near Mulberry, Ohio. He was graduated from Cedarville, Ohio, High School and for short periods of time attended a theological seminary in Dayton, Ohio, and Lawrenceville College at Appleton, Wisconsin. He was chiefly self-educated. He told me on one occasion that he would read a book and then go over it a second time formulating questions and writing them in a notebook. He would then study the book by going over the questions until he could answer each of them without looking at the book. He was ordained a minister at the age of 18. Upon becoming a Mason he found his lifework as he became a full-time Masonic researcher and writer.

He became a Mason in Acacia Lodge No. 176, of Webster City, Iowa, in 1915; later he affiliated with Waterloo Lodge No. 105; with Publicity Lodge No. 1000, of New York; and still later with Mizpah Lodge No. 639 of Cedar Rapids, Iowa. He joined Tabernacle Chapter, R.A.M., of Waterloo, Iowa, and the Scottish Rite Bodies of Davenport, Iowa. He served as editor of *The Builder Magazine* in 1917. Between 1925 and 1930 he was editor of the *New York Masonic Outlook*. For many years he was employed by the Masonic History Company of Chicago and produced many of his books during this period. He later was employed by the Iowa Masonic Library as a researcher and writer, and many of his items appeared in the *Iowa Grand Lodge Bulletin*. Most of these items have been reproduced in two volumes published by the Missouri Lodge of Research under the titles of *Masonic Curiosa* and *The Masonic Essays of H. L. Haywood*. He was a prolific writer and an outstanding Masonic speaker.

He departed this life on February 25, 1956, at Cedar Rapids, Iowa.

REFERENCES

N.Y. Mas. Out., April, 1925, 161, his first issue as editor; has his picture. His memorial table, Phil. Mag., June, 1959, 38. Proc. of the Midw. Conf., 1979. Phil. Mag., Oct., 1956, has his picture on front cover. Mackey's Rev. Ency. of Free., after Preface (1946). STB, Feb. 1957. The Iowa Masonic Library has a file with his biographical data. In this file is a questionnaire prepared by me and sent to him to give me information about his life; he cooperated by answering each question. Later this matter was supplemented by work done by Jerry Marsengill. 1979 Pro. Mid. Conf. 65.

17. RONALD E. HEATON

Ronald E. Heaton was born on November 16, 1898, at Norristown, Pennsylvania. He received his formal education in the public schools of Norristown, Pennsylvania, and was graduated from Norristown High School in 1917. He followed the occupation of accounting and finance and worked as a corporate officer for many years, and for a long period he was secretary and assistant treasurer of the Synthane Corporation.

He is a member of the Valley Forge Historical Society, the Historical Society of Pennsylvania, and the Montgomery County Historical Society. He has been awarded two national Honor Certificates from the Freedom Foundation of Valley Forge. Heaton has written three non-Masonic books relating to history in Norristown and Valley Forge.

He became a Mason in Charity Lodge No. 190 in 1944. At the present time he holds the following memberships: Norristown Chapter No. 190, R.A.M.; Cryptic Council No. 21, R. & S.M.; Hutchinson Commandery No. 32, K.T.; Scottish Rite, Valley of Allentown, receiving the Thirty-Third degree in 1977; American Lodge of Research; Missouri Lodge of Research; Society of Blue Friars; Fellow of the Philalethes Society, and served the Society as treasurer between 1959 and 1979; corresponding member of Quatour Coronati

Lodge; recipient of the James R. Case Medal of Excellence from the Connecticut Research Lodge.

He has been active in the Masonic literary quarries for years and has done extensive research of original records. His book *Masonic Membership of the Founding Fathers* has become a classic since its first publication. He has written many Digests for the Masonic Service Association and has collaborated on several items with James R. Case and Harold V. B. Voorhis.

REFERENCES

7 ALR 416 (1963).

18. ROSS HEPBURN

Ross Hepburn was born in 1898, at Christchurch, New Zealand. He received his formal education at the Christchurch Boys' High School and at Canterbury University. He received the Bachelor of Laws Degree in 1920, the Master of Laws Degree in 1930, the Bachelor of Commerce Degree in 1933, and the Doctor of Laws Degree in 1927. In 1919 he was admitted as a solicitor and in 1920 as a barrister. In 1933 he was admitted as a chartered accountant, and has served in many commercial and civic associations.

He became a Mason in Lodge Riccarton No. 276 in 1927, and served the lodge as Worshipful Master in 1939. He was Exalted in Prince of Wales Chapter, R.A.M., in 1930, and served as an officer for a number of years. He has served the Grand Lodge of New Zealand in many ways since 1940.

He has been active in Masters' and Past Masters' Lodge No. 130, a Masonic research lodge, being a full member since 1939 and serving as secretary between 1939 and 1942; Worshipful Master in 1942; secretary again between 1943 and 1954. His greatest work with the lodge has been as editor of the *Transactions*, serving from 1939 to 1956 and again from 1966 to date.

He has been active in many appendant bodies, and is an honorary member of many Masonic organizations. He is a Fellow of the Philalethes Society, and has written many articles that have appeared in Masonic periodicals all over the world.

REFERENCES

Phil. Mag., April, 1956, 25; has his picture on page 19.

19. MERVIN B. HOGAN

Mervin B. Hogan was born on July 21, 1906, at Woods Cross, Utah. His formal education was as follows: University of Utah, receiving the Bachelor of Science Degree in 1927; University of Pittsburgh, receiving the Master of Science Degree in 1929; University of Utah, receiving the Mechanical Engineering Degree in 1930; University of Michigan, receiving the Doctor of Philosophy Degree in 1936; Yale University, Sterling Fellow in Mechanical Engineering, 1937 and 1938. He has been employed by many large companies in the field of electrical engineering plus a number of schools. He is a registered engineer in many states and a member in many professional societies. In connection with his professional work he has written articles published in engineering magazines.

In 1929 he was married to Miss Helen Emily Reese and they have one son, Edward Reese Hogan.

He became a Mason in 1947 in Wasatch Lodge No. 1 of Salt Lake City, Utah, and served the lodge as Worshipful Master. He has served the Grand Lodge of Utah as follows: Grand Chaplain in 1954, Grand Orator in 1955 and 1956. He joined Utah Chapter No. 1, R.A.M., in 1941; Utah Council No. 1, R. & S.M., in 1941; Utah Commandery No. 1, K.T., in 1942,; and the Scottish Rite Bodies of Utah in 1942, receiving the Thirty-Third degree in 1963. He has been honored with the DeMolay Legion of Honor award. He is a member of the Philalethes Society and a member of the Order of Blue Friars.

He has been a Mason and a Mormon for many years and has written extensively on the subject of the relationship of Freemasonry and the Mormons since he is in a unique position to know the nature of both organizations.

20. ALEX HORNE

Alex Horne was born on December 20, 1897, at Odessa, Russia. He received his college training at Tufts University, Medford, Massachusetts, and received the Degree of Bachelor of Science in Electrical Engineering.

For years he conducted the Horne Machinery Company in San Francisco, California, but is now retired.

He received the Masonic degrees in 1925 in Sinim Lodge (Massachusetts Constitution), then located at Shanghai. He is now a member of Starr King Lodge No. 344 of San Francisco.

He has served the Grand Lodge of California in many ways and was instrumental in setting up and organizing the Grand Lodge Library many years ago. For a number of years he served as chairman of the Library Committee.

Horne is a member of the San Francisco Bodies of the Scottish Rite and at present is Orator Emeritus. He received the Thirty-Third Degree in 1969.

He is a Fellow of the Philalethes Society and a full member of Quatuor Coronati Lodge, and has written many articles which have appeared in the *Transactions* of Quatuor Coronati Lodge, the Philalethes Society magazine, and other publications. His book *King Solomon's Temple in the Masonic Tradition*, published in 1972, is the most complete ever written on the subject.

REFERENCES

Oregon Freemason, Sept., 1977; has his biographical sketch and his picture.

21. WILLIAM J. HUGHAN

William J. Hughan was born on February 13, 1841, in Devonshire, England. As a boy he became an apprentice draper and later joined a wholesale firm in Plymouth; still later he went to Manchester and then to Truro. He retired from business in 1883, settled in Torquay and devoted his full time to Masonic research.

He was made a Mason in St. Aubyn Lodge No. 954, of Devenport, in 1863. The following year he became a member of Emulation Lodge of Improvement, London. When he moved to Truro he joined Phoenix Lodge of Honor & Prudence No. 331, and served the lodge as secretary for a time. In 1866 he affiliated with Fortitude Lodge No. 131, and he served the lodge as Master in 1868 and in 1878. He was Exalted in Glasgow Chapter No. 50, R.A.M., in Scotland in 1865, and became a member of Kilwinning Chapter No. 80. He received many honorary titles from numerous Grand Lodges in recognition of his work as a skilled researcher and scholar. He was made a Senior Grand Warden of the Grand Lodge of Iowa, and an honorary member and Past High Priest of Lafayette Chapter No. 5, of Washington, D.C. He was one of the founders of Quatuor Coronati Lodge. He assisted Robert Freke Gould in the writing of his famous history, and is remembered today for the great amount of original research that he did for the Craft.

He departed this life on May 20, 1911.

REFERENCES

24 AQC 4, 148 (1911). W. R. Denslow, *10,000 Famous Freemasons*, Vol. 2, p. 265.

22. BRUCE H. HUNT

Bruce H. Hunt was born on January 29, 1913, at Forest City, Missouri. He received his formal education in the public schools of Kirksville, Missouri, and was graduated from the high school in New Bloomfield, Missouri, in 1931. He then served an apprenticeship in mechanical dentistry and later operated the Superior Dental Laboratory in Kirksville. On December 26, 1936, he was married to Miss Irene Spencer and born of this union are a son, Stephen Dennis, and a daughter, Suzanne. He has been a member of the Missouri State Historical Society since 1946, and was a charter member and helped form the Missouri State Dental Laboratory Association, serving the group as president for one year and as secretary for two years.

In 1966 he was appointed by the Governor of Missouri to a six-year term on the Board of Regents of Northeast Missouri State Teachers College and served the board as secretary in 1969. He has also served as a director of the National Bank of Kirksville.

He became a Mason in Adair Lodge No. 366, of Kirksville, in 1935-1936, and served the lodge as Worshipful Master in 1940. He has served the Grand Lodge of Missouri in the following ways: District Deputy Grand Master, 1940-1946; Masonic Home Board, 1957-1961; Grand Master in 1960. He joined Caldwell Chapter No. 53, R.A.M., in 1936; serving as High Priest in 1941; Grand Lecturer of the Grand Chapter, 1946-1960; and Grand Secretary in 1960. He joined Kirksville Council No. 44, R. & S.M., in 1937; served as Master in 1942; Grand Master of the Grand Council in 1951; Grand Lecturer, 1952-1960; Grand Recorder, 1960; General Grand Recorder of the General Grand Council, 1966. Hunt joined Ely Commandery No. 22, K.T., in 1939 and was Commander in 1944; and in the Grand Commandery he was Grand Recorder in 1960. He was elected a member of St. Chrysostom Conclave No. 36 of the Red Cross of Constantine in 1945, and served as Sovereign in 1952. He joined the Scottish Rite Bodies of St. Louis in 1957 and received the Thirty-Third Degree in 1971. He joined Moila Shrine in 1944 and is an honorary member of Ararat Temple. He was named a Fellow of the Philalethes Society in 1964, and holds honorary memberships in many Masonic groups.

Since 1946 he has been a full-time employee of the York Rite Masonic Bodies of Missouri.

Since 1962 he has prepared a review of the Grand Lodge proceedings of the Grand Lodge of Missouri, which has been printed as part of the Grand Lodge *Proceedings*. These have been an excellent summary of what has taken place within the Craft during the year. A selection of these reviews was edited by Earl K. Dille and appeared as Volume 33 of the *Transactions of the Missouri Lodge of Research* in 1977. He has also written numerous articles which have appeared in various Masonic periodicals over the years.

REFERENCES

Masonic Review of Bruce H. Hunt, pp. 212-214; also has his picture.

23. ALBERT G. MACKEY

Albert G. Mackey was born on March 12, 1807, at Charleston, South Carolina. He received a classical basic education. He taught school for a time and was graduated from the Charleston Medical College in 1834 and practiced medicine until 1854. In 1836 he was married to Miss Sarah Pamela Hubbell. In 1842 he started to devote a great deal of his time to writing. In 1865 he was appointed Collector of the Port of Charleston and was elected a delegate to the Reconstruction of the Constitutional Convention and served as its president. When the legislature met under the new Constitution to choose a United States Senator, he lacked one vote to being elected.

He became a Mason in 1841 in St. Andrews Lodge No. 10 of Charleston; later affiliated with Solomon's Lodge No. 1, and served as its Master in 1842. He helped form Landmark Lodge No. 76. After he moved to Washington, D.C., he affiliated with La Fayette Lodge No. 19, and served as Grand Secretary of South Carolina from 1842 to 1847. Mackey was active in all branches of the Craft. He served as Grand High Priest of South Carolina, 1855-1867, and as General Grand High Priest, 1859-1868. He was active in the work of the Scottish Rite, becoming an active member of the Supreme Council in 1844, and later that year becoming Secretary General, a position he held until his death.

His first Masonic book was *A Lexicon of Freemasonry*, written in 1845, which was later to be expanded to his *Encyclopedia of Freemasonry*.He was to write many other Masonic books over the years. He was a pioneer in doing Masonic research before doing any Masonic writing. Many of his works have been revised and expanded by others from time to time.

He departed this life on June 20, 1881, at Old Point Comfort, Virginia.

REFERENCES

C. S. Lobinger, *History of the Supreme Council*, pp. 157-162. W. R. Denslow, *10,000 Famous Freemasons*, Vol. 3, p. 116. Tex. Grd. L. Mag., Feb., 1951. Tom V. Canfield, *Albert Gallatin Mackey*, 1 Proc. of Ohio L. of Res. 7. Alvin B. Lowe, *Albert Gallatin Mackey*, K. T. Mag., Nov., 1973, 7. New Age Mag.,

April, 1932, 233; March, 1937, 153. Carter and Harris, *History of the Supreme Council*, Vol. 1, has many references to his work.

24. JERRY MARSENGILL

Jerald Edmond Marsengill, popularly known as "Jerry Marsengill" by his many friends, was born on April 20, 1930, at Russell, Iowa. He attended Trenton Junior College, graduating in 1960; later he attended Drake University, receiving a Bachelor of Arts Degree (summa cum laude) in 1977. He then did graduate work at Drake University, and has done writing and editing work for a number of non-Masonic magazines. For many years he was employed as a train dispatcher for the Chicago Rock Island Railroad. He was, for a time, president of the Young Republicans of Iowa and a member of the board of directors of Shut-Ins, Inc. He served two years in the United States Army in Korea.

He was made a Mason in Hiram Abiff Lodge No. 183, in 1958, and in 1963 joined Home Lodge No. 370. He was Worshipful Master of Hiram Lodge in 1962 and Worshipful Master of Home Lodge No. 370 in 1971. In 1971 he served on the Grand Lodge Committee on Review of Publications and for years has assisted the Iowa Committee on Masonic Education in its work. He has been active in York Rite Bodies, serving as Grand Royal Arch Priest in 1969. He joined the Scottish Rite Bodies in Des Moines in 1963, and was decorated with the rank of Knight Commander of the Court of Honour in 1979. He is a member of many Masonic organizations, including the following: The Grotto, serving as Monarch; Fellow of the Philalethes Society; Corresponding Member of Quatuor Coronati Lodge; the American Lodge of Research; the Order of the Eastern Star; and the Allied Masonic Degrees.

He was the leader in forming Iowa Research Lodge No. 2 and started it on its successful work. He has been a writer of many Masonic items for Masonic periodicals for years, and recently has been working as editor of the *Philalethes Magazine* and also of *The Royal Arch Mason* magazine.

REFERENCES

Iowa Grand Lodge Bulletin, Dec., 1978, p. 595; has his picture. 10 ALR 463 (1968).

25. ROB MORRIS

Robert William Peckham, known to us as Rob Morris, was born on August 31, 1818, near Boston, Massachusetts. He changed his name to Robert Morris and later changed it to Rob Morris to avoid being confused with another person with the same name. He was educated for the ministry, tried several business ventures, and then became a teacher; for a time he was the principal of Sylvan Academy, at Oxford, Mississippi. Then he became president of Oldham College in La Grange, Kentucky. Eventually he devoted all his time to writing on Masonic subjects.

He became a Mason in Oxford Lodge No. 33, in 1846, and later affiliated with other lodges. He was Grand Master of Kentucky in 1858-1859. He joined the Royal Arch in 1848 and the Cryptic Rite in 1850, and was a member of Robert Morris Commandery No. 8, K.T., in 1855-1857. He joined the Scottish Rite by becoming a member of the Fonda Yates group in 1855. For a time he was a controversial figure in the Craft when he sought to bring about a uniformity of the ritual by the formation of the Masonic Conservators and caused much divisiveness within the Craft all over the country.

He is remembered today as a prolific writer and publisher of Masonic books. He was the author of the most famous Masonic poem, and published a volume of Masonic poems. He rendered a valuable service to the Craft by publishing his 30-volume *Universal Masonic Library* containing some of the popular Masonic books of his day. Most members in the United States remember him as the author of the ritual of the Order of the Eastern Star.

He departed this life on July 31, 1888.

REFERENCES

The Families of Rob Morris and Robert Macoy, Phil. Mag., June, 1963, 47; also 8

ALR 409 (1960); with his picture. Lucien C. Rule *Pioneering in Masonry; the Life of Rob Morris*. Harold V. B. Voorhis, *The Eastern Star*, 1976 ed., pp. 5-15, has a good statement of his life and work. Charles S. Guthrie, *Rob Morris and the Early Years of the Grand Lodge of Kentucky*, Phil. Mag., Feb., 1975, 19. Iowa Grand Lodge Bulletin, Nov., 1939, pp. 291-301. STB, May, 1957.

26. JOSEPH FORT NEWTON

Joseph Fort Newton was born on July 21, 1880, at Decatur, Texas. His formal education as as follows; Coe College, Iowa, graduating in 1912; Tufts College, 1918; Temple University, 1929. He became an ordained clergyman in 1893 and served in churches in Paris, Texas and St. Louis, Missouri. He was the founder and pastor of the People's Church in Dixon, Illinois, in 1901 and lived there until 1908. He then served a church in Cedar Rapids, Iowa, from 1908 to 1916. Between 1916 and 1919 he served the City Temple of London, England. Between 1919 and 1925 he served the Church of the Divine Paternity of New York City, and between 1925 and 1930 served the Church of St. Paul, in Philadelphia. Between 1930 and 1935 he served St. James Church, in Philadelphia, and served Luke and Epiphany Church, of Philadelphia, from 1938 until his passing.

While serving as a minister during these years he wrote a religious column for a daily newspaper, books on religious subjects, collections of sermons, and other books of general interest.

He became a Mason in Friendship Lodge No. 7, of Dixon, Illinois, in1902; later he affiliated with Hermon Lodge No. 263 of Cedar Rapids, Iowa, and then affiliated with Lodge No. 51 of Philadelphia. He served the Grand Lodge of Iowa as Grand Chaplain, 1911-1913. He became Grand Prelate of the Grand Encampment in 1933. He joined the Scottish Rite in Cedar Rapids, Iowa, in 1909 and received the Thirty-Third Degree in 1933.

While living in Cedar Rapids he discovered the world of Masonic books and realized that there was a need for a small book explaining the Craft to new members. The result was that he wrote *The Builders*, which has become the most widely read Masonic book in the world. At the beginning a copy was presented to each new member who joined a lodge in Iowa. He was to be active in the work of the National Masonic Research Society and wrote a monthly column for its magazine, *The Builder*. He was to write many *Short Talk Bulletins* for the Masonic Service Association.

He departed this life on January 24, 1950.

REFERENCES

Autobiography: River of Years, published in 1946; reviewed in New Age Magazine, May, 1946, p. 311. H. L. Haywood, *Masonic Essays*, p. 109. Altar Light, March-May, 1979. Phil. Mag., April-May, 1950, page 8. Supreme Council, NMJ, ed. of *The Builders* has a biographical sketch. The *New Age Magazine* published a series of monthly articles while he was in London in which he told of his experiences there.

27. STEWART M. L. POLLARD

Stewart M. L. Pollard was born on May 31, 1922, at Lyman, Maine. His family and ancestors for many years had been members of the Craft and his father, Ralph J. Pollard, served the Grand Lodge of Maine as Grand Master and also wrote a history of Freemasonry of that state plus other books on Masonic subjects.

He received his formal education in the public schools of Wenonah, New Jersey; Lowell, Massachusetts; Waldoboro, Maine; and then went to Bowdoin College, at Brunswick, Maine. On December 6, 1946, he was married to Miss Margaret Louise Russell and of this union there has been born a daughter, Carol Le, and a son, Bruce Edward.

Early in life he became a professional soldier, following in the footsteps of his illustrious father. He served in the Pacific Theater during World War II and later was on occupation duty in Japan and Germany. He received a battlefield commission in Korea and was awarded the Silver Star for "gallantry in action." On the literary side he has written articles for numerous military periodicals. Upon his retirement from the army he was secretary of the National Sojourners and retained this position until he became secretary-treasurer of the Masonic Service Association on the passing of Conrad Hahn.

He is a member of the following associations: The National Society of the Sons of the American Revolution; National Association for Uniformed Services; Knox Memorial Association; Pearl Harbor Survivors Association; Waldoborough, Maine, Historical Society; and the Reserve Officers Association..

He became a Mason in King Solomon's Lodge No. 61, of Waldoboro, Maine, in November, 1944. In 1947 he dimitted and affiliated with Columbia Lodge No. 200 of Greenville, Maine. In 1967 he dimitted and affiliated with Ralph J. Pollard Lodge No. 217 of Orrington, Maine (the lodge is named after his father). In 1963 he affiliated by dual membership with Alt Heidelberg Lodge No. 821, Germany, and served this lodge as Worshipful Master in 1965. He is an honorary member in: Carl zur Eintracht Lodge, Mannheim, Germany; Arminius Lodge No. 25 of the District of Columbia, a German-speaking lodge; Amity Lodge No. 1, Tapei, China; Major General Henry Knox Lodge, Boston, Massachusetts; an Honorary Past Master of Ruprecht zu den Funf Rosen Lodge No. 372 of Heidelberg, Germany; Pythagorous Lodge of Research, Washington, D.C.; Masonic Veterans' Association of South Dakota; Grand Lodge of Montana with the title of Past Senior Grand Warden; Grand Lodge of South Dakota; and The Virginia Craftsmen.

He is a Fellow of the Philalethes Society and a member of the Masonic Club of Delaware. In 1979 he was the Anson Jones Lecturer at a meeting of the Texas Lodge of Research, and the Louis A. Prese Lecturer, Scottish Rite Bodies of Dallas, Texas. He is a member of all the York Rite Bodies. He is a member of the Scottish Rite, and has received the Thirty-Third Degree. He is active in the Order of the Eastern Star, the Order of DeMolay, and many other Masonic groups.

In the Masonic literary quarries he is best known as the author of *Tied to Ma-sonic Apron Strings*, published by the Missouri Lodge of Research, being a collection of humorous Masonic items.

REFERENCES

Sketch appears in *Tied to Masonic Apron Strings* with his picture. STB, September, 1967 (about his father and mother).

28. AEMIL POULER

Aemil Pouler was born on April 20, 1916, at Istanbul, Turkey. He received his formal education in the University of Byazit and Halki and was awarded the degree of Master of Philosophy; he then took postgraduate work towards a doctorate degree.

He is an Honorary Citizen of Texas and has been named an International Peace Gardner of North Dakota.

Pouler is a registered indexer of the Society of Indexers, London, England; a member of the Society of American Archivists; and a member of the Mid-Atlantic Regional Archivist Conference.

He is a member of St. John's Lodge No. 11 of Washington, D.C., and a member of the Scottish Rite. He has been honored by the Scottish Rite, Southern Jurisdiction, with the Thirty-Third Degree and the Grand Cross. He is a Member of the Philalethes Society.

For years he has been the managing editor of the *New Age Magazine,* official publication of the Scottish Rite Supreme Council, and has done an excellent job of classifying and indexing all original material in the House of the Temple, Washington. He has also supervised the chemical treatment of much of the material located there in order to preserve the items permanently. In recent years he has made index cards of all material in the *New Age Magazine* and also the *Transactions* of the Supreme Council, Southern Jurisdiction.

For years he has taken an active part in Scottish Rite Workshops and has presented papers of value at these meetings. He has written articles for *The New Age Magazine* plus a history of the Order of DeMolay in Maryland.

29. ALLEN E. ROBERTS

Allen E. Roberts was born on October 11, 1917, at Pawtucket, Rhode Island, received his formal education in the public schools of Rhode Island, and then continued his studies in the United States Navy with journalism and accounting as his major studies. He has made his home in Virginia since 1945. He is a certified administrative manager and has been producing audio-visual aids for business groups. He is also a certified photographer and a member of the Academy of Administrative Managers. He has served the State of Virginia in a number of capacities.

He joined Freemasonry in 1948 and served his lodge as Worshipful Master in 1959. He has served as a District Grand Master and as Deputy Grand Secretary of the Grand Lodge of Virginia. He has also served as High Priest and Grand High Priest; as Master and Secretary of Virginia Research Lodge No. 1777. He is an honorary member of: Lodge St. Thomas No. 306, Scotland; Alexandria Lodge No. 33, New Brunswick, Canada; Research Lodge No. 104, Atlanta, Georgia; Masonic Lodge of Research, Connecticut; and Josiah H. Drummond Council No. 1, Allied Masonic Degrees, of Norway, Maine. For 14 years he served on the Grand Lodge of Virginia Education Committee. He has been active in many of the youth groups. He founded the Virginia Craftsmen, a travelling Masonic degree team which has worked in many parts of the United States, in Canada, and in Scotland.

Many Masonic honors have come to him: He is a Fellow of the Philalethes Society, a Blue Friar, has received the certificate of literature of the Philalethes Society, and the Honorary Legion of Honor and Cross of Honor from the Order of DeMolay. He has received the following medals: Josiah H. Drummond from the Grand Lodge of Maine; Silver Medal of the General Grand Chapter of Royal Arch Masons, International; John Dove Distinguished Medal of the Grand Chapter of Royal Arch Masons of Virginia; the Virginia Craftsmen Distinguished Service Medal; the Gold Medal of the Glasgow (Scotland) Compass Association; and the James R. Case Medal of Excellence from the Lodge of Research of Connecticut.

He has been the author of articles on Masnic subjects appearing in many Masonic periodicals and has done a great deal of work in the field of Masonic leadership.

30. DWIGHT L. SMITH

Dwight L. Smith was born on January 30, 1909, near Pennville, Jay County, Indiana. He received his formal education in the public schools of Pennville and was graduated from Pennville High School in 1927. He then received professional training in journalism at Indiana University, and received a Bachelor of Arts Degree in 1931. He then engaged in newspaper work for 12 years. On November 24, 1934, he married Miss Adalene Griffith and they are the parents of two girls, Joanna and Alice Jane.

He is a member of the following: Sigma Delta Chi, a society of professinal journalists; Sons of the American Revolution; Society of Indiana Pioneers, serving as its president in 1979; and many historical societies. In 1949 he was commissioned a Sagamore of the Wabash by Governor Henry F. Schriker, of Indiana.

He became a Mason in Pennville Lodge No. 212 in 1934, and later that year transferred his membership to Salem Lodge No. 21. He served Salem Lodge as Worshipful Master in 1937; and then as secretary for three years. He was elected Grand Master of Masons of Indiana and served in 1945-1946. On December 29, 1947, he became Grand Secretary of the Grand Lodge of Indiana and served until January 31, 1979, at which time he was designated as Grand Secretary Emeritus. From 1966 to the present he has served as editor of the *Indiana Freemason* and has been responsible for the excellent comments made about this fine Masonic magazine.

He served as secretary-treasurer of the Conference of Grand Secretaries in North America from 1954 to 1976, except for 1968-1969 when he served as president of the Conference. Upon retiring he was named secretary-treasurer emeritus.

He is a member of the York Rite Bodies

at Indianapolis and of the Scottish Rite Bodies, Valley of Indianapolis; he received the Thirty-Third degree in 1949. In 1966 he was elected a Fellow of the Philalethes Society, and was elected president of this Society in 1979 to serve for three years. He became a member of the Society of Blue Friars in 1968; and became Grand Abbot of this group in 1977.

He has been the recipient of many honors. Here are some of them: James R. Case Medal of Excellence from the Masonic Lodge of Research of Connecticut, in 1974; the Anson Jones Lecturer, Texas Lodge of Research, 1978; decorated by the Grand Lodges of Massachusetts, Maine, New Jersey, and Indiana; received the first Honor Award of the General Grand Council, Royal and Select Masters, International, in 1978; received the Virginia Craftsmen Service Award, in 1979.

He has been the author of many articles appearing in the *Indiana Freemason* and other publications. *Goodly Heritage,* a detailed, excellent history of Freemasonry in Indiana, was published in 1968. He is the author of two booklets that have enjoyed a wide readership over the years: *Whither Are We Traveling?* and *Why the Confusion in the Temple?* He is the author of *Look Well,* a guide for senior wardens, published in 1977, plus several Masonic plays with an historical theme.

REFERENCES

The Indiana Freemason, Dec., 1978, p. 8.

31. J. FAIRBAIRN SMITH

J. Fairbairn Smith was born on January 30, 1902, at Hawick, Roxburghshire, Scotland. He received his formal education in Hawick and later in England with special courses at Rutherford Technical College and the Royal Society of Arts, in London. He was graduated from the National College of Music in 1923, and left Scotland in January, 1924, for Calgary, Alberta, Canada, but on arriving at Toronto decided to visit Detroit. He remained there to make his home. For the next 12 years he taught music and became a director of the Bedford Branch of the Detroit Conservatory of Music and an associate instructor of the Detroit Foundation School. He was active in many music festivals and musical groups.

As a lewis (the son of a Mason who, under the rules, could petition for the Masonic degrees at the age of 18 years) he was made a Mason in the lodge at Hawick, Scotland, when he became 18 years of age. He was Exalted at Cyrus Chapter No. 133, of Detroit, in 1925, and served as High Priest in 1934, and as Grand High Priest of Michigan in 1945. He was Greeted in Monroe Council No. 1, R. & S.M., in March, 1926, and was Knighted in Detroit Commandery No. 1, K.T., in November, 1926. He joined the Scottish Rite Bodies of Detroit in 1934, and served as Commander-in-Chief in 1953-1956. He received the Thirty-Third degree in 1946. He is a member of St. Clements Conclave No. 3, a Fellow of the Philalethes Society, the Royal Order of Scotland, Moslem Temple of the Shrine, Royal Order of Jesters, and a Blue Friar.

For years he served as editor of *The Masonic World,* published in Detroit, and retired around 1975, to spend all his time on Masonic matters.

REFERENCES

W. R. Denslow, *10,000 Famous Freemasons.* Phil. Mag., Aug.-Sept., 1949, has his picture; April, 1979, 12. *Dateline 1774,* Michigan Masonry Vol. 2, 275 (1979).

32. FREDERICK HENRY SMYTH

Frederick H. Smyth was born on June 19, 1919, in Exeter, Devon, England. He received his formal education at St. John's Hospital School, and Exeter School. He entered the civil service in 1937, and in 1947 became associated with the Ministry of Defense where he has been serving ever since. He served in the British Army during World War II. On March 9, 1946, he was married to Miss Doris Edith Cooper, of Harrow, Middlesex, England, and they have two daughters: Jennifer Ann and Ghislaine Rosemary. He is an associate member of the British Institute of Management. He is also a member of the Society of Indexers and he has use this skill in preparing the index for AQC for years.

Smyth became a Mason in Lodge Devon 1999, English Constitution, Jullundur, India, in 1943. In 1945 he affiliated with Lodge Wallace 1279, Scottish Constitution, Barrackpore, India. Upon returning to England he joined The Hazara Lodge 4159, in 1958, serving as Worshipful Master in 1966; and he has served this lodge as organist from that time to the present. In 1963 he joined Connaught Army and Navy Lodge 4323, and has served this lodge as organist since 1963.

He is a member of numerous Masonic groups. Here is a partial list: Mark Master Mason; Grand Master's Lodge of Instruction for Mark Master Masons and Royal Ark Mariners, London; Jullundur Chapter 1999, E.C., Royal Arch Masons; Prince Rose Croix in the Lilly of Kasauli Chapter 200, India; Order Knight of the Temple; St. Raphael Tabernacle 40; Allied Degrees; Order of the Secret Monitor, and many research lodges. He is an Honorary Fellow of the Grand College of Rites of the U.S.A. and a member of the Society of Blue Friars. He has been active in the work and has served as an officer of Quatuor Coronati Lodge. He is a member of the Masonic Book Club.

He has done a great deal of work on Masonic music and has written many outstanding papers. His most outstanding literary effort for the Craft has been the revisions of the *Pick & Knight Pocket History of Freemasonry*.

33. HAROLD VAN BUREN VOORHIS

Harold Van Buren Voorhis was born on January 3, 1894, at Red Bank, New Jersey, a descendant of a family from Hess, Holland, which came to America in April, 1660, on the ship *Spotted Cow*. He received his formal education in the public schools of Red Bank, graduating from the high school there in 1912 and then attended Cooper Union for two years before attending Columbia University. He has engaged in numerous business enterprises and was with Bull & Roberts, Chemists, in New York, from 1912 to 1920, and also from 1943 to 1967. He served in the United States Navy in World War I. He has been a member of the Chamber of Commerce of Red Bank for many years, and has been an officer of the Macoy Publishing and Masonic Supply Company for many years.

He is a member of many professional, social, patriotic, and educational organizations. He has been interested in radio and boating and has been active in many organizatins relating to these activities.

He became a Mason in Mystic Brotherhood Lodge No. 21, Red Bank, in 1920, and served the lodge as Worshipful Master in 1937. He joined Hiram Chapter No. 1, R.A.M., Redbank, in 1921, was High Priest in 1937, and served as secretary for 25 years. He joined Field Council No. 12, R. & S.M., Red Bank, in 1921, was T.I.M. in 1926, and served as recorder for 19 years. He joined Corson Commandery, K.T., in 1921 and served as E.C. in 1945. He joined the Trenton Bodies of the Scottish Rite in 1925 and received the Thirty-Third Degree in 1950.

He is a Blue Friar and a Fellow of the Philalethes Society. It has been said that he belongs to every Masonic organization and that he has received more Masonic degrees than any person living during his lifetime.

REFERENCES

Altar Light, June-Aug., 1978. 7 ALR 127 (1958), has his picture. Phil. Mag., Jan., 1951, 1-3.

34. WENDELL K. WALKER

Wendell K. Walker was born on January 9, 1908, in Battle Creek, Michigan. He received his formal education in the public schools of Battle Creek, and then attended Western Michigan University, receiving the Bachelor of Arts Degree in 1930. He then studied at the University of Exeter, England, the following year and received a certificate. Years later he attended the Columbia University School of Library Service, and received a Bachelor of Science Degree from that school in 1947. He is a member of The American Library Association, the American Management Association, and the Special Library Association.

He served in the United States Army during World War II and is a veteran of the Seventh Regiment of New York, holding the rank of lieutenant colonel in the United States Army Reserve.

He received his Masonic degrees in A. T. Metcalf Lodge No. 419 of Battle Creek, Michigan, receiving the third degree in April, 1932. After moving to New York he affiliated with Independent Royal Arch Lodge No. 2, retaining dual membership in his Michigan lodge; he served his New York lodge as Worshipful Master in 1947. He joined the Scottish Rite and has received the Thirty-Third Degree. He has served his Grand Lodge in many capacities. He is a member of Orient Chapter No. 138, R.A.M., Brooklyn; Columbia Council No. 1 R. & S.M.; Coeur de Lion Commandery No. 23, K.T.; and Kismet Temple Shrine. He is a Fellow of the Philalethes Society.

He has written extensively for Masonic publications and has rendered outstanding service to the American Lodge of Research, serving as Worshipful Master in 1951, 1954-1955.

For years he was Assistant Grand Secretary and Librarian of the Grand Lodge of New York. For many years he has served as Grand Secretary of the Grand Lodge of New York.

REFERENCES

6 ALR 303 (1956); has his picture.

35. DEWEY HAROLD WOLLSTEIN

Dewey H. Wollstein was born on May 25, 1898, at Harrodburg, Kentucky, the son of Abraham and Agnes Nathan Wollstein. He served in World War I, and moved to Rome, Georgia, in 1920. On April 22, 1928, he was married to Willie Mae Farmer and of this union two children were born: Nancy Bruno and Harold Wollstein.

On October 6, 1925, he received the third degree of Masonry in Cherokee Lodge No. 66, and later served this lodge as Worshipful Master. He then served as Master of the Floyd County Convention and as Master of the Seventh District Convention; he served both Conventions as secretary-treasurer from 1957 until his passing.

He was a member of Rome Chapter No. 26, R.A.M., and joined the Scottish Rite in 1926 at Atlanta. In 1951 he received the Rank and Decoration of Knight Commander of the Court of Honor, and in 1955 received the Thirty-Third Degree. He became a Shriner at Yaarab Temple and was the founder of the Rome Shrine Club serving as its first secretary. He was Grand Master of the Grand Lodge of Georgia in 1944.

He was an outstanding Masonic writer and served the Craft in many ways over the years. In 1934 he founded the *Masonic News,* a publication of Cherokee Lodge No. 66 issued for the benefit of the Masons of Floyd County, and served as editor until his passing. In 1949 he became the editor of the *Masonic Messenger,* official magazine of the Grand Lodge of Georgia, and served until 1969 when he was named editor emeritus. For years he served as a member of the Georgia Grand Lodge Educational and Historical Commission, and he was its chairman for many years.

He was an able writer and while he was editor each issue of the *Masonic Messenger* had an editorial with an important message. Many of these have been reprinted in magazines all over the country. He also wrote poetry and one volume of his collected poems has been published. It was my pleasure to meet him on one occasion and I still remember one casual remark he made: "Freemasonry is basically a spiritual organization, and if you remove this element from the Craft it will have no justification for its existence."

He departed this life on May 5, 1971.

Book Author's Index

Missouri Lodge of Research

OFFICERS 1977-1978

Ovid H. Bell, Worshipful Master, 1201-05 Bluff St., Fulton, MO 65251
Bert Casselman, Senior Warden, 6001 Hilltop Rd., Platte Wood, Parkville, MO 64151
Elvis Mooney, Junior Warden, 117 N. Prairie St., Bloomfield, MO 63825
A. W. Griffith, Secretary-Treasurer, P.O. Box 480, Fulton, MO 65251
Olin S. McDaniel, Senior Deacon, 117 E. School St., Bonne Terre, MO 63628
Thomas J. Davis, Junior Deacon, P.O. Box 217, Piedmont, MO 63957
Stanton T. Brown, Senior Steward, Rt. 1, Box 225, Buckner, MO 64016
Richard Calvert, Junior Steward, Federal Aviation Administration, American Consulate General, APO New York 09757
Richard B. Ramage, Senior Marshall, 110 Old Oaks, Ballwin, MO 63011
Lloyd L. Schainker, Junior Marshal, 7333 Balson Blvd., St. Louis, MO 63130
William H Chapman, Senior Director of Ceremonies, 250 Blackmar Pl., Webster Groves, MO 63119
Earl K. Dille, Junior Director of Ceremonies, 10258 Butterworth Lane, St. Louis, MO 63131
Albert H. Van Gels, Chaplain, 24 Spring Dr., Florissant, MO 63031
John B. Vrooman, Tiler, P.O. Box 402, St. Louis, MO 63166

TRUSTEES

Forrest Donnell	William H. Chapman
Morris Ewing	Harold M. Jayne

ADVISORY BOARD

Harry Gershenson	Martin Dickinson
Earl K. Dille	William H. Utz

BOARD OF PUBLICATION

Lewis C. Wes Cook	Ovid H. Bell
Alfred W. Griffith	William R. Denslow
Bruce H. Hunt	

OFFICERS 1978-1979

Bert W. Casselman, Worshipful Master, 6001 Hilltop Rd., N.W., Parkville, MO 64151
Elvis A. Mooney, Senior Warden, 117 N. Prairie St., Bloomfield, MO 63825
Olin S. McDaniel, Junior Warden, 117 E. School St., Bonne Terre, MO 63628
A. W. Griffith, Secretary-Treasurer, P.O. Box 480, Fulton, MO 65251
Thomas J. Davis, Jr., Senior Deacon, P.O. Box 217, Piedmont, MO 63957
Stanton T. Brown, Junior Deacon, Rt. 1, Box 225, Buckner, MO 64016
Richard W. Calvert, Senior Steward, Federal Aviation Administration, c/o American Embassy, APO New York 09667
Richard B. Ramage, Junior Steward, 110 Old Oaks, Ballwin, MO 63011
Lloyd L. Schainker, Senior Marshal, 7333 Balson Blvd., St. Louis, MO 63130
William H. Chapman, Junior Marshal, 250 Blackmer Pl., Webster Groves, MO 63119
Earl K. Dille, Senior Director of Ceremonies, 10258 Butterworth Lane, St. Louis, MO 63131
Robert D. Jenkins, Junior Director of Ceremonies, 2609 W. 70th St., Shawnee Mission, KS 66208
Albert H. Van Gels, Chaplain, 24 Spring Dr., Florissant, MO 63031
John B. Vrooman, Tiler, P.O. Box 402, St. Louis, MO 63166

1977-1978

SECRETARY-TREASURER COMBINED REPORT CONDENSED

Balance Callaway Bank, July 1, 1977 .... $ 1,274.63
Deposits July 1, 1977 to June 30, 1978 .... 11,730.10
Receipts plus balance $13,004.73

DISBURSEMENTS

Paid out by checks No. 1096 through 1159, inclusive $11,490.56
Balance Callaway Bank, Fulton, Mo., June 30, 1978 .... $ 1,514.17

OTHER ASSETS

Callaway Bank
 Certificate of Deposit (No. 18417) 6% .... $ 500.00
 Certificate of Deposit (No. 24396) 6% 400.00
Total C/D—Callaway Bank .... $ 900.00
Kingdom Federal Savings & Loan
 Pass book No. A 1721. Balance 6/30/77 .... $29,992.44
 Interest Received during year 1,535.74
 Transfer from Checking a/c Callaway Bank 2,900.00
 Transfer To Checking a/c Callaway Bank .... (2,500.00)

Balance Passbook No. A 1721 June 30, 1978   <u>31,928.18</u>
Total cash assets, June 30, 1978 $34,342.35

These figures are supported by bank statement, letter from The Callaway Bank, passbook and letter from Kingdom Federal Savings and Loan.

A. W. GRIFFITH,
Secretary-Treasurer.

STATISTICAL

	Life	Active	Corr.	Subs	Exch.	Total
Membership 7/1/77	4	797	719	137	3	1,660
New	1	49	54			104
	5	846	773	137	3	1,764
Transfer	+2		−3		+1	
	7	846	770	137	4	1,764
Deduct						
Died		15	12			27
Resign		161	107	8		276
		176	119	8		303
Membership 7/1/78	7	670	651	129	4	1,461

REPORT OF AUDITING COMMITTEE
September 23, 1978

To the Master, Wardens and Brethren
  Missouri Lodge of Research

We have this date examined the report of the Secretary-Treasurer of the Missouri Lodge of Research for the period of July 1, 1977 to June 30, 1978. We find the report in good order and complete.

FRANK HAZELRIGG
JOHN B. LaMAR

1978-1979
SECRETARY-TREASURER'S COMBINED REPORT

Balance Callaway Bank, June 30, 1978 .... $ 1,514.17
Deposits July, 1978 through June 30, 1979 .... 22,388.97
Receipts plus balance $23,903.14

DISBURSEMENTS

Paid out by checks No. 1160 through 1241 inclusive $22,251.43
Balance Callaway Bank Checking Account, June 30, 1979 .... $ 1,651.71

OTHER ASSETS

Callaway Bank
  Certificate of Deposit No. 18417 .... $ 500.00
  Certificate of Deposit No. 24396 .... 400.00
Total C/Ds at The Callaway Bank, Fulton, Missouri .... $ 900.00

Kingdom Federal Savings & Loan
  Pass Book No. A 1721
    Balance June 30, 1978 .... $31,928.18
    Interest Received 1,588.50
    Transfer from Ck A/C 6,500.00
    Transfer to Ck A/C .... (8,000.00)
Balance Kingdom Federal S & L 6/30/79 .... 32,016.
Total cash assets, June 30, 1979 .... $34,568.

These figures are supported by bank statement and cancelled vouchers. Letters from T
Callaway Bank and Kingdom Federal Savings & Loan Association.

In order to save printing costs the above financial statement is condensed. Detailed figures
expenses and receipts may be seen by any member at the office of the Secretary-Treasurer.

A. W. GRIFFITH,
Secretary-Treasurer.

STATISTICAL

	Life	Active	Corr.	Subs.	Exch.	To,
Membership 7/1/78	7	670	651	129	4	1,4
New		83	57	5		1,
	7	753	708	134	4	1,6
Transfer			−1	+1		
	7	753	707	135	4	1,6
Deduct						
Died		6	9			
Resign		96	76	12		1{
		102	85	12		1'
Membership 7/1/79	7	651	622	123	4	1,4(

REPORT OF AUDITING COMMITTEE
September 22, 1979

To the Master, Wardens and Brethren
    Missouri Lodge of Research

We have this date examined the report of the Secretary-Treasurer of the Missouri Lodge
Research for the period of July 1, 1978 to June 30, 1979. We find the report in good condition ai
complete.

FRANK W. HAZELRIGG, JR.
JOHN B. LAMAR

Related Titles from Westphalia Press

Ancient Mysteries and Modern Masonry: The Collected Writings of Jewel P. Lightfoot, Edited by Billy J. Hamilton Jr.

Jewel P. Lightfoot. Former Attorney General of the State of Texas. Past Grand Master of the Masonic Grand Lodge of Texas. From humble beginnings in rural Arkansas, he worked to become an educated man who excelled in law and Freemasonry. He was a gentleman of his time, well-known as a scholar, public speaker, and Masonic philosopher.

Essay on The Mysteries and the True Object of The Brotherhood of Freemasons
by Jason Williams

This isn't a reprint of a classic. It's a new rendition with new life breathed into it, to be enjoyed both by the layperson trying to understand the Craft and Masonic scholars taking a deeper dive into the fraternity's golden years—when the concepts of liberty and equality were still fresh.

Female Emancipation and Masonic Membership:
An Essential Collection
By Guillermo De Los Reyes Heredia

Female Emancipation and Masonic Membership: An Essential Combination is a collection of essays on Freemasonry and gender that promotes a transatlantic discussion of the study of the history of women and Freemasonry and their contribution in different countries.

Freemasonry, Heir to the Enlightenment
by Cécile Révauger

Modern Freemasonry may have mythical roots in Solomon's time but is really the heir to the Enlightenment. Ever since the early eighteenth century freemasons have endeavored to convey the values of the Enlightenment in the cultural, political and religious fields, in Europe, the American colonies and the emerging United States.

Masonic Myths and Legends
by Pierre Mollier

Freemasonry preserves the teachings of a primitive Judeo-Christian gnosis. In order to better understand these legends and myths and their significance, Pierre Mollier has studied their origins and attempted to find their sources.

Exploring the Vault: Masonic Higher Degrees 1730–1800
by John Belton and Roger Dachez

The study adopted a forensic approach to the available evidence, and the discoveries exceeded expectations. The book details their 'archaeological finds' and offers a novel perspective on the development of the Higher Degrees during the eighteenth century.

Étienne Morin: From the French Rite to the Scottish Rite by Arturo de Hoyos and Josef Wäges

All extant Masonic records have been consulted and using this meta-data, a comprehensive reconstruction emerges, revealing that Étienne Morin was a founding masonic figure in Saint Domingue and creator of his own high degree system, that operated for a time as a defacto Grand Lodge.

The Impact of Freemasonry on the Secular and Liberal Discourse in Mexico
by Guillermo De Los Reyes, Translated by Bradley L. Drew

In this thought-provoking book, De Los Reyes argues that Freemasonry, through its lodges, played a decisive role in shaping Mexico's national thought, contributing to the creation of a liberal and secular State and fostering anticlerical sentiments among the laity that endured well into the twentieth century.

The French Rite: Enlightenment Culture
Cécile Révauger, Editor

This book, focused on the French Rite, covers the founding principles of the Enlightenment and their influence on the birth of modern Freemasonry as we know it today. The authors revisit the fundamental values of the Enlightenment, from a rational approach to religious tolerance and cosmopolitanism.

The Great Transformation: Scottish Freemasonry 1725-1810
by Dr. Mark C. Wallace

This book examines Scottish Freemasonry in its wider British and European contexts between the years 1725 and 1810. The Enlightenment effectively crafted the modern mason and propelled Freemasonry into a new era marked by growing membership and the creation of the Grand Lodge of Scotland.

Getting the Third Degree: Fraternalism, Freemasonry and History
Edited by Guillermo De Los Reyes and Paul Rich

As this engaging collection demonstrates, the doors being opened on the subject range from art history to political science to anthropology, as well as gender studies, sociology and more. The organizations discussed may insist on secrecy, but the research into them belies that.

Freemasonry: A French View
by Roger Dachez and Alain Bauer

Perhaps one should speak not of Freemasonry but of Freemasonries in the plural. In each country Masonic historiography has developed uniqueness. Two of the best known French Masonic scholars present their own view of the worldwide evolution and challenging mysteries of the fraternity over the centuries.

Worlds of Print: The Moral Imagination of an Informed Citizenry, 1734 to 1839
by John Slifko

John Slifko argues that freemasonry was representative and played an important role in a larger cultural transformation of literacy and helped articulate the moral imagination of an informed democratic citizenry via fast emerging worlds of print.

Why Thirty-Three?: Searching for Masonic Origins
by S. Brent Morris, PhD

What "high degrees" were in the United States before 1830? What were the activities of the Order of the Royal Secret, the precursor of the Scottish Rite? A complex organization with a lengthy pedigree like Freemasonry has many basic foundational questions waiting to be answered, and that's what this book does: answers questions.

A Place in the Lodge: Dr. Rob Morris, Freemasonry and the Order of the Eastern Star
by Nancy Stearns Theiss, PhD

Ridiculed as "petticoat masonry," critics of the Order of the Eastern Star did not deter Rob Morris' goal to establish a Masonic organization that included women as members. Morris carried the ideals of Freemasonry through a despairing time of American history.

Brought to Light: The Mysterious George Washington Masonic Cave
by Jason Williams MD

The George Washington Masonic Cave near Charles Town, West Virginia, contains a signature carving of George Washington dated 1748. This book painstakingly pieces together the chronicled events and real estate archives related to the cavern in order to sort out fact from fiction.

Dudley Wright: Writer, Truthseeker & Freemason
by John Belton

Dudley Wright (1868-1950) was an Englishman and professional journalist who took a universalist approach to the various great Truths of Life. He travelled though many religions in his life and wrote about them all, but was probably most at home with Islam.

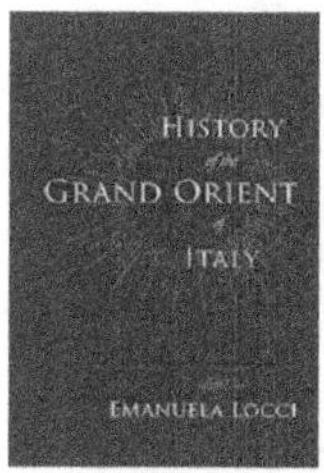

History of the Grand Orient of Italy
Emanuela Locci, Editor

No book in Masonic literature upon the history of Italian Freemasonry has been edited in English up to now. This work consists of eight studies, covering a span from the Eighteenth Century to the end of the WWII, tracing through the story, the events and pursuits related to the Grand Orient of Italy.

westphaliapress.org